CULTURE OF HONOR

ALSO BY DANNY SILK

Loving Our Kids On Purpose

AVAILABLE FROM DESTINY IMAGE PUBLISHERS

CULTURE OF HONOR

SUSTAINING A SUPERNATURAL ENVIRONMENT

DANNY SILK

DESTINY IMAGE® PUBLISHERS, INC.

P.O. Box 310, Shippensburg, PA 17257-0310

"Speaking to the Purposes of God for This Generation and for the Generations to Come."

This book and all other Destiny Image, Revival Press, MercyPlace, Fresh Bread, Destiny Image Fiction, and Treasure House books are available at Christian bookstores and distributors worldwide.

For a U.S. bookstore nearest you, call 1-800-722-6774.

For more information on foreign distributors, call 717-532-3040.

Reach us on the Internet: www.destinyimage.com.

ISBN 10: 0-7684-3146-8   ISBN 13: 978-0-7684-3146-9

For Worldwide Distribution, Printed in the U.S.A.

2 3 4 5 6 7 8 9 10 11 / 13 12 11 10

DEDICATION

To Bethel Church: thank you for your tireless efforts and participation in this grand experiment called "Bethel."

ACKNOWLEDGMENTS

Bill Johnson and Kris Vallotton—thank you for your courageous leadership!

Bethel's senior management team—you are the "masters" at making all this work. It is a perpetual honor to work at your side.

Allison Armerding—you never cease to amaze me with your life of honor toward others. Thank you for pointing it at me!

Dann Farrelly and Andre Van Mol—to your gift of critique I am forever in debt.

ENDORSEMENTS

God is in the process of restoring Kingdom mentality to the church, and those who "get it" will move under the blessed order of God's government. This book is both an indication of this process and a clarification of the strategic issue of honor as it relates to how Christians work together in church. Chapter 2, entitled "The Funnel From Heaven," is an absolute must-read for those who not only are wondering why the fivefold ministry is not working as we had hoped, but for all who have not seriously considered this vital approach to church life. Danny's contribution toward the Kingdom Church will help us all navigate this adventure of Kingdom life together.

Jack Taylor
President, Dimensions Ministries
Melbourne, Florida

In this book, *Culture of Honor,* Danny Silk unearths the ancient foundations of the Kingdom of God. With great wisdom and insight he examines and explains the fundamental building blocks of a supernatural society and constructs the framework for a powerful Christian life. This is more than a book; it is a manifesto of reformation, destined to become a classic that will be a reference for generations to come. *Culture of Honor* is a must-read for every serious believer. It is essential that this book find its way into every seminary in America!

Kris Vallotton
Senior Associate Leader of Bethel Church,
Redding, California
Author of several books, including
The Supernatural Ways of Royalty and
Developing a Supernatural Lifestyle

Pastor Danny Silk has written a wonderful book sharing one of the core values of Bethel Church in Redding, California, that has been foundational to the revival that Bethel has been experiencing for a number of years. I believe the "culture of honor," as Danny presents it, can bring and sustain revival and reformation to anyone who lives out this biblical principle. I highly recommend this book.

Ché Ahn
Senior Pastor and Founder, Harvest Rock Church
Pasadena, California

Sometimes I read a book, and many times my experience is that the book reads me. *Culture of Honor* is one of those books. I want to live this book! Bethel Church has been an open Heaven for many years, and I am grateful to be a part of the family at Bethel Church. The Kingdom of God is a "family business," and in this book Danny Silk gives us the DNA of Heaven on earth. *Culture of Honor* is destined to be a classic that will be read and lived from generation to generation. Read the book, and let the book read you!

Dr. Leif Hetland
President, Global Mission Awareness
Florence, Alabama

Culture of Honor is a revolutionary book that will transform the leadership paradigms that have been so prevalent in every institution, including the church. I believe Danny Silk captures the essence of how Jesus led His disciples and how the disciples led as apostles in the early church through honor.

Culture of Honor will transform the way you think about leadership and the way you lead. You will learn how to be an empowering leader, through practical Kingdom core values that are taught throughout the book. Your leadership lid can't help but to increase as you apply these biblical principles of honor.

Every leader should read this book! Every church leader should read this book! Every husband and wife should read this book! Every parent should read this book! Everyone should read this book!

And then, read it again!!

Kevin Dedmon
Author of *The Ultimate Treasure Hunt: Supernatural Evangelism Through Supernatural Encounters* and *Unlocking Heaven: Keys to Living Naturally Supernatural*

Danny had me hooked from the stunning first-chapter demonstration of how a jaw-dropping, leadership-imploding fall was redeemed through application of a culture of honor. In both its fullness of content and crafting of delivery, this is the finest book from any Bethel author yet. Danny's call and challenge is for the Church to purposefully live empowered and empowering in the New Covenant through a compassionate, safe, liberating, relational culture free of fear, legalism, control, shame, and impotent victimhood. Danny makes the scriptural basis, conceptual models, and successful applications—on congregational, leadership, family, and individual levels—robustly and disarmingly clear. This book is a catalyst for transformation.

André Van Mol, MD
Family Physician
Elder, Bethel Church of Redding
Vice President, Pray North State

I am grateful to Danny Silk who, in *Culture of Honor,* has explained the "recipe" that is the backbone of a 10-year-plus revival that is rapidly accelerating into a movement—and already impacting the nations of the world. In 40 years of being a Christian, I have not witnessed a "movement" that has been sustained for more than 10 years. It is not for lack of gifting or anointing, for that was present in abundance, but it was for lack of an understanding of the "culture of honor" that could allow leaders and followers to flourish in the empowering atmosphere it brings.

Andrew Sievright
President, Heroes of the Nations

The church has for the longest time been in need of governmental reconstruction. Not only are we in need of having our notions of "Kingdom government" conceptually and structurally redefined, we also need to have our heart language of Kingdom definition revisited and restated. It is out of our hearts that we will speak and therefore live. Danny Silk, in his book *Culture of Honor,* goes a very long way in giving us an inspired, informed, and creative approach to understanding what needs to be the heart culture of the Kingdom. His wit and intelligent authorship will seduce you into your own moments of revelation. "Free people cannot live together without honor" is a truth that is non-negotiable and in need of application. This book could be one of the most significant to come out of Bethel Church. An essential read for those who desire supernatural fruitfulness. That fruitfulness will come out of the context of honor.

David Crabtree
Senior Leader of DaySpring Church
Castle Hill, New South Wales, Australia

In 2003, when I first came into contact with Bethel Church and this revival, my life and ministry went through a tremendous and sometimes painful transformation, mainly because I was deeply immersed in religiosity and legalism. Seeing and experiencing the supernatural really impressed me and caused me to wonder about my beliefs and core values. I saw miracles and healings, but I also saw freedom, unconditional love, empowering, acceptance, healthy confrontation, and many other elements of a genuine "culture of honor" that had not been a part of my life. It was actually the culture of honor in every one of these "weird people"—as they appeared to me in the beginning—that pushed me to make the choice of accepting revival and submitting to this transformation and all that it means.

About a year later I met Danny Silk, whom I consider to be one of the most authorized spokespersons of the culture of honor in the midst of this amazing revival. He has become one of my best friends and one of the most influential people in my life and ministry. From him I have learned what the culture of honor looks like, and that revival without this culture of honor is like new wine in an old wineskin.

What this book contains needs to be learned and embraced by every person, whether a leader or not, whether a believer or not. It is urgent that every one of us get tuned in to this culture of honor while seeing Heaven invading earth.

Angel Nava
Senior Pastor, Seeds of Life Church (Semillas de Vida)
La Paz, Mexico

This book could turn your world upside down and help you extend the Kingdom of God wherever you live. The "culture of honor" talked about in this book has the power to lead you on an adventure that will result in the transformation of you, your church, and your city.

As you read this book, be prepared to be challenged to think anew, to review your Christian thought and practice, "to be transformed by the renewing of your mind." As you do so you will be better equipped to transform the culture in which you live.

Dr. Pete Carter
Senior leader of North Kent Community Church
United Kingdom

"*Perhaps the sentiments contained in the following pages, are not yet sufficiently fashionable to procure them general favor; a long habit of not thinking a thing wrong, gives it a superficial appearance of being right, and raises at first a formidable outcry in defense of custom. But tumult soon subsides. Time makes more converts than reason.*"

Thomas Paine in *Common Sense*
Philadelphia, Pennsylvania
February 14, 1776

CONTENTS

FOREWORD

An adulterous woman was thrown at Jesus' feet. She knew the punishment for her sin was public stoning. The fact that she was caught in the very act only heightened the shame and intensified her fear of a painful death. Her accusers stood with confidence because the law of God supported their position. They held the stones that would soon take her life, while she waited for them to display their outrage for her complete disregard of God's standard of holiness. Then the Master began to write in the sand.

We don't know what He wrote. All we know is that the atmosphere created by the writings of the "grace giver" completely disarmed her accusers. They fled as the grace of God drove away the judgments of men as quickly as light displaces darkness. Grace is that superior.

No one needed to tell her to put her faith in Christ. The atmosphere of grace made faith in Jesus the most logical response. Perhaps this is why the apostle Paul taught us that faith is *"according to grace"* (Rom. 4:16). ***Grace is the atmosphere created by love that makes faith the only reasonable response.***

Few things overwhelm me more than an authentic display of the grace of God. Whenever the presence of God enables a person to become free from lifelong issues, you can't help but be amazed at such a wonderful Savior. But grace goes beyond healing from the past: it also launches us into our divine destinies.

I read this manuscript with great joy. But I also read it with many tears as I recalled the impossible situations that we faced together as a church family. They were the kinds of problems that only God could heal. And He did, again and again. It's that same grace that leaks from the pages of this book. It is not a new theology. It is just a clearer manifestation of the original—the heart of God as revealed in the person of Jesus Christ. But that is only half of the story, for grace is but one of the expressions of this revolutionary force of His Kingdom come to earth—the culture of honor.

When I teach on the culture of honor, most everyone says "amen" to show support for what they already believe. Soon after the message they proceed to tell me that they too have a culture of honor. But the response is much different once they've had a chance to come to Bethel for a week or two and they watch the interaction of the staff and the church family. Invariably they leave asking us to please mentor them on developing this as a reformational way of life. Giving honor actually releases the life of God into a situation.

Many people live in atmospheres void of honor and desperately seek our help in creating such a culture. Pastors often ask us to come and teach their church and staff how to show honor. The need is real, and the desire is genuine. But this culture is never built around "what I need." It is built around "what I can give." And if I don't learn to give it to those who deserve it the least, I will continue to live in an environment without honor.

I absolutely love *Culture of Honor*. I've waited a long time to see this revolutionary way of life captured and put into words. While many on my staff teach on this subject, God has given Danny Silk the best language for it. And the spoil he obtains for the Master through his wonderful insights is becoming legendary. In carrying the empowering presence of Jesus in everything he does, he lives to show God's value upon each person he serves, regardless of his or her station in life.

The church is in need of a radical reformation. I believe that this book is a part of God's prescription to address this need. As we succeed, we'll be positioned to help bring the cities of our world into transformation. And it's a transformation through honor—that which communicates the grace of God so beautifully.

Bill Johnson
Senior Pastor of Bethel Church,
Redding, California
Author of *The Supernatural Power of a Transformed Mind* and
When Heaven Invades Earth

PREFACE

I realize that in this book I am challenging what many understand to be true. I am messing with long-standing paradigms. Nonetheless, I find myself undaunted in a course to shed light on many topics long held in a type of darkness by my beloved community, the Church. As a first-generation Christian there are many cultural traditions that have not directly affected my life or family. Equally so, there are many that have not yet taken hold and strengthened my legacy. But as for some of these traditions that I have come across, unfortunately I find them to be highly unjust and a poor representation of who I have come to know as my Lord. The "culture of honor" is a contest to those long-held approaches and core values one can easily find in the historic and contemporary Christian church culture.

I mean no disrespect in presenting this perspective. It is confronting and reforming what we've come to know about church leadership, authority, and church discipline for literally centuries. Please know that I know this is a "grand experiment" at Bethel Church and we have much to learn about how to steward an environment of freedom. Nonetheless, I will present what we've learned thus far.

Peace!

INTRODUCTION

Within these pages you will find what one of my friends calls a "recipe." The *ingredients* in this recipe are a set of beliefs and practices. The *steps* in this recipe combine these ingredients in such a way that they create something powerful—an environment that is uncommon on the earth today. It is an environment that attracts and hosts the presence of God. We at Bethel Church, in Redding, California, call this environment the *culture of honor*. By no means is our "recipe" the only one that creates a culture that hosts the presence of God, but we can tell you that it is one that works.

When God first speaks of honor, in the Ten Commandments, He promises that long life will be our reward for honoring our parents. At Bethel, we believe that this command reveals a principle of honor in general. We often say, "Life flows through honor."

> **The Principle of Honor** states that: *accurately acknowledging who people are will position us to give them what they deserve and to receive the gift of who they are in our lives.*

Honor creates life-giving and life-promoting relationships. The key here is "accurately acknowledging who people are." We can only do this when we recognize their God-given identities and roles. This is what we see in the statement of Jesus: *"He who receives a prophet in the name of a prophet shall receive a prophet's reward. And he who receives a righteous man in the name of a righteous man shall receive a righteous man's reward."*[1] Names and titles are important. Mother, father, son, daughter, apostle, prophet, Christian, human being—such names define a person's role and identity and when used correctly, establish God-designed relationships in which specific "rewards" are given and received to build and strengthen us.

A culture of honor is created as a community of people learns to discern and receive people in their God-given identities. Throughout this book we will explore some of the "names" that have enabled us to establish very specific kinds of relationships in the Bethel community. These are the relationships that attract and sustain the outpouring of God's presence and power in our midst. The names "apostle," "prophet," "teacher," "pastor," and "evangelist" and their distinctive anointings, mindsets, and gifts create a network of relationships designed to bring the focus and priorities of Heaven to earth. Names like "free sons" and "children of light" define the way we must honor and relate to one another, particularly when addressing areas of behavior and relationships that need discipline and restoration. Descriptive names like "royalty," "wealthy," and "benefactor" shape our relationships with our resources and with the wider community that the Church is called to bless and encounter with the love and power of Heaven.

In a culture of honor, leaders lead with honor by courageously treating people according to the names God gives them and not according to the aliases they receive from people. They treat them as free sons and daughters, not slaves; as righteous, not sinners; as wealthy, not poor. Leaders also acknowledge their interdependence on the diverse anointings God has distributed among His leadership and their design for functioning as a team that creates a "funnel" from Heaven to earth. They lead in teaching and preaching a Gospel that accurately acknowledges God's identity as good, as love, as *shalom,* and look for clear manifestations of these realities as signs that God's presence is truly welcome in the culture. And in the safety and freedom that grow as His presence grows, leaders lead by developing ways to help people get along with one another in a free culture. They have tools for confrontation that are congruent with people's God-given identities and are motivated by the passion to protect and grow the connections that God is building among us. Finally, leaders in a culture of honor naturally lead their people in extending the honor of the Kingdom to the wider community, creating ways for our cities to experience the life that is flowing among us.

Life flows through honor. The clear fruit of establishing a culture of honor is that the resurrection life of God begins to flow into people's lives, homes, and communities, bringing healing, restoration, blessing, joy, hope, and wholeness. If we are not seeing this fruit, then we must ask ourselves whether we are truly honoring those around us as we ought. As you will find in the coming pages, I am convinced that there are some patterns of relating in the Church that are based on false versions of who people are, and we must confront and dismantle these if we hope to see abundant life growing in our midst.

My prayer and hope is that this book will guide you as you seek the ingredients and steps for creating a culture around you that hosts the presence of God. Admittedly, this book is just a start, but it's a great start!

CHAPTER 1

A SUPERNATURAL CULTURE

'Not by might nor by power, but by My Spirit,'
says the Lord of hosts.
(Zechariah 4:6)

If you've heard of Bethel Church in Redding, California, chances are that you've heard testimonies of the supernatural happenings that take place there on a regular basis, particularly miracles of healing. What you may not have heard is that these supernatural events are directly related to the *supernatural culture* that the community of saints at Bethel has been developing for over a decade. The heart of this culture is the conviction that Jesus modeled the Christian life for us. Jesus explained that all the supernatural things that happened through Him flowed directly from His intimate connection with His Father, and that same connection was what He came to give us through His death and resurrection. Sustaining a supernatural lifestyle, where signs and wonders follow us, is therefore totally dependent on living out our true identities as sons and daughters of God. Armed with these truths, the leaders at Bethel understand that their primary role is to empower the saints to know God and walk in the fullness of who He says they are. As these core values have been taught and demonstrated, a group of people has grown up with faith and courage to bring Heaven to earth.

In order to help you understand Bethel's culture of supernatural empowerment, I want to show you what it's like. I am going to share something that happened in our School of Supernatural Ministry several years ago. Since this incident, hundreds just like it have been added to the list, but this particular story is the classic case that we refer to in teaching our staff to *create a safe place*. (Creating a safe place will be further explained in the chapter entitled, "The Top Priority of Leadership.")

To set the stage for this story, I need to mention that every member of our staff shares a great mutual delight in our First Year graduates. We are so proud of their zeal and love for revival. After each summer break, our staff interviews the graduates returning for Second Year, and this always reignites their excitement to spend another year with the amazing people we call our students. These Second Year students are the cream of the crop and are leaders to our fresh batch of First Year students.

One year we had two First Year students, amazing people, who were leaders in worship and other ministry activities. After graduating from First Year, they decided to get married in December while attending Second Year. So they applied for Second Year and were accepted. Of course they were—they are amazing!

Shortly after Second Year began, Banning Liebscher, the Second Year pastor, came to me and said, "We have a problem. I have two students who have confessed to me that they had sex over the summer."

I asked him what he was going to do.

Banning then said, "Well, if having sex was all that was going on, that wouldn't be as much of a problem. They stopped about a month before school started and are truly repentant. And I really believed this guy when he told me that."

"What else is going on?" I asked.

"I just found out that she is pregnant," he said.

Now this was a *situation*—an unmarried, pregnant Second Year Bethel School of Supernatural Ministry student roaming the halls. That was something we would have to explain. I could see a certain dread in Banning's eyes. He knew that we would have to remove these two students from the school. This was the first time he'd been the leader in a scenario quite so extreme.

I said, "Let's get together with them and talk about it."

So Banning and his co-pastor, Jill, came into my office with these two students. Now, I did not know them and they did not know me. Neither of them made eye contact with me as they entered my office. Their heads were slumped low, and their eyes were pointed to the floor. It was clear that they were absolutely ashamed of what they had done, and they came in expecting us to punish them for their mistakes. Not only did they believe they deserved judgment for their sin; they were aware of the commonly held conviction that church leaders must protect the whole from the rebellious few. They knew they had been rebellious and that this would most likely be "the talk." What else could we do but tell them we love them and show them the door?

I began the process by saying, "Thank you both very much. You don't know me, or what is going to happen. Thank you for the vulnerability and trust that you have just offered. I know this is scary, and I don't want you to feel scared. We have not made any decisions because we don't really know what the problem is. Do you need any water? Are you okay?"

After they had responded, I addressed the young man. "Now, let me ask you this. What is the problem?"

He looked at Banning, stunned, and asked, "Didn't Banning tell you what happened? Didn't he talk to you?"

I could tell this question made him uncomfortable.

"Yes, he has. Banning has talked to me," I replied.

He asked, "You want me to say it?"

"If you know what the problem is, I want you to tell me," I said. My hunch was that he probably didn't yet know what the problem was.

"We had sex this summer—a bunch of times!" he exclaimed.

"Now, I thought you stopped doing that."

He said, "Yes, we totally did. We stopped doing it about a month before school started."

"So, what's the problem?" I asked again, trying to send him searching further into his heart for the problem.

"Well, she is pregnant," he said, searching for the next thing I might not know.

I asked, "Well, is there anything we can do about that?"

"No!" he fired back emphatically, sending me a clear message that abortion was not an option. He was clearly frustrated by my

questions. Apparently, he had not intended to do so much thinking through this process. He had anticipated punishment, and this was catching him completely off guard.

"Okay, so what is the problem?" I asked once more.

He looked at me for a few moments, shook his head and said, "I don't think I understand the question."

I chuckled. Banning and Jill chuckled. We all chuckled. No one seemed to know what the problem was, and everyone was wondering where I was going with my question.

Finally I said, "If we were going to spend our time today solving a problem, what would that problem be?"

"I don't know."

I asked him if he had repented.

"Yeah. Of course I have," he replied, as if this was a no-brainer question.

"What have you repented of?" I asked.

After a long pause he admitted, "I don't know."

I said, "All right. Well, that is part of the problem, isn't it? How can you repent from a problem unless you know what that problem is?"

"I see what you are saying. Yeah."

"So, we need to find a problem here to solve," I said. "That is what this is about. Let me ask you some more questions."

My whole plan was simply to ask him questions. I was not going to tell him what I thought or tell him what to think. I was not trying to convince him of my amazing perspectives or my powerful discernments. I was searching for the glory, wisdom, and capability in this young man. It needed to be raised to the surface so that he could remember who he was in this house. The shame of his mistake had made him forget who he was. He thought he was one of those people who needed to be kicked and spit on, and he was ready for our leadership team to kick him to the curb. Questions led him, with the aid of the Holy Spirit, to run around and search for the wisdom and knowledge inside of him and find a solution that would change his life forever.

I lofted a couple of slow balls to him. "Tell me, did you not know it was a bad idea to sleep with your girlfriend?"

"I totally knew that," he shot back.

"Well, then, what happened?"

"I don't know." He lowered his head, breaking eye contact.

I gave him a choice to consider and an opportunity to stay with me. "You don't know, or are you not wanting to think about it anymore?"

"Well, it is probably because we were staying up until like 2:00 in the morning watching movies at her house."

"You think?" I raised my eyebrows.

"But I tried to leave. I tried to leave over and over. I would say to her that we shouldn't be in this situation. We shouldn't be here doing this. I told her that we went too far last time and we shouldn't be doing this." As he sheepishly looks over at her, she is pursing her lips and her face is flushed, but the fear of the unknown of being in this room has her in a bit of verbal paralysis.

He continues, "She would get so mad at me! She would call me names, tell me that I was rejecting her, and it was just hellish for days afterward. So I just wouldn't say anything and stayed there. I am not saying that I didn't like it or wasn't a part of it. I totally was. It just wasn't worth fighting with her about it."

"All right. So what you are telling me is that you were more concerned about her being mad at you than you were concerned about doing your job of protecting her from you."

Slowly, he answered, "Yeah."

"So what you are telling me is that when you are around angry people it is easy for you to let them control who you are. Is that what you are telling me?"

"Yeah," he said sheepishly.

"So all it takes for you to abandon your character and your integrity is someone who is upset at you."

"Yeah." He was starting to get a revelation.

I asked, "Dude, is that a problem?"

"Yeah."

"So if we could build a solution to that problem, would that make our time today worth something to you?"

"Totally." He looked up again and made eye contact, trying to hide a smile. I could tell he was unsure about feeling better when this was supposed to be a process that made him feel worse about what he'd done.

"Fabulous. Then let's work on that," I said, with a big smile on my face.

The whole room felt hopeful. Banning and Jill were smiling. I could sense their expectation and sense of responsibility to help this young man deal with the problem he had just identified. But instead, I turned to the girl, who had been watching this whole process with her boyfriend. I could see that she did not want to go through the same thing. Her arms and legs were crossed and her chin was lowered to her chest. I ventured in anyway.

"What is the problem?"

"I don't know," she quickly shot back, defensive.

"You don't know, or you are afraid to think about it?"

"I don't know."

I gently said, "I can see that you are scared. I don't want you to feel afraid. I do want to help you find out what is causing you to add so much pain to your life. Will you let me help?"

For the sake of time, I'll cut the dialogue down and simply say that we eventually got down to the revelation that she did not trust people. It was a stronghold in her life and showed up in numerous behaviors. She struggled with suspicion, and it kept her from letting people speak into her life. Several students had tried to address their situation over the summer, but she did not allow it to affect her decisions. She felt like those people were trying to control her, and her fear blinded her to the care and concern they had for her. This issue had wreaked havoc with her for many years. She was fearful, isolated, often stubborn, and guarded. I got to the bottom of things with her through the same process: questions. I only asked questions—lots and lots of questions, but the right questions.

Asking the right questions in the right way is one of the keys to creating a safe place. A successful confrontation depends on how safe those being confronted feel. If we ignore their need for a safe place, we set them up to act like defensive, blaming, unloving, selfish people who are more interested in saving their own lives than cleaning up messes they've made. We then completely miss who they really are and blame them for their behavior. A process that respects the need for trust and honor will have an entirely different outcome because it allows them to be free—free from control, punishment, and fear. This is how we do Kingdom confrontation. (We will explore this process more fully in a later chapter.)

We had two people in the same situation with two completely different problems. He was afraid of other people being upset with him, and she was afraid of other people controlling her. By the time we discovered these problems, they no longer expected to be beheaded over them. We had created a safe place for them to be themselves, the amazing people they truly are. It was then time to help them fix their problems and set them free from the shame of their mistake.

I asked them another question. "Who is affected by these problems in your life? It's like you walked through a room with a big bucket of paint and then dropped it. Paint has splashed all over the place. Who has paint on them?"

They began to remember the people they loved, the people who didn't yet know that she was pregnant. These were people who loved them, who believed in them, and who had honored them. These were the relationships they wanted to protect—their parents, siblings, leaders in the School of Ministry, and leaders back home. His small home church had been taking a monthly offering to help pay for his school tuition. She had a newly saved brother who thought she had hung the moon. These two represented Jesus to him.

It was as though Banning, Jill, and I could see these two remembering all these people in succession, and as they came to mind, they realized how this situation was going to hurt them. They wept as they listed the names, finally experiencing the pain that this problem had created in their lives. Our team just sat silently, recognizing that this was the *"godly sorrow"* that the Bible talks about.[1] It was leading these two to repentance, and we needed to let it do its work and bear its fruit.

They continued to sob. No amount of threat or punishment could have created what was happening inside of them in that moment. It was a beautiful thing, and it all happened from the inside out. No one forced them to see anything. No one tried to talk them into repenting. This all came to the surface because we trusted them to have a great deal of love and respect inside of them, and because we asked them the right questions.

After they listed the people in their lives who would be most impacted by the news that she was pregnant, Banning, Jill, and I mentioned some people they didn't get to, people who were important to us. I asked, "What about the rest of the Second Year students? How are they going to be affected by this?"

"This news will totally affect them. They are our classmates," he said.

But she retorted, "Some of them will care, but most of them don't even need to know about it!"

"Ah, is this some more of that same problem?" I asked her.

"What?" she asked, seeming not to understand.

"Is this another time when you think that you need to defend yourself from the people who most likely do care about you?"

"I don't know," she said, knowing she had been busted.

"You don't know, or you see what I am saying?"

"I see what you are saying," she admitted.

"Good. Thanks for taking a look at that. Now, what about the First Year students who see you as leaders in this community? How will they be affected by this problem?" I specifically addressed her with this question.

"What! They are a bunch of strangers to us! Why would they be affected by this?" she barked out, upset by my audacity.

But her boyfriend said, "You're right. We are supposed to be leaders in this school. They will totally be affected by us and what we've done."

I asked her what she thought of that perspective. She didn't like it but did agree that it might affect some of them.

"Might? Or *will* affect them?" I asked her. I was committed to pinning her down each time that issue of trust and vulnerability tried to keep her from showing her best self in the situation.

"Will!" she blurted out, followed by a half smile to thank me for not letting her get around it.

I then asked, "What are you going to do? You made a pretty good-sized mess here. We know who has paint on them. What are you going to do to clean it up?"

They went through the list and began to come up with solutions. "We are going to call these family members and we are going to write letters to these people. We will inform them of what's going on, repent, and ask them for forgiveness."

I asked them, "How much time do you need?"

After they conferred together, he said, "One week. We want a week to be able to contact our family and clean up this mess."

"All right," I said. "We will wait and take care of the School of Ministry students involved in the mess later."

And so they did what they had said. Within the week, they contacted their family members and their church leaders, and also went to Pastors Bill Johnson and Kris Vallotton, and some other school staff members. No longer were these people ready to be kicked out of the school. No longer were these people who deserved to be punished. They were met by a stream of loving responses and affirmation by almost every person they approached. There were a couple of unfavorable responses, but this couple had more than enough grace toward those folks.

You see, ***shame is removed through love.*** Shame tries to keep people trapped in their mistakes by convincing them that there is nothing they can do, that they are powerless. When we lovingly removed the shame over them, these two became powerful again, faced their consequences, and went around cleaning up their mess. All they could do was clean up their mess. They could not change the past, but they could go to those they loved and ask for forgiveness. In asking forgiveness, they were saying, "Please allow me to manifest my love toward you and protect this relationship. Please let me clean up this mess." Love cast out their fear and made them powerful again.

The following week they came back to school. Banning and Jill found a break in the class schedule. Banning called my office and asked me to come up to Second Year and facilitate the "clean up." I knew how difficult this might be for some of the students. I knew that some of them would have no place to put what was about to happen. So I wanted to put the experience in a context for them to consider over the next few minutes and months. I gathered the class together and said, "All right, everyone. Something is about to happen that many of you may have never experienced before. Before they say a word, I want all of you to remember something very important. It may be tempting to judge these two for what they are about to share with you. So, please, remember this: each and every one of you in this room, without exception, is a low-life scumbag without Jesus in your life. Please keep that in mind while you listen to what they have to share with you. If any of you have judgments toward them, I want you to come and talk to me personally, before I hear it coming from somebody else that you spoke with."

Then I signaled for the couple to come up. The young man started by saying, "I want to apologize to this class because I know that we are a part of you and you are a part of us. Over the summer we ended up messing up and now we're going to have a baby."

I was struck by his humility and vulnerability. He was truly repenting to this group of peers. He went on to say, "I've discovered a problem in my life I didn't know I had. It has been causing a lot of problems for me. I am working on it now. I have more hope now than I have ever had about solving this problem. But as it stands, this is what's going on." He explained the whole thing. She stood there with him, humble and vulnerable, and after he had finished, did the same thing.

I invited one of their fellow students, Brandon, who held a fatherly role in the class, to come pray for them, forgive them, and restore them to a heavenly standard in relationship with the rest of the class. When he got up, 47 other students—the whole class—got up with him and surrounded these two, pressing in on them. Some began to weep. Brandon began to pray prayers of forgiveness and love. He welcomed them back into fellowship with the community of the class. Someone else told them how much they loved them and thanked them for not leaving the school. Another student thanked them for trusting the class with this part of their lives.

Then the students prophesied over them and the baby. They accepted the baby into the community. The whole class wept together. It was truly an amazing time. I was stunned by the response, but at the same time I knew these people, and that all of them were amazing!

The room felt much lighter as people hugged and smiled through tear-covered faces. Then someone came in from First Year and said, "Hey! First Year has time to do this now."

"Do you want to do this now?" I asked them.

They said, "We might as well."

"All right, let's go."

I led the way. As the two of them headed to the First Year class, the 47 Second Year students followed them. The First Year students could not help but be aware of a huge presence entering their classroom. The 47-student entourage lined the walls of the room like an army of guardian angels as this couple stood before 100 strangers and repented.

I asked Kevin Drury, a pastor who had taken a year off from his ministry to come to BSSM, to pray for them, bless them, and forgive them. As he got up, 100 First Year students stood up and gathered around the couple to pray and bless them. Kevin began to pray and prophesy over them, breaking the curse of shame and illegitimacy over this baby and severing the enemy's legal right to access and destroy this child through shame. It was a powerful time of love and reconciliation.

One hundred strangers embraced and loved on this couple that day. They had done all they could to clean up their mess, and carried on as some of the prime examples amongst our Second Year students for the remainder of the year.

Months later, they got married and shortly after, welcomed a daughter into the world. But from the day she was born, she was fighting for her life. Something was wrong with her blood, and she was dying day by day. Her light was going out. They were living at a specialty children's hospital in Northern California, sending us report after report that the baby was dying. Wherever we were when these reports came in, as well as in our church services and staff meetings, we prayed. But she continued to decline for weeks.

There was desperation in the last phone call we received from this new mother. "She is going to die. The doctors have all said that she won't make it through the night. Please pray!" After this call, I specifically remembered and declared Kevin's prayer. I remembered that there was no shame on this child. I remembered that the enemy had no right to this baby. I reminded our team of the process of restoration they had gone through. We remembered the honor and protection that we had given to this family. Our team prayed in our staff meeting and declared that Kevin's prayer canceled the shame. Death and destruction had no jurisdiction over this child's life.

The next day we got a call.

"The doctors don't know what happened, but they are calling our baby 'The Lazarus baby,'" said a very excited new mother. To this day, their baby girl is alive and well. She is strong, beautiful, and full of life.

The following year, this same young mother was one of the speakers at a Third Year gathering. She got up and, through tears, said, "I just want to thank the leaders in this house. You transfer strength and life from this culture to everybody who comes into it. You build strength in other people. You've given us an inheritance. We will never be the same because of how you managed a situation in our life. Not many other leaders would have handled our situation the way you did. You will never know how deeply that has affected us. You gave us life in a situation that could have easily derailed us for many years to follow. You've given us a relationship that we will die for. Thank you!"

The miraculous recovery of this child was nothing short of supernatural. But the environment in which it occurred is what we simply call "Bethel." As I mentioned, it's becoming a place known for its many miraculous testimonies. But it's the stories of the people who make up this miraculous culture that illustrate the lifestyle and relationships that actually create an environment that draws Heaven to earth. Our culture is what this book is about. Without understanding the core values that drive us, you won't understand the fruit we are getting.

At the heart of this culture is a value for freedom. We don't allow people to use this freedom to create chaos. We have boundaries, but we use these boundaries to make room for a level of personal expression that brings what is really inside of people to the surface. When people are given choices, it reveals the level of freedom they are prepared to handle. When people discover their true capacity for self-control and responsibility, they then have the revelation and opportunity they need to grow toward the freedom that God desires for each of His sons and daughters.

Before we begin to explore the core values of Bethel's culture, however, I feel it's important to expose you to our leadership structure. Our leadership is responsible for empowering and equipping the saints with the revelation and impartation they need to exercise their freedom in a safe place, and I believe we have been successful in this because our leadership has been aligned with the *apostolic* and *prophetic anointings*. I will explain these terms and how they work in the following chapter.

CHAPTER 2

THE FUNNEL FROM HEAVEN

There is nothing like returning to a place that remains unchanged
to find the ways in which you yourself have altered.
(Nelson Mandela, South African Statesman)

I believe that one of the primary factors that has kept Bethel Church in a state of *preparation for* and *stewardship of* the outpouring of the Spirit is the "wineskin" of its leadership, which has been established with an *apostolic and prophetic foundation* and with an expression of each of the other fivefold ministry graces described in Ephesians 4:11—the *pastor, teacher,* and *evangelist.* I believe this is true because I, as a member of this team, have seen firsthand how these diverse anointings each address an essential part of the identity and purpose of the Church through their specific areas of focus and motivation. Without a complete, mature expression of these graces that equip the saints, the people of God cannot be adequately prepared to contain what God is pouring out and release it to the world around them.

I am convinced that one of the reasons senior church leaders experience the disheartening cycle of great outpourings that gradually return to business as usual is a lack of understanding of the fivefold ministry, of their own ministry anointings and callings, and of how their anointings shape the direction of their churches. I hope in this chapter and throughout this book to lay a foundation for understanding these roles and anointings so that leaders can recognize how they themselves and others on their teams can begin to draw on and administer the grace God has deposited in them.

Before I do that, lest you think that every leader at Bethel grew up knowing that he or she was called to ministry and exactly how God had anointed him or her, I want to share the story of my own calling to pastor.

My history as a church leader started in March of 1995. At the time, I was working in a foster care agency called Remi Vista in Mt. Shasta, California. I had just completed eight years of college to complete my Master's degree in social work from UC-Sacramento. My wife, Sheri, our children Brittney, Levi, and Taylor, and I were finally ready to pursue my career in marriage and family therapy. Sheri's litany through that extremely stressful eight-year journey was to joke, "Show me the money!" We were ready for some payoff.

One weekend in March, we made our annual two-hour trek through the mountain roads toward home: Mountain Chapel in Weaverville, California. Sheri and I both grew up in this small community and attended the same high school there together. We had many "Before Christ" memories of this little town, and we had both accepted the Lord under Bill Johnson's ministry at Mountain Chapel within a month of each other.

Going to church in Weaverville was always worthwhile for us. This particular trip, like all of them, was filled with great fellowship, catching up on the lives of so many friends, and informing them of all the current events in our own young family. After church that

Sunday, Kris Vallotton asked Sheri and me to join him for lunch because he had a "proposition" for us. We were excited just to catch up with another dear friend, but we were also certainly curious to find out about this new idea Kris had up his sleeve that, as he had hinted, could possibly alter our whole lives.

After some small talk, he asked us if we knew that Bob Johnson, Bill's brother, was leaving Mountain Chapel to start a new work in Redding. We hadn't known this. He then went on to inform us that he had permission from Bill and the church board to ask us if I would consider replacing Bob as the new associate pastor under Bill. My hands and nose started to get cold. I could see Kris's mouth moving, but I couldn't hear what he was saying. I was going into shock. We told him that we would need some time.

I remember lying in total darkness that night next to Sheri. We were silent, which was unusual, since Sheri, the ultimate verbal processor, was still awake. Finally, out of the dark silence she asked, "Are you thinking about what I am thinking about?"

"Yes," I said, and we burst into nervous laughter. We couldn't believe what was happening.

Within a few months we moved our family to Weaverville so the kids could start school fresh in September. I continued to work in Mt. Shasta and drove home on the weekends. In November, I began my new staff position at Mountain Chapel. But in between those two events, something interesting happened.

One Saturday in September, Bill and Beni Johnson called us into Bill's office to talk. We figured there would be many of these "little chats" to help us get our bearings, keep us informed of our new position, and spell things out for us, as we were coming completely fresh and untrained into the ministry. We were mistaken.

We noticed that Bill and Beni seemed to be laughing nervously as we began the meeting. Beni opened the conversation by telling us how glad they were that we were there. She said that they had never felt the peace that they now did and were so comforted by our presence on the team. She and Bill talked about our pastoral gifts and said that the people would be loved and well cared for under our leadership. I felt something rising up inside me as they went on, but it wasn't pride or great satisfaction. It was fear. The more they talked to us, the more I sensed what was coming. The bomb finally dropped when Beni said, "We've been feeling like the Lord is going to move us on from here. We've felt it for many years, but up to now could never feel good about who we would trust to lead the church. But now that you two are here, we feel so relieved."

I could feel the blood running out of my head. I felt like I was going to faint. Had I just heard what I thought I had just heard? My thoughts raced in my head. *Do you think I came back here to ruin the church that I love, the home where I got saved? Do you have any idea what it would be like to pastor this church of radicals in the small town where you grew up as an unbeliever?* **Are you kidding me?!**

Bill and Beni were laughing. I am sure my face was frozen with shock and terror, in spite of my greatest efforts to conceal what I was feeling. Suddenly, I had a clear thought. *What was the time frame they had in mind for this change?* I asked, "Are you talking about five years from now? Three years?"

Beni answered, "February. We think we are leaving in February. We have no idea why, but that's the month we keep getting."

"February 2000?" I whispered.

"No," she laughed, "February, six months from now. 1996."

At that point I thought for sure I was going to faint or vomit.

That was the last "little chat" about our coming on board. Sure enough, six months later they were gone. Bethel Church interviewed Bill in December of that year, 1995, and offered him a position as senior pastor. He informed them that he had to "train" a new pastor back at Mountain Chapel and would need some time. "February," he told them, "will be the earliest that I can come to Bethel." Just like that, we were sliding toward the leadership role as pastors. I guess we could have said no, but we knew that the Lord had a plan.

After our meeting with Bill and Beni that September morning, however, I was mad. I was spitting mad, mainly because I was so scared. I had thought that we would come to Weaverville and learn from the "Master Pastor." This hope had been dashed in a few moments and suddenly turned into an unexpected, terrifying...promotion. I worked to master my fears by telling myself, *Maybe God is in this. Maybe He is going to stay here even if Bill leaves. Maybe this is going to turn out all right. Maybe He will be with me. Maybe this is what He was trying to tell me 13 years earlier.*

Thirteen years earlier, I was 21 years old and had just given my heart to the Lord. I began helping Kris Vallotton, who was already a leader at Mountain Chapel, with the high school youth group, and at one point Kris prophesied this over me: "One day you will pastor here in Weaverville." I could hardly imagine that at the time, but I did my best to make the word come to pass by looking for a Bible college that I could afford. After some time of fruitless effort, however, I gave up, and in a couple of years I forgot all about that word—until it came crashing back into my mind early in the process of returning to Weaverville. Eventually, it became the weapon with which I fought my fears and inadequacies.

Remembering "He is with me" changed the way I perceived everything. After I forgave Bill for luring me into a situation I could not escape, I started to see what he saw in me—a pastoral anointing. I didn't call it that, but I started to recognize that the peace and comfort that he and Beni mentioned in our "little chat" that day was actually coming from this anointing they could see on our lives. They knew that our hearts would be focused on the people. We would make sure that their flock, the people in whom they had invested 17 years of their lives, were going to get our best.

Thankfully, they were right. As the pastor, I began teaching and preaching material from my counseling background. I started building true identity as dearly loved children of God into the hearts and minds of the people. My schedule was filled with appointments to meet with people. Couples, families, parents, men, and women were continuously coming to my office to get healed and strengthened. Our leadership team began a series called "The Search for Freedom" and started a journey to heal the wounds and lies of their pasts. One of our elders went through a radical transformation during this time that led our whole church to another level of healing, freedom, and community.

The kind of growth I have just described is the passion of the *pastoral anointing*. The pastor needs to know that the people are healthy and strong. He or she knows that the Gospel comes alive as the saints apply and manifest true love and freedom in their lives. This anointing allows God to cultivate His heart in His people. The Good Shepherd is at work through the anointing of pastors.

Bill and Beni had known that their church had been without a strong pastoral anointing for years. Bill's *apostolic* anointing had been growing stronger over the previous decade, and his focus was increasingly more caught up with Heaven's concerns than human concerns. His associate pastor and brother, Bob Johnson, carried a strong *evangelistic* anointing, and his focus was on the lost. And the other leader with a strong anointing was a *prophet,* Kris Vallotton. Each of these anointings turns the attention and priority away from the saints and places that urgency elsewhere, as I will explain in more detail in just a moment.

Stepping into that pastoral vacuum was a little heady. Because I wasn't replacing the apostle but was providing a fresh perspective that met different needs, it was easy for the church to value and receive me as a leader. I remember Bill telling me that the transition of leadership was supernatural, describing it as "scary smooth." He was right. Mountain Chapel was ready for what the pastoral anointing would bring. We were both expecting much more fallout after his 17-year stint as the senior leader. There was none. This was my first lesson in understanding the nature and importance of each member of the fivefold ministry, and the Lord has only continued to build on this understanding since then.

The Fivefold Anointings

I think I can best introduce the attributes of the fivefold anointings by describing what might happen if they all arrived together at the scene of a car accident:

> *The pastor* is the first one out of the car. He scrambles to assess the situation and begins a triage approach in applying First Aid to injured victims. He gathers blankets, jackets, water, and anything else he can find to try to comfort them. He surveys the situation to see if anything is threatening the safety both of those who are receiving care and those who have been drawn to the scene of the accident. He talks with each person to find out his or her name, marital status, and whether he or

she has children. He gathers vital sign information and any available emergency contact information in order to help the emergency response team when they arrive. He brings a sense of calm to the situation, and each person there feels a genuine feeling of care and connection to the pastor. He wonders whether he should have been a doctor.

The teacher is next on the scene. He studies the situation in order to figure out what caused the accident. He steps back, notices the patterns of the skid marks and the distance each car moved before and after the impact, and estimates the speed of each car at the point of impact. Drawing from his deep knowledge of the driver's manual and traffic laws, he develops a theory about who was at fault. His conclusion is that, overall, drivers need more training and would most likely benefit from mandatory classes and continuing education requirements.

The evangelist arrives on the scene and asks everyone lying in a safe, comfortable place (thanks to the pastor), "If you were to die as a result of your injuries, do you know where you would go—Heaven or hell?" He then notices that there is a large gathering of bystanders and people in their cars who have pulled over to watch. He begins to address the larger crowd with the same question. "There are no guarantees that you will make it home safely. Do you know where you would go?" People give their hearts to the Lord right there on the side of the road. He explains to all these new believers that the greatest gift you can ever give to someone else is the gift of salvation. He trains them to lead others to Christ and prays for the baptism of the Holy Spirit to come upon them all. Afterward he says, "This was great!" and decides to go purchase a police scanner when he gets back to town.

The prophet knew this was going to happen because he had a dream about it the previous night. Because everyone in the dream had survived the accident, he rebukes a spirit of death and declares with great faith and unction that all shall live and none shall die. He also proclaims that there are angels surrounding the scene of the accident and prays that the eyes of all the people's hearts will be opened to see in the Spirit. Then he walks around and starts to call the destiny out in various people. He releases a spirit of revelation within the group. And finally, and quite naturally, he begins to ask around to find out who is in charge at the scene. When he discovers the one in charge, he discerns whether this is God's chosen leader or not. Or if he finds that no one is in charge, he will appoint a leader.

The apostle prays for the injured. He invites the supernatural healing touch of God into the scene. He begins to tell testimonies of when he has been on the scene of car accidents and witnessed the power of God manifest itself in those situations. The faith level of the people begins to rise. He then asks if anyone can feel heat in his or her hands. He puts those who raise their hands to work praying for others to be healed. He demonstrates to all who are near that the Kingdom of Heaven is at hand. He then opens a school for those who arrive at car accident scenes and sends them all over the world to do signs and wonders.

Hopefully this scenario displays the reality that each anointing is also a *mindset*. Each anointing determines how a person will see various circumstances and situations, and as a result, makes different solutions available and applicable to the same situation. No anointing is more important or more correct. They are simply God's gifts to His Church to help bring Heaven's perspective to the earth.

Apostles and Prophets

Before we explore the five primary anointings in more detail, along with their strengths and weaknesses, let me point to the scriptural basis for both the offices and the priority order of the apostle and prophet:

> *Now you are Christ's body, and individually members of it. And God has appointed in the church, **first apostles, second prophets**, third teachers, then miracles, then gifts of healings, helps, administrations, various kinds of tongues.*[1]

Paul clearly lays out an order of priority in this passage, and this order is related to the realms of the supernatural that correspond to each particular office. As you could see in the previous illustration, the anointing on the apostle and prophet creates a perspective that is primarily focused on perceiving what is going on in Heaven and bringing that to earth. The teacher is focused on being able to describe everything that happened accurately, and the evangelist and pastor are focused on the people. Each of these areas of focus is vitally important, but in order for them to function together as God intended, they must relate to one another according to His order of priority. The areas of heavenly focus come first and influence the areas of earthly focus.

When Paul makes apostles first, prophets second, and teachers third, he is describing a flow. The flow streams through the teacher, is released in miracles and healing, and continues through helps and administrations and tongues. Tragically, in many churches today, the practices of teaching, helps, and administration have become largely devoid of the supernatural. It seems as though these gifts were plucked out of the list and separated from the *flow* of the supernatural supply of Heaven, and actually, that is exactly what has happened. In order to protect this flow, the Church needs to be founded upon leaders who carry a primary core value for the supernatural.

Rather than having the apostle and prophet at the foundation of church culture, today the American church has largely placed the *teacher, pastor,* or *evangelist* at the helm. But effectively divorcing the supernatural from ministry in this way has drastically impacted the general understanding of the true role of each anointing. Today in most churches the role of a teacher is to state clearly and accurately the truths of the Bible in a theologically sound message in an effort to build security into the lives of believers. The role of the pastor is to create a church that has strong family values and systems in place to nourish strong character and relationships. The role of the evangelist is to emphasize church growth and to train church members to share their faith and lead others to Christ.

The problem is that these are earthly-focused models of leadership. Without the flow of grace from the apostles and prophets, who are not only focused on seeing what is going on in Heaven but also on releasing that reality here on earth, these models will inevitably lead us to focus on what we know God has done in the past and miss out on what He is doing now. They lead us to care more about knowledge than experience.

It's even harder to avoid this imbalance when we live in a society that is permeated with it. Most of the schools, colleges, and universities of our land have embraced a dualistic worldview that separates knowledge from experience. This worldview reduces the goal of teaching to the mere transmission of information. This paradigm is certainly present in the Church, and the result is that much of the teaching ministry in the Church today is devoid of supernatural revelation and power. It is limited to what can be done from earth's authority and resources.

But the fivefold anointing of teaching, one of the gifts of Christ, who modeled just what each anointing does, is very different. Jesus exercised His teaching gift by both *preaching* and *demonstrating* His message with miracles. Those who experienced His teaching were shocked by how different it was, and it was different because, unlike their other teachers, He taught with authority.[2] Christ is the model that defines the ministry of teaching in His church, and the implication of His teaching model is that unless we bring people into the tangible, supernatural reality of the Gospel, we have no authority to teach it.

I realize that the kind of government I am describing, in which there is a clear order of priority in the various roles, is difficult to understand and embrace in American culture. Our American style of democratic government is designed to keep all its governing members in a system of checks and balances, where each branch of government must be accountable to another branch so that no one legislator, judge, or president can gain control of the whole government. I understand that and value this in an earthly model. Nonetheless, it is there in the Scripture: "first apostles, second prophets, third teachers…." I believe that much of the Church has ignored this Scripture and has been using templates gleaned from earth's governors in an attempt to replicate Heaven. But only Heaven's template can reproduce Heaven on the earth.

When we use other models, the Church becomes no more than what people already expect from their earthly experiences. This is a huge and fundamental mistake, with serious consequences. I think we've been duped! When we use man's governing systems to define or reproduce Heaven, we've started down the path of implementing an inferior system. Heaven will not conform to or replicate an inferior system. Heaven must be the source.

In the passage from First Corinthians 12 quoted previously, Paul pointed to Heaven's template for government. He clearly stated an order in church ministry, of which I've heard little outside my immediate environment throughout my 20 years as a Christian. This order is supported by Ephesians 2:17-22 (NASB):

> *And He came and preached peace to you who were far away, and peace to those who were near; for through Him we both have our access in one Spirit to the Father. So then you are no longer strangers and aliens, but you are fellow citizens with the saints, and are of God's household, **having been built on the foundation of the apostles and prophets**, Christ Jesus Himself being the corner stone, in whom the whole building, being fitted together, is growing into a holy temple in the Lord, in whom you also are being built together into a dwelling of God in the Spirit.*

"God's household" literally rests on the foundation or leadership of the apostles and prophets. This design allows the Body of Christ to be built up into a "holy temple" and ultimately to become a "dwelling place of God." Isn't this what we desire?

As I've been hinting, the critical flaw I see in the American design for church structure and government, though it's not limited to America, is *disorder,* meaning that the roles and relationships of leaders are out of order according to Scripture. The foundations and leadership of most churches today consist of pastors, teachers, and administrators.

We've empowered the wrong portion of the list in First Corinthians 12 to be the primary leaders, and the reasoning behind this decision is not spiritual, but earthly. James 3:13-18 (NASB) warns us against this practice of pulling earthly wisdom into our lives:

> *Who among you is wise and understanding? Let him show by his good behavior his deeds in the gentleness of wisdom. But if you have bitter jealousy and selfish ambition in your heart, do not be arrogant and so lie against the truth.* **This wisdom is not that which comes down from above, but is earthly, natural, demonic. For where jealousy and selfish ambition exist, there is disorder and every evil thing.** *But the wisdom from above is first pure, then peaceable, gentle, reasonable, full of mercy and good fruits, unwavering, without hypocrisy. And the seed whose fruit is righteousness is sown in peace by those who make peace.*

When Heaven is the model for our culture, the primary result is *peace*. Peace is the goal of Heaven because it is the primary quality of the government of God. But the disordered forms of government to which we've all become accustomed create not peace, but *control*, which is their intended goal. Man has the opposite goal of Heaven. Earth's leadership structure is motivated by the desire to protect the rule of those in office. When we primarily structure the environment of God's house to protect the will of the people, we've stepped off the path of the "wisdom from above."

To see the seriousness of doing things according to human reasoning rather than Heaven's, we need only remember one of the strongest rebukes in the Gospels, the rebuke Jesus gave to His good friend Peter. If you recall, Peter tried to talk Jesus out of going to die on the cross. Peter wanted to protect what he could see was a good thing. His primary concern and motivation was to keep the current benefit flowing to earth. Jesus turned to him and said, *"Get behind Me, Satan! ...You do not have in mind the things of God, **but the things of men.**"*[3] It was not one of Peter's finest moments, but it is a clear word to all of us watching. Heaven is the model—not earth.

"...First Apostles..."

You have likely heard the term *apostolic ministry* used more in recent years. I am confident that we will hear and see more of it in the years to come. This term is something that needs defining early in this book because I will make frequent references to it from here on. Through this term, I will be referring to the primary goals and objectives of the apostle's leadership, and therefore, *the goals with which all the people under the apostle align themselves.*

When Jesus taught the disciples to pray, He brought a key phrase into their core values. He told them to pray, *"Your Kingdom come. Your will be done on earth as it is in heaven."*[4] His instructions taught them to long for Heaven on earth. I believe this core value is the primary objective of the apostle's ministry. Apostolic leaders are focused on Heaven, and their mission is to see Heaven's supernatural reality established on the earth. They long to see the evidence of Heaven's touch in the environment they lead or influence. Having this motivation at the foundation of a church leads to an entirely different emphasis in the church's governing priorities. The apostle will make the presence of God, the worship of God, and the agenda of Heaven the top priorities in the environment. An apostolic government is designed to protect these priorities.

The apostle Paul refers to himself as the *"master builder"* in First Corinthians 3:10. This is a translation of the Greek word *architekton,* the word from which we derive the English word "architect."

This perfectly describes the role of the apostolic ministry. It is as though God Himself has given blueprints to certain individuals to reproduce Heaven on the earth. Along with this blueprint, the anointing of the apostle contains a quality that stimulates and draws to the surface the diverse anointings in the people around him. As those around the apostle begin to manifest their own unique anointings, it creates an environment of "sub-contractors" who help the "master builder" to realize the blueprints of Heaven.

The following are some of the key characteristics of an apostolic environment and culture:

1. Worship and supernatural activity are priorities in the environment and the lifestyle of the saints, because God's presence is the top priority.

2. The saints are sent, as Jesus was, to destroy the works of the devil, including disease, sickness, and affliction. The saints live to demonstrate to all the people on earth that God is always the good guy and the devil is always the bad guy.

3. The Kingdom of God is *"joy in the Holy Spirit."*[5] Therefore, church is to be a place of exceeding, abundant joy.

4. God desires those who don't yet know Him to come into a relationship with Him where the primary emphasis is love, not merely service.

5. The Body of Christ is being built up and equipped to become a glorious and victorious Bride, no matter how the conditions of the earth may presently appear.

6. The Church is to create global awakening and impact.

7. Successive generations must be equipped to carry and demonstrate Kingdom revelation.

At Bethel Church we have an "offering reading" that we declare as a congregation over our region each Sunday. A few years ago, Mike and Debbie Adams moved to Redding from another state to attend Bethel's School of Supernatural Business. After being in the congregation and absorbing the culture, Debbie wrote what has become affectionately known as "our second offering reading." It really best sums up what I mean by apostolic ministry:

As we receive today's offering we are believing YOU for:

Heaven open, earth invaded

Storehouses unlocked and miracles created

Dreams and visions

Angelic visitations

Declaration, impartation, and divine manifestations

Anointings, giftings, and calls

Positions and promotions

Provisions and resources

To go to the nations

Souls and more souls

From every generation

Saved and set free

Carrying Kingdom revival

Thank You, Father, that as I join my value system to Yours,
You will shower FAVOR, BLESSING, and INCREASE
upon me so I have more than enough to co-labor with
Heaven to see Jesus get His FULL REWARD!
HALLELUJAH!

An apostolic environment is an exciting place, because the focus on Heaven allows prayer, worship, miracles, signs, and wonders to become normal in our daily lives. However, there is one particular area that the role of the apostle is not designed to address directly: the needs of people. Do you remember what the apostles said when confronted with the needs of the people in Acts 6:4? "But we will devote ourselves to prayer and to the ministry of the word" (NASB). They were acting like apostles. The increasing needs of the people were a distraction to their role and anointing. It's not that they didn't care about the people. They did something to make sure that quality men in their community addressed those needs. But an apostle has to have the freedom to pursue Heaven if he or she is effectively going to fulfill an apostolic call.

The Downside

When an apostle pursues his or her calling without the other ministry graces in place, several real issues creep into the environment and threaten success for the apostolic leader. Unusual manifestations not found in the Bible, unprecedented scenarios and styles, an uncomfortable focus on the supernatural, and a noticeable inattention to the needs of the people begin to create friction for any apostolic leader. All the people can see is the distance growing between them and the apostle. As the people's needs go unmet, they can begin to resent the way the apostle is choosing to use his or her time. Travel, meetings, connection with other apostolic leaders, and prayer seem like luxurious expenditures of time when the needs of the people are screaming in their own ears.

I've heard people say, "Signs and wonders are great. Miracles are amazing. I am happy for all those blind people who can see now. But we are going to another church where they care about people, where they teach the Bible, and where they are less emotional. This church doesn't even have a way for new people to get plugged in." This may seem petty, but it is a real complaint that moves people away from an apostolic leader and a revival environment after a while. Open heavens and open back doors are the sweet and sour of the apostolic leader. This is why they need the rest of the team.

"...Second Prophets..."

The next vital piece in the government of a revival culture is the role of the prophet. This is the next piece of the plumbing that pipes Heaven to earth. The foundation is incomplete without the presence of the prophetic anointing. God emphasizes the vitally important role of the prophet throughout the Scriptures:

> *Listen to me, O Judah and inhabitants of Jerusalem, put*
> *your trust in the Lord your God and you will be established.*
> *Put your trust in His prophets and succeed.*[6]

Success is built through the value we maintain for the prophetic voices in our environment, because our prosperity comes through our agreements with Heaven's culture, and the prophets clarify the reality of that culture for us and invite us to enter it. Our experience of prophetic leadership in Bethel's culture has come in many different forms. The number of prophetic voices poured into the formation of our course and destiny seems enormous, from Bob Jones to Bobby Conner; from Dick Joyce to Dick Mills; from Mario Murillo to Michael Ratliff; from Jill Austin to John Paul Jackson; from Paul Cain to Patricia King, Larry Randolph, Mahesh and Bonnie Chavda, Iverna Tompkins, Cindy Jacobs, Wes and Stacy Campbell, and Rolland and Heidi Baker. Along with these global and national prophetic voices and more, equally important local and regional voices have shaped our culture and destiny, including Wendall

McGowen, Mary Andersen, Deborah Reed, Dan McCollam, Judy Franklin, Nancy Cobb, and many others.

Kris Vallotton is the primary sculptor of Bethel's prophetic environment. He is a gift of Christ to our house and to the Body of Christ. His role as a prophet in our environment has cultivated our expectation to discover the heights and depths of the Good News. The Gospel is more than the words on the pages of Scripture. It is a reality that must unfold in the life of each believer, and one of the primary ways it does so is through prophetic ministry, which apprehends the promises of the Kingdom for individual destinies and calls them into reality through declaration. (In his book *The Supernatural Ways of Royalty,* Kris introduces the world to the core values and revelation by which he has established a prophetic culture at Bethel.)

Kris's leadership and influence as a prophet has also cultivated our expectation for God's presence. We need someone to keep us expectant and aware of the ever-present reality of the Kingdom. Apostles keep us believing, but prophets keep us expecting that God is coming. The dynamic ways in which God speaks to the prophet, including dreams, visions, and trances, create awareness of God's involvement with us. These supernatural tools introduce an infusion of sensitivity toward Heaven's activity and plans.

But more than making us aware of Heaven through his or her experiences, the anointing on the prophet actually equips us to have our own heavenly experiences. Matthew 10:41 tells us, *"He who receives a prophet in the name of a prophet shall receive a prophet's reward...."* What is this reward? The reward is to see and hear what the Spirit is doing and saying. The prophetic anointing carries a *seer* dimension, and it gives people sight to see what was invisible prior to the prophet's influence.

Jesus, who modeled the office of the prophet, walked around giving supernatural sight to others all day long. He often asked His disciples and those around Him, *"Do you not yet see or understand?"*[7] The answer was always no because He was introducing an entirely different view of life, especially to the religious leaders of the day. But that question led those same people to begin looking for something they had never considered seeing before. As a result, they received *eyes to see.*

The prophet and the apostle can get along famously because both are looking into Heaven and recreating what they see there on the earth. They should work together like a bow and arrow seeking the same goals. Doubtless, this is why they are the foundation of the New Testament church.

"...Third Teachers..."

Next we have teachers. As I mentioned, the teacher is generally accepted as the highest anointing level in the American church. But the truth is that it is not the highest anointing, but only the third level of anointing. It is a "C" in a grade scale, and it is what keeps the Church only *average* in its effects and influence. Our need and opportunity to upgrade the anointing to an "A" is growing.

Before I get too far into this section about teachers, I need to confess that this will not satisfy the needs of the teachers reading it. For most teachers, this section would have to be a book in itself, because teachers need lots of information before they can conclude most anything. I respect that about teachers. I am not going to try very hard to convince teachers that I am right or they are wrong. I am simply going to present why I think we've made a big mistake in making the teacher the highest anointing operating in the leadership of the American church.

Our current church culture has a high value for the security we feel when we are able to prove that what we have devoted our life to is right. In order to assert our faith, we assume that we must be able to argue a case to a logical conclusion. But the fact is that our need for so much certainty comes from great *uncertainty*. When Heaven stops manifesting itself in the Church, Christians have to *prove* somehow that they are reasonable for following Jesus. When the power of the Gospel is replaced by arguments, everyone should be concerned. When cancer, paralysis, tumors, and mental illness leave people's bodies and minds, we do not require an argument. A person experiencing the touch of Heaven is proof enough that Jesus is who He says He is.

But when the Church insists on having a logical culture, we demand a logical gospel, and therefore, we turn to the teachers. Most teachers today are fixated on the *written* Word of God. They believe that the Word of God is the source of life and truth on the earth. Their value for the Word is much higher than their need for the supernatural. These are the lawyers, scribes, and Pharisees of our day. They can wield the "Sword" with the best. The teacher has a deep, driving need to be right, and predominantly sees the world in terms of "scriptural" and "non-scriptural." Because the teacher's focus is on the Word, the anointing of the teacher influences the Church to focus on the Word. Please don't misunderstand me; I am not trying to devalue Scripture. But I want us to understand how unimportant Heaven has become because of this dreadful error and disorder. The teachers, as the primary influence in the Church, have turned our attention to the law.

When we focus solely on the Word, eventually we begin to fight amongst ourselves over the Word. We begin to pull apart the Body of Christ because there is a right and a wrong. Each teacher is compelled to be right. As Paul said to the Corinthians, we have "many teachers" in the Body of Christ.[8] And when the teachers disagree, and many do, there is division. Leader after leader begins to assert his or her case of doctrine and theology and builds a case to prove his or hers and disprove the others.

What then is the role of the teacher in the church if it is not to prove that Christians are right to believe what they believe? In order for teachers to play their true role in the culture of the Church, they will first have to be willing to pursue a supernatural lifestyle. They will have to be dissatisfied with the armor of their arguments and the lifelessness of their theology. They will need to increase their courage to risk failure and live a life that is unable to answer all the questions of their world. The teachers must embrace mystery.

The anointing on teachers will always cause them to have a high value for education. They will be those who believe that most problems are solved through training and informing people according to Scripture. But the real change they want to see will come under the leadership of an apostolic and prophetic culture. In a supernatural culture, teachers will teach with supernatural results.

When Jesus taught a crowd about the Kingdom of Heaven, He always *showed* them the Kingdom. His disciples were in a never-ending classroom experience. Jesus took "show and tell" to a whole new level. Our teachers must put the "show" back into their lesson plans. I've heard Bill Johnson say many times, "Jesus is perfect theology." I agree. If we see Jesus doing it, then we are on to something good. If He wasn't doing anything like what we are doing, we'd better ask ourselves, "What went wrong?"

Teachers must take the passion and the revelation of the apostles and prophets and show us how it becomes truth that we apply to our lives. The role of the teacher is to help replicate the processes of the supernatural and then train and equip the saints to cooperate with those processes. The love of Scripture and the knowledge that teachers carry help them to communicate complex processes in simple analogies and applications.

Randy Clark of Global Awakening is a prime example to me of someone with a teaching gift who uses it to help the world and the Church understand the supernatural. Although he is an apostolic leader himself, his teaching gift operates in that higher anointing. Therefore, he uses his understanding of Scripture, history, theology, and people to connect mysterious revelations to practical daily life. His models for training people to pray for the sick are excellent and highly effective methods for mobilizing prayer teams to minister to large groups in his crusades. Believers who have never prayed for others to be healed in their whole Christian experience are, within a few hours of training, seeing miracle after miracle.

A successful revival culture has teachers who are perpetuating the supernatural in it. The days of teaching our limited experiences are over. We now must learn to teach how and what Heaven is doing every day to everyone.

Where Do Pastors Fit In?

Ah, the beloved pastors, where will we put another role that has helped complete the disorder in church government? Senior Pastor. What a strange title when you look at the list that Paul laid out in First Corinthians 12. Actually, if you look at that list, pastor isn't even mentioned, let alone numbered. How is it then that Senior Pastor is the title of the most important person in the church structure? I have a hunch.

When a group of people comes together, whether it is a family, a community, a business, a school, or a church, it isn't long before that group organizes itself in such a way to get its needs met. Imagine a survival scene from a movie: The ship sinks, the plane crashes, and the people are lost. Whatever the incident, the steps are the same. The priorities are food and water, shelter, safety, and then hope for rescue. The longer the rescue delays, the more another priority develops: Who is going to lead us? The nod usually goes to the one who has the most aggressive plan to save the group, the "Indiana Jones," if you will. If that doesn't work, then the group begins to think about long-term survival. The leader they pick for the long haul is much more compassionate, steady, practical, and predictable. This leader will make sure that the needs of the people are met. He will ensure that they are civilized and safe. He will be their pastor.

Pastors emerge as long-term leaders when all hope of rescue is gone. People gather around a leader they believe will tend to their particular needs. It shows up in politics and businesses as well as churches. If the people's primary focus is on themselves, they will elect a leader who has the same focus. When the issue becomes long-term survival, the people will look for a pastoral anointing in their leader. It's as simple as that.

If the pastors are not connected to the apostles and prophets, then their leadership will only lead people back to a self-focus and the pastor will have to give them a natural alternative to a supernatural life. When a pastoral anointing is the primary leader, the people expect to be the center of the universe. And unfortunately, the pastor thrives, for a season, in that expectation, burn-out usually follows.

But when the pastoral anointing is connected to the apostle and prophet, it provides another vital piece of the flow from Heaven to earth. These caring, compassionate leaders are the necessary solution to the "back door" problem that apostles and prophets have in their leadership environments. Pastors in a revival culture bring leadership to the people. The pastoral anointing creates great favor with the people because of the connection pastors develop with them. These are the leaders who will be in their lives, homes, and families. These are the leaders who will sit with them and work out marriage problems. These are the leaders who will know about their struggles with employment or raising teenagers.

If pastors can learn to maintain a dual focus on Heaven and people, then they will be the ones who bring a revival culture to the everyday lives of the saints. Keeping this balanced focus requires effort, because pastors naturally want the people to feel loved, discipled, connected, and protected. But when they are submitted to apostolic leadership, they are able to develop cell groups, for example, without making cell groups the primary focus of the church.

With the expansion of purpose and vision, pastors are far less territorial and empowering. Allowing other pastors to rise up at their side is no longer an opportunity for competition or threat. Pastors in an apostolic anointing can lead many more people, because the people no longer need the power of the presence of the pastor.

Pastors bring the nourishing presence of God into the lives of people. They connect the people to the supernatural environment created by the apostles and prophets. Instead of leading people to themselves and then showing them the love they have for people who are hurting, pastors begin to lead the people into the presence of God to find the solutions for life's problems. It is the pastor's good pleasure to see the saints find the green pastures of freedom and comfort made available by the apostolic ministry.

"What About the Lost?"

Evangelists form the end of the funnel that ensures that Heaven's flow from the apostles through the prophets, teachers, and pastors makes it to its intended target—those held in darkness. The evangelist's anointing causes him or her to focus on the souls who do not yet know Jesus as the primary concern and motivation for ministry. And realistically, unless the ministry of the Church is reaching those who don't yet know the Lord, the function of the other anointings is fairly pointless. Perhaps it is this conviction that, strangely enough, causes evangelists to be Christians who seem to be mad at Christians. It can be an eternal frustration for those with this anointing to see that we are having another Bible study or potluck at church while people around the city are perishing to everlasting damnation. It just doesn't make any sense to them.

Nonetheless, we are all on the same team. Becoming frustrated with one another doesn't help us flow together, so what is the solution? I believe it's time for the ministry of the evangelist—which both reaches the unsaved and equips the saints to do the same—to be more deeply integrated into the larger purposes of apostolic ministry.

It is easy for us to believe that anyone can lead another person to Christ. We have great faith that when we pray with someone to accept Jesus, the person is truly born again, right there on the spot. The vast majority of the Christian church today believes that to be true. This concept has only gained momentum since it was introduced several hundred years ago in revival. It was captured by teachers and pastors and preserved among the people in the church. Today the Methodists, Baptists, and other Evangelicals are champions of salvation throughout the world, and nearly every Christian denomination sends missionaries to carry the message of salvation to the ends of the earth. The culture of most churches has an evangelical practice among the people. Teachers teach it and pastors encourage it. The evangelists beat the drum everywhere they go: "We must go and win souls!" But the bigger question is, "Then what?"

The Kingdom of Heaven invading the earth is the goal, not unsaved people invading the Church. The cooperation between all the ministry gifts is the only way to accomplish the primary objective of the Church. We must cooperate with the Holy Spirit in carefully and intentionally assembling the pipe that funnels Heaven and all its power and freedom to the earth. When we do, the importance of the entire Christian church being fully equipped by all the ministry graces so that the Kingdom of Heaven "leaks" from our lives will soon be a concept as widely accepted as praying a prayer of salvation.

Honor Is the Hardware

Honor is the hardware that bolts all this plumbing together. This "funnel" is actually a network of relationships, relationships in which the "flow" I'm describing only continues as we learn to recognize these God-given roles and anointings, release people to operate in them, and receive what they have to give. Those called to operate in a fivefold anointing, as my personal story shows, need other fivefold ministers, especially the prophets and apostles, to identify those anointings. None of us are self-appointed in the Kingdom. God anoints a person, and His Spirit in the rest of the team creates a corporate witness that acknowledges God's anointing and receives the person in his or her role. Only acts of honor such as these can establish and sustain these relationships.

The fivefold design for leadership is obviously a team design, so the one-man show version of Church leadership is clearly not an expression of it, and neither is the bureaucratic, homogenous, "everyone can do every job" style of leadership. Diverse anointings each contribute something entirely unique to the project of bringing Heaven to earth, and this requires an honoring (and undemocratic) attitude that says, "You have something I don't have, and I need what you have."

When fivefold leaders model this kind of honor amongst themselves, then "equipping the saints" becomes a matter of extending honor by releasing every individual believer into his or her unique identity and destiny. Each believer comes to understand his or her significance in relationship to the whole Body, and the conviction begins to take hold: "I carry something that no one else carries. I must develop and release my gifts into the Church and the world and do my part in bringing Heaven to earth." Honor empowers people.

It is time for everyone in the Church to begin honoring those with fivefold anointings, especially those with fivefold anointings! Apostles, prophets, teachers, pastors, and evangelists must honor each other and receive each other with the right "name." Church leaders and believers alike must come into right relationship with Heaven's government. As we do, those things that are out of joint will be restored to their rightful place and hooked up to the flow of the funnel.

Honor has fallen on hard times in our culture. Independence is worshiped. We focus on our private relationships with God and have a hard time recognizing spiritual authority and considering others as more important than ourselves. The result is that we are cut off from the flow of Heaven. The remarkable growth that Bethel has experienced in the last ten years is a testimony to the remarkable difference people are seeing in an environment where the funnel is connected and people are getting in on the flow.

Like Moses pouring oil over Aaron's head, God is continuously pouring life, joy, health, peace, and all the other blessings of Heaven into His funnel. The many wonderful effects of a supernaturally charged environment are overwhelming. "We are not in Kansas anymore, Toto," is the feeling many have when they experience a church where Heaven fills the room. It is the powerful experience of a wineskin that is fully capable to carry and release the outpouring that God has promised to us all along—an outpouring for which we were made. But only honor will build this wineskin, keep it intact, and get us involved with what is inside it.

CHAPTER 3

GOVERNING FROM HEAVEN

...And the government will be upon His shoulder...
Of the increase of His government and
peace there will be no end,
upon the throne of David and over His kingdom,
to order it and establish it with judgment and justice
from that time forward, even forever.
The zeal of the Lord of hosts will perform this.
(Isaiah 9:6-7)

This whole chapter strikes at the heart of the Accuser. But first, I have to give you a little warning because I'm going to offend you for a few moments. I'm going to mess with your entire paradigm of justice. I'm going to take it out, laugh at it, tickle it, and then I'm going to kick it down the stairs. Okay? You're going to have to chase it down the stairs if you want it back.

Imagine this. Your fifth grader comes to you and says, "Here is my report card." You take his report card, open it up, and there is an F on it. Your fifth grader got an F. *Aaugh!* The spirit of fear manifests in you, just as it would in the heart of every parent. "A fifth grader with an F! He's doomed—doomed! It's over. You can't get F's until high school."

Sure enough, with fear gripping your heart, all you can think about is, "How do I control this child's educational outcome?" This could be the thought of any good parent. How are you going to control your child toward *your* goal, because you love him? This is part of the lesson of love that most of us send to our children: *That which we love, we try to control.*

I'd like to introduce another option. Imagine the parent going to the child and saying, "Oh, nooo! An F in fifth grade? We have an early bloomer, ahead of the curve—I knew this about you. I just want you to know that your mother and I have talked. We've figured something out here, and we want you to know this—we are going to love you no matter how many years it takes you to get through the fifth grade. And son, we figured this out too—if you just wait two more years, your little sister will be in your class with you. You and her buddies could go to birthday parties together and stuff."

Your fifth grader is going to look you in the eye and say, "Years?"

"Uh-huh."

"It's not going to take me years to get through the fifth grade!" And lo and behold, ownership of the problem has settled into the heart of the one who should own that problem.

The way we parent our children when they make mistakes reflects most clearly what we believe about human failure, particularly sin. So many of us think that sin, mistakes, and falling short are more powerful than God's heart for us. So many of us think that human failure is this powerful force that will overcome us, and that therefore we must manifest pseudo-power over it through partnership with a spirit of fear! But when the disciples were going to call down fire on the audience that was disrespectful to Jesus, Jesus just shook His head. *"You do not know what kind of spirit you are of."*[1] Second Timothy 1:7 tells us we have not been given that spirit of fear, but of power, love, and a sound mind, or self-control. Please notice here that it is not a spirit of "other-control."

When we are afraid of other people's sin, it makes us crazy in the presence of sin. We are not ourselves. We are not ourselves when we are dealing with other people's mistakes. This weird thing happens to us, and as a result we end up giving parenting and leadership in general a bad name. Do you know how many people are in counseling because of damaging leadership interactions? It is an all-too-familiar experience for us as leaders to cooperate with a demonic plan motivated by the spirit of fear. When we are confronted with people's mistakes, with something that we might not control right there in that moment, we become scared and exercise our authority in the wrong spirit.

Then we project onto God the idea that He's just as afraid of sin as we are. But what exactly is God afraid of, anyway? Nothing. That's exactly right—nothing. He isn't afraid of anything, because love casts out fear, and He is love.[2] He is the love. If you aren't feeling the love when He's there, something's wrong, because that's Him—*love!* When you're feeling fear, that's not Him.

So we have to decide—what partnerships are we going to make when we are in the presence of sin? This was the thing that made Jesus look like a genius. Jesus could come in and out of sinners' lives. He'd walk into a bar with the harlots and the thieves and go, "Hey guys, how you doin'? Hey, there was this rabbi, this priest, and this Baptist preacher." And those people loved Him! They were going, "I don't know who that guy is, but I love Him, love Him, love Him!"

But the Pharisees were more like, "Here, leper. Ring this bell whenever you come around, because you scare me. Uh-oh, a woman on her period. Uh-oh, dead people. Where can we hide? Where can we go? Let's go in the temple. Don't you sweat on me, don't you sweat on me!" Jesus had the love thing down, but the Pharisees didn't have a clue. So, in the presence of sin, the Pharisees were afraid, but when Jesus was in the presence of sin, He was the solution, the remedy. He was powerful.

We Are Un-punishable

Through the cross, Jesus introduced something into the world that we still don't understand. He has made each and every one of us un-punishable. We are un-punishable. It's not wishful thinking, and you've probably even heard this preached. It is our theology to reach the lost. "Come into the Kingdom of Heaven free and clean of your sins." We declare this from every pulpit in the land.

Sin does not need to be punished. It doesn't need to be controlled. It's not a powerful force. It's just that we don't believe it. It's easy to preach stuff. It's another deal living it!

Let's consider some of what the apostle John had to say about how we deal with sin after the cross:

> *My little children, I am writing these things to you so that you may not sin. And if anyone sins, we have an Advocate with the Father, Jesus Christ the righteous.*[3]

John mentioned something that we don't talk about enough anymore. At least, I haven't heard it in quite a while. He said, "We have an advocate in Jesus Christ. We have the best lawyer in town. We're going to get out of this." Jesus is right there with us at every moment to help enforce the victory He's won over sin in our lives. After making this point, John goes on to spend the rest of the book explaining that, because of the cross, our life is no longer about trying not to sin, but about fulfilling the commandment to love. But we are successful in fulfilling the command to love according to the degree that we really understand and believe what the victory that Jesus won actually means:

> *He Himself is the propitiation for our sins; and not for ours only, but also for those of the whole world.*[4]

Now that verse introduces something, but you have to know what the word *propitiation* means, right? It has to mean something to you. You can't just read over that and say, "Blah, blah, blah. Whatever, something…something old." Propitiation is the word for atonement. He paid the ransom. It literally means that Jesus satisfied the wrath of God toward sin. Jesus' death on the cross satisfied the need for God to punish sin in man. When Jesus went to the cross and gave His life as the perfect sacrifice, He ended an insatiable condition. He also introduced an entirely different reality based on an entirely different relationship between God and mankind. He removed the need for punishment. He removed fear from our relationship with Him.

First John 4:18 says, *"There is no fear in love. But perfect love casts out fear, for fear has to do with punishment. The one who fears is not made perfect in love"* (NIV). If we're going to lead our communities in revival and build a house for the presence of love, we have to know how to interact with one another in such a way that eliminates the punishment option, the need to control people when they fail. When we stand in the presence of sin and respond in fear and control, it makes us look like idiots. This would be a good thing to unlearn. This would be a good thing to break our agreements with. Those who sin do not need to be punished. We have to figure out a response to the real lives of the people around us, the real lives of the people that we shepherd, the real lives of the people in the communities where we live—a response to sin that contains no punishment.

The Fork in the Road

I believe that the primary thing that will help us to change our response to sin is to gain a deeper understanding of the new covenant that Christ established for us. The apostle Paul was passionate about showing us that we have a choice to live in two different kinds of relationships with God, and when we don't understand the nature of those relationships, it causes problems. In Galatians 3, Paul asks the Galatians, "Who has bewitched you? What happened to you? I was just here a minute ago and you were fine. What's going on? Who has deceived you? Who has allowed you to completely alter your belief system?" Then he diagnoses the problem: "You're trying to practice two covenants. You're trying to live in two camps."

In Galatians 4 he distinguishes the Old and New Covenants by comparing them with the two offspring of Abraham. Ishmael, son of Hagar, the slave woman, represents the Old Covenant, and Isaac, son of Sarah, the free woman, represents the New Covenant. In Galatians 4:30 (NASB) he quotes from Genesis: *"Cast out the bondwoman and her son, for the son of the bondwoman shall not be heir with the sons of the free woman."* In other words, the two covenants cannot coexist in the same place. You're either a slave under the law, or you're a free son. Love and fear have no fellowship. You can't do two; you have to choose.

He concludes by identifying those who have embraced Christ: *"So then, brethren, we are not children of a bondwoman, but of the free woman."*5 The next verse, Galatians 5:1, says, *"It was for freedom that Christ set us free; therefore keep standing firm and do not be subject again to a yoke of slavery"* (NASB). He's saying, "All right, you have two choices. If you want to, you can live a life protecting your relationship with the rules. But if you want to commit your life to preserving your relationship with the rules, then you will find yourself in the Old Covenant."

The reason Paul is so concerned is that these two different covenants produce different results. Earlier in his letter he mentions that he had rebuked Peter, who should have known better, for trying to get Gentile believers to obey the rules of the Old Covenant, and then explains why this was causing problems:

> *We who are Jews by nature, and not sinners of the Gentiles, knowing that a man is not justified by the works of the law but by faith in Jesus Christ, even we have believed in Christ Jesus, that we might be justified by faith in Christ and not by the works of the law; for by the works of the law no flesh shall be justified. "But if, while we seek to be justified by Christ, we ourselves also are found sinners, is Christ therefore a minister of sin? Certainly not! **For if I build again those things which I destroyed, I make myself a transgressor.** For I through the law died to the law that I might live to God. I have been crucified with Christ; it is no longer I who live, but Christ lives in me; and the life which I now live in the flesh I live by faith in the Son of God, who loved me and gave Himself for me. I do not set aside the grace of God; for if righteousness comes through the law, then Christ died in vain".*6

He is saying that when we start to obey the rules of the Old Covenant, we allow ourselves to be defined as those for whom that covenant was given, namely sinners. When we define ourselves as sinners, we, by definition, deserve to be judged and punished. When we protect our relationship with the rules, the result cannot be anything but punishment. Not only that, when we choose this covenant knowing that Christ has already dealt with the sin issue and opened the way for us to relate to the Father as sons and daughters, then we are actually saying that Christ's death was pointless and are cutting ourselves off from the only thing that can save us—grace. You can see why Paul was so upset with Peter.

Unfortunately, the same issue still needs to be addressed in many of our churches. The downfall of the teacher's anointing is to elevate the teaching of the rules as supreme in the environment, leading people to pay attention to and cultivate our relationship with the rules of God, of Christ. We say, "Hey, it's not a religion, it's a relationship." We have promoted that on bumper stickers and T-shirts, and car washes that have banners. But look at how most church environments respond when someone breaks the rules. All the responses are to shepherd the person back into a right relationship with the rules. Punishment is the tool *par excellence* to restore a person to a right relationship with the culture of rules.

The problem is that in Christ we have not, in fact, been given a relationship with the rules, but a relationship with the Spirit, a relationship heart-to-heart, a relationship that practices love. In Romans 7, Paul talks about two laws—the law of sin and the law of life in Christ—and declares that the law of the Spirit of life in Christ has set us free from the law of sin and death, from the law of relationship with the rules. But that is not the relationship or the reality for most people. Most people have a relationship with the rules, and thus their behavior is motivated by fear of punishment, rather than love.

I'll give you an innocuous example. You're going down the freeway. Everybody is going with the flow of traffic…except for this one guy dodging in and out. That guy's going a little faster than the flow of traffic. The next thing you know, there's a highway patrol car coming down the on-ramp. There he is. Everyone is extremely aware that the highway patrol is right there. "Oh my gosh, there's a cop here. I'm going be late. I didn't factor this into my time and travel equation. What am I going do?" It's like, "Shark in the water! Okay, everybody, who's he going to get?" And everybody speeds up, right? No. Not usually. Everyone slows down. "I'm just going to stay behind him. I'll just slow down. We'll all try to stay behind him." Why? Everyone wants to protect his or her relationship with the rules and avoid punishment. When the cop either pulls that guy over or pulls off the freeway, everybody goes back to the "flow of traffic."

Of course, everyone knows that traffic laws are good and should be enforced. Similarly, Paul explains that God's law is good in that it revealed the power of sin in his life and his need for redemption. That was the purpose of the Old Covenant. However, the law itself could not bring about that salvation. Only in Christ's death can we die to sin and be free to live according to a different law.

Paul says:

> *For I joyfully concur with the law of God in the inner man, but I see a different law in the members of my body, waging war against the law of my mind and making me a prisoner of the law of sin which is in my members. …Who will set me free from the body of this death?*[7]

He goes on to say:

> *Thanks be to God through Jesus Christ our Lord! So then, on the one hand I myself with my mind am serving the law*

of God, but on the other, with my flesh [that which died with Christ] *the law of sin."*[8]

In the previous chapter he gives us a key for stewarding ourselves to walk in the reality that brings us out of the Old Covenant and into the New—*"Reckon yourselves to be dead indeed to sin, but alive to God in Christ Jesus our Lord."*[9] That word *reckon* means to consider the evidence and make a judgment. God's verdict over every believer is that we're dead to sin in Christ.

Paul explains that the law was only for sinners. Since we're dead to sin in Christ, we have been delivered from a life of protecting a connection with the rules. Romans 8:1 tell us, *"Therefore, there's no condemnation [punishment] for those who are in Christ Jesus...."* Then it tells us that being "in Christ Jesus" means we are *"those who walk according to the Spirit and not according to the flesh."* Our experience of life without condemnation happens according to how we *walk*. We experience no condemnation when we walk, not according to a relationship with the rules, but according to a relationship of love. Being un-punishable is the result of walking, through faith and grace, in a relationship with Spirit. It is all about my heart-to-heart connection, my union, my attention to a relationship with Christ.

As we walk in the Spirit, the question we must constantly ask is, how is my life affecting our relationship? Keeping the law of life in Christ means that I manage myself in order to preserve and protect my connection to His heart. It's not about living to protect myself from the punisher when I break the rules. Many of us believe that when Jesus said, *"If you love Me, you will keep* [obey] *My commandments,"*[10] it meant, "If you love Me, you will let Me control you." If I still have a mindset informed by the law of sin and death, I hear Jesus saying, "Keep your relationship with My rules!"

An Old Testament perspective makes John 14:15 sound like another attempt of God to control us. "If you love Me, you will obey my commandments." The problem is, of course, there is no list of commandments from Jesus. We may attempt to assemble one in an effort to protect our relationship to His rules, but that is not the point of that verse. Jesus is not trying to introduce the New Old Testament to those He's died to make free!

But when we hear this command from the mindset of the law of Christ, we hear, "If you love Me, it's going to show up in how you treat the things that I told you are important to Me. The way you manage yourself in our relationship is going to be a clear indicator to Me of your love. What are you going to do? I don't want control over you and I don't have control over you. This is why I've given you a spirit of self-control. It is your attention to our relationship and your ability to manage yourself in this relationship in order to create and sustain intimacy that manifests the law of life in Christ. Intimacy—'In-to-Me-you-see'—is how you learn what is important to Me, and if you love Me, you'll adjust your behavior to protect My heart."

In the Sermon on the Mount, Jesus laid out some statements that look an awful lot like a stricter version of the old rules. In fact, the kind of behavior He described is impossible for any sinner to hope to exhibit. But Jesus wasn't giving these commands to sinners—He was giving them to the sons and daughters of the New Covenant who would have access to an entirely new nature and supernatural grace. He was simply describing how these new people would behave. Remember, the Old Covenant was an external covenant, a system of controls designed to keep sinners in line. But the New Covenant is an internal covenant for sons and daughters who, because of their new nature, can be trusted with the responsibility to govern themselves and have access to the power of self-control through the Holy Spirit. The behavior Jesus describes is evidence of the superior power to walk in righteousness possessed by sons and daughters of the New Covenant.

Obviously, we do face challenges in learning to walk in the Spirit, but these are not the challenges we face when we are trying to keep the rules. They are the challenges of dying to ourselves and exercising our self-control so that we stay connected to the flow of God's grace that enables us to live sin-free lives. So, in a way, this law of Christ is way harder than simply going with the "flow of traffic." But the rewards are infinite because this is where the Kingdom comes. The law that rules in the Kingdom is the law of Christ, the law of love, not the law of rule keeping, and when we line our lives up with love, the Kingdom of love manifests in our lives. Paul's point is, "If you don't have love, if you don't have this, you have nothing."[11] There's no life in the rules. You can be amazingly obedient to the rules but not manifest the life of the Kingdom because there's no life in the rules.

If you think you have a relationship with Jesus going on and love isn't showing up with your relationships with people, then I don't know what you have. If you cannot cultivate heart-to-heart relationships and practice intimacy with people, guess who is fooling whom? If you don't know God, He'll look a lot like you. You'll make Him up, and you'll be a rock star in that relationship. When we don't know who God is because we don't know His love and how His love works, we get scared and we turn Him and our relationship with Him into what we already know.

And guess what we're going to teach our kids? We're going to teach our kids what we already know. We are not going to teach our children a relationship of heart-to-heart connection. We are not going to teach our children intimacy. We're not going to teach them how to manage their half of "us" if we live life in relationship with keeping the rules. Do you know how unappealing it is to have a relationship with rules? Just ask your teenager. Your teenager will show you.

The truth is that we give everyone in our circle of influence what we know, and this contributes to the development of a relational culture that is either rule-driven or love-driven. And only one promotes honor, because only one accurately acknowledges the fullness of our God-given identities. There is no culture of honor without a strongly shared belief that we are free sons and daughters of the New Covenant, not slaves of the Old. We must do whatever it takes to courageously embrace this truth of who we are, walk in it, and come to know it as our reality. Only then can we create and pass on life, love, and freedom—the Kingdom—to those around us. We always pass on what we know and what we have. If all we know is fear and control, and this is what we keep seeing in our environment, then we must address our core beliefs about ourselves, sin, and the work of the cross.

Generation after generation in the Church has lived life attempting to protect a relationship to the rulebook. You can say you're not all day long. What happens when somebody breaks the rules? That is your barometer. What happens when somebody violates what you're living to protect? That's where it's going to show up. That's your feedback right there. What happens when Johnny brings you an F on his report card? Your "Cuckoo for Cocoa Puffs" response is evidence of how important the rules are to you.

When we panic in the presence of sin, it is evidence of how important the rules are to us. I would say we have enough evidence to assert that the rules are centrally important in much of church culture. It is time for us to look at this evidence and admit that our fearful responses directly contradict the message of Christ that we are preaching. Scripture is clear that we have two options—we can choose either to protect the rules and create a religious culture, or to protect our relationships and create a culture of love. And only one of these options is the covenant that Christ died to make with us.

CHAPTER 4

DEARLY LOVED
CHILDREN OF LIGHT

Too often we give children answers to remember
rather than problems to solve.[1]
(Roger Lewin, Scientific Theorist)

"*For you were once darkness, but now you are light in the Lord. Walk as children of light....* "[2] Paul makes an amazing declaration and presents a piercing revelation with this statement. Many Christians are stuck in the revelation presented in the first half of this verse. We believe that the "nature" of man is dark, and we've had the most difficult time making the New Testament transition from dark to light. We lingered so long in the mentality of *"The heart is deceitful above all things, and desperately wicked; who can know it?"*[3] that we've failed to cultivate the truth that we are "children of light." Yes, we once *were* darkness, but that nature has completely changed. Our fear of sin must be removed and our offenses disarmed before we will allow Heaven to govern through us on the earth.

When people sin, it is offensive. When people break the rules, it is offensive to human nature. The world is offended by sin. Look at the headlines in your newspaper:

"Hollywood starlet is going to jail."

"No, she's not going to jail."

"Yes, she is going back to jail."

"She found God in jail."

"She left God in jail."

"Don Imus—the radio guy most of us had never heard of until he made some infamous racial comments—we're going to crucify him publicly by kicking him down the stairs, and take national polls about firing him."

"School teacher molests child."

"Police officer breaks the law."

People love this stuff. "Put it up there; let me read it! I'm not buying your paper unless there is something offensive in there." It is natural to be offended when someone breaks the rules. We put people in prison and call them *offenders*. Our society is filled with sinners practicing sin, and naturally, our society is caught in a relationship with the rules. Even lawlessness is a relationship with the rules. Some people define their relationship with the rules by breaking them. Their message is "I will not be controlled." But without a relationship with love, the only option our society has is to figure out a way to live life within the confine of rules.

Many rules call for many judges, and people love to play judge. That's what headlines and newscasts are for, to help us sharpen our judgment skills. Just imagine the vast number of people who each evening sit in judgment and disgust as they watch their televisions. Now, imagine how many of these people are Christians.

We as believers living in this wider culture have to be aware of the schemes of the enemy. We have to be aware of how natural it is to be offended, and what offense does to you. What offense does to you is it justifies you withholding your love. I get to withhold my love from you when you have broken the rules, because people who fail are unworthy of love, and they deserve to be punished. In fact, what punishment looks like most often is withholding love. And when I withhold love, anxiety fills the void, and a spirit of fear directs my behavior toward the offender.

When we are afraid, we want control, and our responses to the sin of other people are a set of controls that help us feel like we are still in charge. The typical practices of the family, churches, and the government are to set a series of behaviors called punishments in front of an offender and require the offender to walk through these punishments in order to prove that the family, churches, and government are still in charge in the environment. In doing so, we help to confirm the belief in the person who has chosen to sin that he or she is powerless to change and take responsibility for his or her behavior. This whole business is just what Jesus died to get rid of. He's introduced a whole other world with a whole other way.

A Man After God's Own Heart

Though he lived under the Old Covenant, David was a man who valued his relationship with God more than the rules. And in

Second Samuel we get to see what happened to this man when he broke the rules. In Second Samuel 11 we read the story of the time that David should have gone out to war but stayed home instead. He stayed home and sent Joab out to work.

> *Then it happened one evening that David arose from his bed and walked on the roof of the king's house. And from the roof he saw a woman bathing, and the woman was very beautiful to behold.*[4]

He asked around, "Who's that?" And they said, "Well, that's Uriah's wife." Uriah the Hittite was one of David's mighty men—one of the inner circle, one of his friends. And then we read in Second Samuel 11:4, *"David sent messengers and took her, and when she came to him, he lay with her"* (NASB).

If we know anything about Bathsheba, we know that she was an amazing woman. How do we know that? Because of who she was married to. Uriah was stellar. He wouldn't have been married to some loose woman. David took her, brought her to his room, and lay with her. It is quite likely that David raped Bathsheba.

That same verse goes on to say, *"When she had purified herself from her uncleanness, she returned to her house"*—only to send David a message some time later that she was pregnant. Now, this did not happen in a weekend. This took months. This was before the blue strip came out—no plus and minus could be seen. I'm sure she waited until she knew for certain to tell the king that she was pregnant, so it had to be months later.

When David found out he said, "Where's Uriah? Hey, go get him and let's give him some time on leave. Oh, Uriah! So good to see you! Come on, bring him in here. Uriah, you amazing man you, come here. I just love you. Thanks for all that you're doing supporting the war effort. Now, go sleep with your wife. I heard she's been eating a lot lately. I think she's kind of upset. You might want to comfort her. I need some help covering up the consequence of my sin."

But Uriah wouldn't do it. David sent him some food. "Hey, you know, go be happy." But Uriah slept on the front steps of the king's house. He would not go home. He said, "Why should I go sleep with my wife in my bed when the men are lying in a field? I won't go."

David thought, *Dang! A man with character. I wasn't expecting this.* So he decided, "Hey, let's have a little party. Let's see if we can get him drunk. Maybe if we can get him drunk, we can get him to leave his senses, and then we can get him to cover up my sin. Uriah! Hey, dude, here's some wine, the best I've got. You want me to fill that back up for you? Here you go, buddy. Why did I give you the big cup? Well, it's a cup of honor. Yeah, that's it."

That time Uriah did go sleep in a bed—in the servant's quarters. What was David going to do? "Okay, all right. Okay, we're running out of time here. She's going to deliver soon if you don't get this together. Here, Uriah, take this note and give it to Joab. Take your death warrant and hand it to your commander."

This did not happen in a weekend. This wasn't just a little aberration in the character of David. David was practicing something. Sure enough, Joab sent Uriah to the front, pulled back the troops, and he was killed. The messenger came back and Joab said, "Tell David we lost some really good men in this fight. If he is upset with you, tell him, 'Oh, and by the way, Uriah died.'"

So the messenger went back with the message, "We lost good men...and Uriah died." David said, "You know, good people die.

Tell Joab, 'Good people die in battle. It's part of the war. Take the city tomorrow.' That'll make Joab happy—he likes to kill stuff."

You know the story. At this point, it was time for the situation to be confronted. Nathan the prophet went to him and said, "Dude, it's you." So David spent seven days repenting on the floor, and the child died as Nathan said he would. Then we read Second Samuel 12:24: *"Then David comforted Bathsheba his wife, and went in to her and lay with her, so she bore a son, and he called his name Solomon."*

So…hmm. Yes, the Lord takes the child's life. But something doesn't quite add up here. Where was the "Old Testament" punishment in this story—punishment that really "fits the crime"? The Kingdom isn't torn from him as it was with King Saul. Nor is he struck down by an enemy nation and hauled into slavery. His family is forever scarred by David's actions. But we usually don't feel the weight of what David did with Uriah and Bathsheba because God said he was a man after His heart. But who among us wants David as our modern-day pastor?

We need to see that if David were the president of the United States, he would be equivalent to a modern-day Bill Clinton—except that Bill Clinton has never killed one of his friends and married his friend's wife. Do you remember having any offense with Bill Clinton? Do you remember rejoicing at any thought of Bill Clinton's punishment? Do you see the natural response to sin that lives in man?

There are other examples worth noting in Scripture, examples that defy the expectations of justice created by the rules. Take Abigail. Abigail was an unsubmissive wife, basically. She did what her husband Nabal had refused to do—took her husband's stuff and gave it to David, who was very upset. He was coming to kill Nabal. She did an end run, and this made her a rebellious, unsubmissive wife according to the rules. And what was the response? God killed her jerk husband and she married David.[5]

Then there was Peter. "Peter, you're going to deny Me."

"Oh, that would never happen. I'll never deny You."

"Before the rooster crows."

"Never happen."

"And you know what? If you guys deny Me before men, I will deny you before My Father."

Sure enough, Peter denied Him, and sure enough, what did Jesus do?

"Peter, do you love Me?"

"Yes."

"Peter, do you love Me? Peter, will you protect the things that I told you were so important to Me? Peter, will you manage your life in such a way that you will protect Me?"

"Yes, Lord. Yes, I will."[6]

The adulteress—what was Jesus' response to her? *"Go and sin no more."*[7] Wow! That's going to leave a mark! Or no, actually it's not—certainly not the kind of mark the rest of the people were hoping to make on her.

What's the Difference?

So why did God respond differently to these people? Why did David and Peter get a different deal than they deserved? Why did they get a different deal than other people who made the same mistakes, or even less serious mistakes? What was the difference between David and Saul, for example? Well, Saul, he just didn't kill everybody that he was supposed to kill. What was the difference between Peter and Judas? Peter denied Jesus three times to Judas' one betrayal. So the real difference is something vitally important, and it is not in their sin, but in what they did afterward. It is repentance. But repentance only works when the priority of the environment is a heart-to-heart connection.

Repentance does not satisfy the broken rules. Repentance will not work in an environment where we are protecting a relationship with the rules. In a rule-driven environment, repentance has a different meaning. It signifies your willingness to let me punish you. You are repentant when you allow me to inflict my punishments upon you. And the issue of the heart that led you to make the mistake in the first place is never dealt with, because the issue of relationship and love is never touched. The general attitude toward someone who is repentant in a rule-driven culture is, "You have surrendered your will to me in our environment. I'll never be able to trust you though, because you have proven yourself to be a lawbreaker, and it will rest in my memory for a really long time. Until I begin to forget about how scared I was of you, I'll never be able to empower you again." This attitude is what presides over what we call the "restoration process."

But true repentance is a gift. It's not your option. It's not your call. It is a gift that comes in a relationship. There's no place for repentance in the rules, only for punishment. If you break our rules, then you pay our price. That's just how it works. You pay the price in order to assuage the anxieties of the people in the environment that live within those rules. You do the crime, so you do the time. When we practice this in the Church, we are allowing ourselves to be defined by the limits of earthly government. When you break the law, the best earth's government can do is to say, "We hurt them sufficiently so that you guys would calm down."

The gift of repentance creates the opportunity for true restoration. In fact, it is absolutely necessary in order to heal a relationship that has been hurt by sinful behavior. True repentance can only come through a relationship with God in which we come into contact with the grace of God to change. David spent seven days on the ground repenting to God. Saul also tried to repent to Samuel for breaking the rules. But when David got off the ground, he was another man. How do we know that? He never did it again. There was no other Bathsheba.

So what is true restoration? An old meaning of the word "restoration" is to find someone with a royal bloodline who has been removed from the throne and then restore the person to that throne—to a position of honor. But putting a monarch back in his or her place of authority is rarely what the process we call "restoration" looks like when dealing with leaders in the church who have broken the rules. Most fallen leaders leave their churches or denominations and go find a "fresh start." That means that they find a group of people who are not afraid of them breaking the rules again.

But when God restores those who have repented, His process of restoration looks like reestablishing a royal family member in his or her place of rulership and honor. The restored believer can say, "I am now a son of God again." Restoration for the believer is always a restoration of relationship, because restoration is defined by the cross and restoration to relationship is what the cross did. After John declared that Jesus became the propitiation for our sins, he concluded, *"If God so loved us"*—that is, if God was so willing to protect His relationship with us, instead of protect our relationship with His rules—*"we also ought to love one another"* (1 John 4:11)—to love one another in the same way. The standard of the government of Heaven is that we learn to cultivate and protect our relationship with God, with love, and with each other. And if we can't do it, we won't reflect Heaven to the society we live in. We will just have stricter rules that offend us quicker, and we will judge more often and become famous for being offended judges.

Jesus has given us a key to be free from the law that keeps us tied to an earthly model of government, particularly from how that model responds to sin. In my mind, the reason that an apostolic and prophetic environment is so important is that it constantly renews and refreshes our awareness of and trust in the core values of Heaven so that we can bring them to earth. It seems clear to me that the very best that we can do in an environment where teachers and pastors lead is to justify the behavior of utilizing earth's models to deal with God's people. When we start to implement the core values of Heaven into the culture of our congregations and families, including this core value that we are un-punishable, I believe that these cultures will truly be reformed. People will experience life in a completely different way.

Full of Light

I want to tell you a story that encapsulates what heavenly restoration looks like. A friend of mine, a pastor and teacher—one of the most capable, brilliant teachers that I personally know—called me one day and said, "I have a situation. I have a worship leader who just confessed to his wife about an immoral relationship. It's been going on for four years. It was with his wife's best friend. He and his wife were actually mentors to this woman and her husband when the couple came into the church and took a staff position working with our youth. He just told his wife, and they leave on vacation tomorrow.

"We don't know what to do, because this isn't just your run-of-the-mill worship leader. This guy is amazing. He has been taking our church to new places in God. Over the last four years, the anointing on our house has increased. We've started a school of ministry, and he and his wife run our school of ministry. This is our third year. We've almost doubled the enrollment of our school in three years. This couple is leading in creating an amazing environment."

This pastor had called me because he knew something. He knew what had to happen when the truth came out, because he knew what had to happen when you break the rules and you're in a relationship with the rules. They had to put this man through the "restoration process." But this pastor also knew that the restoration process we had at Bethel looked different than the one he had always known. So he asked if I would be willing to meet with this couple first and then give him some insight about how to proceed.

I said, "We'd be glad to meet with them." My wife, Sheri, and I met with the couple about two days later. When they walked in the door, the wife looked as though she'd been crying for a week. He looked as though he had been wired to the undercarriage of the car during their eight-hour trip on the freeway. He was just wracked with shame. He knew that he had destroyed his relationship with the rules, and he knew that he needed to be punished. She was just distraught—her heart was broken. All the trust that she had ever held was broken; every bit of life that she had lived up until that point was lost and forever changed. *She* was going to lose *her* valuable ministry in the church. *Her* life had been ended because of *his* incredible selfishness.

So we just sat and we listened to them for a few minutes, and he did his best to let us know what an evil scumbag he was. "See, you've got to understand, I knew better. I totally knew better. I knew what I was doing. I was hiding it. There's a war inside of me and I've had this problem my whole life. Eighteen years ago when we got married and she was pregnant with our first child, I committed adultery with her best friend then too." He continued to attempt to convince us that he deserved to be punished.

Eventually Sheri prophesied something over him. She said, "I see this hand coming out of the sky, grabbing this handle and flipping this switch, and then all the lights just coming on. It is like you are full of light and everything is completely different. That is what the Lord is going to do."

He said, "That's really sweet of you to say that. I just can't believe that right now. I feel a million miles from that place right now."

We are watching a clash of two kingdoms: Fear and Love, Freedom and Control, Light and Dark. The earthly kingdom that this couple knew was severely limited in trying to restore a child of light. Once again, the truth is, "You once *were* darkness. You now *are* light. Live as dearly loved children of light."[8] But dearly loved children of light cannot be governed by the very best darkness we can find. The most merciful, fair, just, capitalistic, democratic darkness cannot govern children of light.

Sheri and I had the goal of inviting them to experience the power of an apostolic environment that has made the resources of Heaven permanently within reach. We were aware that we had access to the resource of light in an atmosphere that requires light. When Heaven invades earth, it trumps the limitations of natural man and natural perspectives.

We did not believe that what this man had done was evidence of his true identity. Paul said we once *were* darkness, and we now *are* light. Just because you have darkness in you doesn't change your true identity.

A friend and I were out walking around the property of Mountain Chapel one day. We were trying to figure out where to put the new church building. As we were walking, I stepped on a board and a nail went through my foot. I lifted my foot and saw that there was a board attached to the bottom of my shoe. I could clearly see that a nail had entered my foot. But never once did I think, "I'm a nail!" I was, however, very interested in getting that nail out of my foot. And when a child of light discovers darkness in him or her, it does force the issue: "What are *you* going to do? What are *you* going to do?"

We can help as leaders when we come alongside people in this situation and help them to hear that this is what God is asking them. We send the message, "It isn't my job to control you. I'm not scared. What are *you* going to do?"

So we began the restoration process with this couple by asking some questions. We brought our light with us. Living in an apostolic governing system helps us naturally to pull light from Heaven into our pastoral relationships. Therefore, we have a process that heals our relationships with people who break the rules. It makes us powerful in the presence of sin. We're not afraid of sin. Sin is nothing! Sin is darkness! One flick of the switch and *click*—it's over!

So I asked the question that I ask everyone in these situations: "What is the problem?"

He looked at me like I was drunk, because he thought he had done a stellar job telling me what the problem was. "I just told you. I am a lowlife scumbag, masquerading like a son of light. What do you mean, what is the problem?"

"What's the problem? Didn't you know this was a bad idea?" I asked.

"Yes," he replied.

"Didn't you know that whenever your wife or your pastor found out about this, it was going to end up badly?" I leaned forward in my chair.

"Yes," he replied again.

"And you did it anyway?" I prodded.

"Yes." He wasn't sure if I was setting him up for a punch in the nose or what.

"What's the problem?" I asked again.

"What?" he asked, his brow furrowed and his mouth pulled back on one side.

"What is the problem that would drive a man to do such destructive stuff to his family, to his life, to the church he loves, and to his peace with God? What would make a man get there? What's the problem?"

"I don't know," he responded dejectedly.

"Have you repented?"

"Yes," he replied with adamant fervor, though his tone betrayed doubt that this repentance was ready to stand up to a test.

"Of what?" I asked, boxing him in.

He looked at me, unsure if I was for him or against him, and answered, "I don't know."

"That's what I was thinking. How is this going to change if you don't even know how to repent?" I asked.

"I don't know," he said, resigned.

"That's what I was thinking, too!"

Sheri and I were looking at this man from a perspective of light. We intended to solve this issue from a heavenly context, because that was part of our culture. It was natural for us to approach sin and failure from a perspective that makes God more powerful than sin. He, on the other hand, was convinced that he was darkness. He knew that the government of earth was waiting to have its way with him. He agreed with the paradigm of earth and was ready to welcome its verdict of judgment. It was our job to move him to see himself from another vantage point. He needed to believe he was a dearly loved child of light.

"One more time. What do you think the problem is here?" I asked.

"I really don't know."

At this point in the confrontation, I didn't know what the problem was either. So I decided to explore a little. "Well, tell me this. What is your connection with your wife?" I asked, knowing that it was unlikely that he had much of a connection. Adultery is usually a symptom that a couple struggles to be intimate with each other.

"We don't have one, or much of one," he responded sadly.

"What is your wife's love language?" I asked. I wanted to see if he knew how to love his wife.

"Encouraging words," he said, looking up at her.

His wife, sobbing, said, "In eighteen years he has hardly ever told me he loves me."

We were finally onto something. I could hear the bloodhounds of Heaven barking in my ear. I knew that this man was a passionate man. This man had been leading their ministry into great, anointed places. Their church had grown dramatically over the previous few years, and was vibrant with life under this man's leadership. So I said, "Your wife feels loved when you adore her through words, and you can't squeak out an 'I love you' toward her. Meanwhile she watches you lead the masses in singing 'I love you' to God. Is that what you are telling me?"

I could tell that he wasn't quite with me, so I tried again to help him see the contradiction he was living. "Let me see if I understand what you are telling me. You lead people in the adoration and passionate pursuit of God's heart. You write songs that express this amazing passion and love for God. But you do not point any of this strength toward your wife. How about your kids?"

"I can't tell anybody that I love them, not even my kids," he said through tears. "I've turned out just like my father. My father cannot express love to anyone either."

We had just found the problem. We sat there a little stunned. This was the bottom of the barrel that no one outside of this family knew about or experienced. But we also had another problem. I didn't know what to do next. We sat in silence, interrupted only by the sound of crying and sniffles. Then, all of a sudden, I got a word from the Lord. I didn't know if it was a word of wisdom or a word of knowledge or what it was. All I knew was that I didn't know it before I got it. I leaned forward, now confident that this was the key. I asked, "Are you trying to tell me that you can only love that which you think is perfect?"

He looked at me, paused, and said, "No."

"Let me say it again. Are you trying to tell me that you can only risk loving where there is no chance of failure? Are you telling me that you can only love what you believe to be perfect so there is no chance of getting hurt?"

His wife clearly got what I was asking, and fresh tears began to flow.

He looked at me like I had hit him on the nose with a rolled up newspaper.

I asked again, "Are you telling me that you cannot risk your heart to anything that might not turn out to be perfect?"

He started to shake his head, but then started to nod. Suddenly he said, "I have been deceived. This is the very thing I hated about my father. I've been deceived!" he said again and again.

So at this point I invited him to walk through a few minutes of forgiving his father. After he did that, *wham!* He turned to his wife and said with complete sincerity, "I love you so much. I am so sorry!"

In a moment the whole room lit up. It made you want to start singing, I am free at last, I am free at last! Thank God Almighty, I am free at last! Heaven touched me!

He kept confessing to his wife, "I love you. I love you. I didn't know what was wrong with me…." As he said this, his wife's countenance completely changed. Hopelessness left the room as this woman began to experience that which she had moments ago thought was only going to happen in Heaven. And she was right. That is where they keep that stuff. We just had to go get some and bring it to earth. In a few moments they were a couple of lovebirds, sitting there cooing.

There were two miracles that happened that morning. One was the gift of repentance that just hit him and knocked him down. And the other one was her willingness to forgive him in a moment. In a moment, the lights came on and he had a brand new life—they had a brand new marriage. So we just sat there and watched them. It was awkward. But we just let it go.

He said, "I feel like the lights are on all of a sudden. I can see like I've never been able to before. I feel like I am full of light!" Simultaneously, we all remembered the word that Sheri had given him earlier in our time together. We talked and prayed more with them, and Sheri prophesied over them again. It was a glorious time together with some wonderful people.

Moments later he said, "You know…I don't really know if I should feel this happy! I feel so hopeful. I feel so happy. But I feel bad for feeling happy." A curious look crossed his face and he asked, "Well, now that I am a different man, what is my church's leadership going to do with me?"

That was a very good question. As wonderful a group as they are, I was pretty sure they would have a different perspective on the situation. Thankfully, we had one key advantage to help us guide this process to a successful conclusion—their pastor. As I said, their senior pastor was a teacher—a strong, fivefold teacher. Therefore, he had a strong need to be right and to understand what God was doing. But fortunately, he recognized this about himself and had realized that he could reduce the anointing ceiling on his whole world simply by making his need to be right and understand everything the chief director of his leadership, his life, and decisions. This man had moved that cap off of his life by putting himself under apostolic ministry, which brought an apostolic and prophetic leadership anointing into his environment. This is one of the reasons he called us for help. As I said, he knew what happens here.

This couple returned home and I didn't hear back from them for a while, mainly because I'd taken a group of our pastoral staff backpacking. We were gone for four days. (When I say "backpacking," I need to point out that it was a two-mile hike. We consumed 80 trout in three days. It was more like a cruise. The year before I'd taken them on a 38-mile, six-lake excursion through the Trinity Alps. Our staff team refers to that trip as "Danny's Death March." Now *that* was *backpacking*.) When we got back to the house, I headed straight to the shower because I really needed one. The phone rang as I walked by it. I never answer the phone when I am at home, especially if it's a number I don't know, which this was. But for some reason I answered the phone. "Hello?"

It was my pastor friend. He said, "Danny! Hey, I have been trying to get a hold of you."

"Yeah," I said, "I have been backpacking."

"Do you have a minute? I'd like to ask you a few questions about the couple we sent up your way."

Since I didn't think he could smell me, I said, "Sure."

"Oh, great!" he said, as though he knew I was going to say that. "We have you on the speakerphone right now at our elder's meeting. We are trying to figure out this situation. We heard some of the ideas you were sharing with them. We'd like to have you expound on those a little bit."

"Sure." I accepted that the shower I had been fantasizing about for the whole trip home was going to have to wait. My friend first shared some of the ideas that their board had been pondering. The basic plan was something like this:

1. Inform the congregation of what was going on and have them pray for the restoration of these leaders.

2. Have this couple step down for few months to work on their marriage.

3. Review their progress after three to six months and if favorable, slowly reintroduce them to the ministry.

This is the "from earth to Heaven" model that I know most every church will attempt. It is earth's best effort to build trust and credibility back up for the people. It is designed first to comfort the people and then to address the life of the leader. This is tough to admit, but when the anointing of the senior leader is primarily focused on people, then the needs of the people will rule the environment. Again, this is earth's best effort to bring about justice, fairness, or another necessary human comforter.

When this couple had been in my office a few weeks earlier, I had shared a "Heaven to earth" model of handling this situation. They were encouraged by hearing about the process but could see that it was going to be a near-impossible stretch for their leaders to get their minds around it. I could hear that my pastor friend wanted to understand what it was that I had shared with them. The unspoken explanation for his phone call was, "I think I understand what you shared with them. I want to come over to where you are. I want to address this from the light of Heaven and not the darkness of earth's models. I am just not sure how to prove it scripturally." The need to "prove" something scripturally was part of his ceiling, a limitation that strengthened his focus as a teacher but constrained his ability to operate with other priorities when it came to other tasks of leadership. He recognized this limitation and was working to draw on the perspective of another anointing in order to recognize and operate from Heaven's priorities for this situation.

He said, "We would really like to get some input to help with our decision."

"All right, well, here is what I see," I began. "I see that for the last four years you've had a man who has led your congregation into the heart of God, and God has been pouring His blessing out on your congregation. More and more people have become attracted to the freedom that is growing in your environment. I see that in those four years you have birthed new ministries that are blessed and saturated with life and vigor. And the whole time, you have had a great, big, fat, lying, lowlife, scumbag leader living a double life. You have given him raises and empowered him and his influence more and more in your environment.

"Now what you have is a man who is in the best spiritual shape of his life. He went home from that week's vacation a changed man. He went home, gathered his children, sat them down, looked into their eyes, and said, 'Please forgive me. I have withheld my love for you your whole lives. I am so sorry. I only love you. I only adore you.' He showered love on his children for the first time in their lives, and then invited them to speak up at any point they feel it dimming. Their whole household is filling up with light."

I went on, "This man has repented. He is a changed man. But because you now know what has been hidden for the past four years, you think you have to punish him. If you do that, wouldn't it have been better if he had stayed a lying scumbag, a prisoner of his bondage, for the benefit of your church? What are you going to do with the truth? This man doesn't need punishment, removal, a sabbatical, a vacation, a restraining order, or anything of that nature. This man needs some accountability to make sure he keeps the light on. And he needs to clean up his mess."

They said, "Well that brings up another point. We were going to have him stand in front of the congregation and share what has happened with the church as an accountability measure. What do you think about that?"

I said, "Well, let me see if I understand this. As it stands, it's as if he had a gallon of paint, dropped it, got it all over your elder team, this other couple, you, and his wife and family. You are going to give the man a 500-gallon bucket of paint and a grenade as a way to clean up his mess. Now, I am all for people taking responsibility for their messes. I just don't understand why you would make a bigger mess than you already have. I think this mess is pretty easily cleaned up and I think it is pretty easily repaired. That is what I think."

It was very quiet on the other end of that phone. One of them asked another question about something, and that was it. I said, "Bless you guys. I need to go take a shower."

That happened in August 2006. Three months later at Bethel's Leader's Advance I met with my pastor friend and he said, "You would not believe how amazingly they are doing. His entire family looks like they have been raised from the dead. The light and the nourishment that have come to that home are breathtaking." He also said, "We handled the situation exactly as you suggested. It's awesome and it's working!" As of the writing of this book, it's been nearly two years and they are all getting stronger.

The devil is working to destroy us, and the "earth to Heaven" model will usually help him accomplish his goal in the Church. I know that we are not trying to be destructive, but we are confined to our earthly limitations when our senior leaders are teachers, pastors, administrators, and evangelists who have not been hooked up to the flow of anointing and revelation in an apostolic government.

Now, please understand something. I am not a proponent of "keeping things in the family" as a way of handling destructive behaviors among Christians in the Church. If you throw the lights on and see that someone needs to go to jail, don't send a ministry team in to see the person instead. While I was the senior pastor in Weaverville, I reported five people in as many years to Child Protective Services, and two of them were incarcerated. I have no problem involving the public authorities in situations when I know the Church can neither hold the people accountable nor supply them with the level of services necessary for them to get well. We must set clear boundaries, as Scripture teaches, for dealing with people who do not repent. But we must also learn to stop needing to punish people who *do* repent.

I'm not saying that we give them a "get out of jail free" card. But instead of punishing them, we call people to walk in their higher identity and responsibility as children of light rather than crushing them even further into the life of a sinner. When Heaven confronts us in our mistakes, it is like the Lord encountering Job: *"Prepare yourself like a man!"*[9] Walking in the light is not for wimps. It requires a deep faith in God's love and the power of His grace to give us what we need to change.

A church's discipline culture is built to protect what people think— what they think about leaders and what they think about those who fail. Again, when the comfort or expectations of people are held as the primary concern in the culture, and when the core belief of the people is that people who make mistakes are sinners, not sons, then discipline simply will not be administered in a Kingdom way, for the primary concern in a Kingdom culture is "Your Kingdom come, Your will be done on earth as it is in Heaven."

Punishment's main purpose is to ease the anxiety of the people. We want to call it justice, but it is simply the fear of man in leaders who need to stay in favor with the people. As we saw in the lives of David and Peter, God's justice is baffling to human beings. We can only understand it when we give up trying to protect our relationship with the rules. When we start to protect a relationship with the law of life in Christ, our goal is never to assuage fear, but to restore a broken relationship and to get life and love flowing again, and there is only one process that will accomplish that. There is satisfaction through repentance. *We* have to lose our fear of sin and our fear of man, and *we* have to stop punishing those who repent.

It is for freedom that Jesus set us free.[10] He has given us a way to stay away from the yoke of slavery to the rules and offers us a way to live our lives protecting our relationships—first with God, and then with our families and those in our sphere of influence. Our children are those we influence most profoundly, and that which we model is reflected clearly back to us in them. When our children don't need to be punished for their sin and when they begin to learn that the priority when they fail is restoring relationship rather than accepting punishment, they begin to cultivate a high value for relationships as the priority in our culture. This is how we teach people to live a life of love and liberty, and how we learn the power of trust and intimacy.

CHAPTER 5

FREEDOM PRACTICE—DEVELOPING
A WEALTH MINDSET

I cannot afford to have one thought in my mind that is not in His.
(Bill Johnson, Bethel Church)

After my oldest son, Levi, finished eighth grade at Bethel Christian School, he faced the question of where he would attend high school. His older sister, Brittney, had started at public high school and ended up finishing her high school career in home school. Home school was not for Levi, however, because he wanted to play football. So he asked us if he could go to public high school.

Now, this was a family decision because it would affect our whole family. Issues ranging from transportation to trust were at hand. We also knew that this decision was going to set a precedent for our youngest son, Taylor. The biggest concern for us was the fact that at the public high school, Levi would be faced with freedom and options he'd never faced. He'd have to make successful decisions like never before. Bethel Christian School had had about 145 students while Levi was there, with 40 of those students representing the middle school grades and about 15 his eighth grade class. The public school he wanted to attend had 500 incoming freshman and 1,800 total students—half the population of Weaverville, the small town where he had grown up. Beyond having to get used to a bigger school, he would be moving from a Christian school environment that supported our family's core values to a public high school where it seemed he would virtually be living on the beach set of an MTV program. We were not going to be in Kansas anymore, Toto!

The new level of consequences for his choices in life stared Sheri and me in the face. Did we believe that Levi would protect us with his decisions? Did we trust him with our hearts? Were we willing to allow his learning journey to affect us as deeply as these decisions could? Were we willing to live that vulnerably with a 14-year-old boy?

First, we announced to him that this idea scared us. Then we reminded him of the extreme control freaks we could be when we were scared. And finally, we asked him how he planned to protect us through this proposed venture. Our to-be freshman lowered his brow and began to realize that he was a powerful participant in this conversation and decision. He thought for a moment and then simply stated, "I'll be smart…and I won't break your hearts."

Urgh! That was the right answer. And we believed him.

The summer before his freshman year started with afternoon football practices in the triple-digit heat of Redding, California. Levi began working his tail off to be on the team, surrounded by the 70 other freshmen that were trying out. When the game season began, the coach instructed the freshmen players to attend a varsity game. He wanted to enhance their idea of how to play the game of high school football by showing them how the "big boys" played.

On the day the coach told them to do this, Levi came home and told us. "Coach wants us to go to the game this Friday night and watch the varsity play. Can I go?"

When I looked into Sheri's eyes, I could see what she was thinking. She was thinking the same thing I was thinking. We were both having flashbacks about what we had done at high school football games—and it had nothing to do with the football game! We turned and looked at Levi. We knew that we could not put any of our adolescent mistakes on him, but we were still scared of the numerous possibilities that lay out in that Friday evening waiting to tempt him. So I said, "Son, we are very scared, but you can go."

"I can go!" he shouted, swinging his hand through the air like Tiger Woods putting it in for eagle. "Really? I can go? Awesome!"

I was certain that he hadn't heard me say that we were scared. He was too excited about joining his teammates in their quest to learn more about football. I took him to the game and agreed to pick him up at 10:00 P.M. At that time, I drove back out to the field and with the gift of technology that is the cell phone, found him. There he was, right where he had said he would be. My heart was relieved that my whole night of worry had been for nothing. He jumped in the truck and told me all that he'd learned that night. It mostly had to do with how cool the varsity helmets and uniforms had looked.

We pulled up at home and got out of the truck. As we were heading into the house, Levi reached over, touched my arm and said, "Dad, thanks for trusting me."

"You are welcome, Levi," I said. "Thank you for protecting us tonight, son."

"You are welcome."

The Power of "Us"

Levi knows that he carries tremendous responsibility in our relationship. He knows that no one can do his part of "us" but him. He feels the weight of "us" whenever he is out in his freedom. He knows that he is free to do whatever is in his heart to do. His heart is his to manage. And because it is in his heart to protect his relationship with his mom and dad, he makes decisions with a consideration of how those decisions are going to affect us.

That is freedom training. Paul put it like this to the Corinthians, *"All things are lawful for me, but not all things are profitable."*[1] Freedom causes our personal responsibility to rise to the surface. We either rise with it or lose our freedom. The only way to cultivate freedom is through experiencing and learning how to handle an increasing number of options. Managing increasing options is how we expand our lives into ever-increasing abundance.

Jesus said that the thief is the one that came to steal, kill, and destroy. It's the devil who presents us with limitations, who removes our options and makes us afraid to live free lives. But Jesus came that we *"may have life, and have it abundantly."*[2] Jesus has it in His heart to offer us a life of unlimited options.

Abundance, freedom, and choices are all ways to describe a condition of the soul that we must master if we want a revival culture. The development and expansion of a *wealth mindset* is an essential key to our successful introduction of Heaven coming to earth and having it remain on earth. The practices of wealth are exercises in abundance. If we are to learn to steward the resources of Heaven we must first learn to practice a wealth mentality.

Wealth Creates Freedom

The first mistake so many believers make when someone mentions wealth is to equate it to riches. But the idea that money makes someone wealthy is like suggesting that holding a football makes you an NFL quarterback. Riches or money are external conditions and wealth is an internal reality. Our insides will always manifest on our outsides.

For too many centuries a religious fallacy has tried to rule the mind of believers and convince them that riches are the root of all evil, and thus that the poorer you are, the more spiritual you are. Somehow being a poor, weak, uneducated, lowly Christian is something God is cheering on in Heaven. Yeah, just like you are cheering your kids on to be welfare-dependent, high school dropouts. I am fully aware that in more recent decades, the American church has swung to the other extreme and experimented with a "Wealth Gospel" that has led many to pursue powerful Cadillacs and comfortable lifestyles rather than powerful lifestyles and the Comforter. But a wealth mindset is not really about money or idolatry. It's about freedom.

God and Abram

To help define a wealth mindset, I want to present you with a journey that God led Abraham through. In this journey, Abraham started out as "Abram" and eventually became "Abraham" as God moved him through a process that brought out the full measure of God's intended greatness in Abram's life. When he began this process, Abram was already a rich man. He had many possessions and much land and was faithful in stewarding his wealth. He was a man whose outside already matched his inside. But in order for God to take him to the next level, He introduced a powerful set of instructions and steps that expanded Abram on the inside.

In presenting Abram's journey, I want to challenge you to embrace this same process in your life. This is the process that allows us to confront our own mindsets and the limitations we bring with us into our relationship with Heaven. We limit our life in God so easily and so often because we do not see that which hinders us.

In Genesis 12 we read of God's first interaction with Abram:

> *Now the Lord had said to Abram: "Get out of your country, from your family, and from your father's house, to a land that I will show you. I will make you a great nation; I will bless you and make your name great; and you shall be a blessing. I will bless those who bless you, and I will curse him who curses you; and in you all the families of the earth shall be blessed."*[3]

This is quite a "Hello! How are you?" Up front, God made it clear that He was going to transform Abram's life from something that he thought was pretty good to something he could never fathom: "In you, Abram, all the families of the earth shall be blessed."

In the New Testament, the apostle Paul tied us to this same promise. He wrote in Galatians that if you are in Christ, you are Abraham's seed and heirs to the promise that was given to Abraham.[4] Through your life also, all the families of the earth shall be blessed. That is what you are carrying in your DNA. That is what you are carrying in your Father's name and in your identity as a child of the Most High God.

Four Keys to New Freedom

There are four key aspects to the process that God began with Abram in Genesis 12. The first aspect is Abram's *name*. We focus on the fact that *Abraham* means "father of many nations," but it's important to see that *Abram* means "exalted father." An exalted father is not just a father. Abram was not just a regular guy. His very name reveals that he was willing to take on a higher position with more responsibility than an average father. That was the guy God was working with—"Exalted Father." Similarly, those of us who are taking strides to understand and carry the anointing and the revival that is happening today need to understand that God has asked us to take on a greater level of responsibility than the average person. Understanding this responsibility is what shapes us into people who are willing to follow God to a place *"whose builder and maker is God."*[5]

The second aspect of the process for Abram is the first thing God said to him, and I want you to hear this as though God is saying it to you. He said, *"Abram, I want you to leave your country."* In other words, God said, "I want you to leave your land. I want you to leave your territory, your geography. I want you to leave the limitations that you have come to accept as your container, your security, your realm of comfort and influence."

In a move of God, one of the recurring messages we hear is that God wants us to leave our comfort zone. The reason we must leave our comfort zone is that we must have nothing but God to fall back on if we are going to tap into the wealth of Heaven. I recently spoke at the Spiritual Hunger Conference in Spokane, Washington. Heidi Baker was one of the other speakers, and in one of her talks she gently reminded the North American audience that too many of us have a "Plan B" ready to go in case God doesn't show up. She pointed out that this kills our hunger. It also stops up the heavens when we channel our resources to provide for our own comfort instead of channeling them toward Heaven's agendas. The wealth mindset, the mindset that prepares us to participate in the flow of Heaven to earth, is a mindset that embraces Christ's command to seek the kingdom *first,* knowing that God will take care of our needs and desires.

The third aspect of Abram's process was God's next statement: *"I want you to leave your family."* Interestingly, when Abram obeyed God, he took his family with him. What could God have been saying other than, "I am breaking up your family"? Well, our family defines the circumstances of our birth. You and I gain an identity from those we grow up with, and it's very difficult for that identity to shift and expand once it's been established in the perceptions of those around you.

It looks something like this: Say you are the youngest in a family with five children. Even though you're grown up, everyone still sees you as "little Joey!" When you show up at your family reunions, they grab you, take turns rubbing your head and messing up your hair, and go, "How's our little Joey doing? How ya doing, Joey?"

"But Dad, I am the CEO of IBM."

"I know, son, but you are always going to be our little Joey."

You carry a particular identity in an environment filled with people who are very familiar to you. Whenever you are around them, they look at you in such a way that says, "Ha-ha! Look at you! You will never escape the box that we have put you in." Now, that identity may be a very comfortable box. You may be respected and admired by your family. But the reality is that only God, the One who designed each of us, understands our true identity and calling. And in order to discover and become who He made us to be, we will need to go beyond the limits of what our family expects from us.

The Lord says to us, as He said to Abram, "I want you to leave your physical, geographical limitations, and I want you to leave your authority limitations. I want you to leave the territory that you have become comfortable in and I want you to leave the identity that comes from the people who are most familiar with who you've been." And finally, He says to us, *"I want you to leave your father's house."*

This issue of leaving your father's house is the thing I want to focus on for the rest of this chapter. Our father's house is the place where we receive our father's identity, our father's covering, and in particular, our father's socio-economic status. For example, say that you were born into a family where your father was a blue-collar worker and made $15 an hour. Your mom stayed at home raising you and your four siblings, and had an Internet business selling things on eBay. The combined yearly household income stayed around $50,000 per year. This experience put you in a socio-economic class, and this socio-economic class has given you a lens through which you look at the world and the resources in your life. You naturally function within a particular class of people. You identify what is valuable, what is possible, and what different circumstances mean through your socio-economic class.

Our socio-economic class usually comes with an accompaniment—a group of people who validate what we believe is true and what we see as valuable. We are surrounded by people who see the world the way we do—our neighbors, our parents' friends, our closest friends, and our schools. All of these people, along with numerous other cultural reinforcements of which we are mostly unaware, create our "normal," and we usually have no reason to think things are otherwise. All of us judge or make fun of the other classes and hold on to ours like it is the one true class, the one true worldview. For most of us, our eyes have not yet been opened to the fact that there are more ways to see the world than the one that we are carrying around.

So, what I want to present to you next is something that I hope will open up your awareness to the way you see things now and the way your new identity, your true identity, is designed to see things. I hope to expose and confront the way you see things, because you are called to be rulers. You are called to be princes and princesses. You are royalty. You are wealthy beyond your wildest imagination. But unless you think like a wealthy person, you won't be able to handle your identity, role, responsibility, and resources.

Called to Be Rulers

Proverbs 28:16 says, *"A ruler who lacks understanding is a great oppressor, but he who hates covetousness will prolong his days."* Let me state it this way, *"A prince who does not see himself as a benefactor will punish others with his power, but he who hates gain by violence or controlling others will build a lasting legacy."* When a prince *thinks* like a pauper, he *lives* like a powerful survivalist.

The pauper learns one powerful lesson in life, and that is how to stay alive on this planet. The socio-economic worldview of the poor is completely defined and governed by the fear of running out of their daily supply of resources. And when you throw someone who has been trained to survive a recording deal or a professional sports contract or a winning lottery ticket, he becomes a super-survivor. He has great resources, but he uses them to protect himself instead of to benefit others, because he naturally believes that is what his resources are for. He sees the world as something that is there to serve him. He is an opportunist. What he doesn't realize is that by misusing his resources, he is oppressing those around him. He destroys his life, and often the lives of those around him, because his worldview was formed around how to survive, not how to thrive.

As believers, we are all in danger of being princes who think and live like paupers. Unless we are renewed in our thinking, we not only will be abusing the great power and responsibility that we've been given; we won't even be aware that we are doing so.

Poverty, Middle Class, and Wealth

We are all constrained by the class view that we received in our father's house. In order to understand these constraints and identify both how we think and how we should think, I am going to show you three socio-economic class views—a view that looks through the lens of poverty, a view that looks through the lens of the middle class, and a view that looks through the lens of wealth. I will show you how each of these classes views and experiences things so completely differently.

As we go through this exercise, I want you to understand that the class view you agree with the most is probably yours. You also probably have a case for why the other two are wrong. That is okay, because everyone else reading this is doing the same thing. We are not going to debate what is right or wrong. I simply want to give you the opportunity to see that, while you are now wealthy as a son or daughter of the King of Kings, you, like many of us, may not carry a wealth lens for viewing your life.

On the following page is a chart by Dr. Ruby Payne from her book called *Understanding a Framework of Poverty.* This book is an effort to diagnose and treat some of the root causes behind the educational system failures in inner city schools in Texas. In particular, Dr. Payne wanted to lead middle class teachers to better understand and influence children of poverty in their classrooms. She contended that, because the worldviews and life experiences of the teachers and the students were so completely different, the teachers were hopeless of ever being able to educate the children who were not of their own socio-economic class. So Dr. Payne began a system of introducing the teachers to another set of values, beliefs, and motivations, thereby enabling these teachers to "step outside" their own limitations and reach a class view they knew nothing about.

In her book, Dr. Payne illustrates how the different classes experience and view the world, and I've found her analysis to be extremely insightful and helpful in understanding these differences. She does a great job of describing how we all live in very different worlds while sharing the world in which we live. This chart describes what each class values most in various aspects of life. Once again, as you review the following topics, I think you will find yourself feeling confronted by what you see as most valuable, and challenging the other classes' values. After presenting this chart, I will select a few of these topics and break them down in an effort to show you why we must "leave our father's house" and align ourselves with our new "Father's house."

A Framework for Understanding Poverty

by Ruby K. Payne, PhD[6]

	Poverty	Middle Class	Wealth
Possessions	People	Things	One of a kind objects, Pedigrees, Legacies
Money	To be used, spent	To be managed	To be conserved, invested
Personality	Is for entertainment. Sense of humor is highly valued.	Is for acquisition and stability. Achievement is highly valued.	Is for connections. Financial, political, social connections are highly valued.
Social Emphasis	Social inclusion of people they like.	Emphasis is on self-governance and self sufficiency.	Emphasis on social exclusion.
Food	Quantity most important	Quality most important	Presentation most important
Clothing	Individual style and expression of personality	Quality and acceptance by peers, label important	Artistic sense and expression, designer important
Time	Present most important	Future most important	Traditions and history
Education	Valued as abstract but not as reality	Crucial for climbing success ladder and making money	Necessary tradition for making and maintaining connections

(continued)

	Poverty	Middle Class	Wealth
Destiny	Believes in fate. Powerless to change much	Believes in choice. Power to change future with good decisions	*Noblesse oblige*
Language	Survival	Negotiation	Networking
Family Structure	Matriarchal	Patriarchal	Whoever has the money
Worldview	Local	National	International
Love	Conditional upon being liked	Conditional upon achievement	Conditional upon social standing and connections
Driving Force	Survival, relationships, entertainment	Work, achievement	Financial, political, social connections

I'd like to zoom in on the topics of Food, Destiny, Worldview, and Driving Force—first in order to see the distinctions between these class perspectives more clearly, and second in order to see the influence of these perspectives on us as believers in the Church so that we can recognize where we need to line up with Heaven. All of the 14 areas mentioned above are interesting in their own right, so hopefully my analysis of these four will encourage you to go through the others and make the same kind of comparisons.

	Poverty	Middle Class	Wealth
Food	Quantity most important	Quality most important	Presentation most important

I picked food first just for fun. It's such an everyday experience that I thought we'd laugh at ourselves for a minute. The thing is, the way we relate to food indicates a lot about the way that we relate to all the resources by which we meet our basic needs.

When we go to a restaurant with a poverty mentality, we have a certain expectation. We go there because they give us tons of food:

> "If I am going to spend good money on going out to eat, then I want to leave that place stuffed."

> "Hey Bob! We are going to the Brown Bear tonight. We love that place. They give you huge portions for just about any meal you order. It's great!"

> "We are going to the buffet. We are going to the buffet because it's an 'all you can eat' place where you can get as much food as you can stuff into your torso for $9.99. They are going to be sorry I ever walked in there, I tell you what!"

When our main concern is survival, our relationship with food is one of hoarding. The belief that we are not sure when we will eat again doesn't actually have to correspond to reality for us to behave as though it does. With a belief system built on the priority of survival, I live in an experience that meets my need for "quantity" when I relate to food. Buffet!

When I cultivate the impulse to hoard, whether I am hoarding food or something else, it effectively prevents me from being generous to anyone except those I think are worse off than myself. I have friends who are waitresses. A general consensus is that the "Sunday afternoon crowd" is the worst group to deal with. They are typically demanding, irritable, and stingy with their tips.

Unfortunately, Christians with a poverty mentality go out for lunch after church and share their limited view of Heaven with their community.

I submit that we also often see a poverty mentality at work when we take an offering in church. It goes something like this: "Today we are going to show you a video of starving children in Africa. These kids are way worse off than you. We are going to play sad worship music and show you tragic scenes so you can feel guiltier about keeping your money than you are afraid of giving it. Thank you for your generosity."

The middle class is more than free to eat whenever they want. Their resources give them many more options. Therefore, quantity is not a driving force in choosing what they eat. The middle class recommends a restaurant like this:

"Oh! You have got to go there. They have the best chicken *cordon bleu* in the world! It is so good. They also have the best rib-eye steak I've ever eaten in my life. There is this sauce…Oh my, it is so good. It is like $50, though. But it is so good. You've got to try it."

"Oh yeah, we tried that place when it first opened, but it's kind of dirty now. So, we go to this other place that is much cleaner, and the food is great."

The value placed on food is determined by its quality. If it doesn't taste good, then the middle class will pass. But if it's delicious, they will pay extra and come back later for more. They know that they have the choice of where to spend their money and had better get quality in both food and service, or they simply will not patronize that business in the future. Nor will they recommend that establishment to their friends and family.

This class view shows up commonly in how believers select a church. The middle class knows that they have options. They can attend any church in town. So, the quality of the experience had better be there or they won't be. How was the teaching? How is the nursery? Do they have a quality children's program at this church? How difficult is it to park at this church? Were they friendly and helpful when we arrived? Do they realize that we can choose any church in town and that it is their job to keep our money and us around this place? Do they know that we know people in this town? They do know that we can go somewhere else, right?

The wealthy are some strange birds for most of us. They can have as much of the highest quality food they could ever want. Therefore, they see food as a work of art, something that should have *presentation*:

"If it doesn't impress me in the way that it is presented, then I am not sure I am in the right place. Elegance, style, and beauty are what make an establishment worth patronizing. So, when it comes time to eat, make it do something for me. Make it pop!"

Everyone serving food to the wealthy is competing on how it is dressed up. The restaurants of the wealthy don't have cooks; they have artists and creative sculptors working in the kitchen. Now, if a poor guy goes into a restaurant for wealthy people, he or she is going to be shocked at the dainty portion covered by a bunch of "weeds." He is likely to be furious and think he is being ripped off when he discovers that this drizzle costs a week's salary. Our class perspectives set us up to relate to resources in a certain way. If we have little, then we don't expect much more than getting our most basic needs met. But if we have more than enough, then we expect even the everyday experience of eating food to be an encounter with beauty.

Believers with a wealth class view expect much more in their experience with God than salvation. While that is good and they are happy they are going to Heaven, these believers are very aware of what life on earth is supposed to be like. They know there is more provision, beauty, power, and joy than they could ever exhaust, so they make sure that they are living in it every day, all day long. Anything less would be ridiculous.

	Poverty	Middle Class	Wealth
Destiny	Believes in fate. Powerless to change much	Believes in choice. Power to change future with good decisions	*Noblesse oblige*

Powerlessness is one of the primary effects of poverty. When people live in a resource-starved environment, they soon feel the very real constraints of limitation. Their lack of options makes them feel like victims, that their lives are determined by more powerful external forces. As a result, they live superstitiously, believing that a force they cannot control determines their life. They believe in fate, the idea that their life is something that happens to them, and that their job is to do their best to adapt to what happens. Believing in fate is like driving at night with your lights off. You can't really do much about what happens, so you just try to keep your car from being totaled by whatever you hit.

Destiny is oppressive to the poor, because an external force has all the power and leaves them with no power. The poor are slaves of their lives, and the feeling of powerlessness naturally creates anxiety, leading the poor to look for comfort by hanging their hopes on a lucky turn of events. It's not the wealthy that are buying lottery tickets. It's the poor who want a miraculous rescue from life's conditions, which they cannot change. Life is about surviving within the context of their birth, and everyone they know has the same mindset. The young may hope to escape that context, but the hopes of the older ones among them have been crushed by the cruel life of poverty and they believe it to be immutable. They may know a few gifted and "blessed" individuals who have escaped this oppression, but most are trapped by a set of limitations that have kept them captive for generations.

When believers see their destiny in God through a poverty class view, they live a natural, not a supernatural, life, and find themselves trapped in natural problems with no hope of heavenly intervention. They learn to blame God as the One who has the power to do something about their desperate situation but chooses to do nothing. As they experience a powerless gospel, they create a theology to sanction that experience, a theology where Heaven is a lot like earth, God is a lot like them, and the outcome of their lives is predetermined. Fate is called "God's will" and a life of limitation and powerlessness is called "humility" and "perseverance." These are virtues to live up to and model—after all, it's in the Bible, so it must be true.

The big "lottery ticket" for each generation is the Rapture. Since God is apparently not powerful enough or inclined to change their circumstances, the thing that gives them hope is the idea that He is planning to rescue them out of those circumstances. The concept of being powerful eludes those in a poverty class because life in God is not a supernatural experience, but is just more of what they have experienced so far.

The middle class has a much more powerful interaction with life. They believe that their destinies and the quality of their lives are influenced by the fact that they have choices. Having options creates an expectation of freedom, and access to resources creates an expectation that one has power to change the environment by adding to it. When faced with problems, the middle class expects to be able to change a system or most limitations in order to move ahead with the desire within them. The middle class believes that dreams can come true. They believe that they can have anything they want if they continue in wise choices and moral, healthy practices. They believe that it is a right that they live free and that they keep the power they need to preserve that freedom. Primarily, the middle class supplies wars and economies. They can choose between life and death or the amounts of taxes they will pay to protect their freedom.

But the middle class also experiences limitations. There is a ceiling on the amount of money they have access to, a limitation to their power over their environment. Politics, media, and education are the realms of influence and power they turn to for help in improving their lives. Once these are exhausted, they look for solace in building something new in each of these arenas so the next generation can try for breakthrough. A new lobby, a new campaign, or a new expertise will lead us further into our success of achievement and destiny.

The majority of American believers are caught in the middle class view. We are commonly known for our efforts to manipulate our environment. It is so tempting to try to make people think like us. After all, we love people and we want the best for them. We want people to know Jesus and to have what we have. We want people to come to our church and for the quality of our lives to be made available to everyone. We want our Gospel to fill the airwaves, to be taught in every school, and to be legislated from the highest governors in the land. Perhaps the only thing that middle class believers agree upon is this vision of the Gospel as a social and political panacea. The Christian Coalition as a political movement seemed like a great idea at the time and may still to some. Many of us would love to hear Rush Limbaugh, Oprah, or Bono say "God" or "Jesus" one more time.

The wealthy live in a limitless existence where there is no want. No one keeps them from getting what they set their heart and mind upon. The wealthy are accustomed to getting their way. Whatever they ask for, they receive. This situation creates a mindset in them that few experience—a mindset of abundance. Having more than you could ever use and living in that reality builds a sense of obligation within the life of the wealthy class. They see their role in life as one of *noblesse oblige*. This is the French term for the idea that people born into nobility or upper social classes must behave in an honorable and generous way toward those less privileged.

The wealthy mindset is one of generosity. They see the favor and privilege of their lives as a responsibility to bring nourishment and strength to the environment around them. Destiny, to the wealthy, looks like pouring their lives into the long-term benefit of the society and generation in which they live. They live to honor the momentum of their ancestors and to build on the family inheritance for their descendants. The wealthy understand that prosperity must expand if it is to last.

When we as believers begin to cultivate a wealthy class worldview, we will see what apostles and prophets see. We will see and tap into the absolutely unlimited resources of Heaven. We will also see that these resources are an inheritance, something we have access to because we have been grafted into the royal family line of God. This identity is what defines our responsibility to use these vast resources to benefit those around us. When we start to believe the limitlessness of what we have and the weight of what we are called to do with it, we will come to know and experience the reality of the promise that we will receive whatever we ask for.[7] The supernatural will invade our lives, and we will finally lose the anxiety that has been so much a part of our culture in Christianity—anxiety that naturally results from living a life that is devoid of experiencing all the realities that fill the pages of the Bible we profess to believe and live.

Hopefully you can see that leaving our father's house and entering our new Father's House automatically takes our lives to another experience than our fathers lived. Though we appreciate and understand the legacy of those who have gone before us, we are not longing for the days of old. We are not praying that we would return to the "Book of Acts" church. Can you imagine the leader of General Electric saying, "All right, boys, we need to return to the glorious days of the candle. Get to it. Take us back!"

	Poverty	Middle Class	Wealth
Worldview	Local	National	International

All of us have a worldview. It is the scope and span we concern ourselves with as we live our lives. The Internet and satellite television have helped to expand our consciousness of global affairs, but each class continues in their own priority when it comes to worldview.

The poverty class sees life locally. Because resources are scarce, they cannot afford to be concerned with much outside their immediate realm of responsibility. A neighborhood, a village, a town, or part of a city is the extent of concern and investment for the poverty mindset. Churches with a poverty mentality see the world in the context of their congregation, their property, their denomination, or their missions program. It is limited to what they can directly benefit or benefit from.

The middle class tends to be most concerned with their nation, because they feel most affected by the condition of the national economic and political climate. Voting, national news, and economic forecasts are concerns they most readily take responsibility to invest in. Middle class churches are the ones doing the "Get out and *vote*" campaigns and making sure that Christians know who the candidates are. The concerns for prayer are aimed at the social and political climate of the nation.

The wealthy class thinks internationally. Their lives are invested globally, and they are keenly aware of how activity in places all over the world affects the global economy. The wealthy mindset understands the "big picture" and how a global community must succeed as well as the national and local communities.

Believers with a wealthy worldview travel. They invest their lives in a macro-influence. I think Randy Clark provides a vehicle like no other I know to give believers a wealthy worldview experience. There's something about traveling to other nations, amassing with other believers, and seeing Heaven touch earth as you practice the ministry of miracles and healing that cultivates a limitless expectation in your life. It helps you to connect with the fact that the Gospel, the Church, and the Kingdom of God are global realities. It is a practical demonstration of the commission Christ gave us to *"go into all the world and preach the gospel to every creature."*[8] Your worldview expands as you see that Heaven's agenda and resources are designed for global impact and that you have been called to partner in that global picture.

	Poverty	Middle Class	Wealth
Driving Force	Survival, relationships, entertainment	Work, achievement	Financial, political, social connections

What motivates you? Why do you get up in the morning? We see a variety of motivations in the classes. Each has its own set of core values based on what propels its members through life. The driving force for each class is rooted in how they see the world they live in and how they relate to resources.

For the poverty class, the daily concern for survival creates a compass for their decisions, and because their belief in their powerlessness is so strong, these decisions usually follow the course of finding the path of least resistance in order to avoid pain. The quest for pleasure and escape begins each and every day, because life has too much pain built into it.

The value of relationships to the poor is the experience of love and social connection that they offer. Your family and good friends are your world, and typically, you are together for a good portion of your lives. Building relationships among neighbors is natural and these relationships are vital because they often provide an avenue of resources for survival. Unfortunately, however, the strain of limited resources and the drive for survival usually lead to the erosion and abuse of relationships.

Entertainment provides a fantastic method of escape from the harshness of reality in poverty. An individual's ability to entertain others with skills, humor, or music catapults them to the most desirable places in the poverty class. The value for both entertainment and entertainers keeps this group producing both.

When the driving force for believers is survival and escape from pain, they live in continual chaos. Divorces, rebellious teens, domestic violence, and financial upheavals are the culture of the home. Anxiety and fear threaten to devour anything that attempts to grow in these home environments. Churches with this driving force struggle to create an environment of growth and advancement, tending instead to build a legacy of conflict and strife. Usually the resources are the source of strife. As with many nations who spend decades in civil war, these churches are unable to recover from the last battle with the governing authorities among them. The tattered spoils of what was once a resourceful place tend to mark the remains of a church with a driving force of survival.

The ability to achieve is the driving force of the middle class, which explains why this group is often referred to as the "working class." The middle class finds value in those who are working to contribute to the betterment of society. Few things are as disgraceful or offensive to the middle class as those who do not work for a living. Working hard to make a living soars to the top of this class's value system because of their value for things, planning for the future, and achievement. Education, personality, and even language are driven by the middle class's need to succeed by working their way up the ladder of success.

In a middle class family, the parents work to create opportunities for their children to get an education so that they can get a good-paying job. Once a child finds that career, the loop is complete. These children then work and become successful so they can send their children to a good school that will provide them with an opportunity to get a good-paying job. Love is dispensed through this system. When a child fails to complete the loop, the parents struggle to feel like good parents and the family dynamic suffers a certain confusion and sometimes division because a child has broken the cycle.

Motivated by achievement, believers in the middle class have a "works" gospel that puts them to work for God. He has provided them with a "good education" in church and now expects them to be successful workers in His Kingdom. The plans and goals of the middle class church are filled with work and achievements. The more we achieve "for God," the more successful we are in ministry.

The middle class church seems very businesslike and empowers those who are good business people or high achievers. They usually rally around a successful achiever for leadership: "Dr. So-and-so is our leader because he has numerous credentials and endorsements by other high-achieving Christian leaders that we all know and respect." Without trying, we end up with a gospel of conditional love. This creeps into the environment because we are so busy celebrating the achievers that we don't see how we treat those who are not "ringing the bell." Eventually everyone understands that God loves us all, but He *really* loves those who achieve. And that message is reinforced by our entire class culture.

The wealthy have a driving force that, again, doesn't make much sense to the other classes. They get out of bed in the morning to establish and strengthen their connections with other world changers. The wealthy understand that there are a few powerful decision makers who make the global economic, social, and political climate what it is. They are very concerned that they have connections to those decision makers and work to get as close to them as they can get.

The wealthy don't spend their lives working away at a job. They are not training their children to get a job. Instead, they send their kids to schools where other powerful world changers send their children. Connections are the driving force of the wealthy class. They believe that it's not what you know, but who you know and who knows you that makes you successful.

Protecting and developing these relationships with each other helps them to know what is going on all over the world. World leaders in politics, finances, and society are choosing to spend their time with each other for a reason. Knowing that they direct the largest portion of the world's resources, they work to protect the momentum of their ruling class and its members. They understand ways that the other classes do not. They have lived lives of limitlessness and know what it takes in character and responsibility to keep freedom alive throughout their generation and into the next. The wealthy will do everything they can to teach their children how to handle, protect, and pass on the secrets of living in limitless freedom.

Believers who embrace the priority and power of connections will invest their time and energy to build relationships with other re-vivalists, and invest in training their children to do the same. They will make sacrifices to be where God's anointing is pouring out. They will study and experience the works and wonders of God happening all over the globe. They will not be satisfied to "work" for God, but will not stop until He pours unlimited resources through their life to the lives of those around them. Wealthy-minded believers are melding their hearts with apostolic and prophetic leaders all over the world and directing their life's energies, resources, and time toward the success of these leaders. They know that in order for the knowledge of the glory of the Lord to cover the earth as the waters cover the sea, the Church must be filled to overflowing as a whole.

Those with unlimited resources are not focused on those resources as ends in themselves, but on investing them in the things that really matter—people, cultural legacies, beauty. They are seeking out "worthy" causes—things that deserve *honor.* This is why believers who carry a wealth mindset create a culture of honor. Like most things in the Christian life, honor is not an idea, but a practice, a practice of giving. Believers with a wealth mindset don't practice "random acts of kindness"; they embrace the lifestyle of benefactors. And they find a worthy cause a place to show honor, in every person they meet. This, after all, is what the cross, which released the resources of Heaven to us, teaches us to see in people.

All the poverty and middle class motives for giving can't appreciate what God did for us in sending His Son, for He didn't send Jesus out of pity or because He wanted something from us, and certainly not because we deserved it. God paid the human race the supreme honor by becoming one of us. Then He paid us an even greater honor—in His death and resurrection, He made a way for us to become one with Him. And for those of us who have received this outrageous gift from God, is it *our* supreme honor to imitate the One who has honored us by inviting people into God's generosity and giving them a taste of what we've experienced.

Bill Johnson often declares, "We owe people an encounter with God." We owe them this *honor.* Honor is given on the basis of who people are—not what they have earned, or even what they need. Every person you encounter is one Christ has honored in His life, death, and resurrection. The person may not know who he really is from an eternal standpoint, but we do, and when we have a wealth mindset and a heart of honor, we will treat him accordingly.

I hope you can see that a believer carrying a wealth mindset is one of the most important components in bringing Heaven to earth. This mindset not only trains us to see our immediate circumstances from a limitless perspective; it also grounds us in our connections both to the global Body of Christ and to the generations behind and before us. It enables us to jettison the constraints of our past and create an inheritance for our children so that leaving their father's house for the Father's House isn't such a huge chasm to cross.

Can you imagine how our children might live if they are trained from birth to walk in the limitless freedom of the Kingdom? Can you imagine a generation whose dream it is to benefit the world around them by learning to handle and give away the limitless, transforming resources of the Kingdom?

Genesis 12:1-3 says:

> *Now the Lord had said to Abram: "Get out of your country, from your family, and from your father's house, to a land that I will show you. I will make you a great nation; I will bless you and make your name great. And you shall be a blessing. I will bless those who bless you, and I will curse him who curses you; and in you all the families of the earth shall be blessed."*

CHAPTER 6

THE TOP PRIORITY OF LEADERSHIP

There is no fear in love. But perfect love drives out fear,
because fear has to do with punishment.
The one who fears is not made perfect in love.
(1 John 4:18 NIV)

Thomas Jefferson is credited with saying, "Free people are the most difficult to lead." It is extremely pertinent for church leaders, because free people are precisely the group they are called to lead.

Unfortunately, many church leaders have not mastered the difficulties of leading free people. In order to lead free people, we must establish both an environment for them to gain freedom and a government for them to keep that freedom. Generally, neither is what classic church environments are known for. People watching from outside do not expect to keep their freedoms once inside the "institution." Those who do come in are usually ready to give up whatever they have to in order to get rid of their pain. When these people learn that God is a master who wants to control them, as many do, it makes me suspect that church leaders have failed to understand our own Gospel of freedom. A controlling God, who is usually represented by a controlling church leadership, is just not good news.

How can church leadership create freedom and not more rules? How can we bring out the best in human beings and keep it at the surface even as we deal with their problems and shortcomings? Can we empower others and release them to live from their best natures and from the truest reasons they are alive? Will we as Christian leaders, parents, and employers take on the responsibility to learn how to draw out the dreams and destiny in the people we lead?

Let me show you an example of what leading free people might look like (this may be familiar to you if you've read my book *Loving Our Kids On Purpose*). My daughter, Brittney, was 14 once. And like most 14-year-olds, she had a completely different idea of what getting the dishes done meant than my wife, Sheri, had. For this reason, I often heard a conversation that sounded something like this:

Sheri would say, "Britt, time to do the dishes."

And Britt would reply, "I will in just a minute."

That minute would turn into 20 and Sheri would fire off another, "Britt, it is time to get those dishes done."

Britt would volley back with, "I am doing my homework like you said!" or "I am on the phone! I'll be done in just a minute."

This was part of our evening ritual for several months. It was as if the two of them could not go on into the next day without this exchange. Numerous times, Britt made the verbal commitment to finish the dishes, only to fail and have my wife wake up to dirty dishes in the morning. There are several things that my wife does not like in this life: injustice, sushi, bugs, scary movies, and dirty dishes. She really doesn't want to *wake up* to dirty dishes!

Finally, it happened for the last time. Britt went to bed late on a Friday night and forgot to wash the dishes. Saturday morning, she and Sheri had a little conversation about that shortly after Sheri discovered them. I could hear their "little conversation" at the other end of the house. Once finished with Brittney, Sheri came to tell me what had happened. I told her that I had already heard. Meanwhile, Brittney's friend, Rebecca, came over and was visiting Britt in her room. When Sheri and I came looking for Britt to discuss the dish situation, we discovered that, unannounced, Britt and Rebecca had left our house and gone down the street to Rebecca's house. Sheri looked at me with fire in her eyes. Suddenly, it appeared as though her head burst into flames, her skull split open, and a dragon came out of the top of her head. The dragon looked at me and said, "What are *you* going to do?"

"Me?" I replied, suppressing a smile.

"Yes!" the dragon said. "What are you going to do about *your* daughter?"

"Now you want *me* to deal with this situation? Is that what you are saying?"

"Yes!" the dragon said, breathing fire.

So I ran in and did the dishes.

Now, "doing the dishes" at our house involved moving the dishes from the sink into the dishwasher. That was all I did. It maybe took me six minutes. Maybe.

Brittney and Rebecca came back to our house all dolled up with make-up and matching ponytails. Britt asked, "Mom, Dad, can I go to the mall with Rebecca and her mom?"

I thought we would all get to see the dragon again, but instead Sheri was biting the side of her hand, a sign that I was to handle the whole intervention. I said, "Brittney, sweetie. I did the dishes for you."

She said, "Dad that is not fair! I was going to do them! *Ugh!*" Britt began to do little jumps that never actually got her feet off the ground, but were intended to communicate that she did not like what was happening.

Rebecca watched this exchange with a confused look on her face. She finally asked Britt, "Are you in trouble? How do you even know you are in trouble? Nobody is even yelling."

Brittney said, "He's going to trade me chores!"

"Sweetie, which chore would you like to trade me? Would you like to do the trash shed for me or the chicken coop?"

"Ugh! Well, can I look?"

"Of course you can! Of course you can choose which one you are going to do." And thus I empowered the child. I wanted her to feel powerful around me. Out she went.

For those who might not know, the trash shed is a Weaverville cultural experience. Garbage cans left outside would end up with dogs, cats, or raccoons in them, so you had to put the trash in an enclosed area. The door on the shed had a window in it, and once I saw the trash bags through the window, I knew it was time to go to the dump. It was a big old hassle, so I was always waiting for one of my kids to trade me chores.

Britt went and opened the door to the shed. Ten million flies came flying out around her face. "Gross!"

Rebecca nearly started running backward, yelling, "What the heck are we doing out here?"

Brittney spat a fly out and rolled her eyes. Then she headed toward the chicken pen. By the time she got there she was pretty mad, and kicked at the chickens as she entered. "Stupid chickens!" She opened the chicken coop and was completely grossed out by the stench.

Then she came back into the house and said to me, "Chicken pen."

"Awesome, Britt! Thank you!" I replied, excited that I wouldn't have to do that chore in my life this time. Then I asked, "Now, would you like to do that today or tomorrow after church?"

"I can do it tomorrow? Really? Can I go to the mall today with Rebecca?"

"Sure, if you want."

"I can! Oh, Daddy! Thank you! Thank you!"

You may be thinking, "What? You let a transgressor go? You let a sinner escape the due punishment she had coming? Your child got to have freedom and privilege without first experiencing suffering that teaches a lesson? Don't you know that there is need for the shedding of blood for the atoning of sin? How will this child ever learn her lessons?"

Hang on. The story isn't over.

So, off they went to the mall and had a great time. The next morning we went to church and by the time we got back, it was pouring rain. Why? Because Jesus loves me! Brittney was trying to be invisible.

I said to her, "Hey Britt, sweetie! Would you like to wear my rubber boots or those pretty little slippers you have on there?"

"Your rubber boots."

"Do you want to wear my rain jacket or that pretty sweater you have on?"

"Your rain jacket."

"Do you want to use the pitchfork or the shovel?"

"I'll probably need both."

Off she went. One…two…*three* hours later, in she came, dragging that shovel and pitchfork. She had straw hanging off her sopped head. I met her at the back door and asked her what she needed.

She said, "I'm done."

"Awesome! Thank you very much."

"Whatever!" Off she went to take a shower.

Sometime later that week, I heard Sheri say, "Brittney, get those dishes done."

Then I heard Brittney say, "Ugh. I will in just a minute."

So I got up and said, "Britt, I got them for you!" Just as I got off the couch, she came *flying* through the house, yelling, *"You get away from my dishes!"*

I smiled and said, "Hey, I'm just trying to be helpful. But if you ever need me to do your work for you, I am your man."

There is a way to lead people into freedom in such a way that personal responsibility rises to the surface. It requires us to trust people. But it never ceases to amaze me that when we trust people to rise up and see the wisdom in their choices, then we will see a greater person in our relationships. People want to be trusted and they want to be free.

Create a Safe Place

Why do you suppose free people are so difficult to lead? Well, I can tell you that the problem of leading free people is connected to a question about the universe that philosophers and theologians have worked on for centuries. It's connected to the fact that God, the leader of the universe, created us to be free. In fact, God *trusted* us with freedom. C.S. Lewis presented a concise account of the situation in *Mere Christianity*:

> God created things which had free will. That means creatures which can go either wrong or right. Some people think they can imagine a creature which was free but had no possibility of going wrong; I cannot. If a thing is free to be good it is also free to be bad. And free will is what has made evil possible. Why, then, did God give them free will? Because free will, though it makes evil possible, is also the only thing that makes possible any love or goodness or joy worth having. A world of automata—of creatures that worked like machines—would hardly be worth creating. The happiness which God designs for His higher creatures is the happiness of being freely, voluntarily united to Him and to each other in an ecstasy of love and delight compared with which the most rapturous love between a man and a woman on this earth is mere milk and water. And for that they must be free.
>
> Of course God knew what would happen if they used their freedom the wrong way: apparently He thought it worth the risk.[1]

The difficulty in leading free people is *risk*—the risk that they could use their freedom the wrong way. But unlike God, many of us in the Church do not understand why the risk is worth it. The threat of misused freedom looms larger than the prize of true freedom. And because of that, we get scared. This fear can be endemic in supposedly free societies. In the United States, the supposed leader of the free world, fear is rampant. We as believers need to tap into some pretty powerful stuff if we are going to resist the fear in our culture and extend trust to God and people. We also need to pound Heaven's value for freedom into our belief system.

As Lewis pointed out, the whole value of freedom, the whole purpose for freedom, is love. When we use our freedom to love, as intended, our freedom and the freedom of those around us are protected and cultivated. As leaders we need to accomplish many things, from defining reality to reaching productive goals. But the priority of Heaven is crystal clear: "If you have not love…you're just noisy."[2] Leaders who extinguish love in the process of reaching goals have achieved earth's priorities, maybe. But the higher goals of Heaven require us to cultivate and preserve love, and thus freedom, for you cannot have love without freedom. God is love, and His kingdom is a kingdom of freedom. This would be why the Bible tells us, *"The Lord is the Spirit, and where the Spirit of the Lord is, there is freedom."*[3] This verse is saying that when God shows up, people feel free. If that is not happening, we should wonder why. Why isn't freedom breaking out in more places? Could it be because a lot of people, including leaders, misunderstand the goal of God's leadership in our lives?

I want to propose that the goal of God's leadership in our lives, and consequently, the goal of church leaders, is to create a *safe place* for us to discover who we are and why we are here. A safe place is a place where the fear of misused freedom doesn't get to rise up and intimidate us out of risking trust and love in our relationships with one another. A safe place is what gets cultivated when freedom is expressed through love. The essence of love is *safety* and *connection*. If people don't feel safe to be themselves and don't feel a sense of connection with people around them, then it's hard to convince them that they are in a loving place.

Now, we won't step into experiencing a safe place with God and His people as long as we fail to understand and believe that it's what God wants for us. My experience is that most people, including Christians, think God wants us to line up, stay in line, and be good. We've embraced the idea that He is patient, but still on the verge of anger. For most people, God is a scary character—unpredictable and strict. But consider what God said through the prophet Isaiah: *"The mountains and the hills will be removed, but My kindness shall never leave you, nor shall My covenant of peace with you ever be removed."*[4] The mountains and the hills are going to be taken away? Can you imagine watching a mountain be taken away? Can you imagine what would be required for that to happen? It would require more than a little violence, something pretty scary.

God is saying that He is not unpredictable. He wants us to be completely sure of His attitude toward us: "My kindness and My covenant of peace will never be taken away." God wants us to have a blessed assurance, a truth that positions us to look for the freedom that comes to us when Jesus shows up. This mentality, this expectation, and this security allow us to be free everywhere we go.

No matter what case you make against God, no matter what Scriptures you use to make it, no matter what you do to build a different reality—His kindness and His peace will never be taken from you. That word "peace" is literally the word *shalom*. From this word we get several powerful definitions. Here's what it says in the Strong's Hebrew Dictionary:

> 07965 *shaw-lome*; safe, well, happy, friendly; health, prosperity, peace, well.

Please notice that the first definition of *shalom* is "safe" or "safety." Our covenant with God is a *safe place.* The power in this reality is that we as human beings blossom in safety. This is why *shalom* also means "health" and "wholeness." The nourishing effects of His presence stimulate the deepest parts of the best in us. This is why He says that His covenant is for our welfare and not our calamity.[5] His covenant brings peace, happiness, safety, and completeness, and it will never be taken from us. When He shows up, His presence is a safe place.

This is good news. Go ahead and smile. When the Lord shows up, His atmosphere is charged with *shalom.* He brings a safe place everywhere He goes. It never ceases to amaze me how many people want to make a case that God is scary. But they do. This is why we as leaders at Bethel have understood that one of our primary jobs is to declare God's true nature and attitude toward us on a regular basis. Almost every time we do it, we can feel it directly confronting the wrong thinking in the room. So many times I've heard Bill Johnson declare to a congregation that God is in a good mood, only to hear nervous laughter break out all over the place, as if to say, "He-he. I have never thought of God like that before." I myself have made the same statement in places where I've spoken. "God's in a good mood!" I can see the confusion in some people's eyes. It is as though they want to pick up their Old Testament and yell out, "Not in this part of the Bible He's not." Yes, He is! He is in a good mood, from start to finish, and you can make a case for that too.

This truth would seem to be a no-brainer since Jesus came and introduced a New Covenant. It's been a couple thousand years. We should be getting this by now. God is very familiar with His original design for us to need a safe place. The Garden of Eden was such a place. We are designed to need freedom. We are at our best when we are safe, when we are happy, when we feel whole, and when we have peace. If our peace or safety is disrupted, then our physical body begins a process of shutting down our best and preparing us to show our worst. It works something like this:

God put this little gland inside our brain called the amygdala. It is an almond-shaped mass of nuclei located deep within the temporal lobes of the brain. This gland is important for determining emotional responses, especially those associated with fear. When somebody does something threatening or unexpected in your environment, when somebody is not safe, your amygdala kicks on and begins to flood your body with these messages: *react, defend, disappear, fight,* or *flee.* These are some of the responses in which we show our worst. It doesn't take a rocket scientist to discover that people who are scared are not at their creative best. If you've ever been near a person who is drowning and scared that he or she is going to die, then you know it would be a good idea to keep your distance. Throw a rope or extend a pole, but do not let that person get a hold of you or you will become a buoy. Oh sure, the person will apologize later, if you lived. But scared people are not thinking about the team, family, church, or anyone else beside themselves. Fear is a dangerous element for humans to navigate through. Most do not manage it well.

As you can see, when we do not feel safe, it's likely that we will become dangerous ourselves by allowing fear to start directing our behavior. And just imagine what happens when the *leader* in an environment is directed by fear. A majority of leaders, not just

Christian leaders, are pretty uptight. The same goes for far too many parents. When they need to go somewhere with their kids, many parents are uptight from the moment they say, "It's time to leave!" If you are a pastor preparing for Sunday morning, it's a pretty good chance you are uptight. If there is something important going on, and the outcome matters to you, there is a good chance you are going to bring *uptight* with you. It's quite common.

Of course, another word for *uptight* (or stress, or anxiety) is *fear*. And here's the thing—when we are afraid on the inside, there is more than a good chance we are getting that fear on those outside of us. As people, whether we are believers or not, we are creative and spiritual in nature. We are spiritual conductors, and we create an atmosphere, a reality, a *spirit,* if you will, around us. But we can only reproduce on the outside that which is on the inside. If our thoughts and affections are wrapped up with a spirit of fear, while we may think we are smoothly hiding it, we cannot mask the anxiety we allow to live in our lives.

Unfortunately, too many people become accustomed to living in an environment where the people in charge are uptight. Most of us are trained early in life that people who are in charge aren't safe and can hurt us. Sometimes we learn that powerful people *will* hurt us. From our earliest childhood experiences to our most recent run-in with an authority figure, we build a concept about what to expect from God, the ultimate authority figure. If what we have learned is fear, imagine what our amygdalas are doing the entire time we are in the presence of powerful people. What is this doing to our potential in God? How will we ever become whole, free, or healthy living under those conditions?

The answer is simply that we won't. But the good news is that the conditions are changing. Heaven, the kingdom of love and freedom, is invading earth, and love is directly confronting the fear that has governed us. Fear and love are enemies. These two spirits will not hold the same place together. Love and fear are like light and dark…fresh water and salt water…blessing and cursing. And one of them has to win. Love casts out the fear.[6] Love not only casts out the fear; it brings security and safety and *shalom*. This is the fruit that I am seeing in an apostolic environment. Fear is leaving people's lives. Freedom is growing in worship and in our relationships with one another as people are starting to get it: He is a safe place.

As I indicated in the first chapter, creating a safe place is the essential condition for a revival culture. The fact that miracles, signs, and wonders not only have happened in our midst but have continued to happen for years now points to the fact that something has been established—a wineskin of healthy people and relationships that manifest and carry the *shalom* of Heaven. And as I explained in the second chapter, there is an order for leadership, a structure, that sustains the flow of heavenly reality, of grace, in people's lives and facilitates the core values and truths that an apostolic leadership holds dear. It is not a small thing that our leader is regularly declaring the goodness of God over us. If leaders believe that God is good and in a good mood, then the people will follow and learn this to be true for themselves.

If leaders understand that their top priority is making the house of God a safe place, then, as people encounter the safe place of God's covenant in their lives and their potential, anointings, and creativity start to rise to the surface, there will be room to manifest those things in the church. If leaders can create an environment where people can feel loved, safe, and free to be themselves, then we will start to change the world with the Kingdom of Heaven. Then we will be at our best. Then we will be confronting the principalities and powers that have ruled the planet.

Honor and Conflict

Honor is one of the most vital core values for creating a safe place where people can be free. Honor protects the value that people have for those who are different than they are. This core value is central in an apostolic culture because, as we saw in Chapter 2, the fivefold pattern of ministry is built around understanding, valuing, and making room for the different graces that rest upon and flow through different people. Free people cannot live together without honor, and conversely, honor can only be used successfully amongst powerful people who have a true sense of their personal responsibility in preserving the freedom around them. We must be able to be ourselves in this life and community together.

As you are probably aware, high levels of freedom can generate conflict, usually because we experience others who are living in ways that flood our amygdalas. Without a core value of honor, we find that our discomfort around those who choose to live in ways that we would not leads us to shut down their freedom. It is typical, for example, when a teenager begins to explore his or her freedom, that his or her parents become afraid. The fear stems from the fact that the child is choosing options that the parents either wouldn't ever or wouldn't again choose for themselves. The wrestling match is over how different the child can be so as to individuate from the parents and how much the parents can keep the child looking like them. The further the child moves from how the parents live, the more likely the parents are to step in and shut down the child's choices. The result is conflict. But when the teenager and the parents both practice honor, which contains within it love and trust, fear is not allowed to rule their decisions and freedom can be preserved.

Obviously, when I speak of different ways to live, I am not saying that immorality or violating our relationship with God are viable options for any of us. But many Christians disagree about how to live. When people begin to walk in freedom, they will say and do things that demonstrate to all who are near that conformity is not a priority. This clashes with much of our Christian culture experience. Again, I am not building a case for people to be rude, uncaring, or obnoxious, but I am trying to point out that free people are not terribly interested in putting on a façade for anyone.

From the way we dress to the style of music we listen to, to whether we drink alcohol or not, to whether we speak English or Christianese, to whether the gifts of the Spirit are in operation today or not, the reality is that freedom is going to bring our differences to the surface and cause friction within a community. When the people around us are no longer protecting our paradigms, our amygdalas get jacked up. This is how we often end up showing others our worst.

As you can see, the culture of honor both facilitates a safe place and in turn, creates a place of great conflict. The question is whether we will learn to use honor to navigate through the conflict when it arises. Conflict is not inherently evil. As a matter of fact, when conflict goes away, *life* most likely left with it. Sometimes we hope that peace means the absence of conflict, but true peace is always the result of victory. I cannot think of a victory that did not first begin with a struggle.

Chapter 7

Kingdom Confrontation

*It's harder to make amends with an offended friend
than to capture a fortified city.
Arguments separate friends
like a gate locked with iron bars.*
(Proverbs 18:19 NLT)

There will be no culture of honor without the active use of effective confrontation. The skill of combining these two relational elements—honor and confrontation—is the key to sustaining an environment of grace. Please lock onto this chapter. It will help you immensely to bring about what I believe is your hope.

Paul wrote to the Galatians extensively about the fact that we are a people who are called to walk in freedom and love through the internal government of the Spirit of God. Once again, this idea is not new; it just seems that we, like the Galatians, have a difficult time catching onto it. We covered some of what Paul wrote in discussing why we are unpunishable, and this belief is foundational for walking out Kingdom confrontation. For our present purposes, let's review Paul's description of us as a mature heir:

> *Now I say that the heir, as long as he is a child, does not differ at all from a slave, though he is master of all, but is under guardians and stewards until the time appointed by the father. Even so we, when we were children, were in bondage under the elements of the world. But when the fullness of the time had come, God sent forth His Son, born of a woman, born under the law, to redeem those who were under the law, that we might receive the adoption as sons. And because you are sons, God has sent forth the Spirit of His Son into your hearts, crying out, "Abba, Father!" Therefore you are no longer a slave but a son, and if a son, then an heir of God through Christ.*[1]

We are no longer slaves but sons! Our context for life has moved from needing a guardian and steward (external controls) to that of being powerful, free sons of the living God.[2] And far more is required to operate in the freedom of being a powerful, rich person than in the limitations of a slave.

Remember the film *The Matrix*? In his first encounter with Morpheus, Neo hears, "You are a slave, Neo. Like everyone else, you were born into bondage, born inside a prison that you cannot smell, taste, or touch. A prison for your mind." He then offers Neo freedom from this prison—the red pill. But when Neo wakes up in the "real world," he finds himself on an operating table with all kinds of things sticking out of him. Morpheus explains that they are rebuilding his muscles, which he has never used before. This is a dramatic but clear picture of what it's like for us, who were born "in bondage under the elements of the world," to enter the life of freedom.

As slaves, we followed the path of least resistance and weren't required to take full responsibility for our thinking and behavior. We never developed the moral muscles to handle unlimited options. But in the "real world" of the Kingdom, sons and daughters of God are not only expected to be free, but also to understand why they are free and exercise that freedom toward its purpose—love. As Paul goes on to say:

> *For you, brethren, have been called to liberty; only do not use liberty as an opportunity for the flesh, but through love serve one another. …I say then: Walk in the Spirit, and you shall not fulfill the lust of the flesh.*[3]

Our success in using our freedom to love comes down to *walking by the Spirit.* For this reason, if we as leaders are going to build people who can handle freedom, then our leadership methods must mature to address the *spirit* of a man and not simply his *behavior.*

Paul goes on to say: *"Brethren, if a man is overtaken in any trespass, you who are spiritual restore such a one in a spirit of gentleness, considering yourself less you also be tempted."*[4] He is giving instruction for what to do when any of us happen to cross paths with someone who has fallen into a hole. In the previous chapter, Paul has described those who are led by the Spirit and express His character (fruit) in their lives. Here he addresses "you who are spiritual"—those who know and display the love and character of God—and declares that we are to handle such situations in "a spirit of gentleness"—one of the fruits of the Spirit.

We are also to be very mindful of the cost of judging other people. As Jesus taught, the same judgment that we have issued on somebody else's sin will be measured and used on us.[5] Judging others paints a big target on our faces and affords our enemy a turn at us.

"A spirit of gentleness" is an important phrase. It specifically describes the heart attitude of the one doing the confrontation. Gentleness is the perfect term to describe the attitude we must have with those who have made mistakes or failed somehow. Gentleness does not mean nice, and it doesn't mean polite. The heart of gentleness is the belief that "I do not need to control you." Imagine approaching a deer in an effort to pet it. If that deer for a moment thinks you will capture it, that thing is gone. Those of us who know the heart of God must carry the reality that we will not attempt to control the person who is in trouble into every confrontation. This is the first and most important skill to develop. It is also the most difficult.

Mastery of gentleness begins in our belief system. Do we believe that we can control others? Let's review the simple way to test it out. What happens to you when other people do not let you control them? Do you become angry? Do you interpret it as dishonor? Do you find a way to justify punishing them? A yes to any of these questions exposes that you still believe the lie that you can and should control people. Kingdom confrontation requires that you repent of this and begin to allow others to control themselves.

I had a secret expectation that revival would eliminate all the problems in my environment, and eventually this snuck up on me. One day I felt this wave of unbelief come over me because of the people problems surrounding me—adultery, child abuse, addictions, lying, and more. I thought to myself, "If God is really here and His Kingdom is coming, then why are so many people still messing up their lives?" That question caused me to think about the Kingdom of God like I never had before. Is Heaven a place where God controls all the choices? What about the Garden? That place had choices.

I realized then that Heaven has poor choices in it. There have to be poor choices in Heaven, because it's a free place. Lucifer found a poor choice. I have since heard Bill Johnson say many times, "Grace in a culture gives the sin that resides in people's hearts an opportunity to manifest." When we live in a place of love and acceptance, and are applying God's unconditional love to people's lives 100 percent of the time, the sin that lies dormant in people's lives, or the sin that people have been struggling with or hiding, will come out and end up on the floor.

I believe we can learn a lesson about the culture of grace by looking at the evolution of pig farming. Pigs are famous for their mess and stench. For centuries, pig farms were the most disgusting environments imaginable. Because pigs have no natural way of cooling themselves, farmers provided a mud hole for their pigs to keep them from overheating. These mud holes, where pigs wallowed for a good portion of the day, eventually filled with urine and feces because the pigs couldn't seem to find a toilet. If you've ever been around a pigpen, you know the powerful stench that permeates the area, spreading as far as the wind will carry it. Filth, disease, bacteria, and infection are plentifully found in these places.

But in recent times, someone decided to separate pigs from their mess. Instead of making the mess an accepted part of what it means to raise pigs, today's farmers build facilities designed to protect the pigs from all that is disgusting. Instead of using mud to cool the pigs, they use water. The floors and living areas of the pigs have drains and rinse systems that carry the waste away from the pigs. Pigs can now live in clean environments and be every bit as sanitary as household pets. This was unimaginable just a short time ago, and it still hasn't become universal; many pig farmers still use the old methods because the new systems are so expensive.

The Father paid the highest price to make a new system of dealing with our messes available to us. If mankind can figure out a way to raise clean pigs and be willing to pay the price, then certainly the expense of the blood of Jesus can accomplish the desire of our Father's heart for us. Jesus declared, *"You are...clean because of the word which I have spoken to you."*[6] We are clean!

Therefore, we had better have a mechanism in our Christian culture that deals effectively with the sin when it comes out right in front of us. For whatever reason, we've come to expect that church is a place where there isn't going to be any sin. It is just not true. If we don't know how to deal with sin, then we don't know how to deal with people. We inevitably create a culture of law in order to keep people from sinning. The message of this culture is, "Contain your sin within yourself. Don't show it to me; I can't handle it."

Remember, this was the Pharisees' line. They were famous for being afraid of sin, largely due to the fact that the only remedy for sin in their day was various degrees of punishments. The fear of punishment ruled their hearts, relationships, and culture. Jesus, on the other hand, had a group of unlikely companions. They were the thieves, tax collectors, and the hookers of the day. Compared to the other religious leaders at the time, He was like "Jesus of Vegas." He was not in the least afraid of messes people made in their lives, and of letting them happen around Him. Even the people who spent three years walking personally with Jesus were still making messes the night of His crucifixion. But ultimately, His love and the way He led people empowered them to rise above their mistakes and issues.

If we are going to cultivate a grace culture, we need to have effective ways of dealing with other people's problems. We need environments that move the waste away from people instead of making it a part of who they are. Our methods must move the waste away, however, without reinforcing the expectation that other people control us and we control others. As I've pointed out earlier, no one can control us. We have our hands full trying to control ourselves. Therefore, we also need to have empowering ways of managing *ourselves* in the presence of other people's problems. Our power and peace are rooted in being able to maintain our freedom around each other through self-control. Without a priority of self-control, we live in constant reaction to one another, which creates a culture of blame and irresponsibility. "Your stuff triggers my stuff, and I don't know what to do when you do that. Stop it! Now I am going to blame you for what I do. If you don't do that, I won't have to do this."

People will get their power back most quickly in a culture with powerful leaders who lead in freedom and honor. Such a culture has a high value for confrontation, a value that derives from the understanding that not cleaning up messes creates a toxic environment for everyone. However, I want to describe what confrontation is and what it isn't, because there is confusion on that point and this confusion has created plenty of messes in addition to the messes the mishandled confrontation was meant to address. I am going to show you places in the Bible where it works beautifully. I pray that you receive an impartation of truth in your thinking about how to approach the issue of sin in the lives of those around you and how to manage yourself in relationships.

Goals of Confrontation

First, let's identify the goals of confrontation. These must be in your heart and motivate you as you go into a confrontation. Confrontation is about bringing something to the light. When I come to you, in a *spirit of gentleness*, I have come to turn the lights on for you to have an opportunity to *see*. Again, *gentleness* means that *I do not need to control you*. This confrontation is not an attempt to force your hand or make you do something. It is a loving effort to show you, face-to-face, what you might not see or know about what you are doing or how you are affecting the world around you. Gentleness is going to help the anxiety remain low and the love increase through the whole process.

Traditionally, confrontation and conflict are synonymous. These words trigger thoughts of struggle and injury. Too often, those injured are people who care about each other. The culprit in these struggles is control. The wrong goals will produce an undesired outcome. Therefore, it is important to identify and understand the correct goals of confrontation:

- To introduce consequences into a situation in order to teach and strengthen.

- To bring to the surface what people forget about themselves after they have failed.

- To send an invitation to strengthen a relational bond with someone.

- To apply pressure strategically in order to expose areas needing strength and grace.

Let me explain how *to introduce consequences in order to teach and strengthen*. Once again, this goal cannot be met until I have dealt with my belief that I can control others. I must have no intention to get this person to do something. Instead, this process will help the person see the mess he or she has made and see a helpful ally at his or her side.

Second, I must understand that there is a difference between a *consequence* and a *punishment* and be careful to present the former.

Many of us are confused on this point because we have heard punishment called discipline. We all know that discipline is a good thing—the Bible clearly points out that love and discipline are connected.[7] Unfortunately, our so-called discipline looks and feels like punishment. It helps us to mask our fear and justify our need for control. There is no power given to the one receiving such discipline. The one administering the discipline requires complete compliance from the one being disciplined, and therein lies the difference between discipline that is actually punishment and discipline through consequences. Consequences are different from punishment because power is given to the one who has made the mess.

The process of Kingdom confrontation is a process of empowerment, not domination. When a person fails and generates a consequence for that failure in his or her life, the confrontation leads and empowers the person to clean up the mess. One of our sayings at Bethel is, "Feel free to make as big a mess as you are ready to clean up." This is not a flippant broadcast of irresponsibility. It is simply a message to everyone that personal responsibility is required in this environment. No one will be stuck with your mess, and no one will be able to clean up a mess you have made as well as you can.

At Bethel, our interventions are built upon an expectation that people, motivated by respect for relationships, will respond by taking ownership for their choices and the consequences that come from them. This response is only possible when people know they are free. They are free to blow the whole thing off. Only then can they choose to clean up their mess. Only then can they choose to honor and respect their community and relationships.

If we steal this option from them because we want to control the outcome, then we disempower them and create powerless, irresponsible victims. Powerless victims never own anything and do not change their circumstances. Therefore, our confrontations must carry the goal of empowerment from the start. Our process of confrontation will point to the consequences of their choices and offer strength and wisdom instead of control and punishment.

In the first chapter of this book I told the story of a couple of our ministry students who became pregnant during the summer break between First and Second Year. As you remember, I presented the process we went through with them as an example of how we do most confrontations in our culture. Our team and I had great respect and honor for those two students. Our priority was to protect our relationship with them while we showed them something they did not see: the problem and its consequences. Throughout the confrontation we were pursuing and protecting the above goals. We knew that the confrontation was going to bring them tremendous insight, wisdom, and understanding as we assisted them with solving the problem and cleaning up their mess. We also empowered them in a way that brought hope and joy, which strengthened them both in the midst of the cleanup and on the other side of it.

Our process with this couple also helped to reveal and confirm their true identities as a son and daughter of the King of Kings, thereby achieving the next goal of confrontation: *to bring to the surface what people forget about themselves after they have failed.* In a culture of rules, not only do people expect punishment when they fail; they are overwhelmed by the power of shame. According to the size of their mistake or their sensitivity to failure, shame takes root in the hearts and minds of those who fail. Now, shame isn't just a feeling; it is a *spirit.* It is a spirit that attacks the identity of individuals. This spirit lies to people and leads them to believe that their poor behavior is really flowing from who they are: "You didn't fail; you are a failure. You didn't make a mistake; you are a mistake!"

Our two students are amazing people. They made a huge mistake and they are still amazing people. The people we wanted to show up in our confrontation were the best people they have inside them. Shame had determined to cover those people up and sought to destroy them. Our job was to bring their very best to the surface, and then present them with the reality of the situation, knowing that their best will make the best decisions and turn tragedy into triumph. Because we started with this goal, it only made sense to allow those people to show up and to trust them. If we had had a need to punish them, we would have ended up partnering with shame and requiring them to assume a powerless position that allowed us to control them and make them fulfill our wishes.

The greatness that resides at the core of every believer must come forth if we are to truly represent our Father in Heaven. Putting on the cloak of shame and guilt is not only unbecoming for us as His sons and daughters; it is a trap of powerlessness. Reaching in and grabbing our people by their true identities is an act of love that will live on far longer than the sting of failure and consequences. People can see and think when their identity is clear of fear and shame. Again and again, we have seen the greatness in those who have made mistakes take charge and work evil into good. And right along with this, we see our covenant relationships strengthened and deepened.

This is our next goal in confrontation, to extend *an invitation to strengthen a relational bond with someone.* We must see the process of bringing an issue to the light as an invitation to practice our covenant relationships. It may appear that our priority is settling a matter or changing behavior. But in reality, Kingdom confrontation is a test of the covenant between two or more people, and that relationship is always the true priority. When we hold other people accountable for how they are impacting us, or the community around them, we expose the levels of trust we have with those individuals.

When we test the connection between us through confrontation, we learn the true strength of our covenant with another person.

Too often, we find weak, frail connections when we confront. Sometimes it is shocking how little value people have for their relationships with us. Other times it simply validates what we thought and hoped was there.

Trust is the key to a successful confrontation. Without it, we will discover our limitations quickly. If and when we find a confrontation not going well, the first thing to check is the trust level. When trust is low, anxiety is usually high. When anxiety rises, our priority in the encounter shifts to self-preservation, usually by means of seeking to control each other. If we have someone in front of us who believes that he has to protect himself from us, then we will not be talking to his greatness, but instead to his great survival tactics. To have trust, the person we confront must believe that we are for him or her, and will protect his or her best interests throughout the confrontation.

Our two students were absolute strangers to me when we met that day. Prior to our conversation in my office, I had never spoken to either of them. Those two were gambling all their chips coming into the office of a total stranger—a stranger who had the power to punish them, no less. Aware of their extremely vulnerable position, I thanked them for trusting me. Shame, anxiety, and the expectation of punishment were all elements working against us from the start. I asked their school leaders to attend the meeting with us so that I could "borrow" the trust that the couple had already built with them. I knew I needed to establish trust before I could apply any pressure to them in hopes of finding the source of the problem.

Our final goal is to *apply pressure strategically in order to expose areas needing strength and grace.* We need to find the "broken spots" and work to begin healing them. My best analogy for "applying pressure" comes from my early adult years working in a tire store. One of my duties was to pull logging truck tires apart. I would jack up the truck, take off the wheel, take the sledge and break the bead away from the ring, slide the tire off the wheel, and pull the flap and the deflated inner tube out. I would then connect the air hose to the stem of the inner tube and fill it with air—far more air than the tube could contain while inside the tire. When the tube was stretched to capacity, I would take it over to a tank full of water and begin to submerge portions of the tube under the water. As I held sections of the tube under the water, I rolled the tube under my hands and hunted for something: bubbles. I was trying to find the "broken spot" where the air was leaking out. As soon as I located where the bubbles were coming from, I marked it and began to repair the flat tire.

This process only worked if I filled the inner tube with enough internal pressure. The "broken spot" on the tube never revealed itself if I did not apply the right pressure. External pressure will never expose someone's "broken spot." Yelling at it, threatening to cut it into little pieces, coaxing it, or interrogating it are never going to help me find the spot that needs healing. This work is accomplished from the inside out.

Confrontation is a process of applying pressure to another person's life, on purpose, to expose the broken spots. We need to find these places if we ever hope to change the destructive loops in which people often live. We can't make different decisions and create a different result until we know what is wrong.

Isaiah 1:18 says, *"Come now let us reason together. Though your sins be like scarlet...."* Though your sins are blatantly all over the place, God says, "We can do something about that." There is hope. More importantly, God says, *"Come, let us reason together."* The very heartbeat, nature, and desire of God are that we *come.* In these words *"reason together,"* the Lord invites us to mutually look at something to correct it. "Come, let's look at this thing together to bring correction. Do you see what I see? I hope you do, because until you do, what I say won't make any sense to you. If you don't see what I am looking at, all My advice won't make a lick of sense to you. Do you see what I see? Can you hear Me?"

God does not need to control us, and is He not afraid of our "broken spots." He knows that the only way we can truly change is when we are free to change.

Creating Internal Pressure

The power of confrontation comes from the inside out. It is not a sales job or a manipulative ploy to get someone to do something. It cannot be! It has to be genuinely motivated from the inside if it has a prayer of lasting. A common mistake we make is leading someone to say something magical like "I'm sorry." If you've ever tried to get two siblings to clean up a mess they made with each other by ordering, "Say you are sorry," then you know it doesn't work. They will say whatever it takes to get out of trouble and move on; you can see in their eyes and hear in their voices that they are far from reconciled through such an exercise. The solutions to relational disconnection and injury come from the heart. Getting at the heart requires a process that creates internal pressure.

There is a brilliant example of this in the book of Job. Job had a tough time in his life. His well-meaning friends came along and did their best to create pressure on Job from the outside. Each friend had a point of view delivered in the package of a lecture. Their painful guesses as to what might be the problem only added to the powerlessness and grief of Job's plight. Though his friends did their best to aid him, they only made things worse with each passing dialogue.

Finally, in chapter 38, the Lord of all showed up. If anyone had a prophetic insight or word of knowledge about what the exact problem was, it was God himself. Certainly, if someone could get this right, it would be the All-Knowing One. But the One who knows all things did something very different:

> *Then the Lord answered Job out of the whirlwind, and said: "Who is this who darkens counsel by words without knowledge? Now prepare yourself like a man; I will question you, and you shall answer Me."*[8]

God began His intervention in the situation by rebuking the mob of guessers. *"Who is this who darkens counsel by words without knowledge?"* In essence, God showed up and said, "Shut up! All of you just be quiet!" He followed this up with the secret of creating internal pressure: *"I will question you, and you shall answer Me."* Absolute genius! The process of asking great questions begins the internal combustion machine in humans.

It is a process that avoids triggering the natural defenses we employ against people trying to control us. People can feel the trap of leading questions designed to control them. Most of us have experiences with authority figures wanting us to answer their questions "correctly." This process of confrontation creates fear and eliminates what can happen when people feel safe.

Great questions start the internal journey that leads people into an encounter with Truth. God warns Job that this process will try him to his core: *"Prepare yourself like a man!"* Coming from the

King of Glory, this comment would cause anyone to lose all control of his or her bodily functions. But this is the process of Kingdom confrontation.

My wife and I went to the rodeo a while back with some friends. We had the best seats in the arena. It's cool having some wealthy friends. We sat next to the announcer's booth. I was able to look over the rail and see the bull riders right there below me. I watched as one of these cowboys was stretching out. He put his leg up on the fence like a ballerina or gymnast would do. His boot was above his head. It was then that I realized those guys were athletes. I guess I had never thought about it before. They were preparing themselves like men. Because you know what was about to happen. Whoa! They were about to enter the whirlwind.

God said, "Here we go! Prepare yourself like a man. I am going to ask you the questions and you are going to answer me. There is good stuff in you, Job, and I am going to call it out of you." That is how God handles somebody He loves. This is the kind of confrontation that brings freedom. God applied pressure, but He did it in the spirit of gentleness, in that, through His questions, He clearly communicated the message that He did not need to control Job. He protected the opportunity for Job to discover what was truly going on inside him by inviting him to engage his will in the process.

Over and over we see Jesus demonstrate this process. He asked a man who was so obviously blind that his first name was Blind— Blind Bartimaeus—*"What do you want Me to do for you?"*[9] And of course, Blind Bartimaeus answered, *"I want to regain my sight!"* Why did the Lord ask such an obvious question? Or why, when He approached the lame man at the Pool of Bethesda, who had been waiting there for 18 years hoping to catch the angel stirring the water, did He ask, *"Do you wish to get well?"*[10] Why did the Man whose healing ministry had a 100-percent success rate stop and ask questions that have seemingly obvious answers?

Herein lies the power of internal pressure. Jesus knew and practiced that man was born to be free. If we do not have the power to choose, then we will never be responsible for the choice. God plays by His own rules and design—He *honors* the way He made us. In His presence is freedom—freedom to think, decide, and own our lives.

Jesus stopped and asked these men these questions because there is a *line*. There is a line of demarcation, and it represents where one life stops and another life starts. If we believe that we can control others or that we should to demonstrate our great love, then there is no line. Your life belongs to me when I want something from you. But if I am to honor your life and self-control, then there must be a line where I stop and you start. The practice of healthy boundaries between people is a topic that has been well discussed in other books, so I will not launch into it here. But I do want to emphasize the crucial place boundaries serve in empowering people during a confrontation.

Great questions serve a number of great benefits in a successful confrontation, including the goals I've already discussed:

1. They stimulate thinking within the individual with the problem.

2. They allow the person an opportunity to do most of the thinking about the problem from the inside out.

3. They help the person tap into his or her greatness and put it on display during the confrontation.

4. They remind the person of things they tend to forget about themselves in failure.

5. They demonstrate the covenant relationship between the two parties.

6. They allow the one doing the confrontation to remain an ally.

Who Is "Confrontable"?

In Genesis 18 there is a great story about two friends. It is the story about Abraham and God. It is an absolutely amazing example to me that God is a real person. He is not some cosmic perfection that has zero need or tolerance for me. He is not the "Big Boss upstairs" who gets His way or somebody's got to die. Watch this:

> *Then the men rose from there and looked toward Sodom, and Abraham went with them to send them on the way. And the Lord said, "Shall I hide from Abraham what I am doing, since Abraham shall surely become a great and mighty nation, and all the nations of the earth shall be blessed in him?"*[11]

God was on His way to destroy Sodom. But first He was going to check in with His friend Abraham, who might have something to say about it all. God told him that the outcry against Sodom was great and that He must do something about it. Abraham was stunned! His response?

> *And Abraham came near and said, "Would You also destroy the righteous with the wicked?"*

Abraham then proceeded to ask more questions:

> *"Suppose there were fifty righteous within the city; would You also destroy the place and not spare it for the fifty*

righteous that were in it? Far be it from You to do such a
thing as this, to slay the righteous with the wicked, so that
the righteous should be as the wicked; far be it from You!
Shall not the Judge of all the earth do right?"[12]

God stood there, being confronted by Abraham, and responded, "Yeah, you are right. I would spare the city for fifty righteous men." This is profound! God is confrontable! It is unusual, because we've come to know "leadership" as unconfrontable. We classically interpret confrontation of leadership as dishonor.

At God's response, Abraham continued. Like an auctioneer, Abraham whittled down the size of the group it would take for God to have mercy on the city, "Okay, 40...30...20...10?" He threw in a couple of questions, and clarified that he did not mean any disrespect along the way. In the end, *"The Lord went His way as soon as He had finished speaking with Abraham; and Abraham returned to his place."*[13]

Abraham trusted God, and God trusted Abraham. If God made Himself open to confrontation by a man, it begs the question: who is above confrontation? A safe environment is filled with powerful, free people or it is soon to be an unsafe place controlled by those who think they have all the power.

The Key Ingredient Is Trust

If you know that I have great value for you, then you can invite my input. If you trust that I have your best interest at heart, then we will be able to build a deeper covenant relationship through confrontation. If you get a whiff that I don't respect or value you, you will protect yourself from my help. The classic problem of adolescent/parent dynamics is that, as the child becomes a young man or young woman, he or she can feel the disrespect the parent has for his or her ability to think and make decisions. Because the adolescent doesn't feel trusted, he or she resists confrontation.

The nature of confrontation is truth. The purpose of creating external pressure is to find the truth, not to get a confession. People who cannot trust will not show the truth of what is going on inside them to anyone. They feel safer keeping the "broken spot" concealed. It takes a safe place to expose a vulnerable place, an area that needs healing. For this reason, it matters less that the confronter believes that he or she holds great authority and should be trusted than it matters whether the one who is scared believes he or she is cared for and protected.

In essence, a confrontation is an examination. It is a procedure that trusts another to look at some part of your life that you may not know about or understand. It is both vulnerable and necessary if we expect to build healthy lives and live in peace. It reminds me of turning 40. That was the year I had my first *real* physical examination. My doctor asked me to disrobe and lean over the table. I had known this was going to happen; I just couldn't find a way to pretend that it wasn't really going to be like I had heard. The rubber glove and goop on the tray next to me gave it away. This was going to be invasive! Sure enough, the invasion came and went. I could hardly look my doctor in the eye. Nervous laughter was overtaking me as I tried to play it off. I said, "Should we tell my wife what just happened?"

My doctor laughed right along with me and then *she* said, "Your prostate is smooth. That's a good thing. See you in a year or so."

King David put it this way:

Search me, O God, and know my heart; try me, and know my anxieties; and see if there is any wicked way in me, and lead me in the way everlasting.[14]

Jesus is the Great Confronter. It is no coincidence that He was neither afraid in the presence of people's mistakes nor afraid to confront those people with a loving invasion of the truth. Whether it was His disciples, the rich young ruler, or the woman at the well, He was able to help people identify what was going on below the surface better than anyone. And at the same time, little children came running up to Him as a "safe place." Kids are natural at identifying people who are safe. One of the keys to Jesus' mastery of confrontation is that His interactions with people were motivated by compassion. I remember Bill Johnson saying, "If it doesn't hurt you to confront another person, you probably have a wrong attitude."

Confrontation and empowerment go hand in hand in a culture of honor, and mercy, compassion, and courage are the qualities necessary for maintaining a healthy flow of these two elements in your environment. Successful confrontation builds relationships and strengthens covenant bonds. It is an art built on certain skills, but more importantly, it is a lifestyle that flows from your beliefs and core values. The more you establish Heaven's goals for confrontation in your thinking, the more you will be positioned to release Heaven into your confrontations.

CHAPTER 8

REVOLUTION TO REFORMATION TO TRANSFORMATION

For the earth will be filled
with the knowledge of the glory of the Lord,
as the waters cover the sea.
(Habakkuk 2:14)

There was a time in our nation's history when it was considered normal and acceptable to own other human beings. We adopted and passed down a cultural view and practice that slavery was "necessary" for our commerce and households to function. We enslaved, sold, oppressed, and punished people like animals because it was "normal."

The most difficult aspect of this tragedy was that it is *biblical*. Both the Old and New Testaments apparently condone and show God's blessing on slave owners. The apostle Paul instructed slaves to submit to their masters.[1] He didn't even hint at it being a huge injustice and an offense to Heaven's paradigm. Jesus did not instruct His disciples to "set My people free" and wage a campaign against slavery.

Or did He? He introduced His ministry by stating that He had been anointed *"to proclaim liberty to the captives."*[2] He later commissioned all who would follow Him to imitate His example. This leaves each generation of believers with the question of how to do that. How can we violate our own Scriptures, and especially our traditions, to find a higher place of honor and freedom for people? It usually takes a war. As the history of our nation proves, sometimes it takes a civil war.

Harriet Beecher Stowe wrestled with this question in her book, *Uncle Tom's Cabin*. She said:

> I wrote what I did because as a woman, as a mother I
> was oppressed and brokenhearted, with the sorrows and
> injustice I saw, because as a Christian I felt the dishonor
> to Christianity—because as a lover of my country I
> trembled at the coming day of wrath.[3]

Many historians consider *Uncle Tom's Cabin* a significant influence in the events leading to the Civil War, which ended in the abolition of slavery in America. When Abraham Lincoln finally met Harriet, he said to her, "So you're the little woman who wrote the book that made this great war!"[4] But Stowe's brother and fellow abolitionist, Henry Ward Beecher, gave another man credit for the overthrow of slavery. When Beecher was asked after the Civil War, "Who abolished slavery?" he answered, "Reverend John Rankin and his sons did it."[5]

John Rankin was born in Jefferson County, Tennessee, and raised in a strict Calvinist home. In 1800, Rankin's eighth year of life, his view of the world and his religious faith were deeply affected by two things—the revivals of the Second Great Awakening that were sweeping through the Appalachian region, and the largest organized (though unsuccessful) slave rebellion in U.S. history up to that point, led by an enslaved man, Gabriel Prosser, who was executed along with 27 of his conspirators. Ann Hagedorn writes:

> For Rankin, the events of his eighth year resonated deeply. In his memory, the story of a man losing his life in pursuit of freedom would always blend together with the many nights of manifestation in the woodlands of East Tennessee. There would come a time when enough years had passed that Rankin could look back and know that the passions of the summer of 1800 had inspired his own private awakening.[6]

Convinced as he was that the thrust of the Gospel was to eradicate oppression, and slavery in particular, from the world, Rankin wrestled deeply with the portions of Scripture that seemed to condone slavery—Scriptures that were taught from many a pulpit in his day. Ultimately he resolved this conflict by determining that the balance of the Word taught that God never intended mankind to be enslaved, and that it was the duty of every righteous man and woman to seek God's highest purposes for humankind. In an address to a delegation of anti-slavery societies he said:

> The Scriptures represent all men as having sprung from one common parent—all as "made of one blood"…Consequently all are created equally free. Whatever rights the first man had, all his children must have. God created no slaves. He gave to all men the same original rights…
>
> …Let the church universal as the army of the living God, come up to the help of the Lord against the

mighty; let her voice be heard as the voice of many waters, proclaiming liberty to the captive, and the opening of the prison to them that are bound—and the poisonous fountains of death shall be dried up, the rivers of anguish shall cease to flow, and sorrow and sighing shall flee away. Union in this great work will prepare the church for the rising of millennial glory, when liberty shall be universal, and the song of redeeming love shall ascend from every tongue.[7]

The passion birthed in Rankin's heart as a young boy ultimately led him to brave dangers of all kinds, from angry, rotten-egg slinging mobs to slanderous newspapers and direct physical attacks on himself, his family, and his property. He was not only fearless and unstoppable in preaching the message of freedom, but also in living it. He and his family continuously spent their time and resources to help runaway slaves to freedom—their house and name were among the most well known on the Underground Railroad—and to support other abolitionists in their efforts to do the same. As Henry Ward Beecher, who observed Rankin's heroism firsthand, testified, this one man's message and example were so powerful and far-reaching that the dismantling of an entire system of oppression, a system that many, even those who decried it, had believed was impossible to remove, has been laid to his credit.

The life of John Rankin is evidence that when Heaven touches earth in revival, it creates something inside a person—a vision of how God made the world to be and a cry to take part in the restoration of all things, until a day "when liberty shall be universal." Encountering the living God and receiving a fresh revelation of His heart both give us a greater hunger for freedom in our own lives and require us to "set the captives free." This appetite drives us past the cultural norms and fuels us with supernatural courage to spurn the persecution that comes from those maintaining the status quo. Revival ignites life in people to press against the limitations and boundaries of society. It calls to the deepest parts of mankind and screams "Freedom!" so loudly that the same cry comes out of our mouths. *Revival* launches *revolution* and revolutions initiate *reformation.*

This is where we stand as a movement in our generation. We are in the throes of a reformation. No longer will we tolerate the status quo of an externally governed existence. No longer will we accept training in powerlessness. No longer will we live as servants and slaves. The religious motivation of the pending wrath of God and the ideals of a small life are no longer options for us. We are sons and daughters of the Most High. We are in training for reigning as never before. We now expect to be powerful, living an abundant life in Christ until the kingdoms of this earth become the Kingdom of our God.

I have the privilege of leading the Bethel School of Transformation. This school provides people with a behind-the-scenes peek at the culture of freedom we are building at Bethel. Since we began offering the school in 2005, we've had more than a hundred churches take this four-day adventure of training in what we are doing here. Without exception, there has been a senior leader in every single school who asks, "How in the world are we ever going to do this in our church?" I want to say that you are not alone if you have that question.

I want to share a testimony about a man, a good friend of mine, who had that same question. Steve Doerter, a pastor in North Carolina, got involved in the Bethel culture a couple of years ago. He began to listen to the podcasts, came to some conferences, and began to bring the things he was learning to his congregation and its other leaders. These things represented some significant changes for these people. The church historically was Baptist, had become non-denominational, and under Steve's leadership was pursuing more freedom and power than they ever had before. However, they had not yet come to know what he had experienced at Bethel, and thus were finding it difficult to be on the same page with him.

He asked himself, *How am I going to get this thing moving?* Eventually he decided to expose his leaders to what he was pursuing by bringing them to Bethel's Leader's Advance conference. The Leader's Advance is an invitation-only conference for those leaders who are in relationship with other leaders in our network. It is a powerful time for everyone who attends.

One night at the Advance, my wife Sheri and I were sitting at dinner with Steve, his wife, Joyce, and his leadership board. They were a friendly enough group, but they obviously did not understand much of what was going on around them. One of the things that goes on at the Leader's Advance is that our School of Supernatural Ministry students wait on the tables. These students are constantly "under the influence" of the Holy Spirit, and on this particular night, our table waiters became increasingly "drunk." They were happy—super happy. Finally, Steve's leaders asked, "What is wrong with those people?"

I replied, "They're just happy, and they're drunk."

"They're drunk?" they asked.

I went on to explain, "See, there is this guy and his name is Georgian Banov. He is upstairs in another dining room praying for people, and I would imagine that the whole upstairs is drunk by now.

You should go up there and check it out! You should just go look at it—get close enough to see it."

They said, "Well, we'd like to do that. We'd like to go see what this is." And off they went.

The next report I got was that they eventually had their own pile—their own pile of former Baptist elders. The next time I saw these distinguished people, their hair was all messed up and one had his pant leg tucked into his shoe. It was then I could see that Steve was gaining momentum with his team of leaders.

Since their team came to that conference, there have been several significant miracles in their church. Cancerous tumors disappeared in a woman's body. Financial miracles, inner healings, and deliverances are now a common part of this church's day-to-day experiences. But one miracle caught my attention.

There was a little 3-year-old boy named Pablo who was diagnosed with a developmental disorder that falls within the spectrum of autism. He was so agitated that his mother could not hold him, kiss him, or be affectionate with him at all. He squirmed out of her arms or anyone's and ran away from them as fast as he could. He could only say one-word sentences at a time. He was unable to say his name or age, and had no concept of colors or shapes. He was highly sensitive to the texture of food—so much so that he would spit out any new food introduced and thus could only eat one texture of food at a time. No one could take him out of the house, not even to go shopping, because of the scene he would cause. When he got disturbed or anxious, he started pounding his head on the floor or on the wall. He was oblivious to people around him and completely trapped in his own little world. He had never slept a whole night in his life; he was commonly up at two or three in the morning and awake for the rest of the night. You can imagine how worn out his parents were after three years of unsettled sleep. He had a brother who was totally scared of him. Great disruption had come to this family because of their son's condition.

Pastor Steve got up one Sunday morning to deliver the message. As he reached the podium, the Lord called an "audible" at the podium. So he changed the message and entitled his new sermon, "God Is Good, and I Highly Recommend Him." He began to talk about the goodness of God, the faithfulness of God, and God's heart toward people. It wasn't too long before he was sharing testimonies and stirring the faith in the room. At the end of the message, they began praying for those who wanted what had just been prophesied in the testimonies. Pablo's mom came up and several leaders laid hands on her in proxy for him. They began to command healing and the release of miracles, the release of Heaven, into the situation at her home.

Pablo's mom believed the prayers and headed home after the service. She arrived late that evening and woke up in the morning, failing to realize that, for the first time in three years, everyone had slept through the night! She woke up and thought, "Something is changing." She walked up to her son and asked, "What is your name?"

He replied, "Pablo."

She asked, "How old are you?"

"Three."

The people who had stayed with him while she was gone began to report to her that changes like that had been going on since the previous day—the miracles began as soon as she received prayer. Months later, Pablo is still sleeping through the night. He's not hitting his head against things anymore. He now says his name, his age, and can interact with 80 percent of the questions that someone asks him. The specialists who worked with him expected that he would only ever be able to communicate with one-word sentences and sign language. He is now speaking in complete sentences. He knows the difference between four colors and knows the names of the rest of them. He knows the difference between a circle and a square and a rhombus. (I don't even know what a rhombus is!) He can count up to 20. He's starting to sing songs. He's starting to play with other children for short periods of time. Mom took him to McDonald's for lunch without incident. They're able to hold him and hug him and kiss him and be affectionate with him.

The therapist who had been coming to the family's home and working with Pablo cried as she told this mother what she was witnessing happen to him. She could not comprehend the drastic improvement in him in only three short weeks. But the kicker for this mom, the reason that she wrote it all down, was that the principal of the school Pablo attends came out and met her at her car one day in tears. She said, "This is nothing short of a miracle that has happened in our city."

Revolutionaries

I want to show you why Heaven is invading earth. A revolution is happening, and you are a witness to it. In fact, if you have made it this far in this book, then you are most likely a participant in it. You are a revolutionary! Your involvement as a revolutionary is going to lead us to our next great reformation in the Church. We are in the midst of a great transformation. Heaven is infiltrating the Body of

Christ and stirring up the passion and the hearts of those who have come to expect more.

Every year at our Leader's Advances we ask, "Who is here for your first Advance?" Half the room raises their hand. We are stunned each time. How does it happen that half the room is new every time? The list gets longer and longer and longer, and the room gets smaller and smaller and smaller. There is a momentum developing, where more and more people are hearing about Heaven leaking through. Everywhere members of our team go to minister, people tell us, "Heaven is leaking through, and our own city is starting to hear about it."

There is something powerful happening all over the globe and all of a sudden we're not feeling quite so unique anymore. Churches all over the world are experiencing the same things we are. The testimonies of Heaven's invasion are more and more common. But the encouraging part is that these stories are not just coming from Africa, Asia, and South America. These stories are coming from local churches all over the United States. We are starting to feel like part of a momentum, part of a movement, part of a transformation.

Before I throw the word "revolutionary" around too much more, let me give you a definition straight from the dictionary:

> **Revolution:** forcible, pervasive, and often violent change of a social or political order by a sizable segment of a country's population (*Encarta Encyclopedia*).

This definition is begging to be associated with Matthew 11:12: *"...the Kingdom of Heaven suffers violence, and violent men take it by force."* As the Kingdom advances in revival, it is bringing about a forcible overthrow of a government in the Church, the forcible challenge of a social order that so many of us have been confined to throughout our church experience. There is a way of doing things that has constrained Heaven from blasting the earth. But an increasing number of people from all over the earth have said, "Enough! We've had enough of this!" And it has begun a revolution. We have begun a revolution that is leading to a reformation, and a reformation is simply this:

> **Reformation: 1**. to improve (a law or institution) by
> correcting abuses (*Farlex Dictionary*).

Institutions develop because the way of doing things becomes so comfortable, so predictable, so routine, that we no longer have to think, we no longer have to risk, and we no longer have to believe. It's all simply a matter of rote behavior, and we are carried through our Christian life because it is the way we've always done it. A reformation is something that comes and asks, "Why are you doing what you do? Do you realize that what you are doing is not working? Everything you've established in your traditions needs to change. Now, what are you going to do?" The answer is that we're going to have to create something we've never seen before. And when reformation is complete, it brings transformation:

> **Transformation:** A thorough or dramatic change in
> form or appearance (Encylopedia.com).

Our transformation demonstrates to the world that it's something brand new, something that no one has ever seen before. We are living in a time, in a day, and in a government that allows us to change. We now are living in a posture and in a relationship with our city that looks completely different than in the past. However, I need to be honest about one necessary element in this transformation that can be a deal-breaker for a lot of people. It's common for people to say, "We want to change. We want things to be different. We went to a conference and things are going to be different now. We bought the whole video set, and now, buddy, things are going be different around here." Except there's this piece they miss. They have a whole herd of sacred cows in their world that do not want to budge.

I had a brochure stuck in the screen door at my house recently. It was from a church in our neighborhood. It said, "Not Like Every Other Church" across the top. I opened it up because I hoped it was true. On the front of the brochure was a picture of the pastor and his wife, "Mr. and Mrs. Ed Jones." Below those photos were pictures of several other couples, "Mr. and Mrs. Tom Smith, Mr. and Mrs. Ozzie Wald, Mr. and Mrs. Harry Chin, Mr. and Mrs. etc...." As I read this, I thought. *There are two people in each of these pictures, and only one name. Where did she go? She's just gone. You know what? This isn't any different. In fact, this is the same old malarkey. The closer a woman gets to that church, the more she disappears. That is a scary place if you're a woman.*

The Church is one of the last institutions in our society that practices sexism freely and "biblically." For some reason, it is still tolerated to dishonor or disempower our women. The brochure was a lie. That church wasn't unlike most churches. Dang! It isn't hard to *say* that everything's different—"We're not doing it like every other church, the way our granddaddy did it." Yeah, but it looks a lot the same and it feels about the same. The same anxiety and control are still here. And we end up sounding like one of those silly politicians—you know, the ones who are going to bring about "change" and immediately institute a lot of "same"? Revolutionaries know that transformation comes when we are finally willing to have a "sacred cow barbecue."

Governmental Shifts

In chapter 2 I introduced some of the governmental shifts that are necessary for Heaven to flow to the earth. Transformation has been successful at Bethel to the degree that we have implemented that new set of core values and paradigms. The government that is typically in place in our churches and has been for centuries is what I referred to as a pastoral government, with a pastoral directive, with these players featured at the helm: pastors, administrators, teachers, and even evangelists. Once again, the priorities of this government are where the problems start:

Current Government: Current Priorities:

Pastors—People

Administrators—Things

Teachers—Doctrine

Evangelists—Salvation Message

The first priority in a pastoral government is *people.* How safe, comfortable, and happy are the people in our church environment? We need to know this, because we know these people have choices, and if they aren't happy in that environment, they will go someplace else. We can pretend like we don't care, but this governing system cares about "butts in the seat."

The next priority is our *things.* In a pastoral government, there are many teachings about stewardship and taking care of our money, our parking lot, our building, and our stuff. These are the driving forces of how we do church.

The next priority, *doctrine,* leads us to focus on right and wrong, truth and error. This attitude develops: "What is right or true is everything we teach, and what is wrong is taught by everybody else in town who disagrees with us." We end up trying to teach people to defend themselves against other Christians, to defend their lives as believers, and to defend their choice of and participation in this particular church.

The *gospel of salvation* is the final priority. Getting people saved is generally the only supernatural activity in the pastoral environment. And without the presence of the supernatural, we end up teaching converts, "You were a sinner, you prayed a prayer, and now God's grace is applied to your life. Your sins are forgiven, but you're still a sinner and we're watching you."

The core values of this environment flow from its leadership anointing and structure. For example, here's a core value that has been propagated liberally among the congregations of our nation: "God is always right, so be like Him. Be one of the most difficult people on the planet to talk to. We have taught you the truth, and don't you dare consider anything except what we taught you because you might be deceived. Someone might introduce you to the idea that the supernatural is a part of the Kingdom of Heaven. The 'supernatural' is always suspect and it is full of deceptions. Only the devil has supernatural power on the earth."

Such core values create an environment centered upon the things that can be proved and controlled. This church environment is pervasive throughout the land, and I'm sure all of you reading a book like this are trying to make a break. If you are in a pastoral government, you're going to have some problems trying to introduce contrary core values to that environment.

These priorities I've mentioned are not evil, any more than childhood is evil. They are an inferior Christianity, if you will. But a system that effectively prevents believers from growing up causes symptoms of disorder. People don't grow as God designed them to in a pastoral environment because deep in its core, the pastoral government defines its people as sinners working out their salvation. This means that we are not trustworthy and are essentially servants waiting for further instructions. Our lives are defined by a divine "to do" list. As difficult as this may be, these are some of the sacred cows that need to find the "grill."

It's scary to say that doctrine isn't the most important part of our relationship with God. And even to suggest that the salvation message isn't paramount can seem like heresy. But until we are willing to re-order our thinking, to be renewed in our minds, then yesterday will determine our tomorrow.

We must have permission in our church environments to challenge the sacred cows of our day, just as Jesus did. Remember, Jesus came and confronted the Jews, the people of His day who knew more about God than anyone. He rebuked their love affair with their own interpretation of His Kingdom. Sadly, most of them refused His invitation to the sacred cow barbecue, and we shouldn't be surprised if something similar happens when we start doing the same thing in our generation. Once again, one of the primary things we must confront is the issue of order in the House of God, and we do that with Scripture:

> *And God has appointed in the church, first apostles, second prophets, third teachers, then miracles, then gifts of healings, helps, administrations, various kinds of tongues.*[8]

I'm still not sure how this got passed over for so many years in our approach to governing God's church. I am not sure how Paul could make it clearer than "first...second...third." Where did that go?

How did a pastoral environment become the supreme level in the church? "Pastor" is not even in the list. It's not even a close fourth. So, *all* our cows must die, especially those roaming around in plain view, or worse yet, those standing in our living room.

I remember watching a show about lions on the Discovery Channel one night. It showed footage of two lions fighting in a field, an old lion and a young lion. The young lion beat up the old one, and so the old lion was out and the young lion was in. It was sad to watch the former leader of the pride limp off into the Serengeti sunset. He was battle-worn from years of defending his position, his face covered in scars. What happened next was, I thought, both interesting and barbaric. The first thing the young lion did as the new ruler of the pride was to attack and kill all the cubs of the old lion. It was shocking to see this huge animal breaking the necks of the former leader's offspring. This action caused all of the females to go into heat so the new leader could breed an entire new bloodline—a bloodline that would carry his DNA.

I watched Bill Johnson do that. Stay with me for just a minute. When Bill landed at Bethel, it had a pastoral government, led by an evangelist. When Bill was invited to interview for the senior leader position, the board of elders said, "We think you're the guy."

He said, "I will come here *only* if this board is in 100-percent agreement that I come."

They were stunned. "We've never had a unanimous vote of this nature," they said to him.

He said he would not come unless it was unanimous. That was the first of many changes he would require of this government. They called him back and said, "Hey, it's a miracle. For the first time ever, an unanimous vote!" At the time, the church had 2,000 people. In the next couple of years, Bill grew it down to about 1,000. Meanwhile, the pastoral government that had existed for some 50 years was groaning, "Aaahhhhh!" There was a new sheriff in town and a new government was being established. As a result, the priorities were going to change. These elders deserve as much credit as Bill for a successful transformation. They held on through the *revolution* and all the casualties of war. They made it through the *reformation* of how things were going to be done around here. We live today in that *transformation*.

The new government Bill introduced was aligned with what Paul laid out, "First apostles, second prophets, third teachers…" and thereby introduced a new set of priorities into Bethel's environment:

New Government: New Priorities:

Apostles—Heaven

Prophets—Spirit World

Teachers—Articulating the Kingdom

Workers of Miracles—Supernatural Activity of the Believers

In this government, the priorities are about Heaven, the presence of God, and the blueprint of Heaven being reproduced on the earth. There is a new core value for the activity of the spirit world, for the saints having their eyes and ears opened by the prophet, for hearing the heartbeat of Heaven and becoming aware of the activity of the third Heaven, which supersedes the devil's strategies. Signs, wonders, and miracles bring people into God encounters that radically change the way life is lived here on the earth. No longer is it an environment of fear and reaction, but of proactively establishing the architecture and blueprint of Heaven on the earth—of making the prayer, "Your Kingdom come, Your will be done on earth as it is in Heaven" a reality of life for believers and the community around them.

Once again, the role of the teacher in this new government is no longer to try to build a defensive network for believers against other believers, or even believers against cults. The teacher's job is to help the people see Heaven and a supernatural God at work on the earth in the Scripture. They give people a scriptural context to understand the apostles and prophets and their core values. They teach us that these leaders design a place where Heaven stays the priority, where anything can happen, and where it does. If the people do not understand what is happening, they will be afraid and seek a place where they are in charge again. Teachers help bring this understanding and reduce the anxiety of God's people that can prevent them from entering into all that is available in His presence.

I won't review the role of pastors in an apostolic environment, but I want to give attention to the next role Paul mentions in this particular list—the workers of miracles. I believe that "workers of miracles" is another description for the role of the evangelist in an apostolic government. I believe we have lost the connection between these two roles because, without the leadership of apostles and prophets, workers of miracles generally don't get to operate in their roles. But in an apostolic environment, the apostles and prophets pull the supernatural into the environment, and the workers of miracles run around pushing every button to see what can happen. They bring the priority of supernatural activity into the practical, daily lives of believers, as well as to the lives of all those in their community, along with a high value for protecting that activity. They create a contagion for risk-taking and living in the impossible.

As the new wineskin of apostolic leadership is established, a new wave of evangelism is going to be released through the workers of miracles. For the past century, the Church has emphasized the practice of evangelism. People like D. L. Moody, William Booth, and Charles Finney taught the Church to "win people to Christ." This experience has brought many into the Kingdom—many believers mention it when giving their testimony of salvation. It is also something most modern Christians are trained to do in their local congregations.

But the workers of miracles are bringing a new practice of evangelism into the Church's environment. These radicals of faith are releasing "God encounters" everywhere they go, whether it is the workplace, street corner, supermarket, restaurant, or mall. Healings, miracles, words of knowledge, prophetic ministry, and heavenly revelation are leading people to Jesus in droves. We call these people "treasure hunters" where I come from.

This revolutionary ministry called "treasure hunts" is sweeping the globe. Kevin Dedmon, author of *The Ultimate Treasure Hunt,* has trained thousands of people to do this supernatural work. Simply put, it works like this: pray together and get a "treasure list" from Heaven. This list has things like names, places, colors of clothing, specific areas of the body that have pain, diseases, situations in people's lives, gender, and all kinds of other "clues." The team then goes out into the community to find their "treasure." As soon as a "treasure hunter" locates someone on the list, he or she approaches the person and shows him or her that he or she is on the "treasure list." At this point, the "treasure hunter" asks if there is something he or she can pray about for the person. Time after time, Heaven rocks these people. God shows up in power! Signs, wonders, and miracles are the ongoing testimony of treasure hunting.

It has reached the point in our community where people are anticipating a God encounter. One team of leaders from another community came to Bethel's Transformation School and found themselves out in our city doing a treasure hunt with one of our Second Year students from the School of Supernatural Ministry. While in a popular department store in town, they approached a man who fit one of the items on the "treasure list." When they told him that he was on the list and therefore one of God's treasures, he exclaimed, "I've heard about this. I've always wanted to be the treasure you guys found!"

The man excitedly received what God had for him and the team moved on to the next treasure. There were no arguments about theology, no threats of dying and going to hell. This encounter was just a simple and powerful reminder that God is alive and loves this man. Although many people give their hearts to Jesus in these encounters, it isn't the primary goal. The priority is for believers to be conduits on the earth for Heaven to happen. We are creating opportunities for the blueprint of Heaven to be expressed.

Transforming Cities With Honor

Another priority of an apostolic mission is to leak the Kingdom into the community rather than getting the community to come to our church. This priority is motivated by honor and a wealth mindset, which lead us to look for ways to benefit those around us.

It's amazing to see what can happen when you have a thousand students descending on our community every week doing outreach and treasure hunts. But I want to tell you about a friend of mine who is seeing the blueprint unfold in his Mexican city. His name is

Angel Nava. He and his wife, Esther, lead both a church and school of supernatural ministry in the southern portion of Baja California in a city called La Paz (Peace). In 2003, they met another couple who turned the Christian world they had come to know so well upside down.

Denny and Danette Taylor were sent out from Bethel to start a school of supernatural ministry in La Paz. Their first task was to find the individuals who God was inviting to become catalysts for revival in their city by embracing and replicating what we've stepped into in Redding. Through a series of events they met Angel and Esther Nava. The next several years became a testimony of how the culture of honor transforms a city.

I remember the absolute transformation that first happened in this couple, who had been pastoring a nice, quiet church for a few years prior to meeting the Taylors. When she first saw the power of God at work in a meeting with Bill Johnson and Kris Vallotton, Esther knew she had discovered the reason she was alive. Angel, on the other hand, was scared of the supernatural manifestations and wanted nothing to do with them. But the Lord slowly brought him to a place of curiosity, and finally to the place where he recognized that Heaven was trying to invade his city.

However, with this recognition came the realization that if he turned his heart toward revival, it would cost him everything. First, he would lose his relationship with his leadership; those overseeing his church from a pastoral paradigm would remove themselves from his life if he turned toward the supernatural. He also knew that several of his closest pastor friends would leave simultaneously. Nevertheless, he and Esther purposed to do whatever they needed to do in order to welcome God and Heaven into La Paz.

Their first step was to begin supporting Denny and Danette's efforts to bring a school of supernatural ministry into their city. As they did, they immediately began to see healings and miracles. In the first year of the school, they saw a woman raised from the dead. As new and exciting as this was in their lives and ministry, Angel's heart was to see his city transformed. He devoured everything he could find from Bethel's teachers. He wanted to better understand what was needed on his end for Heaven to be welcome in Mexico. He began to realize that God was in a good mood and wanted people to know His love. He also started to believe that his great city could experience God more effectively if he helped Jesus get out of the church and into the city.

But how was he to do that? All he had known up to that point was how to go into the city and bring people back to his church. Where would he put a quarter of a million people? He needed a strategy change. He needed a way to be "leaven in the lump" of La Paz.

Mexico does not have a blood donor system that works. They have a government official who is responsible to receive blood donations, but no one gives blood. It is customary for Mexican citizens to have to find their own donor if they need surgery. Angel got an idea. He went into his local blood donation department and talked to the new director about how his job was going. Aware that business was slow, Angel asked some questions about how blood donation worked in La Paz. That next week, he shared his new city transformation strategy with his congregation: "We will become the largest donors of blood in our city. Follow me."

Angel became the leader of blood donation in his city. The members of his congregation currently donate blood three times a year. Knowing the competitive nature of churches, Angel invited other churches and pastors to take part in the blood drive. Now several churches compete to be the ones who give the most blood each year. As a result, La Paz now leads the state in blood acquisitions, and the new director of the blood bank received a government award for the spike in donations. Angel made that state official look like a genius. As a result, that man wants Angel to be successful.

It was fun for Angel to introduce his community of believers to a wealth paradigm in which they became benefactors of their city by serving it in a life-giving way. But he wanted to take it to another level. He and Esther began to do outreaches to some of the Indian villages on the mainland of Mexico. They began to teach their people to serve the poor and love those who could never do anything to return the favor.

Now, their church is not like an American church. Material resources are scarce, and people live modest lives. Angel taught his people to give and serve in ways that seemed impossible to the natural mind. They are now taking their own people to new heights of love, service, and sacrifice. They are exporting miracles, healing, and generosity to the states around them.

Staying true to form, Angel got another "God idea" to make an impact on his city. His children go to a Catholic private school in La Paz. This private school has an orphanage associated with it, and the priest of the school is also involved with this orphanage. Angel's conversations with the priest informed him about some of the needs of the orphans; he learned that one of their greatest needs was for new shoes.

Now, Mexican Protestants and Catholics are like cats and dogs. They do not get along. They do not fellowship together and cannot seem to find much value in each other. The Protestants are antagonistic toward the Catholics and have numerous justifications for their disdain toward them. There is an intense separation between the two camps. But when Angel returned to his congregation and shared that the Catholic orphanage needed shoes, his church decided to buy enough pairs of new shoes for all the orphans—70 pairs. They didn't buy cheap shoes, either; they bought Nikes. A local shoe store owner, who was a believer, found out about their gesture and said that he wanted in on the deal. He agreed to sell the shoes to the church at cost.

Angel's church was so excited about blessing the Catholic orphans that they took it to the next level. They invited the children to come to their church on a Sunday morning so they could present the gifts as a family. The priest and the children didn't know what Angel's church was up to, but unexpectedly the priest agreed to bring all his children to the Seeds of Life Protestant church on a Sunday morning. Such a thing had probably never happened in Mexican history!

At the service, the church took things to an even greater level of extravagance. They wanted those children to feel the honor and love God has for them. Families that Angel and Esther knew could not afford to buy bikes for their own children were pooling together money to give a bike as a gift to the orphanage. They lined chairs across the front of the church and had the children come and sit in the chairs, facing the congregation. The people came and washed the feet of the children and then presented them with their new shoes. Then, the children from Angel's church stood behind their guests and prophesied over them. Tears flowed from everyone in the room. Angel then invited the priest to sit in a chair. He washed the feet of the priest in front of his people. The priest could not believe what he and his children were experiencing. No one would ever be the same.

The school of ministry in La Paz continues to grow and the church continues to build new structures to expand their capacity. They are building teams of healing, the prophetic, workers of miracles, and are teaching their people about Heaven and the supernatural. The students have begun to minister the supernatural to the congregation. There is no turning back! This is all quickly becoming the normal Christian life for them. Outreach to the city is flowing, and miracles are happening in everyday environments such as school, stores, and sidewalks. Heaven is invading everyday life in La Paz.

Angel and Esther continue to grow in their own faith and character. They are learning about love and intimacy for each other and their family. They are learning about cultivating freedom and honor as leaders. They are leading in creating a safe place for people who learned that life is about survival. They are challenging an impoverished culture to pull on the unlimited resources of Heaven. They are connecting the powerless with power, the hopeless with hope, and the captives with freedom. The transformation they are living in is now becoming a transforming reality to those around them. They are a catalyst for Heaven.

More recently, Angel and Esther have taken the reconciliation between Protestants and Catholics to a historic level. In October of 2008 I received this e-mail from Angel:

> Just a short note to share how last night's meeting was a success. About 3,000 people gathered in the government plaza in La Paz, most of them Catholics, but lots of Christians too. We all joined to pray for Mexico in a first time ever event. We had never had Catholics and Christians praying together in our country. By the end of the event, I raised my voice to ask forgiveness to the

Catholics because we had built walls instead of building bridges. A great ovation was heard when I hugged the bishop. But it was even more powerful seeing Christians and Catholics hugging each other and expressing forgiveness and reconciliation.

One of the most powerful moments to me was at the very end of the meeting, when my wife Esther and I were walking down off the platform, I found a crowd of people waiting for me to hug me and say thanks…all of them were Catholics.

I know this is a new day…and new things are about to happen here.

Revival is here. We are making history.

Weeks after this unprecedented prayer gathering, the local priest informed Angel that his bishop was sick and in the hospital. He knew that Angel's ministry sees many people healed. He asked Angel to visit the bishop in his hospital room and release the healing power of God to him. Angel was both honored and encouraged by this trust and favor. He is in regular contact and relationship with this bishop now, and they are good friends. A fresh excitement is in the air around the healing and partnership of the Protestants and Catholics in their city.

But change doesn't come without a cost. While I was visiting the Navas the following month, Angel got a call from a group of Protestant pastors with whom he is associated. The leader of the group said that he and several others were coming to La Paz the next week and wanted to meet with him to discuss his recent "prayer gathering" with the Catholics. This leader made it clear that they were not happy about what he had done. As a matter of fact, they were coming to have him repent for his mistake.

Angel's public apology to the Catholics was the most humiliating and upsetting part—they want him to retract his comments and apologize to them right away. His own friends, his brothers in Christ, were upset with him for bringing healing in his community. This was going to be a confrontation, and a test of their honor for each other. After my return from La Paz, I received this e-mail from my friend:

> Thursday I met the [local] pastors, as I told you I was
> going to do. It was very good. They came in a very
> good mood and spirit. They told us the things they
> were not in agreement with. The problem is the way
> they picture God and the church. The religious
> mindset doesn't allow them to see God moving beyond
> "our churches." I confronted their mindset and they
> had no answers for my questions. We got
> breakthrough, mainly because regardless of our
> differences, at the end of the meeting the relationship
> between them and us got strengthened.

They were able to preserve their relationships even through disagreement. This may be the next miracle we see in La Paz—Christian leaders who disagree and continue to honor and love one another. Transformation comes to a region when the leaders can manifest the priorities of Heaven, which leads the people to do the same. Angel and Esther are leading a city into a period of transformation. They are making a powerful impression and impact on city officials, business owners, local citizens, and other church leaders. They are now joining forces with the mayor's office, the state governor, and the police. Yes, the next target for Angel is the Mexican police. *Jesus!*

Building a Vessel of Honor

Those of us who have experienced the current revival know about the miracles that are happening. We see them increase every day all over the world. Now we must build a vessel to transform our communities, our cities, and our nations. Global revival will not have lasting impact unless we see the core values of Heaven show up in our nation's governments.

I don't mean that we simply elect people who say they are believers and go to church. I mean that we build a paradigm that invites a nation to be saved in a day. We classically put into government those who will protect what is important to us. We elect leaders in this nation who will protect our economy, our safety, and our rights. The key ingredient that is missing is a government that will protect the priorities of Heaven and the presence of God in our land.

Sometimes we like to believe that we are doing that in our churches, except for one glaring reality: God's presence and power is missing from many of our churches. Therefore, we are simply creating church governments that protect our precious traditions and theologies. The supernatural is nowhere near most of the largest denominations in our land. How stupid would unbelievers have to be to partner with the Church in making the entire country as limited as most churches are?

The culture of honor is not about giving the church's leaders more control. I hope I have made it clear that it is actually about getting rid of control and cultivating self-control and freedom. The Church is to lead in bringing more freedom to the earth. Heaven is begging to invade the prison so many people live in, whether it is depression, pain, disease, or fear. Our role is to eliminate those things in our lives, homes, and church communities so we can lead others to the peace, joy, freedom, and love we've found for ourselves.

My prayer is that this book has awakened your hope to see that honor is a powerful factor in holding on to what Heaven is pouring into our generation. Without an increase in the practice of loving, honoring relationships that emphasize unlimited freedom and opportunity for all those involved, then we will most likely watch this revival pass through our hands and have to be reinitiated by another generation. We have been privileged to live in such a beautiful moment in the history of mankind. Let's honor it!

ENDNOTES

Introduction

1. Matthew 10:41.

Chapter 1

1. 2 Corinthians 7:10.

Chapter 2

1. 1 Corinthians 12:27-28 NASB.

2. See Mark 1:22.

3. Matthew 16:23 NIV.

4. Matthew 6:10.

5. Romans 14:17.

6. 2 Chronicles 20:20 NASB.

7. Mark 8:17 NASB.

8. See First Corinthians 4:15.

Chapter 3

1. Luke 9:55 NASB.

2. See First John 4:8,18.

3. 1 John 2:1 NASB.

4. 1 John 2:2 NASB.

5. Galatians 4:31 NASB.

6. Galatians 2:15-21.

7. Romans 7:22-24 NASB.

8. Romans 7:25 NASB.

9. Romans 6:11.

10. John 14:15 NASB.

11. 1 Corinthians 13:2-3, my paraphrase.

Chapter 4

1. Braus, Judy A. and Wood, David. *Environmental Educational in the Schools: Creating Programs that Work Peace Corps Information Collection & Exchange.* Manual M0044. (August 1993), 37.

2. Ephesians 5:8.

3. Jeremiah 17:9.

4. 2 Samuel 11:2.

5. See First Samuel 25.

6. See Matthew 10:33, Matthew 26:34-35, John 21:15-17.

7. John 8:11.

8. See Ephesians 5:8.

9. Job 38:3.

10. See Galatians 5:1 NASB.

Chapter 5

1. 1 Corinthians 6:12 NASB.

2. John 10:10 NASB.

3. Genesis 12:1-3.

4. See Galatians 3:29.

5. Hebrews 11:10.

6. Ruby K. Payne, PhD, *A Framework for Understanding Poverty* (Highland, TX: aha! Process, Inc., 2005), 59.

7. See John 14:13.

8. Mark 16:15.

Chapter 6

1. C.S. Lewis, *Mere Christianity* (New York: HarperCollins, 2001), 47-48.

2. 1 Corinthians 13:1, my paraphrase.

3. 2 Corinthians 3:17 NIV.

4. See Isaiah 54:10.

5. See Jeremiah 29:11 NASB.

6. See First John 4:18.

Chapter 7

1. Galatians 4:1-7.

2. See Galatians 3:25-26.

3. Galatians 5:13,16.

4. Galatians 6:1.

5. See Matthew 7:1-2.

6. John 15:3.

7. See Hebrews 12:6 NASB.

8. Job 38:1-3.

9. Mark 10:51 NASB.

10. John 5:6 NASB.

11. Genesis 18:16-18.

12. Genesis 18:23-25.

13. Genesis 18:33.

14. Psalm 139:23-24.

Chapter 8

1. See Ephesians 6:5 and Colossians 3:22.

2. Luke 4:18.

3. Joan D. Hedrick, *Harriet Beecher Stowe: A Life* (New York: Oxford University Press, 1994), 205.

4. Charles Edward Stowe, *Harriet Beecher Stowe: The Story of Her Life* (Whitefish, MT: Kessinger Publishing, 2005), 203.

5. Ann Hagedorn, *Beyond the River: The Untold Story of the Heroes of the Underground Railroad* (New York: Simon and Schuster, 2004), 274.

6. Hagedorn, *Beyond the River,* 22-23.

7. Hagedorn, *Beyond the River,* 106.

8. 1 Corinthians 12:28 NASB.

RESOURCES

Hagedorn, Ann. *Beyond the River: The Untold Story of the Heroes of the Underground Railroad.* New York: Simon and Schuster, 2004.

Lewis, C.S. *Mere Christianity.* New York: HarperCollins, 2001.

Payne, Ruby K. *A Framework for Understanding Poverty.* Highland, TX: aha! Process, Inc., 2005.

Stowe, Charles Edward. *The Life of Harriet Beecher Stowe: Compiled From Her Letters and Journals.* Boston: Houghton Mifflin, 1889.

Stowe, Charles Edward. *Harriet Beecher Stowe: The Story of Her Life.* Whitefish, MT: Kessinger Publishing, 2005.

RECOMMENDED READING

A Life of Miracles by Bill Johnson

Basic Training for the Prophetic Ministry by Kris Vallotton

Basic Training for the Supernatural Ways of Royalty by Kris Vallotton

Developing a Supernatural Lifestyle by Kris Vallotton

Here Comes Heaven by Bill Johnson and Mike Seth

Loving Our Kids On Purpose by Danny Silk

Purity—The New Moral Revolution by Kris Vallotton

Release the Power of Jesus by Bill Johnson

Secrets to Imitating God by Bill Johnson

Strengthen Yourself in the Lord by Bill Johnson

The Happy Intercessor by Beni Johnson

The Supernatural Power of a Transformed Mind by Bill Johnson

The Supernatural Ways of Royalty by Kris Vallotton and Bill Johnson

The Ultimate Treasure Hunt by Kevin Dedmon

When Heaven Invades Earth by Bill Johnson

AVAILABLE FROM DESTINY IMAGE PUBLISHERS

Using Picture Storybooks to Teach Literary Devices

Using Picture Storybooks to Teach Literary Devices

Recommended Books for Children and Young Adults

Volume Two

Susan Hall

ORYX PRESS
1994

The rare Arabian Oryx is believed to have inspired the myth of the unicorn. This desert antelope became virtually extinct in the early 1960s. At that time several groups of international conservationists arranged to have 9 animals sent to the Phoenix Zoo to be the nucleus of a captive breeding herd. Today the Oryx population is over 800, and nearly 400 have been returned to reserves in the Middle East.

© 1994 by The Oryx Press
4041 North Central at Indian School Road
Phoenix, Arizona 85012-3397

Published simultaneously in Canada
Printed and Bound in the United States of America

∞ The paper used in this publication meets the minimum requirements of American National Standard for Information Science—Permanence of Paper for Printed Library Materials, ANSI Z39.48, 1984.

Library of Congress Cataloging-in-Publication Data
Hall, Susan, 1940-
  Using picture storybooks to teach literary devices : recommended books for children and young adults / Susan Hall. — vol. 2.
  Includes bibliographical references and index.
  ISBN 0-89774-849-2
  1. Children—Books and reading. 2. Figures of speech—Bibliography. 3. Children's stories, English—Bibliography. 4. Picture books for children—Bibliography. 5. Style, Literary—Study and teaching. 6. Figures of speech—Study and teaching. 7. Children's stories—Study and teaching. I. Title.
Z1037.H23   1994
[PN1009.A1]
016.808'0083—dc20   94-32803
                                                                      CIP

To Paula, Keeper of the Books

CONTENTS

* * * * * * * * * *

PREFACE

* * * * * * * * * * *

Volume I of *Using Picture Storybooks to Teach Literary Devices* (Oryx Press, 1990) legitimizes the use of picture storybooks in language arts programs at all grade levels. Volume II expands this function of picture storybooks with over 300 new titles—both newer works and selected classics. Although this volume is meant to stand alone, readers may wish to refer to the first five chapters in Volume I for a more extensive discussion of picture book characteristics, the function of pictures in picture books, the literary quality of this genre, and how literary terms and their definitions were selected for inclusion in the bibliography.

Classroom curriculum now encompasses resources beyond the course textbook. When trade books began to enter the educational domain, a new role for picture books emerged. No longer just a first stage toward serious reading, the picture book is now enhancing math concepts, history lessons, art projects, science experiments, human relations development, and, of course, the language arts program. Creative teachers have found ways to use picture books in all grade levels and in all subject areas.

BACKGROUND

Specifically, picture storybooks can effectively illustrate many of the common literary elements found in "mature" literature. Deceptively simple, picture storybooks have the advantage of teaching complex literary devices in an accessible format to students of all ages. Flashback, inference, and rich imagery occur in the art and text of the picture storybook as readily as in the play, the novel, or the short story.

Regardless of age and grade level, students all need careful, step-by-step learning experiences when comprehending a new concept. Even very young students may begin to move beyond the literal interpretation of a story to appreciate its colorful language or its subtle understatement or perhaps the author's unique tone.

For example, by selectively choosing the simpler vehicle of a picture storybook such as *Chrysanthemum* by Kevin Henkes (Greenwillow, 1991), the teacher can show second graders the meaning of irony, defined as a situation which ends up being the opposite of what might be expected.

In this story, Chrysanthemum loves her special name. Everyone tells her how beautiful it is. Then, she starts school. Other children laugh at her for having the name of a flower. She is hurt and embarrassed. The name does not seem good anymore. She becomes a miserable outcast, ashamed of what had once been a source of pride. She wishes she had an ordinary name like the other kids have.

However, when the children's favorite "indescribable something out of a dream" music teacher, who also has the name of a flower, says she likes Chrysanthemum's name, class attitude abruptly changes. The teacher is even going to call her own baby Chrysanthemum if it's a girl.

Suddenly, all the children adore flower names. "Call me Marigold." "I'm Carnation." "My name is Lily of the Valley." The child who was once ridiculed for her peculiar name becomes the object of admiration and envy. How different this situation has turned out from the way it began. This story demonstrates irony in a setting children can relate to.

A picture storybook can be used equally well to explain irony to an eighth grader or even a high school senior. Older readers will enjoy the universal appeal of the slapstick humor in *Rosie's Walk* by Pat Hutchins (Macmillan, 1968). This tale of a lucky innocent is classic irony.

Clearly Rosie the airhead is doomed. This hen takes her morning stroll heedless of imminent danger. She never notices the fox, only a few steps behind her, as she makes her way around the barnyard. By mere inches she escapes his efforts to snatch her. In the process she walks clear of a pond; he falls into it. She escapes stepping on a rake; he gets bashed in the face. She walks safely past the bee hives; he gets attacked.

Something is happening here. Things are not turning out as expected. The stupid hen is having a lovely day. The clever fox is miserable. This is irony. Some teachers might wish to explore with some students the additional possibility that the apparently dumb chicken might just be smart enough to lead a too-clever fox to his own self-destruction. Surely, when they encounter irony in more challenging literature, these students will be prepared to recognize it.

PICTURE STORYBOOK CRITERIA

For inclusion in this bibliography, a picture storybook must exhibit a single original story told in prose or verse and must possess a recognizable opening situation, a conflict, and a resolution.

Some categories of picture storybooks were excluded. Controlled vocabulary "beginning reader" books were avoided. "Toy" books having manipulative or special effects such as textures, holes, smells, shapes, or pop-ups were not included. Wordless picture storybooks do not appear in this bibliography. Neither do the plethora of familiar traditional fairy tales unless they are parodies of a tale. Occasionally, a new or unfamiliar folktale is included, because the story is original to the western world.

Since libraries contain a mixture of new books, older books, and really older "classics," *Using Picture Storybooks to Teach Literary Devices, Volume 2* contains entries from across the copyright date spectrum. Included are enduring titles such as Beatrix Potter's 1902 *The Tale of Peter Rabbit* as well as new titles, such as Allen Say's *Grandfather's Journey*, that have been just recently shelved. This volume contains nearly 300 entries; all are different from the titles listed in Volume 1.

SCOPE AND ORGANIZATION

The picture storybooks are listed in alphabetical order under the literary devices they illustrate. The selection of literary terms were gleaned from examining various literature textbooks for grades six through nine and literature read by children from primary through junior high grades. The definitions were compiled primarily from these four sources:

Beckson, Karl and Arthur Ganz. *Literary Terms, A Dictionary*. New York: Farrar, Straus & Giroux, 1977.

Cuddon, John A. *A Dictionary of Literary Terms*. Garden City, NY: Doubleday, 1977.

Holman, C. Hugh. *A Handbook to Literature*. 4th ed. Indianapolis, IN: Bobbs Merrill, 1980.

Yelland, H.L., S.C. Jones, and K.S.W. Easton. *A Handbook of Literary Terms*, Rev. ed. London: Angus & Robertson, 1983.

SAMPLE BIBLIOGRAPHIC ENTRY

All entries have basic bibliographic information, annotations, examples, and cross-references to other devices used. Three additional pieces of information are included in the bibliographic entries of Volume 2: (1) Following the literary devices exhibited in each book is a brief notation listing the style or mixture of styles employed by the picture storybook artist (discussed in the next chapter under "The Art in Picture Storybooks"). (2) If warranted, any curriculum tie-in suggested by the book's content are also included. (3) A starred entry indicates those all-ages books having special appeal to mature readers.

Shown below as a sample of the format used is an entry for a book listed under the literary device heading "Simile":

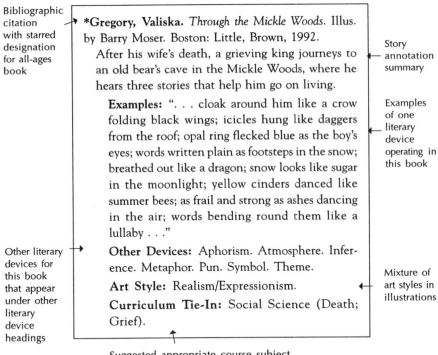

Bibliographic citation with starred designation for all-ages book

*Gregory, Valiska. *Through the Mickle Woods.* Illus. by Barry Moser. Boston: Little, Brown, 1992.

Story annotation summary

After his wife's death, a grieving king journeys to an old bear's cave in the Mickle Woods, where he hears three stories that help him go on living.

Examples: ". . . cloak around him like a crow folding black wings; icicles hung like daggers from the roof; opal ring flecked blue as the boy's eyes; words written plain as footsteps in the snow; breathed out like a dragon; snow looks like sugar in the moonlight; yellow cinders danced like summer bees; as frail and strong as ashes dancing in the air; words bending round them like a lullaby . . ."

Examples of one literary device operating in this book

Other literary devices for this book that appear under other literary device headings

Other Devices: Aphorism. Atmosphere. Inference. Metaphor. Pun. Symbol. Theme.

Art Style: Realism/Expressionism.

Mixture of art styles in illustrations

Curriculum Tie-In: Social Science (Death; Grief).

Suggested appropriate course subject

REFERENCES

Henkes, Kevin. *Chrysanthemum.* New York: Greenwillow, 1991.
Hutchins, Pat. *Rosie's Walk.* New York: Macmillan, 1968.

Using Picture Storybooks to Teach Literary Devices

ABOUT PICTURE
STORYBOOKS

* * * * * * * * * *

PICTURE BOOKS, PICTURE STORYBOOKS, AND ILLUSTRATED STORYBOOKS

Only original stories in the picture storybook format have been chosen for inclusion in both volumes of *Using Picture Storybooks to Teach Literary Devices*. Picture books and illustrated storybooks are not included. There are differences between these three kinds of books, and some definitions are in order.

Picture Storybook

The picture storybook is defined as a 32-page blend of text (prose or poetry) and illustration that works together to tell a story with a beginning, a middle, and an end. The words and pictures ideally share in revealing the story so that what is not said in text is shown in illustration. Ideally, the one could not exist without the other. Practically, a particular book might exhibit more illustration and less text or vice versa. Even though text and illustration are important partners in picture storybooks, these elements do vary in prominence from book to book because of the incredible range and diversity of the genre.

Picture Book (nonstory)

The picture book is defined (for purposes of this bibliography) as a short illustrated book that does not tell a story separate from the concept it is trying to teach. Picture books include alphabet books, counting books, books about the seasons, and books that define shapes, sizes, and colors or emotions such

1

as anger, sadness, and joy. The terms picture book and picture storybook are generally used interchangeably. But, here a distinction is made between them.

Illustrated Storybook

The illustrated storybook is defined as having much more text and pages than the standard picture storybook or picture book and is much less profusely illustrated. Sometimes, the book may even contain multiple stories. Illustrations serve as adornment to the text, which can stand alone without them.

THE ALL-AGES PICTURE STORYBOOK

Though still not widely accepted, especially among children's book publishers who continue to seek material for "age ranges," there are a growing number of educators and other picture book experts who are recognizing that some picture storybooks have an ageless quality about them.

In the literary device section of this book, some entries have been starred (*), alerting educators that here might be a suitable book to use as a model for the more mature student thinkers, writers, or illustrators. Such all-ages books have stories that reflect mature experiences and concerns. Personal issues crucial to older students (and adults) are often explored in picture storybooks. These books demonstrate vivid language, sophisticated humor, quality characterization and plot, and often supply valuable supplementary material for curricular subjects.

Well-known writers on the picture book genre such as college instructor Patricia Cianciolo and editors Barbara Elleman and Betsy Hearne have always contended picture books that examine aspects of life openly and controversially belong in the classroom subject areas. Some picture books may actually be better suited to older children.

For example, Jane Yolen's *Encounter* (Harcourt Brace Jovanovich, 1992) shows the landing of Columbus in 1492 on the island of San Salvador from the point of view of a suspicious young Native American boy, who lives long enough to see his feelings of foreboding confirmed. Older students' skills of analysis are put to work deciphering symbolism in the boy's dream of "three winged birds with voices like thunder" and metaphors describing a "sharp silver stick" that "bit my palm so hard the blood cried out." A good picture storybook can't be depleted; it offers something to readers of any age.

Sixteen school teachers, professors, book reviewers, illustrators, and writers recently expressed their acknowledgment and advocacy of all-ages picture books in *Beyond Words: Picture Books for Older Readers and Writers* (edited by Susan Benedict and Lenore Carlisle, Heinemann Educational Books, 1992).

It may take a novel over 300 pages to convey a message with perfection. A picture storybook has to do it in 32 pages. Thomas Newkirk, contributor in *Beyond Words*, believes the Western world ought to adopt the Asian aesthetic perspective which values economy and suggestiveness over explicitness. From this perspective, brevity of text is not a concession to young readers but, rather, demonstrates the consummate skill of the writer.

Lenore Carlisle, another contributor in *Beyond Words*, said one of her sixth grade students remarked that there are some picture books which probably shouldn't be read by kids until they're in at least fourth grade. Another student believes if a picture book is well written it's for everyone, and you won't outgrow it. Picture books are an easy place to think, said a third student.

David Ludlam's older students use the same factors selecting picture books for class activities as they do when selecting adolescent or adult literature—maturity and presentation of subject matter and connection to personal experiences. He says in *Beyond Words* that it is wonderful that picture books know no limit as to the age of their readers.

Referring to literary complexity and sophistication or possibly to social commentary or emotional depth, Susan Benedict's older students thought that some picture storybooks probably aren't well received by young readers and listeners because they are "too hard."

Linda Rief, who uses picture books with her adolescent students, even goes so far as to say she thinks some picture books are not written for little children. Whether the author intends it or not, the language, the illustrations, and the concepts are more important to older kids and adults. She cites Chris Van Allsburg as an author who writes such books. She suggests older students are better able to appreciate and enjoy the quick access to mood, theme, and superior artwork in these all-ages books. Or, perhaps students confront such serious issues in their lives today that beautiful picture books bring them back to the pleasures of childhood.

Intended for mature readers or not, all-ages picture storybooks do appeal on different levels simultaneously to children and adults. They strike a chord in both, and, if occasionally there is a unique picture book that elicits more chuckles or more tears from the adult reader than the young child, that fact is to be commended as having broadened the range of the genre, not condemned as having missed its targeted child audience.

All-Ages Picture Storybook Characteristics

The all-ages picture storybook often makes a strong impression through pathos. It will engage difficult or complex issues such as death or loss. But, soul-searching serious topics are not the exclusive theme in all-ages picture storybooks.

One delightful surprise is a book by Gus Clarke called . . . *Along Came Eric* (Lothrop, Lee, & Shepard, 1991). It concerns sibling jealousy, which is hardly a unique subject among picture books. What lifts this book above the pre-school crowd is its extremely subtle, understated humor in both the illustrations and in the text.

Older, knowing readers will find this a funny, right-on story. Along came Eric and older brother Nigel is out of sorts. Eventually, Nigel realizes he must bow to the inevitable and accept his younger brother into the family.

He philosophizes, "Life isn't so bad." Eric, the center of attention, of course, "had never thought it was." Until, ". . . along came Alice." The stricken look on poor Eric's face speaks volumes. An older, wiser, and slightly patronizing Nigel is more than ready to initiate young Eric into facing the inevitable.

Anyone who has ever been an older or younger sibling or can empathize with them will share a private smile while admiring this author/illustrator's craftsmanship dealing with one of life's universals.

Subjective as the criteria must necessarily be, the following few characteristics tend to set apart the all-ages picture storybooks from those that are more strictly designed to entertain the very young.

Theme usually deals with universal or sophisticated truths. Topics include self-fulfillment, complicated relationships, multiple levels of comprehension and insight, nostalgia, war, love, and other intriguing "adult" subjects. Stories will speak to the inner child in all of us but will also impart a nugget of mature truth.

Allen Say is such an author who does not pander to youth. In his 1994 Caldecott Award-winning *Grandfather's Journey* (Houghton Mifflin, 1993), he describes similar feelings shared by both a young man and his grandfather who are each torn by a love for two different countries. Both were born in Japan and moved to America as young adults. Neither can stop longing for his first land, nor can they feel content when in their first land and away from their new land. "The moment I am in one country I am homesick for the other," observes the young man. He is the story's narrator, and his life parallels that of his grandfather. Though a generation apart, he remarks simply, "I think I know my grandfather now." And, so does the reader.

Language may be vividly lyrical with rich imagery, understated with precise simplicity, full of emotional allusions. Consider this opening to Valiska Gregory's *Through the Mickle Woods* (Little, Brown, 1992):

> At eventide the king sat on his solitary throne. Winter snow drummed its
> fingers on the windows, and icicles hung like daggers from the roof. "I am

weary," he said. He drew his cloak around him like a crow folding black wings and closed his eyes.

The author is deliberate in the selection of grim, medieval images. The stage is set. Here is a lonely person, disinterested in life. The king's wife has died, and he is bereft with grief. Barry Moser's realistic art is a stunning adjunct to the evocative text. It takes a reader who has lived a while to appreciate this sensitive exploration of a painful topic.

Humor is often bold or delightfully subtle, often visual, sometimes alluded to through text or art, and is even part of secondary action that is not stated in the text. Sometimes there are inside jokes and puns requiring a mature awareness that is lost on very young readers. Sometimes humor is achieved through contrasting the usual with a jarring change.

In Raymond Briggs's *Father Christmas* (Coward, 1973), Father Christmas is grumpy and tired and coming down with a cold, not at all the image of jolly old Santa. He complains bitterly about his obligations, "Blooming snow; Blooming cold; Blooming chimneys; Roll on summer."

Characterization, Plot, Etc. have no special dimensions except, loosely speaking, "maturity." The main character in an all-ages book is often not a child. Harve Zemach's *Duffy and the Devil* (Farrar Straus Giroux, 1973) contains a spunky young servant woman and an annoying imp in a parody of Rumpelstiltskin. When she is finally caught in her lie, the older student will admire her quick-thinking reaction that turns an iffy outcome back in her favor.

In Charlotte Zolotow's *The Moon Was the Best* (Greenwillow, 1993) the only nod to childhood is a young daughter asking her mother about her best memories of Paris. A nostalgic description of the city's sights follows.

Another of Allen Say's books, *A Tree of Cranes* (Houghton Mifflin, 1991), is written from the perspective of an adult recalling experiences that occurred as a child.

One all-ages book in this bibliography has a fish and a flamingo as the main characters. The universal value and appeal of characterization and plot in all-ages picture books depend on the same things that appeal in adult literature—new understandings, acceptance, or a personality change, presented in an appropriate style.

THE ART IN PICTURE STORYBOOKS

Because the picture storybook is a synthesis of both text and art, it is appropriate to make reference in the bibliographic entries to the art style incorporated in each book. Picture storybooks might even be considered a discrete art genre and may serve as a viable means of introducing students to artistic literacy. For a detailed examination of art as it applies to specific picture books, refer to Sylvia S. Marantz's *Picture Books for Looking and Learning: Awakening Visual Perceptions Through the Art of Children's Books* (Oryx Press, 1992).

Teachers who wish to discuss art as integral to narrative should keep in mind that art is composed of *media, technique,* and *style.*

Media refers to such application products as water color, acrylics, gouache, oils, pencil, charcoal, pen and ink, chalk, and pastels.

Technique refers to the method of application of various products: pasting, painting, drawing, stenciling, woodcutting, linocutting, etching, or airbrushing.

Style is that elusive quality of an artist's work based on arrangement of line, color, and mass into a visual image. The artist's manipulation of materials and tools evoke feelings, create a mood, and produce a unique entity that results in an aesthetic response. Style is the complex ordering of media products and media technique, but it is more than the sum of the parts.

Artists gravitate toward similar ways of making visual statements that can be identified by art critics and historians. For example, impressionism and cubism can be recognized as unique and separate art styles. Classifications are based on widely accepted characteristics that demonstrate consistent structural elements governed by technique and tradition.

While some attempt can be made to identify styles because of observable groupings of characteristics, media products and the technique employed in their application are not always so easy to recognize in picture book art. Unless the publisher thoughtfully provides such technical information between the book's covers, it's hard for nonartists to know with certainty what media product was used or how it was applied. Is the color the result of pastel or crayon or chalk? Is the pattern woodcut or linocut? Is the paint oil or acrylic? Are the dark outlines made with magic marker or ink pen or soft pencil or maybe charcoal? One must remember that resultant images in a picture book are not the artist's original piece of art.

Annotations in this bibliography briefly attempt to identify only the style or combination of styles in evidence. If media product and media technique are known, these are added to the annotation.

Picture book artists can re-create the text or add another dimension to the story by taking up where the author has left off. Almost all art styles in existence have been adopted in picture book illustrations, from the most representational realism to the more abstract cubism. This particular bibliography does not contain examples of cubism, but some picture book artists, such as Brian Wildsmith, do employ it.

Even surrealism occasionally appears in picture book art. This bizarre form of illustration produces a double exposure effect through fantastic juxtapositions of incongruous images. For example, an ice skate realistically drawn might have a human head, also realistically drawn, poking out of the top of the shoe and wrapped round with a fur stole.

Styles are meant to enhance meaning. No one style is more or less appropriate for children or preferred by them. Because of its neat simplicity, the cartoon line drawing has always been, and continues to be, a popular art style chosen by picture book artists. But, modern artists like Emily McCully, Donald Crews, Ann Grifalconi, Allen Say, Ruth Brown, and Barry Moser are creating some very exciting impressionistic and expressionistic works mixed with realism. Many artists change their style from book to book, depending on what they believe the text requires.

There is a caveat associated with style identification. No designation of a particular art style can be absolutely precise because of variations within styles and within books that employ a variety of styles. Artists enjoy varying their style within and between books they illustrate.

Consider the dazzling array of styles demonstrated on the pages of *Ben's Trumpet* by Rachel Isadora (Greenwillow, 1979). Realism, impressionism, and expressionism can all be identified, with even a hint of cubism emerging in some of the "far-out" drawings. The author, using only pen and ink, was creating the allusion of sound through art (visual music), and the result certainly seems to have worked.

Ruth Brown is another author/artist, who often mixes styles in her paintings. While they always manage to appear realistic, her illustrations also exhibit occasional touches of both expressionism and impressionism. *The Picnic* (Dutton, 1992) shows the viewpoint of meadow animals looking out of their burrow at a family picnic, which includes a nosy dog. The almost photographic art is, nevertheless, exaggerated to show a unique perspective.

In fact, it's hard to find true realism in picture book art. Artists frequently modify realism with other styles to create special effects.

The following art style definitions are to be considered only practical working definitions for the lay person. Art dictionaries tend to offer detailed and complex definitions that are somewhat less serviceable for the teacher's purposes. Educators in the primary and secondary school settings require plain language and identifiable characteristics that distinguish and separate the styles.

Art Style Definitions

Cartoon is an art form that produces simple, lively, caricature line drawings, colored or not, like those of comic book drawings. The cartoon is employed to depict both serious and humorous topics. Imagination is often expressed through exaggerated features and wonderful detail. Artists who employ the cartoon style in picture books include Stephen Kellogg, Dr. Seuss, Kevin Henkes, and William Steig.

Collage is a pictorial technique in which an arrangement of diverse materials such as bits of newspaper, fabric, paper, photographs, and paint are mounted on a two-dimensional surface such as paper or canvas to create a scene. Sometimes the scene is completed with a linear drawing on top of the multi-textured surface. Artists who employ collage in picture books include Ezra Jack Keats and Leo Lionni.

Cubism is a radical break from the idea of art as the imitation of nature. In analytical cubism the art subject is rigorously dissected in an exhaustive quest to separate it into its basic geometric cylinders, spheres, cones, etc. The various components of the subject overlap each other in a three-dimensional rendering. The effect is an abstract presentation of an object from many different points of view simultaneously. Artists who employ a simplified form of cubism in picture books include Brian Wildsmith and Paul Rand.

Expressionism leans toward distorted proportions and perspectives. There is exaggeration of natural color, shape, and line to create an emotional impact. For example, an enormous hand might thrust out from a small thin arm. Subjects may be bold and splashy or free-flowing and delicate, lined in cartoon-like drawings. Notice Alice's elongated neck drawn by Sir John Tenniel for Lewis Carroll's *Alice's Adventures in Wonderland*. Artists who employ expressionism in picture books include Peter Parnall, Vera Williams, Ruth Brown, and Eric Carle.

Folk encompasses a variety of "looks" dependent more on specific geography and less on cosmopolitan artistic influences. It adheres to perpetuation of a regional collective awareness. The artist deliberately uses traditional media techniques and ethnic decorative motifs, symbols, and patterns common to a specific culture or subculture. This art does not emphasize the artist's own personal preferences or craftsmanship. The effect is to be indistinguishable from others in the same culture. Artists who employ folk in picture books include Ed Young's oriental flair, Margot Zemach's Cornish flavor, Paul Goble's Native American motifs, and Gail Haley's African influence.

Impressionism emphasizes artistic play with light through color. Rather than broad blended strokes, pure pigment is stippled closely in dabs and short dashes which the eye then mixes to suggest, rather than show, precise copies of life.

The effect demonstrates the scintillating, changeable quality of light that occurs through shadows, fuzzy outlines, and fleeting glimpses. Artists who employ impressionism in picture books include Uri Shulevitz, Stephen Gammell, Ronald Himler, and Taro Yashima.

Naive is sometimes called "primitive" because of its unsophisticated, child-like clear outlines that disregard perspective. Human or animal figures are usually depicted in frontal or profile positions with little differentiation in facial detail. Every inch of the page seems filled with simple drawings of extremely detailed intricate scenes. Colors are brilliant rather than a subtle mix of tones. There is no attempt to create shading. Artists who employ naive art in picture books include M. B. Goffstein, Virginia Lee Burton, and Barbara Cooney.

Realism is an attempt to depict figures and objects in close representation to lifelike color, texture, shadows, proportions, and arrangements as perceived in the visible world. But, this style is not necessarily an attempt to create photographically exact images. Objects are permitted the artist's special vitality of expression. Artists who employ realism in picture books include Lynd Ward, Miska Miles, Chris Van Allsburg, and Nancy Carpenter.

Surrealism is the deliberate and unexpected combination of incongruous but meticulously realistic appearing objects assembled in an improbable, supernatural atmosphere that defies everyday logic. Impossibly startling, haunting, somewhat repellent imagery is displayed for shock value. For example, a pair of bedroom slippers with bird wings attached, or a bathroom sink with a human mouth in place of the drain hole, all drawn entirely with photographic accuracy, would demonstrate this style of art. One artist who particularly employs surrealism to good advantage in picture books is Anthony Browne.

REFERENCES

Benedict, Susan, and Lenore Carlisle. *Beyond Words: Picture Books for Older Readers and Writers*. Portsmouth, NH: Heinemann, 1992.

Briggs, Raymond. *Father Christmas*. New York: Coward, 1973.

Brown, Ruth. *The Picnic*. New York: Dutton, 1992.

Carroll, Lewis. *Alice's Adventures in Wonderland*. Illus. by Sir John Tenniel. New York: St. Martin's Press, 1977. c1865.

Clarke, Gus. . . . *Along Came Eric*. New York: Lothrop, Lee, & Shepard, 1991.

Gregory, Valiska. *Through the Mickle Woods*. Illus. by Barry Moser. Boston: Little, Brown, 1992.

Isadora, Rachel. *Ben's Trumpet*. New York: Greenwillow, 1979.

Marantz, Sylvia S. *Picture Books for Looking and Learning; Awakening Visual Perceptions Through the Art of Children's Books.* Phoenix: The Oryx Press, 1992.

Say, Allen. *Grandfather's Journey.* New York: Houghton Mifflin, 1993.

Say, Allen. *A Tree of Cranes.* New York: Houghton Mifflin, 1991.

Yolen, Jane. *Encounter.* Illus. by David Shannon. New York: Harcourt Brace Jovanovich, 1992.

Zemach, Harve. *Duffy and the Devil.* New York: Farrar Straus Giroux, 1973.

Zolotow, Charlotte. *The Moon Was the Best.* New York: Greenwillow, 1993.

LITERARY DEVICES USED IN PICTURE STORYBOOKS

* * * * * * * * * * *

ALLITERATION

A repeated consonant sound occurring at the beginnings of neighboring words or within neighboring words as well; it may be used to establish mood.

Example: Miserable, mizzling, morning drizzle.

SOURCES

Amoss, Berthe. *Old Hannibal and the Hurricane.* New York: Hyperion, 1991.
On board the ship *Sally Sue*, Old Hannibal is describing for his friends the great hurricane he once endured, when they suddenly run into another storm.

> **Examples:** ". . . as sturdy a ship as ever sailed the seven seas; heave-ho on that rope, me hearties; biggest, blowingest, most blustering blast that ever blew; wind began to wail and whine; Bellowing Bertha being born; breathed and blew, groaned and grew; whales wallow; silver sharks slither; safe and snug in Sally Sue by the sea."
>
> **Other Devices:** Hyperbole. Internal Rhyme.
>
> **Art Style:** Colored Cartoon.

Daly, Niki. *Mama, Papa, and Baby Joe.* New York: Viking Penguin, 1991.
In jaunty word rhythms a family's adventure on a shopping trip is described in action-packed pictures full of unlikely hilarious detail.

> **Examples:** ". . . sitting sipping; pick 'n pay; moany, moany macaroni; ziggery-zaggery; clickety-clack; pudding pack; smackety-smack; blue buttons; Billy 'n Barney."

Other Devices: Allusion. Pun. Tone.

Art Style: Cartoon.

Edwards, Hazel. *Snail Mail.* Illus. by Rod Clement. Australia: Collins, 1986.
A mail-eating snail describes his life with "them" and his culinary interests.

Examples: ". . . munching mint; chomping chives; tasting tomatoes."

Other Devices: Inference. Irony. Poetic Justice. Pun.

Art Style: Realism.

Gerstein, Mordicai. *The Sun's Day.* New York: Harper & Row, 1989.
As the sun rises, moves through the sky, and finally sets, an hour by hour description of the activities that take place are explained.

Examples: ". . . chirping chicks; babies want breakfast; horns honk; bees buzz;
wheels whirr; cats curl; peaches are ripe and ready to pick; balls . . . bouncing;
soup pots are simmering; pictures . . . painted; babies take baths."

Art Style: Colored Cartoon.

Curriculum Tie-In: Science (Sun).

Kahl, Virginia. *How Do You Hide a Monster?* New York: Charles Scribner's, 1971.
Sympathetic townspeople join forces to lead astray a group of men sent to investigate a monster in their lake.

Examples: "They'd slip and they'd shout, then they'd skid and they'd scream;
slithered and skidded; fearful, frightful; forest is filled with the finest of fowl;
balefully blinking eyes; deep dark lake; huge and hairy; sniffle-y sort of snuffle."

Other Devices: Ambiguity. Irony.

Art Style: Colored Cartoon.

Curriculum Tie-In: Social Science (Cooperation).

Kahl, Virginia. *Plum Pudding for Christmas.* New York: Charles Scribner's, 1956.
After inviting the king to be their Christmas guest, the duchess and her daughters find themselves unable to serve the promised plum pudding.

Examples: "Plums that are purple; plum that is plump; burned brightly; purple
plums; pudding with plenty of plums."

Other Devices: Foreshadowing. Internal Rhyme. Irony. Understatement.

Art Style: Colored Cartoon.

Curriculum Tie-In: History (Medieval Times).

Lobel, Anita. *Alison's Zinnia.* New York: Greenwillow, 1990.
A series of flowers are passed along from one person to another.

Examples: "Alison acquires an amaryllis for Beryl who buys a begonia for
Crystal" . . . and so on through the alphabet. Each girl's name, the verb connected to the flower, and the flower's name all begin with the same sound.

Art Style: Expressionism water color.

Seuss, Dr. *How the Grinch Stole Christmas.* New York: Random House, 1957.
The Grinch thinks stealing the trappings of Christmas will stop Christmas.

> **Examples:** "Sound wasn't sad; shocking surprise; snarled with a sneer; Christmas from coming; slithered and slunk with a smile; popcorn! and plums!; started to shove; cup of cold water; fib fooled; the ribbons! the wrappings!; the tags, the tinsel; the trimmings! the trappings."
>
> **Other Devices:** Onomatopoeia. Theme.
>
> **Art Style:** Colored Cartoon.
>
> **Curriculum Tie-In:** Social Science (Values).

Shaw, Nancy. *Sheep in a Shop.* Illus. by Margot Apple. Boston: Houghton Mifflin, 1991.
Sheep hunt for a birthday present and make havoc of the shop, only to discover they haven't the money to pay for things.

> **Examples:** ". . . sheep shop; rackets and rockets; try trains; sheep sprawl; ribbon from the rack; swap to pay the shop; hop home."
>
> **Other Devices:** Allusion.
>
> **Art Style:** Colored Cartoon.

Steig, William. *Shrek.* New York: Farrar Straus Giroux, 1990.
Like two peas in a pod, ugly Shrek and his ugly bride are made for each other and live horribly ever after, scaring the socks off all who fall afoul of them.

> **Examples:** ". . . busy boiling bats in turpentine and turtle juice; singing and scything; pheasant, peasant; pleasant present; jabbering jackass; Shrek shrieked; bellowed a blast."
>
> **Other Devices:** Hyperbole. Internal Rhyme.
>
> **Art Style:** Colored Cartoon.
>
> **Curriculum Tie-In:** Social Science (Acceptance and Respect).

ALLUSION

A reference in one literary work that calls forth within the reader an appropriate association to another piece of literature, or a well-known person, or an event from history, or a place; it is used to enrich surface meaning.

> **Examples:** having the patience of Job (biblical character)
> met his Waterloo (historical site of Napolean's defeat)
> Black Monday (event: stock market collapse)
> sour grapes (Aesop fable: work of literature)

SOURCES

Abolafia, Yossi. *Fox Tale.* New York: Greenwillow, 1991.
Donkey, Crow, and Rabbit join forces to prevent Fox from swindling Bear out of his jar of honey.

    Examples: Like the tricks in Aesop fables, Fox cons a crow out of a piece of cheese when he flatters the bird's singing ability, causing it to drop the cheese. Fox trades Rabbit sour grapes for sweet ones, claiming they are full of vitamin C. Fox takes the smaller sack of chestnuts and gives the larger one to Donkey, who later discovers it contains rocks.

    Other Devices: Poetic Justice. Pun.

    Art Style: Colored Cartoon.

    Curriculum Tie-In: Social Science (Consequences; Cooperation).

Ahlberg, Janet, and Allan Ahlberg. *Each Peach Pear Plum.* New York: Viking Kestrel, 1978.
As the story progresses, each page visually hints at a nursery rhyme or fairy tale character that is then fully revealed on the following page.

    Examples: Among characters is Tom Thumb, who hides in a peach tree. In the cupboard is Mother Hubbard. Other appearances include Cinderella, the Three Bears, Baby Bunting, Bo-Peep, Jack and Jill, Robin Hood, and a wicked witch.

    Art Style: Colored Cartoon.

*Briggs, Raymond. *Father Christmas.* New York: Coward, 1973.
Comic strip pictures follow a rather disgruntled Santa on his annual rounds.

    Examples: Father Christmas is careful not to miss anyone on his rounds. As he flies over an elegant palace, he remarks to himself, "Good! the flag's flying. They're in." He then proceeds to make his royal deliveries.

    Other Devices: Point-Of-View.

    Art Style: Colored Cartoon Strip.

Cameron, Polly. *I Can't Said the Ant.* New York: Coward-McCann, 1961.
An ant, encouraged by a kitchen battalion of 89 objects, comes to the rescue of a fallen teapot.

    Examples: "Polly put the kettle on. We'll all have tea." After the pot is mended, the ant calls upon the nursery rhyme characters to test out the workmanship of her restorers.

    Other Devices: Internal Rhyme. Pun. Theme.

    Art Style: Colored Cartoon.

    Curriculum Tie-In: Science (Lever and Pulley).

Daly, Niki. *Mama, Papa, and Baby Joe.* New York: Viking Penguin, 1991.
In jaunty word rhythms a family's adventure on a shopping trip is described in action-packed pictures full of unlikely hilarious detail.

> **Examples:** Illustrations allude to Woody Woodpecker, Peter Rabbit, Buffalo Bill Cody, Noah's ark, and Andy Warhol, among figures from literature and the world of art.
>
> **Other Devices:** Alliteration. Pun. Tone.
>
> **Art Style:** Cartoon.

Goffstein, M. B. *My Noah's Ark.* New York: Harper & Row, 1978.
An old woman fondly remembers a lifetime of experiences related to a carved representation of Noah's ark that she's had since childhood.

> **Examples:** The biblical references include her father's voice "booming like God's" and "make it three hundred cubits long." Now, after the passage of years and loved ones, "Our fun and sorrow seem to form a rainbow, and it warms one like sunshine."
>
> **Other Devices:** Atmosphere.
>
> **Art Style:** Naive.
>
> **Curriculum Tie-In:** Social Science (Aging; Values).

Kimmel, Eric A. *Four Dollars and Fifty Cents.* Illus. by Glen Rounds. New York: Holiday House, 1989.
To avoid paying the Widow Macrae the four dollars and fifty cents he owes her, deadbeat cowboy Shorty Long plays dead and almost gets buried alive.

> **Examples:** "You got as much chance of collecting that money as seeing Custer ride back from the Little Bighorn."
>
> **Other Devices:** Irony. Pun. Simile.
>
> **Art Style:** Impressionism.
>
> **Curriculum Tie-In:** Social Science (Foolish Behavior).

McNaughton, Colin. *Guess Who's Just Moved in Next Door?* New York: Random House, 1991.
A tour is taken through a very peculiar neighborhood where an assortment of wacky neighbors from Superman to a ship of pirates reacts to the arrival of new neighbors.

> **Examples:** There are references to Mr. Scrooge, Humpty Dumpty, Santa Claus, Noah's ark, the Three Bears, and the Hunchback of Notre Dame.
>
> **Other Devices:** Caricature. Irony. Parallel Story. Pun. Satire.
>
> **Art Style:** Colored Cartoon.

Oakley, Graham. *The Church Cat Abroad.* New York: Atheneum, 1973.
For the sake of their friends, two mice and a cat set out to become high-paid actors, so they will earn enough money to fix their leaking church vestry roof.

Examples: Sampson did the "Cheshire Cat's smile," which alludes to the creature from the book classic *Alice in Wonderland.* The mice recite the "Owl and the Pussycat" rhyme and do the Sugar-Plum Fairy's dance.

Other Devices: Tone. Understatement.

Art Style: Colored Cartoon.

Okimoto, Jean Davies. *Blumpoe the Grumpoe Meets Arnold the Cat.* Illus. by Howie Schneider. Boston: Little, Brown & Co., 1990.

A grumpy old man and a shy, but tenacious, young cat form an unlikely friendship at a Minnesota inn that provides its guests with a cat for the night.

Examples: "A bachelor farmer from Lake Wobegon picked Fred," alludes to the popular radio show town and characters created by Garrison Keillor about a fictional place in Minnesota.

Other Devices: Inference.

Art Style: Cartoon.

Curriculum Tie-In: Social Science (Loneliness).

Ringgold, Faith. *Tar Beach.* New York: Crown, 1991.

A young girl dreams of flying above her Harlem home, claiming all she sees for herself and her family.

Examples: Alluding to her heritage of slavery and the slave's "flight" to freedom in times past, "flying" makes Cassie Louise Lightfoot "free to go wherever I want for the rest of my life." By virtue of claiming it for him in her imaginary flights, Cassie can give her father the Union Building, which he worked to build but which excludes him from membership because "Grandpa wasn't a member." This tactic alludes to discrimination by race according to the "Grandfather Clause," so useful in perpetuating inequality.

Other Devices: Metaphor. Symbol.

Art Style: Naive paint.

Curriculum Tie-In: Social Science (Discrimination; Race Relations).

Roth, Roger. *The Sign Painter's Dream.* New York: Crown, 1993.

A spunky old woman's request and a rather unusual dream convince crabby Clarence to make the most glorious and magnificent sign of his career and then give it away.

Examples: Clarence loved to read history books about the Revolutionary War. In a dream, George Washington shows up asking for a big sign: SEND SHOES TO VALLEY FORGE. This historical allusion refers to the famous winter battle during which soldiers were ill clad. When the famous general departs, he says, "We're all in a bit of a hasty pudding," which also refers to language of the Revolutionary era.

Art Style: Expressionism.

*Scieszka, Jon. *The Frog Prince Continued.* Illus. by Steve Johnson. New York: Viking, 1991.

After the frog turns into a prince, he and the princess do not live happily ever after. The prince decides to look for a witch to help him remedy the situation.

Examples: Among the witches the frog prince encounters is one who "can't have him waking up Sleeping Beauty before the hundred years are up." Another one "can't have any prince rescuing Snow White" and says, "Here, eat the rest of this apple." Another witch seems to have a gingerbread house and is expecting Hansel and Gretel for dinner. A final witch is on her way "to see a girl in the village about going to a ball."

Other Devices: Irony.

Art Style: Expressionism.

Shaw, Nancy. *Sheep in a Shop.* Illus. by Margot Apple. Boston: Houghton Mifflin, 1991.

Sheep hunt for a birthday present and make havoc of the shop, only to discover they haven't the money to pay for things.

Examples: Short on cash, but long on ingenuity, sheep swap "three bags full" of their wool for their purchase. This action constitutes a neat nod to Mother Goose and tradition.

Other Devices: Alliteration.

Art Style: Colored Cartoon.

Van Allsburg, Chris. *The Widow's Broom.* New York: Houghton Mifflin, 1992.

A witch's worn-out broom serves a widow well, until her neighbors decide it's wicked and must be destroyed.

Examples: According to historical legend, witches were considered evil and were burned at the stake. When the neighbors carry away the broom they believe is bewitched, they choose an appropriate means of destruction. They bind and burn the broom at the stake.

Other Devices: Inference. Stereotype.

Art Style: Impressionism.

AMBIGUITY

A device that allows for differing, alternative reactions to the same piece of language. It also refers to using an expression that conveys more than one meaning simultaneously.

Example: "Who" is on third base. (This could be a question, or it could be a statement that someone with the last name of WHO is on third base.)

SOURCES

Ada, Alma Flor. *The Golden Coin.* Illus. by Neil Waldman. Trans. from Spanish by Bernice Randall. New York: Atheneum, 1991.
Determined to steal an old woman's gold, a young thief follows her around the countryside and finds himself inadvertently helping others while being transformed in the process.

Examples: The thief hears the woman say, "I must be the richest person in the world." He sees a gold coin in her hand. He hears the people she has attended in sickness claim she gave each a gold coin. He assumes she has many gold coins. When at last he confronts her asking, "Where's the gold?" she surprises him by handing him one coin. She tells him, "I've been trying to give it to someone who might need it." But each person refuses, saying, "Keep it. There must be someone who needs it more." So she tells the thief, "You must be the one who needs it." All week misunderstanding has plagued the young thief.

Other Devices: Irony.

Art Style: Latin American Folk.

Curriculum Tie-In: Social Science (Ethics).

Asch, Frank. *Moon Bear.* New York: Charles Scribner's, 1978.
A bear who falls in love with the moon worries when it diminishes.

Examples: While the bear believes that the honey he is setting out for the moon is helping the moon get fat again, the birds who are really eating it know differently.

Other Devices: Irony.

Art Style: Naive/Cartoon colored pen and ink.

Ball, Duncan. *Jeremy's Tail.* Illus. by Donna Rawlins. New York: Ashton Scholastic, 1990.
Jeremy is determined to pin the tail on the donkey at the birthday party. He is blindfolded and doesn't want any help.

Examples: Jeremy believes he is in the room with the other party kids. "Am I nearly there?" he asks. "Almost, just mind your step." Jeremy has wandered on to a bus. Neither speaker knows what the other really means. And, so it goes as he steps on a boat that ends up in Egypt and later as he wanders around in Africa. He finally ends up back home where he pins the tail on the donkey correctly, but is accused of cheating and told he must do it all again.

Other Devices: Inference. Irony.

Art Style: Folk.

Briggs, Raymond. *Jim and the Beanstalk.* New York: Coward-McCann, 1970.
As a sequel to Jack, another curious climber finds the giant now beset with the inadequacies of old age and endeavors to fill his needs.

Examples: Boy: "Don't you have any glasses?"
Giant: "Only beer glasses."
Boy: "I mean reading glasses."
Giant: "It's my eyes I'm talking about!"
Other Devices: Parody. Pun. Tone.
Art Style: Colored Cartoon.
Curriculum Tie-In: Social Science (Friendship).

Handforth, Thomas. *Mei Li.* Garden City, NY: Doubleday, 1938. [Caldecott Award]
A resourceful young girl wheedles and buys her way along on a New Year's fair
trip to the city and concludes the best part of the trip is getting home.

Examples: Soon after the fortune teller says she will rule over a kingdom,
Mei Li overhears her mother tell her brother, "You have brought us the prin-
cess who rules our hearts." Mei Li thinks, "Even Mama knows that I am a
princess . . . but where can my kingdom be?" She falsely assumes her royalty is
of the physical world.
Other Devices: Stereotype.
Art Style: Impressionism/Chinese Folk.
Curriculum Tie-In: Social Science (Sexism).

Kahl, Virginia. *How Do You Hide a Monster?* New York: Charles Scribner's, 1971.
Townspeople join forces to lead astray a group of men sent to investigate a
monster in their lake.

Examples: The investigating team complains of a very "vile" and "unsteady
and queer" bridge that is "so shaky we slipped and we slid." They never realize
what the townspeople know. The "bridge" is actually the friendly monster's
"slick back."
Other Devices: Alliteration. Irony.
Art Style: Colored Cartoon.
Curriculum Tie-In: Social Science (Cooperation).

Kellogg, Steven. *Pinkerton, Behave!* New York: Dial, 1979.
Pinkerton fails to learn behavior at obedience training, but when he comes face
to face with a burglar, his bad habits become useful.

Examples: All the commands are mixed up in Pinkerton's mind. For example, "Get-The-Burglar" is interpreted as cuddle and lick and "Fetch" means
shake and tear up the newspaper. Using his system, his family yells "Fetch" to
make Pinkerton shake the burglar and "Come" to make him jump out the
window, dragging along the burglar. When they want a hug they say to
Pinkerton, "I'm a burglar."
Other Devices: Irony.
Art Style: Cartoon.

Koller, Jackie French. *Mole and Shrew Step Out.* Illus. by Stella Ormai. New York: Atheneum, 1992.

Mole commits a comic blunder regarding a fancy ball, but his good friend Shrew sticks by him.

> **Examples:** Mole learns the dress is "black tie and tails." He literally secures other "tails" since he is not sure his own is enough—one from a lizard, who will grow another, one from a kite, and one from a spinning silk worm.
>
> **Other Devices:** Pun.
>
> **Art Style:** Cartoon watercolor.
>
> **Curriculum Tie-In:** Social Science (Friendship).

Levine, Arthur A. *All the Lights in the Night.* Illus. by James E. Ransome. New York: Tambourine Books, 1992.

Moses and his little brother Benjamin find a way to celebrate Hanukkah during a dangerous emigration to Palestine.

> **Examples:** The boys had to sacrifice their precious lamp to pay passage on the ship. The older brother expresses sorrow for its loss and the fact that "Now we have nothing to light for Hanukkah." But the young brother looks to the clear star-filled sky and remarks, "We have all the lights in the night." The light from the lamp is substituted by the stars, and the promise of future nights of light is represented by the freedom they will find in their new land.
>
> **Art Style:** Impressionism oil paintings.
>
> **Curriculum Tie-In:** History (Jewish Emigration from Russia, 1914).

Novak, Matt. *Elmer Blunt's Open House.* New York: Orchard Books, 1992.

Several animals and a robber explore Elmer Blunt's home when he forgets to close the door on his way to work.

> **Examples:** Elmer Blunt knew he left his home in a rush the day he overslept. "I really made a mess this morning," he observes. So he unknowingly proceeds to clean up the results of the animals' play and the burglar's hasty exit. He then settles down in "his safe quiet home."
>
> **Other Devices:** Irony. Pun. Understatement.
>
> **Art Style:** Colored Cartoon.

Rosenberg, Liz. *Monster Mama.* Illus. by Stephen Gammell. New York: Philomel (Putnam & Grosset), 1993.

Patrick Edward's fierce mother helps him deal with some obnoxious bullies.

> **Examples:** Due to his mother's reputation, Patrick Edward is sensitive to any aspersions cast against her. When the hapless bullies throw out a common insult, "Aw, your Mother wears army boots," they have no idea what they did to trigger the kind of violent reaction that turns Patrick Edward into a powerhouse of fury.
>
> **Other Devices:** Aphorism. Hyperbole. Inference. Simile.

Art Style: Expressionism water color.

Curriculum Tie-In: Social Science (Parent and Child).

Turnbull, Ann. *The Tapestry Cats.* Illus. by Carol Morley. Boston: Little, Brown & Co., 1992.

Subdued by her mother who always knows what is best, a princess dreams of having pet cats.

Examples: The princess and queen speak the same words but their meaning differs. The queen says the princess shall have gold and silver for her birthday. The princess has named two cats "Gold" and "Silver" and so can honestly say, "That *is* what I want."

Other Devices: Inference. Simile.

Art Style: Naive.

Williams, Barbara. *Albert's Toothache.* Illus. by Kay Chorao. New York: E. P. Dutton, 1974.

Nobody believes Albert when he complains of a toothache.

Examples: His problem with semantics causes Albert's turtle family to think of other possible reasons why he must really be staying in bed. Perhaps he fears a school bully. Maybe he doesn't like supper. Finally his grandmother thinks to ask him *where* his toothache is and learns it's on his toe and that a gopher bit it. The "toothache" is clarified and easily fixed.

Art Style: Impressionism pencil shading.

Curriculum Tie-In: Social Science (Acceptance and Respect; Family Life).

*****Wilsdorf, Anne.** *Princess.* New York: Greenwillow, 1993.

A girl proves that she is a real princess in an unusual way.

Examples: Though his mother has her doubts about "that raggedy girl" being a "genuine princess," the prince gets his lady with his mother's blessing. The girl is appropriately black and blue and miserable the morning after sleeping on a pile of mattresses with a tiny pea under them. Only the skin of a genuine princess would be delicate enough to feel a pea and be bruised by it. Of course, the facts are something else. Princess forgot how high she was and "fell all the way to the floor." Her bruises had nothing to do with a pea.

Other Devices: Foreshadowing. Parody. Pun. Satire.

Art Style: Cartoon water color.

ANALOGY

An illustrative example of something familiar to explain and clarify something unfamiliar by comparing the likeness of the known thing to the unknown thing, as when a camera is compared by analogy to the human eye.

Example: 'Tis with our judgements as our watches, none go just alike, yet each believes his own.   Pope, *An Essay on Criticism*

SOURCES

Burton, Virginia Lee. *The Little House.* Boston: Houghton Mifflin, 1942. [Caldecott Award]
A personified small house sitting on a hill is happy but wonders what life in the city is all about. When she finds out, she is not happy and longs for the way it used to be.

> **Examples:** Like people, the house longs for something different and is "curious about the city." Once achieved, a desired change may not meet expectations and nostalgia results.
>
> **Other Devices:** Foreshadowing. Personification.
>
> **Art Style:** Naive.
>
> **Curriculum Tie-In:** Social Science (Values).

Lionni, Leo. *Matthew's Dream.* New York: Knopf, 1991.
A visit to an art museum inspires a young mouse to become a painter.

> **Examples:** This simple mouse story introduces art and the artist and serves as a how-to for choosing a life as an artist, a dream come true. Matthew confronts color and style. At night he dreams of art. In the morning his real world is transformed to new beauty by his new artist's eye. He becomes a painter.
>
> **Other Devices:** Pun.
>
> **Art Style:** Collage.

Lionni, Leo. *Swimmy.* New York: Pantheon, 1963.
A small brave fish teaches his fellows that there's safety in numbers.

> **Examples:** In fish or in politics what can't be accomplished by individual action can be achieved through joint effort. By themselves small fish are weak and defenseless against power. But combining and working as a single unit makes them defeat "big fish."
>
> **Art Style:** Collage.
>
> **Curriculum Tie-In:** Social Science (Cooperation).

Williams, Garth. *The Chicken Book.* New York: Delacorte, 1946, 1970.
Some baby chicks express wishes for food and grit.

> **Examples:** Like the baby chicks who want things, people, too, learn they must "scratch" (work) to get their desires. Nothing comes without effort.
>
> **Other Devices:** Foreshadowing. Theme.
>
> **Art Style:** Expressionism/Cartoon.

Yolen, Jane. *Welcome to the Green House.* Illus. by Laura Regan. New York: G. P. Putnam's Sons, 1993.
  Describes the tropical rainforest and the life found there.

  Examples: The wet, hot, green world of the deep rainforest is compared to a greenhouse. Treetops make a roof. Vines frame the window view. Strong lianas make impenetrable walls. Like the plants in a greenhouse, there are accents of bright colors in the animal and bird life found in the rainforest.

  Other Devices: Atmosphere. Imagery. Internal Rhyme. Onomatopoeia. Pun.

  Art Style: Realism/Expressionism.

  Curriculum Tie-In: Science (Rainforest; Ecology).

APHORISM

A brief statement expressing some general truth, sometimes putting a new twist into an old saying. It means the same as "maxim" or "proverb."

  Example: The proper study of mankind is man.
                  Don't count your Boobies before they're hatched.

SOURCES

Baker, Keith. *Who Is the Beast?* New York: Harcourt Brace Jovanovich, 1990.
  When a tiger suspects he is the beast the jungle animals are fleeing from, he returns to them and points out their similarities to his characteristics.

  Examples: "We are all beasts—you and me."

  Art Style: Expressionism.

  Curriculum Tie-In: Social Science (Discrimination; Self-Discovery/Esteem).

Chaucer, Geoffrey. *Chanticleer and the Fox.* Adapted and illus. by Barbara Cooney. New York: Crowell, 1958. [Caldecott Award]
  This is a cautionary tale about a rooster who listened to flattery to his detriment.

  Examples: Chanticleer learns the lesson: "Never again shall you with your flattery get me to sing with my eyes closed. For he who closes his eyes when he should watch, God let him never prosper." Fox learns: "God, bring misfortune to him who is so careless about his self-control as to prattle when he should hold his peace." Don't trust in flattery is the message in this tale.

  Other Devices: Foreshadowing. Simile. Understatement.

  Art Style: Cartoon scratchboard technique with color overlay.

  Curriculum Tie-In: Social Science (Values; Consequences).

Duvoisin, Roger. *Petunia*. New York: Knopf, 1950.

A silly goose carries around a book thinking that it will make her look smart.

> **Examples:** When she discovers finally that simply carrying a book is not sufficient to make one wise, she concludes: "It is not enough to carry wisdom under my wing. I must put it in my mind and in my heart."
>
> **Other Devices:** Irony. Symbol.
>
> **Art Style:** Colored Cartoon.
>
> **Curriculum Tie-In:** Social Science (Values; Self-Discovery/Esteem).

***Gregory, Valiska.** *Through the Mickle Woods*. Illus. by Barry Moser. Boston: Little, Brown & Co., 1992.

After his wife's death, a grieving king journeys to an old bear's cave in the Mickle Woods, where he hears three stories that help him go on living in contentment.

> **Examples:** Whether we are born high or low, the same things come to us all. "The cloth will pattern itself whether we will or no"—life is made up of the good and sad and is only meaningful with each. "My song requires them all"—the fearful as well as the beautiful make up the richness of life.
>
> **Other Devices:** Atmosphere. Inference. Metaphor. Pun. Simile. Symbol. Theme.
>
> **Art Style:** Expressionism/Realism.
>
> **Curriculum Tie-In:** Social Science (Death; Grief).

Ikeda, Daisaku. *The Cherry Tree*. Illus. by Brian Wildsmith. English version by Geraldine McCaughrean. New York: Knopf, 1992, 1991.

After a war destroys their Japanese village and kills their father, Taichi and Yumiko find hope by nursing a cherry tree through a harsh winter and seeing it blossom into new life.

> **Examples:** "With love and patience, nothing is impossible." Through nursing the tree, an old man teaches the village never to give up hope.
>
> **Other Devices:** Symbol.
>
> **Art Style:** Impressionism line drawings.
>
> **Curriculum Tie-In:** Social Science (Coping; War).

Rosenberg, Liz. *Monster Mama*. Illus. by Stephen Gammell. New York: Philomel (Putnam & Grosset), 1993.

Patrick Edward's fierce mother helps him deal with some obnoxious bullies.

> **Examples:** "Strength is for the wise, not the reckless." Patrick Edward is taught to use special skills, but it is his righteous indignation that makes his strength superior to that of the bullies. "Always use your powers for good, never for evil." When he is standing up for his rights and defending his mother's honor, he can roar loudly and even break baseball bats.
>
> **Other Devices:** Ambiguity. Hyperbole. Inference. Simile.

Art Style: Expressionism.

Curriculum Tie-In: Social Science (Parent and Child).

Say, Allen. *Grandfather's Journey*. Boston: Houghton Mifflin, 1993. [Caldecott Award]

A Japanese American man recounts his grandfather's journey to America, his eventual longing to return to his homeland, and his restlessness when he does. The man, too, learns how it feels to be torn by love for two different countries and can empathize with his grandfather.

Examples: It is possible to love two lands and yet not quite feel at home in either. The narrator and his grandfather find themselves in a cross-cultural dilemma. "The moment I am in one country I am homesick for the other." The grown grandson has learned what his grandfather found out.

Other Devices: Atmosphere. Foreshadowing. Irony. Paradox. Parallel Story. Symbol.

Art Style: Impressionism/Expressionism/Folk water color.

Curriculum Tie-In: Social Science (Cross-Cultures; Continuity of Life).

Wolkstein, Diane. *White Wave, a Chinese Tale*. Illus by Ed Young. New York: Thomas Crowell, 1979.

A young Chinese farmer discovers a goddess living in a snail shell.

Examples: "When we die, all that remains is the story." When the old man who experienced moon goddess died, the shell is lost, the shrine to her disappears, and only the story remains through time, which "is how it is with all of us."

Art Style: Impressionism.

ATMOSPHERE

The prevailing mood or feeling developed through descriptions of setting and details about how things look, sound, feel, taste, and smell in order to create an emotional climate that establishes a reader's expectations and attitudes.

Example: Referring to the celebrated jumping frog of Calveras County: "like a solid gob of mud" (light, humorous).

SOURCES

Armstrong, Jennifer. *Hugh Can Do*. Illus. by Kimberly Bulcken Root. New York: Crown, 1992.

Hugh wants to seek his fortune in the city, but first he must find a way to pay the toll-taker at the bridge.

Examples: In a sort of "agricultural period" style, the rhythmic language suits folktale expectations: "Humm, there, young sprout. Say you get me a nice loaf of bread for my lunch. Was you to do that, why, then I'd let you cross! . . . He nibbled and frowned and he pondered and chewed till his loaf was no more than a pile of crumbs. . . . The Toll Man popped out. His long pointed nose sniffled left, sniffled right."

Other Devices: Foreshadowing. Poetic Justice. Pun. Simile.

Art Style: Cartoon water color.

Curriculum Tie-In: Social Science (Coping).

Booth, Barbara. *Mandy.* Illus. by Jim Lamarche. New York: Lothrop, Lee & Shepard, 1991.

Hearing-impaired Mandy risks going out into the scary night during an impending storm to look for her beloved grandmother's lost pin.

Examples: The tender, gentle affection and easy acceptance between these two is demonstrated when the dance music quits before Mandy is ready, and her grandmother senses Mandy's disappointment. Grandma "took her hands and started dancing again . . . their eyes told each other of the fun they were having." After going out to search for the pin, "tears fall on Mandy's head" when Grandma rushes into her arms when she returns safely.

Other Devices: Point-Of-View.

Art Style: Impressionism.

Curriculum Tie-In: Health and Safety (Hearing Impaired).

Brown, Ruth. *The World That Jack Built.* New York: Dutton Children's Books, 1991.

A cat's playful romp after a butterfly provides counterpoint to a cumulative tale about the environment.

Examples: A world of beauty and natural wonders begins the story about the trees, meadow, stream, woods, and hills that are beside the house Jack built. Ominous color changes frighten the cat as the reader sees the land sicken. Next to the factory Jack built, the forest dies; the meadow is sterile; the stream is polluted. This becomes a somber cautionary tale.

Art Style: Impressionism.

Curriculum Tie-In: Science (Environment; Ecology).

Bunting, Eve. *The Wall.* Illus. by Ronald Himler. New York: Clarion (Houghton Mifflin), 1990.

A boy and his father come to the Vietnam Veterans Memorial to find the boy's dead grandfather's name.

Examples: The somber respectful nature of a mysterious monument impresses a little boy. They take a paper rubbing of his grandfather's name with "parts of other guys' names on there, too." But his grandfather won't mind because as his dad tells him, "They were probably friends of his anyway." The wall is viewed from a child's simple perspective. "A bunch of big girls in school uniforms" carry little flags to the monument. The child watches another boy and his grandfather look at the wall. He wishes his own grandfather was there with him and his dad looking together at it.

Other Devices: Point-Of-View.

Art Style: Realism.

Curriculum Tie-In: History (Vietnam Memorial)
Social Science (War).

Caudill, Rebecca. *A Pocketful of Cricket.* Illus. by Evaline Ness. New York: Holt Rinehart Winston, 1964.

A small child's affection for his world is beautifully expressed as a young farm boy loves the sights and sounds of everything around him.

Examples: "The dirt under his feet felt soft and warm. He spread his toes and watched the dust squirt between them." A gentle, slow-paced, bucolic environment is evoked. He watches a yellow butterfly "fan its wings—open and shut, open and shut." He follows behind the cows. "Nodding their heads and switching their tails, they walked, one behind another, along the cow path beside the fence."

Other Devices: Imagery.

Art Style: Expressionism.

Curriculum Tie-In: Science (Ecology).

Crews, Donald. *Shortcut.* New York: Greenwillow, 1992.

Children taking a shortcut by walking along a railroad track find excitement and danger when a train approaches.

Examples: A real sense of fear and heightened emotion is created by the progression of events and the large-print type. First is the apparent sense of safety: "We looked. . . . We listened. . . . We decided to take the shortcut home." Then the small note of concern: "whoo." And then one child definitely hears it. "I HEAR A TRAIN!" Finally, the strong warnings: "THE TRAIN! THE TRAIN! GET OFF! GET OFF! GET OFF THE TRACKS!"

Other Devices: Foreshadowing. Inference.

Art Style: Impressionism paint spatter.

Curriculum Tie-In: Social Science (Fear).

DePaola, Tomie. *Nanna Upstairs and Nanna Downstairs.* New York: G. P. Putnam's, 1973.

Tommy loved weekly visits to his grandmother downstairs and his great-grandmother upstairs. When Nanna upstairs dies, it is the closeness of his loving family that comforts him and helps him accept her death.

Examples: The tender description of these and other relatives indicates a gentle reverence for their unique differences. The upstairs grandmother always invites him to open her sewing box and help himself to candy mints inside. When 94-year-old Nanna has to be tied into her chair, 4-year-old Tommy asks to be tied into his chair. "They would eat their candy and talk." He would watch the grandmothers as they combed out their long silver-white hair and make of it a "cow's tail." He strongly refutes his brother when he says the hair made them look like witches. "She does not! She's beautiful." The whole family is remembered with love. There is lap time with mother, who explains, "Died means that Nanna Upstairs won't be here anymore" and "she will come back in your memory whenever you think about her."

Other Devices: Flash-Forward. Pun.

Art Style: Cartoon.

Curriculum Tie-In: Social Science (Death; Aging; Grandparents).

Dunrea, Olivier. *Eppie M. Says.* . . . New York: Macmillan, 1990.
Life on the farm is never dull for Ben, who faithfully follows his big sister's advice.

Examples: The illustrations mark a contrast to the quiet text. Zany, incongruous, hallucinatory art abounds. There are flying chickens and eggs with feet.

Art Style: Cartoon/Surrealism.

Ets, Marie Hall, and Aurora Labastida. *Nine Days to Christmas.* New York: Viking, 1959. [Caldecott Award]
Ceci experiences her first Christmas *posada* party with the pinata of her choice.

Examples: The ambience of the traditional Mexican market life is shown through descriptions of people and events. At the corner tortillas are being made and bought. At the gate to the street is an "old man too poor to have shoes . . . carrying such a heavy load on his back that he almost had to run to keep from falling." There are two village women "with babies on their backs and their arms full of flowers for the market." On Sunday, the servant "Maria went home to her village." The market sells "candies and toys and sparklers and painted clay figures of Joseph and Mary and the donkey." And, "swinging and turning in the wind, were the pinatas."

Art Style: Spanish Folk.

Curriculum Tie-In: Geography (Mexican Culture).

Fowler, Susi Gregg. *Fog.* Illus. by Jim Fowler. New York: Greenwillow Books (William Morrow), 1992.
A visitation by deep fog traps a family in their house and enables them to rediscover their love of making music.

Examples: The fog makes the family uneasy. Dad says "better stay inside." Little sister looks scared. "What's going to happen?" she cries. Mama says, "Nothing's going to happen," but "she was worried." The dog whimpers. Grandma enigmatically says, "The fog wants something." Mama doesn't "like the sound of that" and shudders. They all get "the shivers." The mood changes at once when Grandma announces the fog "came for music." There is laughing, dancing, and the "house didn't seem gloomy and frightening anymore." Mama and Daddy "haven't had so much fun in ages."

Other Devices: Theme.

Art Style: Expressionism.

Curriculum Tie-In: Social Science (Family Life; Values).

Goffstein, M. B. *My Noah's Ark.* New York: Harper & Row, 1978.
An old woman fondly remembers a lifetime of experiences related to a carved representation of Noah's ark that she's had since childhood.

Examples: There is tender nostalgia and whimsical humor in these reminiscences. The Noah her father carved "had a hammer in one hand and a mop in the other, and Mrs. Noah carried a saw." The gray horse he carved "looked sad, and I always stroked her with my finger until to this day there is not much paint left on her, except for her two little eyes, which look grateful." Though the woman's new husband teased her about the toy, ". . . how gently he carried the ark to my new home." And, now at aged 90 with everyone gone, "the ark holds their memories." It "warms one like sunshine."

Other Devices: Allusion.

Art Style: Naive/Cartoon.

Curriculum Tie-In: Social Science (Aging; Values).

Graham, Lorenz. *Song of the Boat.* Illus. by Leo Dillon and Diane Dillon. New York: Thomas Crowell, 1975.
Momolu's father Flumbo lost his canoe in a fight with an alligator. The two set out to find the special tree from which a new canoe can be fashioned.

Examples: Ambience is of traditional West African life style. When the father lost his boat, "him heart no lay down, cause he no got boat." In politeness, people offer him the use of their boats. He pretends he doesn't need a boat. "Flumbo laugh for him mouth. But Flumbo no laugh for him heart." The son and father each show respect for the other on their long journey. The boy doesn't wish to show his tiredness: "Leg be strong past belly; leg say 'go,' belly say 'stop.'" The father understands and to enable the boy to save face, says: "Belly got sense."

Art Style: African Folk woodcut.

Curriculum Tie-In: Geography (West African Culture).

***Gregory, Valiska.** *Through the Mickle Woods.* Illus. by Barry Moser. Boston: Little, Brown and Company, 1992.

> After his wife's death, a grieving king journeys to an old bear's cave in the Mickle Woods, where he hears three stories that help him to go on living.

>> **Examples:** The motif of the Middle Ages comes through strongly in the gloomy, mystical bowing to fate. The image of a dark crow's wing is compared to a cloak. Icicles are described like daggers. Though his traveling companion tries to lift the king's mood by remarking how his breath "makes words in the air," the king merely reminds him that "the way is hard. . . . You'd best save your breath."

>> **Other Devices:** Aphorism. Inference. Metaphor. Pun. Simile. Symbol. Theme.

>> **Art Style:** Expressionism/Realism.

>> **Curriculum Tie-In:** Social Science (Death; Grief).

Hall, Donald. *Ox-Cart Man.* Illus. by Barbara Cooney. New York: Viking, 1979. [Caldecott Award]

> Narration describes day-to-day life throughout the changing seasons of an early nineteenth-century New England family.

>> **Examples:** In this thrifty era, "everything they made or grew all year long that was left over," went to market, even the cart that hauled the goods and even the ox that pulled the cart. Then the whole process begins all over again when the new year begins. It starts with new harness for the young ox, a new cart, and all the goods produced on the farm. Life is fulfilling and purposeful. Personal gains and improvements are shown in small, steady progress. Besides the necessary needle for embroidery, there is peppermint candy simply for pleasure. Everyone has worth and importance in the family unit.

>> **Art Style:** Naive.

>> **Curriculum Tie-In:** History (Nineteenth-Century America-Frontier Life).

Johnson, Angela. *One of Three.* Illus. by David Soman. New York: Orchard Books, 1991.

> The youngest of three sisters reflects candidly about her daily relationships with her older sisters and her family.

>> **Examples:** She likes doing things with the two sisters but is devastated and angry to be left behind when they go off by themselves. Mom helps by inviting her to paint together. Dad says she has to be the baby, just sometimes. A new threesome is "fine too." The tenderness of helping a child overcome abandonment is evident in text and art.

>> **Art Style:** Realism.

>> **Curriculum Tie-In:** Social Science (Acceptance and Respect; Jealousy; Parent and Child; Self-Discovery/Esteem; Siblings).

Johnston, Tony. *The Cowboy and the Black-Eyed Pea.* Illus. by Warren Ludwig. New York: G. P. Putnam's, 1992.

The wealthy daughter of a Texas rancher devises a plan to find a real cowboy among her many suitors.

> **Examples:** Colorful western language evokes a stereotyped view of how the hard-hitting, jolly Old West may never have been. "Her daddy was fixing to leave her all his worldly goods, . . . rich men will flock here like flies to pralines, seeking your hand in marriage, bristling with pistols and brag, . . . didn't know the front end of a horse from the rear, . . . fetched another blanket . . . sorely needed more, . . . just a-working and a-rubbing and causing him no end of pain, . . . thunder spooked the longhorns something awful, . . . set up a fearsome bawling, . . . produced by that vexatious black-eyed pea, . . . like as not, the rampaging longhorns would squash both man and horse, . . . the pea commenced to work at him."
>
> **Other Devices:** Caricature. Inference. Parody. Simile.
>
> **Art Style:** Colored Cartoon.

Keats, Ezra Jack. *The Snowy Day.* New York: Viking, 1962. [Caldecott Award]

The magic and sense of possibility in a first snowfall are evoked—snowmen to build, snowballs to pack, mountains to climb, snow angels to carve, and snowbanks to collapse in.

> **Examples:** There is ephemeral delight in the simplicity and newness of snow as it's savored for the first time. There is the promise of added enjoyment when the child invites a friend to play with him. A stick makes an interesting track and interesting effect on the snow. He watches a snowball fight and "knew he wasn't old enough—not yet." He slides down a "heaping mountain of snow" and is delighted to find snow still falling the next day.
>
> **Other Devices:** Imagery.
>
> **Art Style:** Collage.
>
> **Curriculum Tie-In:** Science (Seasons—Winter).

Lamorisse, Albert. *The Red Balloon.* Garden City, NY: Doubleday, 1956.

A lonely boy and a red balloon become companions.

> **Examples:** A harsh and dangerous environment for gentle things is depicted in a city devoid of understanding. A resourceful child isn't allowed to keep pets. So the boy and his balloon cope loyally against gangs of young thugs and insensitive adults who try to separate them. His mother tries to throw away the balloon; school masters and bus drivers won't let it inside; kids try to steal it and finally to destroy it. An instinct for survival wins out over all.
>
> **Other Devices:** Poetic Justice. Symbol.
>
> **Art Style:** Photography.
>
> **Curriculum Tie-In:** Social Science (Loneliness).

Mahy, Margaret. *Keeping House.* Illus. by Wendy Smith. New York: Margaret K. McElderry Books (Macmillan), 1991.

Lizzie Firkin has no time to keep house because she works at night at a famous club singing and tap dancing and playing trombone. So she is too tired to sweep the floor or clean cupboards.

Examples: What kind of place is it? It is "a rough-and-tumble house—unwashed, undusted, and topsy-turvy." And the cupboards must be nailed shut to keep things from falling out. Lizzie is too busy practicing her trombone, dying her hair, painting a few extra designs on her clothes. "The cat was curled up in the breadbox, asleep on the sliced bread. The parrot was molting." No place is more in need of Robin Puckertucker, the answer to a busy person's housekeeping needs.

Other Devices: Hyperbole. Inference. Simile. Stereotype.

Art Style: Impressionism.

Martin, Jacqueline Briggs. *Good Times on Grandfather Mountain.* Illus. by Susan Gaber. New York: Orchard Books, 1992.

Mountain man Washburn insists on looking on the bright side of things, even as disaster after disaster befalls him.

Examples: The mountain man takes life casually and ends up just fine. He could make "a spider out of a stick of wood—he was that good." Each time trouble comes, he is philosophical. The cow jumps the fence and he remarks, "I guess she got an itch to travel." When a fierce mountain storm blows down his cabin, he says, "I've slept under stars before." There was "some pretty good wood in this pile," so he makes himself "a fancy fiddle." And, of course, his casual, accepting attitude is just right. He makes music and the neighbors "romped and stomped . . . and danced until their shoes fell off." The animals return; the neighbors help him rebuild, and life is grand, mountain style.

Other Devices: Tone.

Art Style: Expressionism.

Curriculum Tie-In: Social Science (Coping).

McCloskey, Robert. *One Morning in Maine.* New York: Viking, 1952.

A little girl experiences the loss of her first baby tooth one Maine morning.

Examples: This is simply an ordinary day in the life of a child who is loved and comfortable in her environment by the sea. She digs clams with her father, gets an ice cream cone from the store clerk, watches a fish hawk, a loon, a seal, and gulls, falls down on slippery seaweed, listens to folks' everyday talk about lobster trapping and biting fish, and goes to the repair shop with her father to get a spark plug for their outboard motor. The vivid setting makes the difference in this common event in the life of all children.

Other Devices: Inference.

Art Style: Impressionism/Cartoon pencil shading.

Curriculum Tie-In: Health and Safety (Maturation).
Geography (Maine).

McCully, Emily Arnold. *Mirette on the High Wire.* New York: G. P. Putnam's Sons, 1992. [Caldecott Award]
Mirette learns tightrope walking from Monsieur Bellini, a guest in her mother's boarding house. She does not realize he is a celebrated artist who has withdrawn from performing because of fear.

> **Examples:** Through art and language the reader is drawn into the magic of Parisian society "one hundred years ago, . . . when theaters and music halls drew traveling players from all over the world." The boarding house becomes a cozy dining salon where folks "devoured . . . kidney stews" and reclined on "feather mattresses." The child Mirette sits in the shadows on stair steps enthralled "to overhear the vagabond players tell of their adventures in this town and that along the road." And, when she goes out to retrieve laundry and sees the enchanting stranger "crossing the courtyard on air," she knows instantly "of all the things a person could do, this must be the most magical."
>
> **Other Devices:** Inference.
>
> **Art Style:** Impressionism water color.
>
> **Curriculum Tie-In:** Social Science (Courage).

Say, Allen. *Grandfather's Journey.* Boston: Houghton Mifflin, 1993. [Caldecott Award]
A Japanese American man recounts his grandfather's journey to America, his eventual longing to return to his homeland, and his restlessness when he does. The man, too, learns how it feels to be torn by love for two different countries and can empathize with his grandfather.

> **Examples:** Told in short, spare, straightforward sentences, the simple, unadorned facts produce poignant reminiscences. The man recounts, "The last time I saw him, my grandfather said that he longed to see California one more time. He never did." First the grandfather, and later, the grandson return to the country they miss when they "can not still the longing in my heart."
>
> **Other Devices:** Aphorism. Foreshadowing. Irony. Paradox. Parallel Story. Symbol.
>
> **Art Style:** Impressionism/Expressionism water color.
>
> **Curriculum Tie-In:** Social Science (Cross-Cultures; Continuity of Life)

*Say, Allen. *Tree of Cranes.* Boston: Houghton Mifflin, 1991.
A Japanese boy learns of Christmas when his mother decorates a pine tree with paper cranes.

Examples: A quiet, sensitive, loving dignity exists between mother and child. Mother knows he has visited the forbidden pond. "Mama frowned and gave me a silent stare. . . . She knew." The boy knows when his mother is thinking about California. "She was remembering. She was seeing another tree in a faraway place where she had been small like me."

Other Devices: Flash-Forward. Inference. Point-Of-View.

Art Style: Oriental Folk/Realism.

Curriculum Tie-In: Social Sciences (Cross-Cultures).

Shulevitz, Uri. *Dawn.* New York: Farrar Straus Giroux, 1974.
A grandfather and his grandson awake on a peaceful morning to experience dawn arrive in a mountain lake setting.

Examples: A sense of day beginning is shown and described. The "moon lights a rock, a branch, an occasional leaf." The shadow of the mountain beside the lake "stands guard, dark and silent." A light breeze "shivers" the lake and "vapors" arise. Soon a bat circles, a frog jumps, and a bird calls. "Suddenly" the mountain and lake turn brilliant green as the sun brings about an everyday miracle.

Other Devices: Imagery.

Art Style: Impressionism pen and ink water color.

Curriculum Tie-In: Science (Meteorology; Environment; Sun).

Steig, William. *The Amazing Bone.* New York: Farrar Straus Giroux, 1976.
A talking bone saves a charming piglet from being food for a fox.

Examples: The language is redolent with ghoulish, deliciously gross, humor. "You coward," the bone sneers. "You worm, you odoriferous wretch." The fox retorts, "It would be amusing to gnaw on a bone that talks . . . and screams with pain." He says to the piglet, "You're exactly what I've been longing for . . . young, plump, and tender. You will be my main course at dinner tonight. And he seized Pearl in a tight embrace."

Other Devices: Caricature. Foreshadowing. Inference. Irony.

Art Style: Cartoon water color.

ver Dorn, Berthea. *Moon Glows.* Illus. by Thomas Graham. New York: Arcade (Little, Brown & Co.), 1990.
Moonlight falls on city and country. Creatures snuggle down to sleep in their own special night light but all share the moon's glow.

Examples: This is a soothing, peaceful day's end. A sleepy cat curls up at the window. A sleepy fish is silent and still. A sleepy turtle tucks himself in his shell. Etc.

Art Style: Impressionism.

*Yolen, Jane. *Encounter*. Illus. by David Shannon. New York: Harcourt Brace Jovanovich, 1992.

A Taino Indian boy on the island of San Salvador recounts the landing of Columbus and his men in 1492.

Examples: "A clap of thunder woke me from my dream." This ominous sign of trouble ahead begins the boy's account. Immediately, he doesn't trust the stranger who "made a funny noise with his mouth, not like talking but like barking of a yellow dog." He observes how the strangers "touched our golden nose rings and golden arm bands but not the flesh of our faces or arms." He sees the chief's eyes were "blue and gray like the shifting sea." They are patted on the head much like a child would pat a dog. He sees no respect from these strangers and predicts that "our blood would cry out in the sand."

Other Devices: Flash-Forward. Foreshadowing. Metaphor. Point-Of-View. Stereotype. Theme.

Art Style: Realism/Expressionism acrylic.

Curriculum Tie-In: History (Columbus-Discovery of America).

Yolen, Jane. *Welcome to the Green House*. Illus. by Laura Regan. New York: G. P. Putnam's, 1993.

Describes the tropical rainforest and the life found there.

Examples: The lush, wet, warm world of shades of green is compared to the feeling of being inside a humid, colorful greenhouse. The richness of animal and plant life living in harmony and fullness creates a feeling of canopies, walls, windows, and paths for the sunshine to filter through.

Other Devices: Analogy. Imagery. Internal Rhyme. Onomatopoeia. Pun.

Art Style: Realism/Expressionism.

Curriculum Tie-In: Science (Rainforest; Ecology).

*Zolotow, Charlotte. *The Moon Was the Best*. Photographs by Tana Hoban. New York: Greenwillow Books, 1993.

A mother visiting Paris brings back to her daughter all her best memories of beautiful fountains, the sparkling Seine, parks, and paintings.

Examples: Here is depicted the special ambience that is Paris. Birds "waken people in the middle of the city!" The sky can be seen everywhere "because the buildings are low." The Seine sparkles from one side of Paris to the other. Bookstalls line the stone wall above the riverbank. People carry unwrapped bread "like sticks under their arms." And flowers are part of everyday life, even in the "window of the corner butcher shop."

Other Devices: Imagery.

Art Style: Photography.

Curriculum Tie-In: Geography (Paris, France).

CARICATURE

Use of exaggeration or distortion (physical characteristic, eccentricity, personality trait, or exaggerated act) to make a figure appear comic or ridiculous.

Example: "Droll little mouth drawn up like a bow . . . belly, that shook like a bowl full of jelly." ("Night before Christmas" Santa description.)

SOURCES

Goble, Paul. *Iktomi and the Berries, a Plains Indian Story.* New York: Orchard Books (Franklin Watts, Inc.), 1989.
Iktomi shows how not to go hunting for buffalo berries or much of anything else.

Examples: The boastful Iktomi is the epitome of the poor hunter, as he is meant to be, to teach youth how not to behave. He sets out to impress relatives by getting prairie dogs to make a feast. (Who would want to eat them?) His wolf costume is so cumbersome he succeeds in scaring away his prey and then accuses the white men of spoiling the habitat for his quarry. He falls into the water while stalking the ducks and sees the reflection of berries from some bushes growing on shore. Maybe fruit soup would impress the relatives. He dives into the stream after the berries, finally realizes his mistake, and angrily beats the bushes that are growing along the shore. All the berries drop into the water and float away for a snack the ducks enjoy.

Art Style: Folk pen and ink.

Curriculum Tie-In: Social Science (Foolish Behavior).
History (Native Americans).

Johnston, Tony. *The Cowboy and the Black-Eyed Pea.* Illus. by Warren Ludwig. New York: G. P. Putnam's, 1992.
The wealthy daughter of a Texas rancher devises a plan to find a real cowboy among her many suitors.

Examples: "Out where coyotes serenade the moon and sagebrush grays the land, there lived a young woman of bodacious beauty." In western-style exaggerated motifs there exists "the biggest spread in the great state of Texas." Callers came as "tall as a tree . . . with a moustache as big as tarnation, prideful as roosters, spurs a-jingling, bristling with pistols and brag, fringes galore, neckerchief a-flying, and fresh as a Texas morning."

Other Devices: Atmosphere. Inference. Parody. Simile.

Art Style: Colored Cartoon.

McCloskey, Robert. *Make Way for Ducklings.* New York: Viking, 1941. [Caldecott Award]

A mallard family chooses to raise its family in a rather inappropriate setting.

Examples: "She was so proud she tipped her nose in the air and walked along with an extra swing in her waddle." This mother duck appreciates the admiring glances from those she passes and makes herself and her children the center of attention. It is of no concern to her that she brings all the city's street traffic to a halt when she wishes to take the children to the park.

Other Devices: Foreshadowing. Point-Of-View.

Art Style: Cartoon.

Curriculum Tie-In: Literature (Pacing of Story).

McKissack, Patricia. *A Million Fish ... More or Less.* Illus. by Dena Schutzer. New York: Knopf, 1992.

A boy learns that the truth is often stretched on the Bayou Clapateaux and gets the chance to practice what he has learned when he tells his own version of a bayou tale.

Examples: Such folk as the southern bayou produces will lean back on old cane chairs on their houseboat front porch and prop their feet on the railing. They swap tales about the "mighty peculiar place" where "strange things do happen." When the outrageous story is finished, they always snap their suspenders and wink.

Other Devices: Foreshadowing. Hyperbole. Inference.

Art Style: Impressionism/Expressionism paint.

Curriculum Tie-In: Social Science (Self-Discovery/Esteem).

McNaughton, Colin. *Guess Who Just Moved in Next Door?* New York: Random House, 1991.

A tour through a very peculiar neighborhood where an assortment of wacky neighbors from Superman to a ship of pirates reacts to the arrival of new neighbors.

Examples: There are recognizable renderings of Hell's Angels, Humpty Dumpty's egg family, graveyard ghosts, Frankenstein's monster, outer space aliens, and pirates, all of whom are super stereotypes.

Other Devices: Allusion. Irony. Parallel Story. Pun. Satire.

Art Style: Cartoon.

Steig, William. *The Amazing Bone.* New York: Farrar Straus Giroux, 1976.

A talking bone saves a charming piglet from being food for a fox.

Examples: The fox is endowed with all the classic, cunning, heartless traits attributed to his species: "grinning so the whole world could see his sharp white teeth, . . . not so easily duped, . . . determined she would be his dinner,...

Why should I be ashamed? I can't help being the way I am. I didn't make the world. . . . I regret having to do this to you, . . . It's nothing personal."

Other Devices: Atmosphere. Foreshadowing. Inference. Irony.

Art Style: Cartoon water color.

Zemach, Harve. *The Judge.* Illus. by Margot Zemach. New York: Farrar Straus Giroux, 1969.

A judge's mistrust of people leads to a disastrous confrontation with a monster.

Examples: In a terrible indictment on justice, the judge behaves with foolish obstinacy, railing at innocent witnesses and accusing them of ignorance and untruthfulness. He has made up his mind without listening to evidence. In his blind arrogance he must face alone the monster he has declared does not exist.

Other Devices: Foreshadowing. Hyperbole. Poetic Justice. Satire. Theme.

Art Style: Expressionism.

Curriculum Tie-In: Social Science (Consequences; Foolish Behavior).

FLASHBACK

Interruption of present action to insert an episode that took place at an earlier time for the purpose of giving the reader information to make the present situation understandable or account for a character's current motivation.

Example: "In compliance with the request of a friend of mine, who wrote me from the East, I called on good-natured, garrulous old Simon Wheeler and inquired after my friend's friend, Leonidas W. Smiley. . . . I have a lurking suspicion that Leonidas W. Smiley is a myth . . . and that he only conjectured that if I asked old Wheeler about him, it would remind him of his infamous Jim Smiley, and he would go to work and bore me to death with some exasperating reminiscence of him. . . . If that was the design, it succeeded. I found Simon Wheeler dozing comfortably by the bar-room stove . . ."

Mark Twain—*The Notorious Jumping Frog of Calaveras County*

SOURCES

Ballard, Robin. *Gracie.* New York: Greenwillow, 1993.

Gracie describes life in her two separate homes, one with her mother and one with her father.

Examples: Gracie says, "I wonder what it was like when my parents were together." The illustrations, occurring in gray tones of yesteryear, show a school romance, a wedding, and a hospital room with parents holding a new infant.

Art Style: Naive colored line drawings.

Curriculum Tie-In: Social Science (Divorce; Family Life).

Baylor, Byrd. *One Small Blue Bead.* Illus. by Ronald Himler. New York: Charles Scribner's, text: 1965, illus.: 1992.

A boy makes it possible for an old man in their primitive tribe to go in search of other men in far-off places.

Examples: "Listen to the wind . . . and try to let time blow away, away back to a dim and ancient day." Thus, begins a story that moves immediately from the present to the distant past and back to the present again.

Other Devices: Flash-Forward

Art Style: Realism/Impressionism.

Curriculum Tie-In: History (Pre-History).

Dragonwagon, Crescent. *Home Place.* Illus. by Jerry Pinkney. New York: Macmillan, 1990.

While out hiking, a family comes upon the site of an old house and finds some clues about the people who once lived there.

Examples: "Can you listen, back, far back?" People from another past time suddenly live again. They sing, eat fried chicken, braid long hair, swing in an uneven swing in the black walnut tree, wash dishes, swat at mosquitoes, and watch thunderstorms—just like now.

Other Devices: Imagery.

Art Style: Impressionism.

Curriculum Tie-In: Social Science (Continuity of Life).

Johnston, Tony. *The Promise.* Illus. by Pamela Keavney. New York: A Charlotte Zolotow Book (HarperCollins), 1992.

While helping her neighbor assist one of the cows in giving birth, Ramie hears a story of another birth helped by a young person also interested in cows.

Examples: During the long night of calving, Mr. Gates begins, "Once, long ago . . . a rancher named Willis had a cow." Thus begins a story that ties together the past and the present.

Other Devices: Foreshadowing. Inference. Stereotype (Reverse).

Art Style: Impressionism.

Kellogg, Steven. *The Mystery of the Missing Red Mitten.* New York: Dial, 1974.

When Annie loses her fifth mitten of the winter, she begins to backtrack her day's activities to see where she left it.

Examples: Her activities throughout the day are revealed as she returns to search for the red mitten. There was sledding with Ralph, castle building with Ruth and Herman, making snow angels, and constructing the snowman to surprise Miss Seltzer. By the time Annie drinks hot chocolate with Miss Seltzer, the reader is up to date on her ventures and the mystery is about to be solved.

Art Style: Cartoon.

Pirotta, Saviour. *Solomon's Secret.* Illus. by Helen Cooper. New York: Dial, 1989.
When Solomon visits his neighbors for afternoon tea, he discovers their back-yard harbors exotic adventure.

Examples: Most of his friends think the Zees are strange and a bit scary. But Solomon "knew the secret. . . . It had all started the summer before, when Solomon and his Dad baked cinnamon rolls." The reader learns what happens when folks visit the interesting Zees.

Art Style: Expressionism.

Schermbrucker, Reviva. *Charlie's House.* Illus. by Niki Daly. New York: Viking Penguin, 1989.
After some men build Charlie's house with cement, pole supports, and iron sheet walls and roof, Charlie fashions his own version of a house from clay mud and scraps of trash.

Examples: The story opens with the family living in their tin shelter and flashes back to one summer when men constructed it.

Other Devices: Inference.

Art Style: Expressionism.

Weiss, Nicki. *Stone Men.* New York: Greenwillow, 1993.
Grandma tells Arnie how a poor peddler, with the help of the stone men he always made for companions, saved a village from being destroyed by soldiers.

Examples: Near the conclusion of the story, when Arnie asks if it really happened, "Grandma reached over to the bookcase. She took something from a shelf . . . a man made of stone." Grandma says she had been a child back then and witnessed it all. Grandma concludes the story in the present time.

Art Style: Colored Cartoon/Naive.

FLASH-FORWARD

Sudden jump forward in time from chronologically narrated events to a later time in which the story usually progresses to its conclusion.

Example: Martha angrily threw the toy locomotive, and although it missed her brother Albert, a tiny piece of mama's precious mantel clock disappeared. One dainty leg was gone. The clock listed clumsily.

Martha tenderly touched the rough place where the missing leg had been. Carefully rewrapping the clock in its tissue, she laid it back into the old trunk as her grandchildren slammed the kitchen door. Someday she would share her memories with them.

SOURCES

Ackerman, Karen. *Just Like Max.* Illus. by George Schmidt. New York: Knopf, 1990.

When Great Uncle Max, the tailor, becomes sick and can no longer sew, nephew Aaron becomes his "hands," and together they create something special.

Examples: "Forty years later" begins the jump into the future. The narration then changes to first person as history repeats itself. Now it's Uncle Aaron in the 4th-floor loft who sits working at a long table, the way his Uncle Max had done, and it's now Uncle Aaron who hears a mother admonish, "Don't be a bother—he has a living to make."

Art Style: Impressionism/Realism.

Curriculum Tie-In: Social Science (Continuity of Life; Family Life).

Baylor, Byrd. *One Small Blue Bead.* Illus. by Ronald Himler. New York: Charles Scribner's, text: 1965, illus.: 1992.

A boy makes it possible for an old man in their primitive tribe to go in search of other men in far-off places.

Examples: "Now the blue bead lies in a sandy place . . . if you find it please take care not to leave it just anywhere, for the boy named Boy would be happy to know that his bead goes with you wherever you go." After the long-ago events are narrated, the author uses the blue bead as a bridge between then and now.

Other Devices: Flashback.

Art Style: Realism/Impressionism.

Curriculum Tie-In: History (Pre-History).

DePaola, Tomie. *Nanna Upstairs and Nanna Downstairs.* New York: G. P. Putnam's, 1973.

Tommy loved weekly visits to his grandmother downstairs and his great-grandmother upstairs. When Nanna upstairs dies, it is the closeness of his loving family that comforts him and helps him accept her death.

Examples: The story setting begins showing young Tommy's relationship with his two grandmothers. At the end, time has skipped to "a long time later, when Tommy had grown up."

Other Devices: Atmosphere. Pun.

Art Style: Cartoon.

Curriculum Tie-In: Social Science (Death; Aging; Grandparents).

Lyon, George Ella. *Cecil's Story.* Illus. by Peter Catalanotto. New York: Orchard Books, 1991.

A boy thinks about the possible scenarios that exist for him at home if his father goes off to fight in the Civil War.

Examples: The boy sits at breakfast and imagines his life if his father gets injured and his mother must go fetch him home.

Other Devices: Point-Of-View.

Art Style: Expressionism.

Riddle, Tohby. *Careful with That Ball, Eugene!* New York: Orchard Books, 1991.

Eugene's ball heads for the neighbor's window.

Examples: Eugene pictures all the appalling fates that await him when the ball strikes the window. In that split second after his disastrous kick, he sees himself in exile for the rest of his life.

Other Devices: Hyperbole.

Art Style: Cartoon.

***Rylant, Cynthia.** *An Angel for Solomon Singer.* Illus. by Peter Catalanotto. New York: Orchard Books, 1992.

A lonely New York City resident finds companionship and good cheer at the Westway Cafe where dreams come true.

Examples: "Solomon Singer went to the Westway Cafe every night for dinner that first year *and he dines there still.*"

Other Devices: Irony. Symbol.

Art Style: Impressionism water color.

Curriculum Tie-In: Social Science (Loneliness).

***Say, Allen.** *Tree of Cranes.* Boston: Houghton Mifflin, 1991.

A Japanese boy learns of Christmas when his mother decorates a pine tree with paper cranes.

Examples: The story begins, "When I was not yet old enough to wear long pants," but ends, "And like the snowman we made, many years have melted away now."

Other Devices: Atmosphere. Inference. Point-Of-View.

Art Style: Oriental Folk/Realism.

Curriculum Tie-In: Social Sciences (Cross-Cultures).

Scheller, Melanie. *My Grandfather's Hat.* Illus. by Keiko Narahashi. New York: Margaret K. McElderry Books (Macmillan), 1992.

A boy's relationship with his grandfather is remembered through vignettes with a 17-year-old hat.

Examples: The boy describes in detail his relationship with his grandfather, then says, "My grandfather died two months ago." The rest of the story covers the time without his grandfather.

Other Devices: Symbol.

Art Style: Impressionism.

Curriculum Tie-In: Social Science (Grandparents; Acceptance and Respect; Aging).

Yashima, Taro. *Umbrella.* New York: Viking, 1958.

Momo is three when she receives red rubber boots and an umbrella for her birthday. She eagerly looks forward to a chance to use them.

Examples: Near the end, the author says, "Momo is a big girl now, and this is a story she does not remember at all."

Other Devices: Onomatopoeia. Simile. Tone.

Art Style: Impressionism paint.

Curriculum Tie-In: Social Science (Self-Discovery/Esteem).

*****Yolen, Jane.** *Encounter.* Illus. by David Shannon. New York: Harcourt Brace Jovanovich, 1992.

A Taino Indian boy on the island of San Salvador recounts the landing of Columbus and his men in 1492.

Examples: "So it was we lost our lands to the strangers from the sky. That is why, I, an old man now dream no more dreams." The story starts with the boy young and awakened from a dream. It ends many years later with an old island man wearing western clothes and sitting on a tree stump looking off into the ocean.

Other Devices: Atmosphere. Foreshadowing. Metaphor. Point-Of-View. Stereotype. Theme.

Art Style: Realism/Expressionism acrylic.

Curriculum Tie-In: History (Columbus-Discovery of America).

FORESHADOWING

A device that provides clues to alert the reader about events that will occur later in the narrative. It serves to build suspense.

Example: Nothing could go wrong on such a perfect day. Or so I, in my childlike innocence, thought.

SOURCES

Agee, Jon. *The Return of Freddy Le Grand*. New York: Farrar Straus Giroux, 1992.
Pilot Freddy's adventures come full circle when he is found and befriended by the farm couple who rescued him the first time he crashed.

> **Examples:** Luckily Freddy is found by Sophie and Albert, farmers who reveal a down-to-earth flair for aerodynamics. "Late into the night, Freddy told them all he knew about airplanes" including "basic flying principles." This knowledge will prove helpful to the hapless Freddy when the couple fly to his rescue yet again.
>
> **Other Devices:** Understatement.
>
> **Art Style:** Cartoon.

Armstrong, Jennifer. *Hugh Can Do*. Illus. by Kimberly Bulcken Root. New York: Crown, 1992.
Hugh wants to seek his fortune in the city, but first he must find a way to pay the toll-taker at the bridge.

> **Examples:** The young man who wished to seek his fortune in the city is "poor as a rabbit but quick as a fox." Surely, one so confident as to dream about "his fortune, and how he would make it, and where, and how soon" will prevail.
>
> **Other Devices:** Atmosphere. Poetic Justice. Pun. Simile
>
> **Art Style:** Cartoon water color.
>
> **Curriculum Tie-In:** Social Science (Coping).

*****Babbitt, Natalie.** *Phoebe's Revolt*. New York: Farrar Straus Giroux, 1968.
Stubborn Phoebe detests her dresses "of fluff and lace . . . and everything to do with girls." But when her father permits her to wear his clothes, they don't quite suit either.

> **Examples:** The women of the household are too close to the problem and can only see a rebellious child who must be made to see how her clothes are like other girls' clothes. These girls all seem "to be content enough." Only father "has his doubts" when the women plan a party designed to "change her mind" so she will "want to be like the rest." Father is described as "a most resourceful man." When things do go awry at the party, it is not surprising when the man is able to put things right for the women and little Phoebe.
>
> **Other Devices:** Poetic Justice. Satire. Stereotype.
>
> **Art Style:** Cartoon.
>
> **Curriculum Tie-In:** Social Science (Anger; Acceptance and Respect; Self-Discovery/Esteem; Sexism).

Bottner, Barbara. *Bootsie Barker Bites.* Illus. by Peggy Rathmann. New York: G. P. Putnam's, 1992.

Bootsie Barker likes to play only intimidating games in which she can bite. One day her friend comes up with a better game.

Examples: Just when Bootsie announces another distasteful game, "Tomorrow . . . you get to be a worm," her friend says, "Charlene and I spent the morning inventing a new game." Suddenly the "worm" has turned. A few shadows on the wall, using her pet salamander Charlene and an archeologist's lantern, change the victim into the aggressor.

Other Devices: Inference. Poetic Justice. Understatement.

Art Style: Colored Cartoon.

Curriculum Tie-In: Social Science (Bullies; Friendship).

Bunting, Eve. *Night Tree.* Illus. by Ted Rand. New York: Harcourt Brace Jovanovich, 1991.

A family makes its annual pilgrimage to decorate an evergreen tree with food for the forest animals at Christmas time.

Examples: On the night before Christmas the family always goes "to find our tree." "Our box" is in the back of the truck with "the rest of our stuff." They take a blanket when they get out of the truck at the forest. They find the tree that "has been our tree forever and ever." "It's grown since last year." This is not going to be the usual family tree-cutting experience. When they open the box, the truth is confirmed. Out come strings of food for the wild animals. The tree will be decorated on the spot.

Art Style: Realism.

Bunting, Eve. *Someday a Tree.* Illus. by Ronald Himler. New York: Clarion (Houghton Mifflin), 1993.

A young girl, her parents, and her neighbors try to save an old oak tree that has been poisoned by chemicals.

Examples: The first hint that the tree is in trouble occurs when the child narrates, "I turn on my stomach and bury my face in the grass. Why does it smell so funny? I sniff." Will the tree survive? The animals have left. "Each night I watch. . . . If the deer come back . . . but they don't." The reader knows the efforts to save the tree will fail. But there is hope for other trees. She grabs acorns from her collection. ". . . they seem to be beating, bursting with tree life."

Other Devices: Inference.

Art Style: Impressionism.

Curriculum Tie-In: Science (Ecology; Trees).

Burton, Virginia Lee. *The Little House.* Boston: Houghton Mifflin, 1942. [Caldecott Award]

A personified small house sitting on a hill is happy but wonders what life in the city is all about. When she finds out, she is not happy and longs for the way it used to be.

> **Examples:** Though the lights of the city seem far off, the little house "was strong and well built" and could "never be sold for gold or silver." It will not be long before the city engulfs the little house, which then watches many changes occur in her environment.
>
> **Other Devices:** Analogy. Personification.
>
> **Art Style:** Naive.
>
> **Curriculum Tie-In:** Social Science (Values).

Burton, Virginia Lee. *Mike Mulligan and His Steam Shovel.* Boston: Houghton Mifflin, 1939.

Mike Mulligan and his steam shovel Mary Anne make canals for boats, flat ground for trains and airplanes and cars, but become obsolete when gasoline, diesel, and electric shovels come along. There is only one job left for Mike and Mary Anne.

> **Examples:** Mike Mulligan "always said that she could dig as much in a day as a hundred men could dig in a week, but he had never been quite sure that this was true." He will get a chance to prove it. "When people used to stop and watch them, Mike Mulligan and Mary Anne used to dig a little faster and a little better." This will prove helpful on the biggest project of their career. And when Mr. Henry B. Swap "smiled in rather a mean way," Mike and Mary Anne have their work cut out for them to win the contest and prove their boast.
>
> **Other Devices:** Poetic Justice.
>
> **Art Style:** Cartoon/Naive.
>
> **Curriculum Tie-In:** Science (Machine Technology).
> Social Science (Values).

Chaucer, Geoffrey. *Chanticleer and the Fox.* Adapted and illus. by Barbara Cooney. New York: Crowell, 1958. [Caldecott Award]

A moral tale about a rooster who listened to flattery.

> **Examples:** Just before danger arrives, Chanticleer has a vivid warning. He dreams of a frightening "beast like a hound which tried to grab my body and would have killed me. His color was between yellow and red, and his tail and both ears were tipped with black." But this warning will be dismissed because his favorite hen said, "Do not fear dreams."
>
> **Other Devices:** Aphorism. Simile. Understatement.
>
> **Art Style:** Cartoon scratchboard technique with color overlay.
>
> **Curriculum Tie-In:** Social Science (Values; Consequences).

*Clarke, Gus. ... *Along Came Eric*. New York: Lothrop, Lee & Shepard, 1991.
Nigel is used to being the center of attention. A new baby upsets Nigel's security. He adjusts and must help young Eric adjust when baby Alice arrives.

Examples: On the final page, the worried look on Eric's face when baby Alice enters the family indicates the whole thing will happen again. The confident arm around his brother's shoulder and the we'll-survive-together look on his face hints that Nigel will be there to assist his brother through the trauma of a younger sibling. His own experience will be his guide.

Other Devices: Inference.

Art Style: Cartoon.

Curriculum Tie-In: Social Science (Siblings; Jealousy).

Cole, Sheila. *When the Rain Stops*. Illus. by Henri Sorensen. New York: Lothrop, Lee & Shepard, 1991.
Setting off to pick blackberries, a child and her father encounter animals before a rain storm and afterward.

Examples: "It was cloudy when Leila and Daddy went out to gather blackberries for a pie." This portends the likelihood of future rain. And so does, "The sky grew darker. . . . Leaves trembled in the breeze . . . rumble of thunder."

Other Devices: Onomatopoeia.

Art Style: Impressionism.

Curriculum Tie-In: Science (Rain).

Crews, Donald. *Shortcut*. New York: Greenwillow, 1992.
Children taking a shortcut by walking along a railroad track find excitement and danger when a train approaches.

Examples: "We should have taken the road. But it was late." The freight trains don't run on schedule and are apt to come at any time. These warnings hint that there will be trouble on the tracks.

Other Devices: Atmosphere. Inference.

Art Style: Impressionism paint spatter.

Curriculum Tie-In: Social Science (Fear).

Daugherty, James. *Andy and the Lion*. New York: Viking, 1938.
A boy's interest in lions and his early encounter with one help save the day when a lion escapes its high steel cage during a circus performance.

Examples: At the same time Andy is enjoying reading about lions, his father is reading a newspaper headline about a lion that has escaped from a circus. Not long after, Andy encounters the lion and befriends it on his way to school. Later when the circus comes to town, a lion leaps over its high cage. Could it be the one with a penchant for fleeing? Of course, Andy and the lion do quickly recognize each other from their previous encounter.

Art Style: Cartoon caricature and brown tone.

DePaola, Tomie. *Strega Nona.* Englewood Cliffs: Prentice-Hall, 1975.
When Strega Nona leaves her bumbling apprentice Big Anthony alone with her magic pasta pot, he is determined to show the townspeople how it works.

Examples: Things are not likely to go well between Big Anthony and the forbidden pasta pot since he "didn't pay attention" and "too bad for Big Anthony, because he didn't see Strega Nona blow three kisses to the magic pasta pot."

Other Devices: Poetic Justice. Tone.

Art Style: Cartoon/European Middle Ages Folk.

Curriculum Tie-In: Social Science (Consequences; Ethics).

Flack, Marjorie. *Angus and the Ducks.* New York: Doubleday, 1930.
A curious Scottish terrier wants to find out what made the noise coming from the other side of the hedge.

Examples: Angus discovers that a loud "woo-oo-oof!!!" will send the ducks "all of a flutter." And he enjoys the effect of chasing them away from the water trough. But he fails to notice that "the ducks talked together." After this, the advantage Angus has over them is abruptly reversed.

Other Devices: Onomatopoeia. Poetic Justice.

Art Style: Expressionism colored line drawings.

Curriculum Tie-In: Social Sciences (Consequences).

Flack, Marjorie. *Angus Lost.* New York: Doubleday, 1932.
A little Scottish terrier is bored with the same things at home and is curious to see what the outside world has to offer.

Examples: "Faster ran the other dog, faster ran Angus, but Angus's legs were too short." The other dog's "legs were too long." When the big dog disappears around the corner, the reader is not surprised with the result. Angus is lost. The milkman will help Angus get home again. All he has to do is follow the cart to his own house porch.

Other Devices: Onomatopoeia. Point-Of-View.

Art Style: Expressionism colored line drawings.

Fleischman, Paul. *Time Train.* Illus. by Claire Ewart. New York: A Charlotte Zolotow Book (HarperCollins), 1991.
A class takes a field trip back through time to observe living dinosaurs in their natural habitat.

Examples: When the modern train pulls out of New York and reaches Philadelphia, the narrator says, "We knew we were in for an unusual trip." The scene outside the train window shows people in horse and carriages and early autos. The longer the train travels, the farther back in time the landscape becomes.

Other Devices: Understatement.

Art Style: Expressionism.

Curriculum Tie-In: History (Pre-History).

Freeman, Don. *Dandelion*. New York: Viking, 1964.
Jennifer Giraffe sent out party invitations that read, "Come as you are," but that doesn't stop Dandelion from indulging in a make-over.

> **Examples:** Disregarding the wording on his invitation, Dandelion immediately begins to "improve" his appearance. Trouble is expected.
>
> **Other Devices:** Pun. Theme.
>
> **Art Style:** Cartoon.
>
> **Curriculum Tie-In:** Social Science (Self-Discovery/Esteem).

Hutchins, Pat. *Rosie's Walk*. New York: Macmillan, 1968.
Rosie the hen strolls through the barnyard oblivious to the fox who follows her in spite of a series of mishaps.

> **Examples:** Rosie's near misses and the fox's near fatalities are shown through the art, though neither one knows what awaits. A rake, a pond, a haystack, a heavy bag of flour, a cart, and a hive of bees all foil the fox and protect the unwary Rosie from disaster.
>
> **Other Devices:** Irony. Poetic Justice. Satire. Stereotype.
>
> **Art Style:** Expressionism.
>
> **Curriculum Tie-In:** Health and Safety (Accident Prevention).

Hutchins, Pat. *Tidy Titch*. New York: Greenwillow, 1991.
Titch helps his older brother and sister clean their rooms.

> **Examples:** Titch, whose room was tidy, carries away all the rejected toys his siblings are too old to use while they clean their rooms. Now their rooms are neat. What has happened to Titch's room?
>
> **Art Style:** Cartoon.

Johnston, Tony. *The Promise*. Illus. by Pamela Keavney. New York: A Charlotte Zolotow Book (HarperCollins), 1992.
While helping her neighbor assist one of the cows in giving birth, Ramie hears a story of another birth helped by a young person interested in cows.

> **Examples:** Mr. Gates shares the story of the boy long ago who got a chance to begin raising cattle when he received his first calf as a thank-you for assisting in a difficult delivery. He tells Ramie, "The boy made a promise to himself . . . when he was grown, if ever he met another child who would truly love a calf, he would do just what Willis had done." Ramie, too, will receive her first calf.
>
> **Other Devices:** Flashback. Inference. Stereotype (Reverse).
>
> **Art Style:** Impressionism.

Kahl, Virginia. *Plum Pudding for Christmas*. New York: Charles Scribner's, 1956.
After inviting the king to be their Christmas guest, the duchess and her daughters are unable to serve the promised plum pudding.

> **Examples:** "But no one kept watch on the little Gunhilde." The plum pudding can't be made without plums. And, Gunhilde is licking her lips. There will be serious trouble if the king cannot have his promised pudding.
>
> **Other Devices:** Alliteration. Internal Rhyme. Irony. Understatement.
>
> **Art Style:** Cartoon.
>
> **Curriculum Tie-In:** History (Medieval Times).

Kasza, Keiko. *The Rat and the Tiger*. New York: G. P. Putnam's, 1993.
In his friendship with Rat, Tiger takes advantage and bullies Rat because of his greater size. But one day Rat stands up for his rights.

> **Examples:** One last event will bring about a showdown between the two friends. When Rat lets Tiger see his fine castle, Tiger is happily reading a book called *The Art of Karate*. The reader is prepared for what happens on the next page.
>
> **Other Devices:** Irony.
>
> **Art Style:** Colored Cartoon.
>
> **Curriculum Tie-In:** Social Science (Friendship; Bullies).

Leaf, Munro. *The Story of Ferdinand*. Illus. by Robert Lawson. New York: Viking, 1936.
Ferdinand is a bull who would rather sit and smell the flowers than fight.

> **Examples:** As soon as we read, "All the other little bulls . . . would run and jump and butt their heads together" while Ferdinand preferred to "sit quietly and smell the flowers," the reader suspects Ferdinand is heading for trouble.
>
> **Other Devices:** Irony. Satire.
>
> **Art Style:** Expressionism/Cartoon.
>
> **Curriculum Tie-In:** Social Science (Acceptance and Respect).

Lionni, Leo. *Alexander and the Wind-Up Mouse*. New York: Pantheon, 1969.
Alexander thinks it would be more pleasant to be an appreciated wind-up toy than a hated real mouse until he sees what fate the toy faces when new toys arrive.

> **Examples:** Maybe being "cuddled and loved" is not quite enough reason to want to be a toy mouse. "I can only move when they wind me," the toy says. Alexander finds him in a "box full of old toys" when the new gifts come. Alexander must decide about whether to change into a mouse like Wind-Up Willie.
>
> **Other Devices:** Theme.
>
> **Art Style:** Collage.
>
> **Curriculum Tie-In:** Social Science (Self-Discovery/Esteem).

Mahy, Margaret. *The Boy Who Was Followed Home.* Illus. by Steven Kellogg. New York: Franklin Watts, 1975.

A witch's pill is supposed to cure Robert of the hippopotamuses who daily follow him home from school. But there is one disadvantage to the treatment.

> **Examples:** Mrs. Squinge, the witch, tries to warn that the pill will cure the problem of hippos following Robert home, "but . . ." Unfortunately, Robert's father "grandly" says, "No buts!" Too bad they don't heed her warning.
>
> **Other Devices:** Understatement.
>
> **Art Style:** Cartoon pen and ink.

Mantinband, Gerda. *The Blabbermouths.* Illus. by Paul Borovsky. New York: Greenwillow, 1992.

Although he swears not to reveal the source of his new-found wealth, a poor farmer can't help telling his wife and then a neighbor, and soon even the chief magistrate finds out.

> **Examples:** As soon as that first neighbor remarks, "It's a good thing you've not told anyone else. . . . But now I must run," it is clear the secret is out. The only way the gold can remain safe is by convincing the magistrate her husband is crazy. The wife proceeds to stage an elaborate plan by first raining down doughnuts for her husband to find. From then on, convincing the magistrate is not that hard to do.
>
> **Other Devices:** Tone.
>
> **Art Style:** Naive.
>
> **Curriculum Tie-In:** Social Science (Foolish Behavior).

Mark, Jan. *Silly Tails.* Illus. by Tony Ross. New York: Atheneum, 1993.

Vegetables do not talk today thanks to vain and rude carrots who once hurled insults over the hedge separating their garden from formerly peaceable rabbits.

> **Examples:** The carrots, not willing to let well enough alone, chide the insulted rabbits for their "silly" ears, tails, eyes, and, as the reader soon comes to expect, their teeth. Soon the "outraged" rabbits take revenge in a way that is predictable between a rabbit and a carrot.
>
> **Other Devices:** Personification.
>
> **Art Style:** Colored Cartoon.

McCloskey, Robert. *Lentil.* New York: Viking, 1940.

Lentil saves the day when the band can't play to welcome home the town's most important citizen.

> **Examples:** Jealous Old Sneep deliberately sabotages the welcome by noisily eating a lemon. The sounds of sour slurping prevent the musicians from playing because "their lips were all puckered up." But Lentil never could pucker up to whistle and doesn't have the lemon problem. He does have a harmonica, however.
>
> **Art Style:** Cartoon/Impressionism pencil.

McCloskey, Robert. *Make Way for Ducklings.* New York: Viking, 1941. [Caldecott Award]

A mallard family chooses to make a home in a city environment and causes concern among the human inhabitants.

> **Examples:** Fortunately, the mallard family made a friend of policeman Michael, who fed them peanuts when they met him at the riverbank park. Later, his services come in handy when the family attempts to cross a busy street. Mrs. Mallard "knows all about bringing up children," which will be put to the test when she takes them to the Public Garden.
>
> **Other Devices:** Caricature. Point-Of-View.
>
> **Art Style:** Cartoon.
>
> **Curriculum Tie-In:** Literature (Pacing of Story).

McKissack, Patricia. *A Million Fish ... More or Less.* Illus. by Dena Schutzer. New York: Knopf, 1992.

A boy learns that the truth is often stretched on the Bayou Clapateaux. He gets the chance to tell his own version of a bayou tale when he goes fishing.

> **Examples:** Hugh Thomas recalls his elders' parting words, "Remember . . . strange things do happen on the Bayou Clapateaux." Sure enough, some strange things begin to happen as Hugh Thomas commences his day of adventures.
>
> **Other Devices:** Caricature. Hyperbole. Inference.
>
> **Art Style:** Impressionism/Expressionism paint.
>
> **Curriculum Tie-In:** Social Science (Self-Discovery/Esteem).

Polacco, Patricia. *Just Plain Fancy.* New York: Little Rooster (Bantam), 1990.

Naomi, an Amish girl whose elders have impressed upon her the importance of adhering to the simple ways of her people, is horrified when one of her hen eggs hatches into an extremely fancy bird.

> **Examples:** No one knows how the fancy egg got into the hen yard. But the book's front papers show a Pennstate Bird Hatchery truck being forced off the side of the road by a horse and buggy. The truck's door opens and an egg flys out into the grass. A sign indicates that it came from the "exotic" box. When the hatched chick grew up, it "ruffled up his feathers and did something that took their breath away." The bird, of course, is a peacock.
>
> **Other Devices:** Pun.
>
> **Art Style:** Expressionism.
>
> **Curriculum Tie-In:** Geography (Amish Culture).

Potter, Beatrix. *The Tale of Peter Rabbit.* New York: Frederick Warne, 1902.

Disobedient Peter suffers consequences in Mr. McGregor's garden.

Examples: The other bunnies have cute names; Peter's name is bluntly different and separates him from the others. The warning not to go to McGregor's garden hints that the "different" child will find this adventure irresistible. And, when he does come to grief, losing his jacket, which "was a blue jacket with brass buttons, quite new," it bodes ill for him when he faces his mother.

Other Devices: Imagery. Irony. Metaphor. Onomatopoeia. Poetic Justice. Understatement.

Art Style: Cartoon/Realism water color.

Curriculum Tie-In: Social Science (Consequences; Parent and Child).

Rathmann, Peggy. *Ruby the Copycat.* New York: Scholastic, 1991.

Ruby insists on copying Angela, until her teacher helps her discover her own creative resources.

Examples: The reader suspects when Ruby smiles admiringly "at the top of Angela's head" that she will come back to school after lunch wearing a red ribbon like Angela's because she copies everything Angela does or wears.

Other Devices: Theme.

Art Style: Cartoon.

Curriculum Tie-In: Social Science (Self-Discovery/Esteem; Acceptance and Respect).

Reiser, Lynn. *Dog and Cat.* New York: Greenwillow, 1991.

A dog learns never to chase cats.

Examples: The straightforward "Once there were two neighbors, a big dog and a little cat. . . . One day they met . . ." intimates conflict.

Other Devices: Poetic Justice.

Art Style: Cartoon.

Curriculum Tie-In: Social Science (Consequences).

Sakai, Kimiko. *Sachiko Means Happiness.* Illus. by Tomie Arai. San Francisco: Children's Book Press, 1990.

Although at first Sachiko is upset when her grandmother no longer recognizes her, she grows to understand that they can still be happy together.

Examples: "I don't like sunsets, even if they are so beautiful. Trouble always comes in the evening." Sachiko clearly dreads something: facing her "changed" grandmother who suffers from Alzheimer's disease.

Other Devices: Inference.

Art Style: Realism/Impressionism.

Curriculum Tie-In: Health and Safety (Alzheimer's Disease).

***Say, Allen.** *Grandfather's Journey.* Boston: Houghton Mifflin, 1993. [Caldecott Award]

A Japanese American man recounts his grandfather's journey to America, his eventual longing to return to his homeland, and his restlessness when he does. The man, too, learns how it feels to be torn by love for two different countries and can empathize with his grandfather.

Examples: ". . . my favorite weekend was a visit to my grandfather's house. He told me many stories about California." The grandfather's last wish was "to see California one more time." When the boy is nearly grown, it is inevitable that he, too, will go "to see California for myself."

Other Devices: Aphorism. Atmosphere. Irony. Paradox. Parallel Story. Symbol.

Art Style: Impressionism/Expressionism/Folk water color.

Curriculum Tie-In: Social Science (Cross-Cultures; Continuity of Life).

Seuss, Dr. *The Cat in the Hat.* New York: Random, 1957.

A cat shows tricks and other amusements to two bored children on a rainy day.

Examples: The fish bowl fish, who serves as a Jiminy Cricket conscience, warns, "He should not be here when your mother is out." And, very soon the house gets trashed.

Other Devices: Hyperbole. Imagery.

Art Style: Cartoon.

Curriculum Tie-In: Social Science (Ethics).

Steig, William. *The Amazing Bone.* New York: Farrar Straus Giroux, 1976.

A talking bone saves a charming piglet from being food for a fox.

Examples: The bone, who "fell out of a witch's basket," may have learned something useful that will help an escape from the fox when all seems bleak. The bone, for example, can speak in "any language" and is able to "imitate any sound there is." Later, these critical skills prove both life saving and then pleasant after the bone "became part of the family" and provided "music whenever they wanted it."

Other Devices: Atmosphere. Caricature. Inference. Irony.

Art Style: Cartoon water color.

Steig, William. *Sylvester and the Magic Pebble.* New York: Windmill Books (Simon & Shuster), 1969. [Caldecott Award]

A young donkey inadvertently causes himself to turn into a large rock. His family doesn't know where their child is and nearly gives up hope that he will return.

Examples: From the beginning paragraph, pebbles figure importantly in Sylvester's life. His hobby is "collecting pebbles of unusual shape and color." One of them proves magic and leads to his unfortunate change into a rock.

Later, his father finds "a fantastic pebble" which Sylvester would have "loved for his collection." This signals the reuniting of the family. Finally, the magic pebble is put in the safe, because "no magic is now needed."

Other Devices: Imagery. Personification. Pun. Stereotype. Symbol. Theme.

Art Style: Cartoon water color.

Curriculum Tie-In: Social Science (Parent and Child).

Ward, Lynd. *The Biggest Bear.* Boston: Houghton Mifflin, 1952. [Caldecott Award] Johnny Orchard goes out to acquire a bearskin, comes home with a cute little cub instead, and has to contend with its growing appetite.

Examples: "I suppose you know what a bear likes to eat," says the boy's father. Trouble lies ahead trying to appease the bear's hunger. The bear especially likes maple sugar.

Other Devices: Pun. Stereotype. Understatement.

Art Style: Realism/Impressionism.

Curriculum Tie-In: History (Nineteenth-Century America Frontier Life).

Williams, Garth. *The Chicken Book.* New York: Delacorte, 1946, 1970.
Some baby chicks express wishes for food and grit.

Examples: Some chicks wish for things, and what they desire is shown by the illustrations that are nearby. Once they follow their mother's advice, they achieve their needs by scratching (working).

Other Devices: Analogy. Theme.

Art Style: Expressionism/Colored Cartoon.

*__Wilsdorf, Anne.__ *Princess.* New York: Greenwillow, 1993.
A girl proves that she is a real princess in an unusual way.

Examples: Each princess is "guarded by an evil monster who must be vanquished before the princess will be free to marry." As the prince approaches each one, its name says something about the character of the princess it guards. First there is the horrible "Videopteryx." Its mistress can't be bothered to answer the prince because she would rather watch television. The "Antiseptyx" guards a girl who comes waving a dishcloth and duster and fusses about dirty feet on clean floors.

Other Devices: Ambiguity. Parody. Pun. Satire.

Art Style: Cartoon water color.

Woodruff, Elvira. *The Wing Shop.* Illus. by Stephen Gammell. New York: Holiday House, 1991.
After his family moves to a different part of town, Matthew tries to get back to his old house by trying on various pairs of wings in an unusual wing shop.

Examples: A "pair of lovely gray and white ones" dunk him headfirst in the ocean. They once belonged to a gull and won't work for him. Neither will a pair of leathery black ones. They hang him upside down in the barn rafters. A bat's wings aren't quite right. The bee's wings bring his face into a geranium, and so on.

Art Style: Impressionism.

*Yolen, Jane. *Encounter.* Illus. by David Shannon. New York: Harcourt Brace Jovanovich, 1992.

A Taino Indian boy on the island of San Salvador recounts the landing of Columbus and his men in 1492.

Examples: A boy wakens from a dream featuring "three great winged birds with voices like thunder and with white teeth." Soon, "great-sailed canoes" land. The boy dreads their arrival and warns, "Do not welcome them." But trouble is unavoidable when people dismiss him with, "All children have bad dreams." He watches "their chief smile. It was the serpent's smile—no lips and all teeth." "One of the strangers let me touch his sharp silver stick. . . . It bit my palm so hard the blood cried out." Repeatedly, the boy sees danger in welcoming these white men. But no one listens because he is "only a child."

Other Devices: Atmosphere. Flash-Forward. Metaphor. Point-Of-View. Stereotype. Theme.

Art Style: Realism/Expressionism acrylic.

Curriculum Tie-In: History (Columbus).

Zemach, Harve. *The Judge.* Illus. by Margot Zemach. New York: Farrar Straus Giroux, 1969.

A judge's mistrust of people leads to a disastrous confrontation with a monster.

Examples: The monster chews stones, belches flame, has claws and jaws, growls and groans, and "does bad things," but the judge refuses to listen to warnings. With all the prisoners marched off to jail, there is no one to help him when he faces the monster.

Other Devices: Caricature. Hyperbole. Poetic Justice. Satire. Theme.

Art Style: Expressionism.

Curriculum Tie-In: Social Science (Consequences; Foolish Behavior).

HYPERBOLE

Obvious and extravagant exaggeration not meant to be taken literally.

Example: I'm so hungry I could eat a horse.

SOURCES

Amoss, Berthe. *Old Hannibal and the Hurricane.* New York: Hyperion, 1991.
On board the ship *Sally Sue*, Old Hannibal is describing for his friends the great hurricane he once endured, when they run into another one.

Examples: Like a typical tall tale sea adventure, Hannibal describes a hurricane that sinks his ship into the deep "where Neptune rules his kingdom," but he "bailed quick and Sue rode high." He captures carpentry tools and materials out of the "flotsam and jetsam" and turns the boat into an airborne sailing ship. He gets to shore ahead of the collapsing hurricane.

Other Devices: Alliteration. Internal Rhyme.

Art Style: Colored Cartoon.

Charlip, Remy. *Fortunately.* New York: Four Winds Press, 1964.
Good and bad luck accompany Ned from New York to Florida on his way to a surprise party.

Examples: There are a series of cliff-hanging escapades involving an exploding airplane, a hole in a parachute, a haystack with a protruding pitchfork, water teeming with sharks, tigers who chase him into a cave, and a fancy ballroom where a huge birthday party is being held for him.

Art Style: Naive.

De Regniers, Beatrice Schenk. *May I Bring a Friend?* Illus. by Beni Montresor. New York: Atheneum, 1964. [Caldecott Award]
No matter who the young friend brings to tea with him, the king and queen welcome them.

Examples: Friends who accompany the young guest include a giraffe, a hippo, a seal, monkeys, lions, and an elephant who all ate and ate "till there wasn't any more to eat."

Other Devices: Poetic Justice.

Art Style: Impressionism.

Curriculum Tie-In: Social Science (Acceptance and Respect).

Gag, Wanda. *Millions of Cats.* New York: Coward-McCann, 1928.
The old man seeks just the right kitten for his wife.

Examples: "Hundreds of cats thousands of cats, millions and billions and trillions of cats."

Other Devices: Paradox. Theme.

Art Style: Folk/Cartoon.

Gross, Theodore Faro. *Everyone Asked about You.* Illus. by Sheila White Samton. New York: Philomel, 1990.
Nora's friend Charlie claims that everywhere he went in the universe they asked about her.

Examples: Even the Empress of Jupiter and the Martian platoon have asked about her.

Other Devices: Internal Rhyme.

Art Style: Folk.

Kraus, Robert. *Milton the Early Riser.* Illus. by Jose Aruego and Ariane Aruego. New York: Windmill Books (E. P. Dutton), 1972.

Milton copes with his early morning loneliness in a manner that exhausts him by the time everyone else awakens.

Examples: A whirlwind has put all the sleepers into unnatural positions. Milton "worked and worked and he put things right."

Other Devices: Irony. Pun.

Art Style: Colored Cartoon.

Lindbergh, Anne. *Tidy Lady.* Illus. by Susan Hoguet. New York: Harcourt Brace Jovanovich, 1989.

An unusually tidy lady is obsessed with making her new home neat.

Examples: She rolls up the lawn, rakes down the stars, and removes the sky. She bends all twigs and branches in one direction then cuts down the old tree. She removes windows and doors from the house and shoves the house together into a tiny square. Everything goes out in trash bags.

Art Style: Expressionism.

Mahy, Margaret. *Keeping House.* Illus. by Wendy Smith. New York: Margaret K. McElderry Books (Macmillan), 1991.

Lizzie Firkin has no time to keep house because she works at night at a famous club singing and tap dancing and playing trombone. She is too tired to sweep the floor or clean cupboards.

Examples: Lizzie "couldn't even walk across her own floor because of the mess. She had to jump from one bare spot to another. When she opened the cupboards, a thousand things with sharp corners fell out on her." She "yawned so hard that she nearly sucked the parrot off his perch." The "spiders packed their bags and moved to the house next door."

Other Devices: Atmosphere. Inference. Simile. Stereotype.

Art Style: Impressionism.

McKissack, Patricia. *A Million Fish ... More or Less.* Illus. by Dena Schutzer. New York: Knopf, 1992.

A boy learns that the truth is often stretched on the Bayou Clapateaux. He gets the chance to tell his own version of a bayou tale when he goes fishing.

Examples: ". . . caught a wild turkey weighed five hundred pounds . . . a lantern that'd been left by Spanish conquistadors back in the year 15 and 42. And it was still burning!" Other exaggerations include a cottonmouth snake with legs. The boy caught three fish and "a million more," which he would have brought home if a grandfather alligator and his kin and an "army of raccoons" and crows and some cats hadn't all taken their share, leaving him with only three small fish.

Other Devices: Caricature. Foreshadowing. Inference.

Art Style: Impressionism/Expressionism paint.

Curriculum Tie-In: Social Science (Self-Discovery/Esteem).

Ratz de Tagyos, Paul. *A Coney Tale.* New York: Clarion Books (Houghton Mifflin), 1992.

The inhabitants of a rabbit village in seventeenth-century Flanders discover the biggest carrot in the world and work to dig it up.

Examples: The town square tree is said to be "hundreds and hundreds of years old." To get the "biggest carrot in the world" out of the ground, "hundreds of coneys pulled." "Thousands of coneys" feed for months on the carrot. It is so big "it reached through the earth to China."

Other Devices: Tone.

Art Style: Colored Cartoon.

Riddle, Tohby. *Careful with That Ball, Eugene!* New York: Orchard Books, 1991.

Eugene watches his ball speeding right for the neighbor's front window.

Examples: In his imagination, Eugene sees the ball punching through the neighbor's wall, landing in a bowl of oatmeal, and causing Eugene to be "in very big trouble." He might have to join a circus and run away to South America or be a Himalayan hermit or a monk or a gangster on the run.

Other Devices: Flash-Forward.

Art Style: Cartoon.

Rosenberg, Liz. *Monster Mama.* Illus. by Stephen Gammell. New York: Philomel (Putnam & Grosset), 1993.

Patrick Edward's fierce mother helps him deal with some obnoxious bullies.

Examples: His mother "zoomed out of her cave like a fast-moving freight train" to come to his rescue. She lives in a cave at the back of the house. They call her a monster.

Other Devices: Ambiguity. Aphorism. Inference. Simile.

Art Style: Expressionism.

Curriculum Tie-In: Social Science (Parent and Child).

Sendak, Maurice. *Where the Wild Things Are.* Harper and Row, 1963. [Caldecott Award]

Max is a little boy dressed in a wolf suit who is sent to his room for behaving ferociously. Suddenly, the walls disappear, and he finds himself in a magic forest of wild creatures.

Examples: "That very night in Max's room a forest grew and grew and grew until his ceiling hung with vines and the walls became the world all around." "And in and out of weeks and almost over a year" he sails on a private boat to "where the wild things are." "They roared their terrible roars and gnashed their terrible teeth and rolled their terrible eyes and showed their terrible claws."

Other Devices: Inference. Point-Of-View. Theme.

Art Style: Expressionism pen and ink colored drawings.

Curriculum Tie-In: Social Science (Self-Discovery/Esteem; Anger; Consequences; Forgiveness; Parent and Child).

Seuss, Dr. *The Cat in the Hat.* New York: Random, 1957.

A cat shows tricks and other amusements to two bored children on a rainy day.

Examples: The cat balances books, a toy ship, a cake, the household pet fish, some milk, and numerous other items before they finally crash down.

Other Devices: Foreshadowing. Imagery.

Art Style: Cartoon.

Curriculum Tie-In: Social Science (Ethics).

Steig, William. *Shrek.* New York: Farrar Straus Giroux, 1990.

Like two peas in a pod, ugly Shrek and his ugly bride are made for each other and live horribly every after, scaring the socks off all who fall afoul of them.

Examples: They are endowed with "wicked eyes livid red, horny warts, rosy wens, and full of rabid self-esteem." They "bellowed a blast of fire, putrid blue flame" and "could spit flame a full ninety-nine yards." Any snakes dumb enough to bite Shrek got convulsions and died.

Other Devices: Alliteration. Internal Rhyme.

Art Style: Cartoon.

Curriculum Tie-In: Social Science (Acceptance and Respect).

Zemach, Harve. *The Judge.* Illus. by Margot Zemach. New York: Farrar Straus Giroux, 1969.

A judge's mistrust of people leads to a disastrous confrontation with a monster.

Examples: This monster can "chew stones." Its "paws have claws." It "belches flames," "spreads its wings," "growls," "groans," and "does bad things."

Other Devices: Caricature. Foreshadowing. Poetic Justice. Satire. Theme.

Art Style: Expressionism.

Curriculum Tie-In: Social Science (Consequences; Foolish Behavior).

Zimelman, Nathan. *Treed by a Pride of Irate Lions.* Illus. by Toni Goffe. Boston: Little, Brown & Co., 1990.

Animals like Mother but not Father. Perhaps tame animals are too refined and Father must go among wild animals in Africa to find one that will love him.

Examples: Father is butted fiercely by a rabbit, is balanced between the open jaws of a crocodile, hangs on to the neck of a tall giraffe, is ensnared in coils of a boa constrictor, and in general is excessively abused.

Other Devices: Irony. Understatement.

Art Style: Cartoon.

IMAGERY

A device that provides mental pictures summoned up by terms and expressions that appeal to the senses so that we see, hear, smell, feel, and taste much of what the characters experience. Such images can create a writer's tone.

> **Example:** Even the usually cool green willows bordering the pond hung wilting and dry.

SOURCES

Aylesworth, Jim. *Country Crossing.* Illus. by Ted Rand. New York: Atheneum, 1991.

Re-creates the sights and sounds at a country crossing one summer night, as an old car patiently awaits the passing of a long, noisy freight train.

> **Examples:** "Summer moon softened the night with quiet light; moonlight sparkled in the puddles; gleamed like silver on the rails; strong yellow light began to poke its way through the trees; roar of an engine began to rumble out of the darkness; passed with a rush and a swirl of dust; leaf flew into the air, then skidded to a stop."
>
> **Art Style:** Expressionism.
>
> **Curriculum Tie-In:** Social Science (Nostalgia).

*** Baylor, Byrd.** *Your Own Best Secret Place.* Illus. by Peter Parnall. New York: Charles Scribner's, 1979.

A girl discovers that the hollow at the foot of a cottonwood tree was first someone else's secret place before it was hers. She begins to understand how William Cottonwood felt there.

> **Examples:** ". . . tangle of shadowy thickets; damp leaf smell; sudden swoop of pinon jays; straight shafts of sunlight through the treetops; curled up like a fox, cozy and warm; sand looks like waves and changes every day and always seems magic."
>
> **Other Devices:** Theme. Tone.
>
> **Art Style:** Expressionism pen and ink line drawings.

Curriculum Tie-In: Social Science (Self-Discovery/Esteem; Continuity of Life; Acceptance and Respect).
Geography (American Southwest).

*Bedard, Michael. *Emily.* Illus. by Barbara Cooney. New York: Doubleday Book for Young Readers (Bantam, Doubleday, Dell), 1992.

When mother and child pay a visit to their reclusive neighbor Emily, who stays in her house writing poems, there is an exchange of special gifts.

Examples: Prose resonates with mystical wonder and terse rhythm of Emily Dickinson's poetry. The child peaks through the window of her front door. "There was no one there but winter, all in white." She overhears her parents chatting at night. "Voices drifted up the dark." Her father sang the night song for her. "Like flakes of flowers the words fell to the sheets." When the snow melts, "the hedge had lost its veil." Mother's new silk dress "whispered when she walked." The road "was full of mud and mirrors where the sky peeked at itself."

Other Devices: Point-Of-View.

Art Style: Naive.

Curriculum Tie-In: Literature (Emily Dickinson).

Caudill, Rebecca. *A Pocketful of Cricket.* Illus. by Evaline Ness. New York: Holt Rinehart Winston, 1964.

A small child's affection for his world is beautifully expressed as he shares the sights and sounds of everything around him.

Examples: The hickory nut "smell tingled in his nose like the smell of the first frost." He "heard bugs and beetles ticking," a cicada "fiddling high notes in the August heat," an "owl hooting in the dusky woods," and the wind "rustling in the ripening corn." The beans "felt cool like morning." A "brown caterpillar looped fast along a corn blade." He "took a bite from one apple, then a bite from the other—sweet and sour, sweet and sour."

Other Devices: Atmosphere.

Art Style: Expressionism.

Curriculum Tie-In: Science (Ecology).

Chall, Marsha Wilson. *Up North at the Cabin.* Illus. by Steve Johnson. New York: Lothrop, Lee & Shepard, 1992.

Summer vacation up north at the cabin provides memorable experiences on the water, with the animals, and through the other faces of nature.

Examples: We "watch the loons dance down the sun." "Sunshine sits on my lap all morning." A moose "shakes his great head, rocking branches of bone as he bellows a warning." Papa "skims the silver water on only one ski." Other images include: "when frosted windows cloud the sun," and "tufted island in the bay."

Other Devices: Metaphor. Simile.

Art Style: Impressionism paint.

Curriculum Tie-In: Science (Ecology).

Dragonwagon, Crescent. *Home Place.* Illus. by Jerry Pinkney. New York: Macmillan, 1990.

While out hiking, a family comes upon the site of an old house and finds some clues about the people who once lived there.

Examples: ". . . daffodils in a row, a yellow splash brighter than sunlight, or lamplight, or butter in the green and shadow of the woods; flower cups lifted to trumpet the good news of spring; raccoons who rustle at night; deer who nibble delicately; scratchy-sweet singing; long, long hair, unpinning, unbraiding, and combing by an oval mirror; uneven swing hanging vacant."

Other Devices: Flashback.

Art Style: Impressionism.

Curriculum Tie-In: Social Science (Continuity of Life).

Ets, Marie Hall. *Play with Me.* New York: Viking, 1955.

A little girl tries to play with animals she finds in the meadow, but when she reaches, grabs, or runs toward them, they run away.

Examples: A rabbit was "wiggling his nose and nibbling a flower." A blue jay "jabbered and scolded." A chipmunk was "shelling an acorn with his sharp little teeth." A turtle was "just sitting still, getting warm in the sun" before he "plopped into the water." A bug was "making trails on the water."

Other Devices: Inference. Irony.

Art Style: Naive/Cartoon pencil and charcoal drawings.

Curriculum Tie-In: Science (Ecology).

Freschet, Berniece. *The Web in the Grass.* Illus. by Roger Duvoisin. New York: Charles Scribner's, 1972.

A fragile and friendless little spider lives out her life in strangely silent and busy beauty.

Examples: She is described with "legs long and slender" having a "handsome coat with bright orange spots." She produces "filmy threads of gossamer lace." She "spun more silk and patted it into a soft blanket around the eggs." Soon, "hundreds of baby spiders were ballooning through the sky."

Other Devices: Simile.

Art Style: Collage.

Curriculum Tie-In: Science (Spiders).

George, William T. *Fishing at Long Pond.* Illus. by Lindsay Barrett George. New York: Greenwillow, 1991.

While fishing for bass, Katie and her grandfather observe a deer, an osprey, a goose, and other pond visitors.

> **Examples:** ". . . oarlocks groaned and creaked leaving behind a trail of double whirlpools; boat glided by noiselessly; deer snorted and bounded off; osprey hovered with quick, backward wing beats."
>
> **Art Style:** Realism.
>
> **Curriculum Tie-In:** Science (Ecology).

Goble, Paul. *The Girl Who Loved Wild Horses.* Scarsdale, NY: Bradbury, 1978. [Caldecott Award]

A romantic tale of a Native American girl who ran free with the wild horses on the plains.

> **Examples:** "Birds were singing about the rising sun." "Horses were rearing up on their hind legs and snorting in terror." Other expressions include ". . . drumming hooves; our thoughts fly with them; everything was awake; lightning flashing in the darkness; horses eating and moving slowly among the flowers."
>
> **Other Devices:** Simile. Symbol.
>
> **Art Style:** Native American Folk Motif.
>
> **Curriculum Tie-In:** History (Native Americans).

Keats, Ezra Jack. *The Snowy Day.* New York: Viking, 1962. [Caldecott Award]

Here is the magic and sense of possibility in a first snowfall: snowmen to build, snowballs to pack, mountains to climb, snow angels to carve, snowbanks to collapse in.

> **Examples:** Expressions include ". . . crunch, his feet sank in the snow; a stick that was just right for smacking a snow-covered tree; down fell the snow—plop! a smiling snowman; a great big tall heaping mountain of snow; picked up a handful of snow—and another, and still another."
>
> **Other Devices:** Atmosphere.
>
> **Art Style:** Collage.
>
> **Curriculum Tie-In:** Science (Seasons—Winter).

MacDonald, Golden. *Little Island.* Illus. by Leonard Weisgard. Garden City, NY: Doubleday, 1946. [Caldecott Award]

Narration about an island in foggy weather.

> **Examples:** Expressions include ". . . fog came in from the sea and hid the little Island in a soft wet shadow; little waxy, white-pink, chuckleberry blossoms; tickly smelling pear tree; seals came barking down from the north; seaweed squeaked at low tide; herring and mackerel leaped out of the water all silver in the moonlight; wind whistled; fireflies flashed in the darkness."

Other Devices: Metaphor. Paradox. Simile.

Art Style: Impressionism.

Curriculum Tie-In: Science (Geology).

Maestro, Betsy. *Bike Trip.* Illus. by Giulio Maestro. New York: HarperCollins, 1992.

A family takes a bicycle trip and experiences the sights, sounds, and smells of town, country, and seashore.

Examples: ". . . bright yellow helmet with real racing stripes; wind whistling gently; whirring of tires; sweet smell of grass and hay; clackety hollow sound of a wooden bridge; blast of a truck driver's air horn; bright paintings of sailboats at the art sale; bell ringing and red light flashing on the raising bridge; salty smell of marsh grass; turtles running on a large rock."

Art Style: Colored Cartoon.

Curriculum Tie-In: Health and Safety (Accident Prevention—Bike Safety).

McCloskey, Robert. *Time of Wonder.* New York: Viking, 1957. [Caldecott Award]

A summer season on a north coast island is enjoyed through the last days before fall.

Examples: Expressions include ". . . rain begins to spill down coming closer across the bay; millions of splashes, the drops visible on the water; growing ferns pushing aside dead leaves, unrolling their fiddle-heads slowly unfurling, slowly stretching." A foggy morning hides the sound of snorting porpoises "having an acrobatic breakfast of herring under the bay."

Art Style: Impressionism paint.

Curriculum Tie-In: Science (Ecology).

Parnall, Peter. *Alfalfa Hill.* Garden City, NY: Doubleday, 1975.

Winter comes in a whisper. Hour after hour snow fell, transforming a fall landscape into new arrangements.

Examples: Expressions include ". . . ripped crisp leaves from the whipping trees and hurled them crazily, crazily; crackled and scraped and nestled, covering the forest floor. . . . Squirrels skittered, deer browsed, grouse leaped, mice raced, screech owl peered. When winter settled in, there were no squeaks, chatters, peeps, clucks, rustling, scratching, chewing, caws, preening, combing, or washing one's paws."

Other Devices: Metaphor. Simile.

Art Style: Expressionism pen and ink line drawing.

Curriculum Tie-In: Science (Seasons—Winter; Environment).

Parnall, Peter. *The Great Fish.* Garden City, NY: Doubleday, 1973.

A beloved grandfather's poetic explanation for the cause of spawning salmon that saved the Indians from starvation is a poignant reminder of a heritage lost.

Examples: Expressions include ". . . yellow leaves dipped and bucked through the air; dry cornstalks chattered; fermenting apples; deer became fat on the wastes of his harvests; crusty shells guarded the sleeping seeds; a battered old rifle, rusting its usefulness away; dyes made from nut husks and berry juices by women long since gone; spring sun smiled and broke the grip of the river ice; tears of the mothers were carried in the swift river waters to the sea; water gave way to flesh, so great were the numbers of fish that swarmed toward our mountains."

Other Devices: Inference. Understatement.

Art Style: Expressionism pen and ink line drawing.

Curriculum Tie-In: Science (Environment; Ecology).

Potter, Beatrix. *The Tale of Peter Rabbit.* New York: Frederick Warne, 1902.
Disobedient Peter suffers consequences in Mr. McGregor's garden.

Examples: Expressions include ". . . ran straight away to Mr. McGregor's garden, and squeezed under the gate; feeling rather sick, he went to look for some parsley; was on his hands and knees planting out young cabbages; Peter was most dreadfully frightened; he rushed all over the garden, for he had forgotten the way back to the gate; it was a blue jacket with brass buttons, quite new; gave himself up for lost, and shed big tears; implored him to exert himself; now and then the tip of her tail twitched as if it were alive; flopped down upon the nice soft sand on the floor of his rabbit-hole and shut his eyes."

Other Devices: Foreshadowing. Irony. Metaphor. Onomatopoeia. Poetic Justice. Understatement.

Art Style: Cartoon/Realism water color.

Curriculum Tie-In: Social Science (Consequences; Parent and Child).

Radin, Ruth Yaffe. *High in the Mountains.* Illus. by Ed Young. New York: Macmillan, 1989.
Description of a day spent near Grandpa's house in the mountains.

Examples: Expressions include ". . . serious firs stretching tall, not caring about the deer at all; alpine flowers hiding in between the green, they can't be seen from far away; afternoon sun touches the peaks and misses the valleys; a line that curves and hides but still connects the near and far, going higher to the tundra where no trees can ever grow."

Other Devices: Metaphor. Simile.

Art Style: Impressionism paint.

Curriculum Tie-In: Science (Ecology).

Ryder, Joanne. *Winter Whale.* Illus. by Michael Rothman. New York: Morrow Junior Books (Just-For-A-Day series), 1991.

A child transforms into the animal for a day and discovers what life is like as a whale; also bear and goose. Others in series include *Lizard in the Sun*, 1990; *White Bear, Ice Bear*, 1989; *Catching the Wind*, 1989.

> **Examples:** ". . . wild bird soaring; slippery bank; wind-tossed feathers; thick shaggy fur; long dark tongue; spicy scent; ribbons of light; rain whispers; roar through the sea; fine white mist; light as a pencil; light as a handful of popcorn; feeling hot sunlight creep."
>
> **Other Devices:** Point-of-View.
>
> **Art Style:** Expressionism.
>
> **Curriculum Tie-In:** Science (Ecology).

Seuss, Dr. *The Cat in the Hat.* New York: Random, 1957.

A cat shows tricks and other amusements to two bored children on a rainy day.

> **Examples:** Expressions include ". . . mother's new gown with the pink white and red dots; the cake, rake, gown, milk, books, fan"; and other long lists of things fallen on the floor.
>
> **Other Devices:** Foreshadowing. Hyperbole.
>
> **Art Style:** Cartoon.
>
> **Curriculum Tie-In:** Social Science (Ethics).

Shulevitz, Uri. *Dawn.* New York: Farrar Straus Giroux, 1974.

A grandfather and his grandson awake on a peaceful morning to experience dawn arrive in a mountain lake setting.

> **Examples:** Expressions include ". . . lake shivers; slowly, lazily, vapors start to rise; lonely bat circles in silence; a bird calls, another answers; moon lights a rock, a branch, an occasional leaf; mountain stands guard, dark and silent; oars screak and rattle, churning pools of foam."
>
> **Other Devices:** Atmosphere.
>
> **Art Style:** Impressionism pen and ink water color.
>
> **Curriculum Tie-In:** Science (Meteorology; Environment; Sun).

Steig, William. *Sylvester and the Magic Pebble.* New York: Windmill Books (Simon & Schuster), 1969. [Caldecott Award]

A magic pebble, a fierce lion, and a wish made in panic lead to separation from loved ones.

> **Examples:** "Clap of thunder, and the rain came shooting down; went away confused, perplexed, puzzled, and bewildered; thoughts began to race like mad; into every nook and gully of the neighborhood; flowers showed their young faces."

Other Devices: Foreshadowing. Personification. Pun. Stereotype. Symbol. Theme.

Art Style: Cartoon water color.

Curriculum Tie-In: Social Science (Parent and Child).

Tresselt, Alvin. *Hide and Seek Fog.* Illus. by Roger Duvoisin. New York: Lothrop, Lee & Shepard, 1965.

The worst fog in 20 years temporarily disheartens grownups, but the children take it in stride.

Examples: The fog turned "off the sun-sparkle on the waves; terns flew back to their roosts on the craggy rocks." Children ran in and out of the water "blue-lipped and shivering." Other expressions include ". . . spoddled in the lazy lapping waves on the beach; dulled the rusty scraping of the beach grass; muffled chattery talk of the low tide waves."

Other Devices: Metaphor. Simile.

Art Style: Impressionism/Naive.

Tresselt, Alvin. *Rain Drop Splash.* Illus. by Leonard Weisgard. New York: Lothrop, Lee & Shepard, 1946.

Narration of rain as it progresses from a puddle to pond, to brook, to lake, to river, and to ocean.

Examples: The rain "dripped from shiny leaves . . . dropped from a rabbit's nose . . . splashed from a brown bear's tail . . . fell from a daisy's face . . . trickled down tree trunks . . . splunked on a green frog's back." "Dragonflies skimmed; turtles floated; ferry boats puffed."

Art Style: Naive/Cartoon.

Curriculum Tie-In: Science (Rain; Environment; Geology; Meterology).

Tresselt, Alvin. *White Snow Bright Snow.* Illus. by Roger Duvoisin. New York: Lothrop, Lee & Shepard, 1947. [Caldecott Award]

A spring snow storm is described with lively text.

Examples: Snow "filled the cold tree branches with great white blossoms." Snowflakes "sparkled in the light of the street lamps." Frost made "pictures of ice ferns on the window panes." Other expressions include ". . . grey pussy willows pushed out of their brown shells; fence posts lost their dunce caps; smell of wet brown earth filled the warm air."

Other Devices: Metaphor. Simile.

Art Style: Naive.

Curriculum Tie-In: Science (Seasons—Winter; Environment).

Turner, Ann. *Rainflowers.* Illus. by Robert Blake. New York: A Charlotte Zolotow Book (HarperCollins), 1992.

Animals, trees, flowers—all react to a thunderstorm and its aftermath.

Examples: "Mice chittered to grass nests; chipmunks squeaked to low stone walls; birds skittered to the tree line; woodchucks lumbered to deep dry holes; the sky tumbled and rolled with the weight of the thunder; rain dripped from the barn door onto the child's tongue."

Other Devices: Simile.

Art Style: Impressionism.

Curriculum Tie-In: Science (Rain).

Warnock, Natalie Kinsey. *When Spring Comes.* Illus. by Stacey Schuett. New York: Dutton Children's Books, 1993.
A child living on a farm in the early 1900s describes some of the activities that mark the approach of spring.

Examples: ". . . pour hot syrup, making swirls on the snow and we'll eat the waxy candy with Grandma's sweet milk doughnuts and sour pickles; Canada Geese will fly north honking a long sad song; music of tree toads will fill the night; chase the swallows from the porch but they'll swoop and squawk and build a nest there anyway; strawberries nestle all sugary on Grandma's rich biscuits; swoop down the hill in the silvery light."

Other Devices: Simile.

Art Style: Expressionism acrylic and pastel.

Curriculum Tie-In: Science (Seasons—Spring; Ecology).

Wright, Betty Ren. *The Cat Next Door.* Illus. by Gail Owens. New York: Holiday House, 1991.
After Grandma dies, the annual visit to the summer cabin is not the same. But the cat next door remembers how things used to be and cheers a grieving grandchild.

Examples: Expressions include ". . . gulls glide up and down, riding a roller coaster made of air; drove through a dark tree-tunnel; dog stood up slowly, with his tail flip-flopping."

Other Devices: Simile. Symbol.

Art Style: Realism/Expressionism.

Curriculum Tie-In: Social Science (Death; Grief; Grandparents).

Yolen, Jane. *Welcome to the Green House.* Illus. by Laura Regan. New York: G. P. Putnam's, 1993.
Describes the tropical rainforest and the life found there.

Examples: Expressions include ". . . strong lianas bar the way; ropey vines frame the views; canopy of leaves where the sun and rain poke through narrow slots; in the dark green, light green, emerald green, bright green, copper green, blue green, ever-new green house."

Other Devices: Analogy. Atmosphere. Internal Rhyme. Onomatopoeia. Pun.

Art Style: Realism/Expressionism.

Curriculum Tie-In: Science (Rainforest; Ecology).

*Zolotow, Charlotte. *The Moon Was the Best.* Photographs by Tana Hoban. New York: Greenwillow Books, 1993.

A mother visiting Paris brings back to her daughter all her best memories of beautiful fountains, the sparkling Seine, parks, and paintings.

> **Examples:** A child asks her mother to remember scenes of Paris that show "things I'd like if I were there." There are "flowering chestnut trees along the streets"; a man feeding "a cluster of silvery pigeons"; people carrying "long loaves of unwrapped bread, like sticks under their arms"; "parks like paintings and paintings like parks"; a "tiny carousel like a birthday cake, with white animals waiting for the music to start"; fountains spraying water "in a curving white mist over prancing horses and glistening gods."
>
> **Other Devices:** Atmosphere.
>
> **Art Style:** Photography.
>
> **Curriculum Tie-In:** Geography (Paris, France).

INFERENCE

A device that allows for reasonable conclusions drawn by the reader about characters or events based upon certain limited clues or facts presented in the story by the author. Inference allows readers to make their own discoveries without direct comment from the author.

> **Example:** It rained heavily and steadily for three full days. Mark had set out hours ago to cross the hundred-year-old weakened wooden bridge. Susan was startled when the phone rang; her face paled as she listened to the caller.

SOURCES

Aardema, Verna. *Why Mosquitoes Buzz in People's Ears.* Illus. by Leo Dillon and Diane Dillon. New York: Dial, 1975. [Caldecott Award]

Mosquito tells Iguana a nonsense tale, annoying Iguana and setting off a chain reaction that causes a jungle tragedy. Mosquito's guilty conscience makes it adopt an annoying habit, which exists to this day.

> **Examples:** The mosquito whines in people's ears: "Is everyone still angry at me?" When it does that, "she gets an honest answer." People, of course, smack the mosquito.
>
> **Other Devices:** Poetic Justice.

Art Style: Expressionism/African Folk.

Curriculum Tie-In: Social Science (Foolish Behavior).

Allen, Judy. *Tiger*. Illus. by Tudor Humphries. Cambridge, MA: Candlewick Press, 1992.

When a rumor starts that there is a tiger in the woods, the villagers plan to kill it. Eating the meat, they believe, will make them brave, and selling its skin will make them rich. So when another rumor begins that a famous hunter is coming to town, the villagers decide to ask him to hunt the tiger for them.

Examples: The "hunter" stalks the tiger but "the angle is difficult and the tree is in the way." Then it is in his sights, but at the last second, "the tiger moved and spoiled his shot." Next, "the light is bad, and the shadows make it hard to judge distance." Finally, conditions are just right, and "that was when the hunter got his second shot. The tiger faced him." The fine head and great chest are just right in his sights for a "third shot." The tiger "snarled to warn him not to come any closer." All of these shots and no dead tiger? At last, the hunter "packed away his camera and rested."

Other Devices: Irony. Satire. Stereotype.

Art Style: Realism.

Curriculum Tie-In: Science (Endangered Species).

Ball, Duncan. *Jeremy's Tail*. Illus. by Donna Rawlins. New York: Ashton Scholastic, 1990.

Jeremy is determined to pin the tail on the donkey at the birthday party. He is blindfolded and doesn't want any help.

Examples: Jeremy has taken a bus trip, balloon trip, and ship rides into foreign countries and back home again in order to pin the tail on the donkey. Now he is told that his correct placement of the tail means he must have peeked. He must try it again. Poor Jeremy is seen staggering out the house door. Down the path in front of him is an alien space ship with its door open. New adventures are about to begin all over.

Other Devices: Ambiguity. Irony.

Art Style: Folk.

Bottner, Barbara. *Bootsie Barker Bites*. Illus. by Peggy Rathmann. New York: G. P. Putnam's, 1992.

Bootsie Barker likes to play only intimidating games in which she can bite, until one day her friend comes up with a better game.

Examples: Bootsie's visits are not anticipated with joy. Mother says she has a "wonderful" surprise. Bootsie will be staying overnight. The girl's eyes look startled and she knocks over her glass of juice. How would she feel if Bootsie takes a rocket to outer space? "It's fine with me." Clearly, she would be pleased to be quit of her.

Other Devices: Foreshadowing. Poetic Justice. Understatement.

Art Style: Colored Cartoon.

Curriculum Tie-In: Social Science (Bullies; Friendship).

Bunting, Eve. *Someday a Tree.* Illus. by Ronald Himler. New York: Clarion (Houghton Mifflin), 1993.

A young girl, her parents, and her neighbors try to save an old oak tree that has been poisoned by chemicals.

Examples: The end of the big tree doesn't mean the end of all trees. As the title suggests, even after the tree has died, it will live on through some of the seeds saved each year. The girl tells the tree, "I don't know, Tree, ... But maybe.... If even one of these grows, we'll have a tree, big as this!"

Other Devices: Foreshadowing.

Art Style: Impressionism.

Curriculum Tie-In: Science (Ecology; Trees).

Butler, Dorothy. *My Brown Bear Barney in Trouble.* Illus. by Elizabeth Fuller. New York: Greenwillow, 1993.

A little girl and her toy have fun all week, getting into all kinds of mischief, almost always displeasing someone. Sunday comes and things quiet down, but Barney is bored.

Examples: "Never mind," the little girl tells him. "It's Monday again tomorrow." A new week promises fresh excitement, and folks are sure to again be displeased.

Art Style: Colored Cartoon.

*Clarke, Gus. ... *Along Came Eric.* New York: Lothrop, Lee & Shepard, 1991.

Nigel is used to being the center of attention. A new baby upsets Nigel's security. He adjusts and must then help young Eric adjust when baby Alice arrives.

Examples: "Father Christmas liked Nigel very much." A huge stocking full of toys proves it. But, suddenly, "it seemed ... nobody liked Nigel much anymore," because the family can only coo over baby Eric and ignore Nigel. The huge stocking full of gifts in Eric's crib proves that Father Christmas likes Eric best of all. In the passing years the boys become closer in abilities. Nigel decides life isn't so bad, and Eric has never thought it was. But then "... along came Alice." Nigel is the expert here and knows just how to help Eric through the adjustment.

Other Devices: Foreshadowing.

Art Style: Colored Cartoon.

Curriculum Tie-In: Social Science (Siblings; Jealousy).

Corbalis, Judy. *The Cuckoo Bird.* Illus. by David Armitage. New York: HarperCollins, 1988.

A little girl and her grandmother try to outwit a shape-changing, greedy cuckoo bird who had tricked his way into their house.

Examples: Even though the cuckoo is shaped like a soldier, an old man, and a baby, telltale bird characteristics are still present: a beak nose, spur heel, some dropped feathers, a head crest, and tail feathers. These imply his true nature.

Other Devices: Poetic Justice. Theme.

Art Style: Expressionism.

Curriculum Tie-In: Health and Safety (Stranger Danger).

Crews, Donald. *Shortcut.* New York: Greenwillow, 1992.

Children taking a shortcut by walking along a railroad track find excitement and danger when a train approaches.

Examples: When the train arrives, the event is traumatic. "We jumped off the tracks onto the steep slope. We didn't think about the briers or the snakes." Fear for life takes precedence over lesser fears, and the event becomes for each of them a powerful, life-lasting memory. "We walked home without a word. We didn't tell Bigmama. We didn't tell Mama. We didn't tell anyone. We didn't talk about what happened for a very long time. And, we didn't take the shortcut again."

Other Devices: Atmosphere. Foreshadowing.

Art Style: Impressionism paint spatter.

Curriculum Tie-In: Social Science (Fear).

Dickens, Lucy. *Go Fish.* New York: Viking Penguin, 1991.

Herbert the polar bear doesn't like water and can't swim to catch fish. He depends on his parents, the penguins, and fishermen. One day he accidentally ends up in the water and discovers he has no trouble fishing or swimming.

Examples: Herbert sits on a "nice and warm" rock. Everything in the landscape is white and blue except this gray "rock." Soon the rock swims off taking Herbert into the sea. This "rock" turns out to be a whale.

Art Style: Cartoon.

Edwards, Hazel. *Snail Mail.* Illus. by Rod Clement. Australia: Collins, 1986.

A mail-eating snail describes his life with "them" and his culinary interests.

Examples: When the lady puts a "No Junk Mail" sign under her mail slot, poor snail must go on a diet because the majority of the household's mail is obviously unsolicited. Later he happily resumes eating "To-the-Householder" envelopes again. Why? Snail has neatly chewed off the "No" on the lady's junk mail sign.

Other Devices: Alliteration. Irony. Poetic Justice. Pun.

Art Style: Realism.

Ehlert, Lois. *Feathers for Lunch.* New York: Harcourt Brace Jovanovich, 1990.
An escaped house cat encounters 12 birds in the backyard but fails to catch any of them and has to eat feathers for lunch.

    Examples: The cat's bell goes jingle-jingle. It's not surprising he doesn't catch any prey. Seeing the feathers drop hint that they are all he'll get of any bird.

    Art Style: Folk.

    Curriculum Tie-In: Science (Bird and Plant Identification).

Ets, Marie Hall. *Play with Me.* New York: Viking, 1955.
A little girl tries to play with animals she finds in the meadow, but when she reaches, grabs, or runs toward them, they run away.

    Examples: When she gives up trying to play with them and simply sits quietly, they come round. The only way to make them "play" is by letting them come to you rather than actively seeking them.

    Other Devices: Imagery. Irony.

    Art Style: Naive/Cartoon pencil and charcoal drawings.

    Curriculum Tie-In: Science (Ecology).

Flack, Marjorie. *Angus and the Cat.* New York: Doubleday, 1931.
Angus the Scottie dog spends three days chasing the new cat that has come to live at his house, but when the cat disappears, Angus misses his new friend.

    Examples: Though Angus looks and can't find the cat inside or outside the house, the reader sees where it's hiding and knows the cat is not gone. There seems no doubt the cat is merely waiting its own time to show up and that when it does the two will be happy to be together again.

    Other Devices: Irony. Paradox.

    Art Style: Expressionism colored line drawings.

    Curriculum Tie-In: Social Science (Friendship; Acceptance and Respect).

Fleming, Denise. *Lunch.* New York: Henry Holt, 1992.
A very hungry mouse eats a large lunch comprised of colorful foods.

    Examples: After stuffing himself on a variety of foods, "he took a nap." There is a clear trail of messy food smears to his mouse hole. He emerges later sniff-sniffing. His gustatory activities of lunchtime are about to be repeated for dinner.

    Art Style: Expressionism colored paper pulp and stencils.

Greenfield, Eloise. *She Come Bringing Me That Little Baby Girl.* Illus. by John Steptoe. New York: J. B. Lippincott, 1974.
A child's disappointment and jealousy over a new baby sister are dispelled as he becomes aware of the importance of his new role as a big brother.

Examples: Though his mother hugs him, "she didn't put that little girl down for a minute." And, he doesn't like the way his parents look at her, "like she was the only baby in the world." The "presents all over the place" are "really making me sick." His jealousy is apparent. When he finally comes to terms with her, that, too, becomes clear. "She can have one of Mama's arms... as long as she knows the other one is mine."

Art Style: Expressionism.

Curriculum Tie-In: Social Science (Jealousy; Siblings).

*Gregory, Valiska. *Through the Mickle Woods.* Illus. by Barry Moser. Boston: Little, Brown & Co., 1992.

After his wife's death, a grieving king journeys to an old bear's cave in the Mickle Woods, where he hears three stories that help him go on living.

Examples: The king's dark, deep pain prevents him from talking about or facing his grief. The boy tells the king he misses the queen. The king says, "I will not talk of this." The boy says, "The Queen used to tell me stories." The king "turned his back as if the boy had not spoken." Finally, after listening to the bear he can hear the morning bells and is able at last to say, "Mark you, how merrily they ring." His mind has opened to appreciate the beauty of the world around him.

Other Devices: Aphorism. Atmosphere. Metaphor. Pun. Simile. Symbol. Theme.

Art Style: Expressionism/Realism.

Curriculum Tie-In: Social Science (Death; Grief).

Hoban, Russell. *Bedtime for Frances.* Illus. by Garth Williams. New York: Harper & Row, 1960.

Bedtime is 7:00 PM, but Frances is not ready to sleep.

Examples: She needs milk, another kiss, her dolls. When her parents have run out of patience with her, there is the threat of a spanking. Then something makes a fluttering noise at the window. Frances thinks about going to tell her parents but "she thought about it some more and decided not to tell them." This is a sensible decision.

Art Style: Cartoon.

Curriculum Tie-In: Social Science (Parent and Child; Self-Discovery/Esteem).

Holl, Adelaide. *The Rain Puddle.* Illus. by Roger Duvoisin. New York: Lothrop, Lee & Shepard, 1965.

Gazing at their own images, each barnyard animal thinks a similar poor creature has fallen into a rain puddle.

Examples: When the puddle dries up, each animal assumes the fallen creature must have escaped. But a "wise old owl looked down from a tree above and chuckled to himself." He, alone, seems to understand what has really happened.

Art Style: Naive.

Isadora, Rachel. *Ben's Trumpet*. New York: Greenwillow, 1979.

Ben wants to be a trumpeter, but he plays only an imaginary instrument until the neighborhood night club trumpeter discovers his ambition.

Examples: After neighborhood children tease him, Ben is ashamed of his pretend playing and "puts his hands in his pockets and walks slowly home." For-real playing becomes feasible when the club trumpeter invites him to "come on over to the club, and we'll see what we can do."

Art Style: Expressionism pen and ink/Impressionism/Realism.

Curriculum Tie-In: Music (Jazz).

Johnston, Tony. *The Cowboy and the Black-Eyed Pea*. Illus. by Warren Ludwig. New York: G. P. Putnam's, 1992.

The wealthy daughter of a Texas rancher devises a plan to find a real cowboy among her many suitors.

Examples: They prepare to go on their honeymoon with a full-blown Texas moon in front and a full-grown Texas mule in back, who is "piled high with saddle blankets—in case the need should arise." Why? Because, of course, a real cowboy has sensitive skin and will "bruise like the petals of a desert rose."

Other Devices: Atmosphere. Caricature. Parody. Simile.

Art Style: Colored Cartoon.

Johnston, Tony. *The Promise*. Illus. by Pamela Keavney. New York: A Charlotte Zolotow Book (HarperCollins), 1992.

While helping her neighbor assist one of the cows in giving birth, Ramie hears a story of another birth helped by a young person interested in cows.

Examples: When Mr. Gates begins a story about another night in which someone helped a farmer with a difficult calving, we sense that boy might be Mr. Gates, himself. Later, he uses the same tincture on the cow that the boy of long ago was taught to use. Finally, when the boy of long ago got older, "he bought more cattle. Herefords. Always Herefords," just like Mr. Gates owns.

Other Devices: Flashback. Foreshadowing. Stereotype (Reverse).

Art Style: Impressionism.

Kennedy, Richard. *The Porcelain Man*. Illus. by Marcia Sewall. Boston: Little, Brown & Co., 1976.

Each time the poor girl mends the broken porcelain vase, it turns into something different, and provides a new possible means of escape from her dreary life of repairing junk.

Examples: The porcelain vase serves its purpose but can't compete with a real man. A young man pushing a wheelbarrow stops to "comfort her" while she's mending the porcelain during one of its breaks. As they work together gluing it, the girl "admired how well and how quickly the young man worked with his hands." When they cook supper, "their eyes met often as they moved about."

Other Devices: Tone. Understatement.

Art Style: Colored Cartoon.

Kroll, Virginia. *Masai and I.* Illus by Nancy Carpenter. New York: Four Winds Press, 1992.

Linda, a little girl who lives in the city, learns in school about East Africa and the Masai. She imagines what her life might be like if she were Masai.

Examples: After comparing her life to that of the Masai, maybe the similarities are understandable given the hint that the Masai heritage could be her own. ". . . smooth brown skin over high cheekbones and black eyes that slant up a little when I smile . . . I would look just like this if I were Masai."

Other Devices: Paradox.

Art Style: Expressionism/Realism.

Curriculum Tie-In: Geography (East African Culture).

Lionni, Leo. *Inch by Inch.* New York: Obelensky Astor-Honor, 1960.

A clever inchworm uses his talent for measuring things to escape being eaten.

Examples: When the vain nightingale threatens to eat him for breakfast if he refuses to measure her song, he tells her to "go ahead and sing" while he "measured and measured . . . inch by inch." The reader sees the increasing camouflage of green stems separating and hiding the tiny worm as he moves safely out of her view.

Other Devices: Poetic Justice. Pun.

Art Style: Collage.

Curriculum Tie-In: Science (Measurement).

Mahy, Margaret. *Keeping House.* Illus. by Wendy Smith. New York: Margaret K. McElderry Books (Macmillan), 1991.

Lizzie Firkin has no time to keep house because she works at night at a famous club singing and tap dancing and playing trombone. She is too tired to sweep the floor or clean cupboards.

Examples: The housekeeper despairs that he'll never make a fortune in his profession, because all his employers clean their homes before he arrives so that he won't know how messy they really are. Will it be the same with Lizzie Firkin who "shook crumbs off the cat, dusted the parrot . . . ?" But wait; why are all the cupboards nailed shut? Maybe there is possible employment here after all.

Other Devices: Atmosphere. Hyperbole. Simile. Stereotype.

Art Style: Impressionism.

McCloskey, Robert. *One Morning in Maine.* New York: Viking, 1952.

A little girl experiences the loss of her first baby tooth one Maine morning.

> **Examples:** When Sal loses her first tooth, she makes a wish. Later, when she is offered an ice cream cone at the store, she believes her tooth wish has come true. "And it's supposed to be chocolate," she tells the store owner, who has no idea why it's "supposed" to be any such thing.
>
> **Other Devices:** Atmosphere.
>
> **Art Style:** Impressionism/Cartoon pencil shading.
>
> **Curriculum Tie-In:** Health and Safety (Maturation).
> Geography (Maine).

McCully, Emily Arnold. *Mirette on the High Wire.* New York: G. P. Putnam's, 1992. [Caldecott Award]

Mirette learns tightrope walking from Monsieur Bellini, a guest in her mother's boarding house, not knowing that he is a celebrated tightrope artist who has withdrawn from performing because of fear.

> **Examples:** A moment comes when Mirette and Bellini are together on the high wire. She recognizes that he has frozen, and she wishes to help him get across the wire. "They were thinking only of the wire, and of crossing to the end." And what about the future. Does Bellini conquer his fear? Does Mirette develop into a high wire artist herself? The final book illustration shows a promotional poster "Mirette and Bellini" with another young girl looking closely at it. The two seem to have found success together. And, perhaps interest has awakened in another young person, who is also dreaming of such a career.
>
> **Other Devices:** Atmosphere.
>
> **Art Style:** Impressionism water color.
>
> **Curriculum Tie-In:** Social Science (Courage).

McKissack, Patricia. *A Million Fish ... More or Less.* Illus. by Dena Schutzer. New York: Knopf, 1992.

A boy learns that the truth is often stretched on the Bayou Clapateaux. He gets the chance to tell his own version of a bayou tale when he goes fishing.

> **Examples:** Did those mighty peculiar things really happen, and did he really catch a million fish? Maybe, but the reader learns "a smile broke across Hugh Thomas's face, and he winked his eye," after finishing his story.
>
> **Other Devices:** Caricature. Foreshadowing. Hyperbole.
>
> **Art Style:** Impressionism/Expressionism paint.
>
> **Curriculum Tie-In:** Social Science (Self-Discovery/Esteem).

*Miles, Miska. *Annie and the Old One.* Illus. by Peter Parnall. Boston: Little, Brown & Co., 1971.

A Navajo girl tries to stop the passage of time when her grandmother announces that after "the new rug is taken from the loom, I will go to Mother Earth."

Examples: When she finally comes to realize she can't forestall the future, Annie picks up her weaving stick and tells her mother she is "ready to weave." She has accepted the approaching death of her grandmother and recognizes the continuing pattern of life "slipping the weaving stick in place, as her mother had done, as her grandmother had done."

Other Devices: Theme.

Art Style: Expressionism.

Curriculum Tie-In: Social Science (Death; Aging; Grandparents). Geography (Native American, Navajo Culture).

Nomura, Tukaaki. *Grandpa's Town.* Trans. by Amanda Mayer Stinchecum. Brooklyn: Kane/Miller, 1991.

A young Japanese boy, worried that his widowed grandfather is lonely, accompanies him to the public bath.

Examples: Slowly the boy realizes his grandfather actually has a large network of friends where he lives and doesn't need to go live with him and his mother. The fish man says, "So, Gen, this is your grandson?" The greengrocer asks, "On your way to the bath, Gen?" The lady in the attendant's booth says, "My, Gen, you're very early today." All through the day, people talk to his grandfather in a familiar way. Finally, the boy concludes, "You aren't alone after all, are you, Grandpa?"

Art Style: Expressionism/Japanese Folk.

Curriculum Tie-In: Social Science (Grandparents). Geography (Japanese Culture).

Okimoto, Jean Davies. *Blumpoe the Grumpoe Meets Arnold the Cat.* Illus. by Howie Schneider. Boston: Little, Brown & Co., 1990.

A grumpy old man and a shy young cat form an unlikely friendship at a Minnesota inn which provides its guests with a cat for the night.

Examples: Though it wasn't easy, shy, persistent Arnold finally manages to break through Blumpoe's angry loneliness. At last, Blumpoe can smell Dutch cinnamon rolls baking again, which he has not noticed since his cat Raymond died. He even "sleepily . . . stroked Arnold's fur."

Other Devices: Allusion.

Art Style: Cartoon.

Curriculum Tie-In: Social Science (Loneliness).

Oppenheim, Shulamith Levy. *The Lily Cupboard.* Illus. by Ronald Himler. New York: A Charlotte Zolotow Book (HarperCollins), 1992.

Miriam, a young Jewish girl, is forced to leave her parents and hide with strangers in the country during the German occupation of Holland.

> **Examples:** It is obvious that the family who cares for Miriam is loving and understanding of the Jewish situation. The woman "has a broad, kind face" and the man "has a million wrinkles around his eyes," and puts his arm around her shoulder when he explains the importance of the hiding cupboard. Their son "grins" in a friendly manner and gives her a rabbit to help her pain lessen at being away from her parents.
>
> **Other Devices:** Symbol.
>
> **Art Style:** Impressionism water color gouache.
>
> **Curriculum Tie-In:** History (German Occupation—Netherlands). Social Science (War).

Parnall, Peter. *The Great Fish.* Garden City, NY: Doubleday, 1973.

A beloved grandfather's poetic explanation for the cause of spawning salmon that saved the Indians from starvation is a poignant reminder of a heritage lost.

> **Examples:** The grandfather does not have to explain the reason why the spawning salmon do not return up the mountain stream. He merely says, ". . . a mother's tears are not enough." The reason is expressed through the illustrations, which show water polluted by waste dumping of all kinds.
>
> **Other Devices:** Imagery. Understatement.
>
> **Art Style:** Expressionism pen and ink line drawing.
>
> **Curriculum Tie-In:** Science (Environment; Ecology).

Rayner, Mary. *Mr. & Mrs. Pig's Evening Out.* New York: Atheneum, 1976.

The babysitter is not what she seems to be, and it takes the quick wits and resourcefulness of the 10 brave piglets to avert dreadful consequences.

> **Examples:** When Mr. Pig invites the sitter to have "something to eat later," Mrs. Wolf says, "Thank you, I shall." Later in the piglets' room she looks "longingly at Garth, all rosy, plump, and pink."
>
> **Art Style:** Colored Cartoon.
>
> **Curriculum Tie-In:** Health and Safety (Stranger Danger).

Rosenberg, Liz. *Monster Mama.* Illus. by Stephen Gammell. New York: Philomel (Putnam & Grosset), 1993.

Patrick Edward's fierce mother helps him deal with some obnoxious bullies.

> **Examples:** Monster Mama's reputation helps teach the bullies responsibility. When they harass Patrick, taking his dessert in the paper bag and his cap, she thunders and frightens and informs the bullies that "I still want something lovely for dessert!" Soon, they are in the kitchen where they "feverishly sifted and stirred and baked a strawberry tea cake with French whipped cream on

top." Later, as they eat together the boys declare, "Your mother is something else." And, they're not thinking bad thoughts.

Other Devices: Ambiguity. Aphorism. Hyperbole. Simile.

Art Style: Expressionism.

Rosenberg, Liz. *The Scrap Doll.* Illus. by Robin Ballard. New York: A Charlotte Zolotow Book (HarperCollins), 1991.

A little girl fixes up her mother's old scrap doll and learns that one made at home with love can be much better than the most beautiful store-bought doll.

Examples: Lydia thinks her creative efforts resulted in an "ugly old thing," but this attitude changes when her mother asks what the doll's name is. The reader knows Lydia has come to accept the doll when she names it Sarah because the name "suits her."

Other Devices: Theme.

Art Style: Cartoon.

Curriculum Tie-In: Social Science (Values).

Sakai, Kimiko. *Sachiko Means Happiness.* Illus. by Tomie Arai. San Francisco: Children's Book Press, 1990.

Although at first Sachiko is upset when her grandmother no longer recognizes her, she grows to understand that they can still be happy together.

Examples: The girl understands at last that in her mind, the grandmother "is a little girl, only five years old." She realizes "it must be hard . . . to suddenly discover that everyone is a stranger to you." At this point, her anger against this strange turn of events dissolves and a new relationship of acceptance develops. She feels love for someone helpless and pretends to meet her for the first time and to invite her to come home with the family. Her father, also, realizes a change is in order and plays along with her as he "nodded, nodded knowingly."

Other Devices: Foreshadowing.

Art Style: Realism/Impressionism.

Curriculum Tie-In: Health and Safety (Alzheimer's Disease).

****Say, Allen.** *Tree of Cranes.* Boston: Houghton Mifflin, 1991.

A Japanese boy learns of Christmas when his mother decorates a pine tree with paper cranes.

Examples: On the day the story begins the narrator, speaking of a time when he was a child, says, "The last time I went there was a gray winter day." His mother does not want him to go near the neighbor's pond. She fears he will drown. He disobeys her warning. But when the story concludes, he makes her a Christmas promise not to do it again. Apparently, he has kept that promise, for it is many years later after that first Christmas.

Other Devices: Atmosphere. Flash-Forward. Point-Of-View.

Art Style: Oriental Folk Realism.

Curriculum Tie-In: Social Science (Cross-Cultures).

Schermbrucker, Reviva. *Charlie's House.* Illus. by Niki Daly. New York: Viking Penguin, 1989.

After some men build Charlie's house with cement, pole supports, and iron sheet walls and roof, Charlie fashions his own version of a house from clay mud and scraps of trash.

> **Examples:** Charlie's dreams of how things can be better are apparently realized when "he put his foot down . . . and kept going." A grown up Charlie is wearing sunglasses and is leaving shantytown in his car. People are waving good-bye. Perhaps Charlie has realized his dreams of a better life.
>
> **Other Devices:** Flashback.
>
> **Art Style:** Expressionism.

Sendak, Maurice. *Where the Wild Things Are.* New York: Harper & Row, 1963. [Caldecott Award]

Max is a little boy dressed in a wolf suit sent to his room for behaving ferociously. Suddenly the walls disappear and he finds himself in a magic forest of wild creatures.

> **Examples:** Max "made mischief of one kind and another." He pounds a nail into the wall making a sizable hole, chases the family pet dog, threatening it with a fork, and he gets sent to his room for sassing his mother. But he is not submissive. "I'll eat you up," he shouts at her and gets nothing to eat for supper. In retaliation, his imaginative "wild things" are ordered to bed without supper to show his power over them.
>
> **Other Devices:** Hyperbole. Point-Of-View. Theme.
>
> **Art Style:** Expressionism pen and ink colored drawings.
>
> **Curriculum Tie-In:** Social Science (Self-Discovery/Esteem; Anger; Consequences; Forgiveness; Parent and Child).

Shulevitz, Uri. *One Monday Morning.* New York: Charles Scribner's, 1967.

A lonely boy's daydream brings a whole pack of playing-card visitors to his drab city apartment.

> **Examples:** Not until the end does the reader observe how it came to be that the "King," "Queen," and the entire entourage who visit the boy on Sunday have been conjured up through looking at the pictures on playing cards.
>
> **Art Style:** Cartoon/Impressionism pen and ink.
>
> **Curriculum Tie-In:** Social Science (Loneliness).

Spinelli, Eileen. *Somebody Loves You, Mr. Hatch.* Illus. by Paul Yalowitz. New York: Bradbury, 1991.

An anonymous valentine changes the life of the unsociable Mr. Hatch, turning him into a laughing friend who helps and appreciates all his neighbors.

Examples: Before the valentine, his life is narrow and colorless. Every day he gets up 6:30 sharp, leaves his brick house and walks eight blocks to the shoelace factory where he works. "At lunchtime he would sit alone in a corner, eat his cheese and mustard sandwich, and drink a cup of coffee. Sometimes he brought a prune for dessert." This bleak person certainly needs a valentine in his life.

Other Devices: Irony.

Art Style: Naive.

Curriculum Tie-In: Social Science (Self-Discovery/Esteem; Loneliness).

Steig, William. *The Amazing Bone.* New York: Farrar Straus Giroux, 1976.
A talking bone saves a charming piglet from being food for a fox.

Examples: "It would be amusing to gnaw on a bone that talks . . . and screams with pain." The bone wisely took the implied warning and "kept quiet the rest of the way, and so did Pearl." It seemed that Pearl was about to be the fox's main course in his meal. She could smell "vinegar and oil" as the fox prepared a salad. She could hear him "sharpening a knife" and "wood being put into a stove."

Other Devices: Atmosphere. Caricature. Foreshadowing. Irony.

Art Style: Cartoon water color.

Steptoe, John. *Stevie.* New York: Harper & Row, 1969.
When his mother takes on a babysitting job and announces that he will have "a little friend come stay with you," Robert can only see him for a nuisance. Little Stevie stops coming and Robert finds he actually regrets his absence. He was "kinda like a little brother."

Examples: Maybe Robert doesn't really hate having Stevie, the nuisance, around as much as he pretends. He says, "Sometimes people get on your nerves and they don't mean it or nothin' but they just bother you. . . . He couldn't help it cause he was stupid." Robert stands up for Stevie in front of his buddies. "He's just my friend and he's stayin' at my house."

Other Devices: Irony. Paradox.

Art Style: Expressionism heavy black outlines suggestive of stained glass.

Curriculum Tie-In: Social Science (Self-Discovery/Esteem; Jealousy).

Tobias, Tobi. *Pot Luck.* Illus. by Nola Malone. New York: Lothrop, Lee & Shepard, 1993.
Rachel learns her grandmother's definition of "pot luck" when she helps Gram prepare dinner for an old friend.

Examples: It is obvious that Sophie is Gram's very special friend, and pot luck for her will not be according to the general understanding of the concept. Rachel watches Gram buy the perfect chicken, the best fruit and vegetables, and ingredients for a home baked cake (not one wrapped in plastic from the store). Gram says Sophie has "red hair, blue eyes, and a smile like sun in the morning." When they are nearly ready for their guest, Gram tells Rachel to put on something nice because "pot luck doesn't mean blue jeans" for Sophie and it doesn't mean "last night's stew."

Other Devices: Irony.

Art Style: Colored Cartoon pencil lines.

Curriculum Tie-In: Social Science (Friendship).

Turkle, Brinton. *Obadiah the Bold.* New York: Viking, 1965.

A young Quaker boy in nineteenth-century Nantucket dreams of becoming a pirate.

Examples: Not until Obadiah's older siblings demonstrate the harsher side of being a pirate, does he rethink his career goals. They tie him up, put him in the "brig," and make him "walk the plank." Afterwards, Obadiah no longer "takes his spy glass to the supper table" or "to bed with him." His father tells him a real hero's tale about his seafaring grandfather, and Obadiah says of the Cape Horn, "Someday I'll see it." He still plans a life at sea but is cured of wishing to be a pirate.

Art Style: Impressionism.

Curriculum Tie-In: History (Nineteenth-Century New England—Quaker Life).

Turnbull, Ann. *The Tapestry Cats.* Illus. by Carol Morley. Boston: Little, Brown & Co., 1992.

Subdued by her mother who always knows what is best for her, a princess dreams of having pet cats.

Examples: Her fairy godmother "smiled at the princess as if she guessed all her thoughts." She understands the princess wants for her seventh birthday "Silver" and "Gold," the two cats pictured in the tapestry. The queen also thinks silver and gold would be appropriate gifts but thinks the fairy godmother needs a new wand. When she receives "Silver" and "Gold," the princess "knew there was nothing wrong with the old one." Only the upstairs chambermaid complains about needing to moth-proof the tapestries. "There are holes in two of them as big as cats."

Other Devices: Ambiguity. Simile.

Art Style: Naive.

Van Allsburg, Chris. *The Garden of Abdul Gasazi.* Boston: Houghton Mifflin, 1979.

Does the retired magician change dogs into ducks? Or is Miss Hester right that Alan has only been fooled?

Examples: When the bad tempered dog/duck grabs his hat and flies off with it, Alan notes, "You really haven't changed so much." But the dog Fritz is waiting at Miss Hester's door, very much himself. Still, after Alan leaves, thinking the garden owner has teased him, Fritz has something in his mouth that he drops at Miss Hester's feet. "What are you doing with Alan's hat?" she asks.

Art Style: Impressionism carbon pencil light and dark tones.

Van Allsburg, Chris. *The Widow's Broom.* New York: Houghton Mifflin, 1992.
A witch's worn out broom serves a widow well, until her neighbors decide it's wicked and must be destroyed.

> **Examples:** The widow must think quickly how she will save her broom. She "could tell by their faces that the men would not be leaving without the broom." She does provide them with a broom, which they promptly destroy. Later, she tells the neighbors she's seen a ghost of the broom "as white as snow . . . carrying an axe." They flee in terror, and she smiles at her magical broom, not the one she gave them to destroy. Her special broom is "not a ghost at all, but still covered with the coat of white paint she'd given it." The widow and her former witch's broom have no more problems with nosy neighbors.

> **Other Devices:** Allusion. Stereotype.

> **Art Style:** Impressionism.

Wells, Rosemary. *Benjamin and Tulip.* New York: Dial, 1973.
Benjamin is bullied by Tulip until he has nothing to lose and takes action that earns her respect.

> **Examples:** A new understanding has been achieved between the two when Benjamin jumps out of a tree and "accidentally" lands on Tulip and then "accidentally" bounces a watermelon off her head. Pretty soon they're both eating watermelon and spitting seeds at each other.

> **Other Devices:** Understatement.

> **Art Style:** Colored Cartoon pen and ink.

> **Curriculum Tie-In:** Social Science (Bullies; Friendship; Anger; Self-Discovery/Esteem).

Zion, Gene. *Harry the Dirty Dog.* Illus. by Margaret Graham. New York: Harper & Row, 1956.
A white dog with black spots takes a tour of his town and gets so dirty he becomes unrecognizable as a black dog with white spots.

> **Examples:** He begins his adventures by hiding the scrub brush because he hates baths. It ends with his retrieving the brush so he can rejoin his family as a clean dog they recognize. Still, there is no sense overdoing the clean thing. He keeps control of the brush under his sleeping pillow. No future baths unless he wants them.

> **Other Devices:** Irony.

> **Art Style:** Naive/Cartoon.

INTERNAL RHYME

Two or more words rhyme within a single line.

Example: I bring fresh showers to thirsting flowers.   —Shelley

SOURCES

Amoss, Berthe. *Old Hannibal and the Hurricane.* New York: Hyperion, 1991.
On board the ship *Sally Sue,* Old Hannibal is describing for his friends the great hurricane he once endured, when they run into another one.

    Examples: ". . . south-mouth; a hurricane of tremendous fame and Bellowing Bertha was her name; ready to scare . . . then and there; other boats and fishing floats; clippers and kippers; trees and debris; woe, I'm feeling low; glided to rest on the very next crest."

    Other Devices: Alliteration. Hyperbole.

    Art Style: Cartoon.

Cameron, Polly. *I Can't Said the Ant.* New York: Coward-McCann, 1961.
An ant, encouraged by a kitchen battalion of 89 objects, comes to the rescue of a fallen teapot.

    Examples: Among many, many one liners: "She went kerplop said the mop."

    Other Devices: Allusion. Pun. Theme.

    Art Style: Cartoon.

    Curriculum Tie-In: Science (Lever and Pulley).

Gerrard, Roy. *Rosie and the Rustlers.* New York: Farrar Straus Giroux, 1989.
Rosie's herd of steers won't be safe until the rustlers are tracked down and brought to justice.

    Examples: "Where the mountains meet the prairie, where the men are wild and hairy." Etc.

    Art Style: Expressionism.

Gross, Theodore Faro. *Everyone Asked about You.* Illus. by Sheila White Samton. New York: Philomel, 1990.
Nora's friend Charlie claims that everywhere he went in the universe, they asked about her.

    Examples: ". . . hitched a trip on a rocket ship; All right, all right, Mister Sunshine Bright; I took a hike to the peak of Mt. Pike."

    Other Devices: Hyperbole.

    Art Style: Folk.

Kahl, Virginia. *Plum Pudding for Christmas.* New York: Charles Scribner's, 1956.
After inviting the king to be their Christmas guest, the duchess and her daughters are unable to serve the promised plum pudding.

> **Examples:** ". . . a big clump of plump purple plums in a sack . . . each bumpy lump is a plum that is plump."
> **Other Devices:** Alliteration. Foreshadowing. Irony. Understatement.
> **Art Style:** Colored Cartoon.
> **Curriculum Tie-In:** History (Medieval Times).

Southey, Robert. *The Cataract of Lodore.* Illus. by David Catrow. New York: Henry Holt & Co., 1992.
At the request of his children, the author creates a descriptive poem evoking the beauty and feel of water that flows on its way to a famous waterfall in England.

> **Examples:** Several pages of "recoiling, turmoiling" and "toiling and boiling" and "thumping and plumping" and "bumping and jumping." Etc.
> **Art Style:** Colored Cartoon.
> **Curriculum Tie-In:** Science (Geology).

Steig, William. *Shrek.* New York: Farrar Straus Giroux, 1990.
Like two peas in a pod, ugly Shrek and his ugly bride are made for each other and live horribly ever after, scaring the socks off all who fall afoul of them.

> **Examples:** ". . . in here a fearless knight, in there a well-born fright; do me the honor to step aside, so Shrek can go to meet his bride; magicians mercury, plumber's lead, I smite your stupid, scabby head."
> **Other Devices:** Alliteration. Hyperbole.
> **Art Style:** Cartoon.
> **Curriculum Tie-In:** Social Science (Acceptance and Respect).

Vozar, David. *Yo, Hungry Wolf! A Nursery Rap.* Illus. by Betsy Lewin. New York: Delacorte, 1993.
A retelling in rap verse of "The Three Little Pigs," "Little Red Riding Hood," and "The Boy Who Cried Wolf."

> **Examples:** ". . . they see and flee him; blows at his foes; at the door with a roar; shack is intact; clothes are soilin' and Wolfie's recoilin'; though weak in physique; eyes are the size of those mean wolf guys."
> **Other Devices:** Tone.
> **Art Style:** Colored Cartoon.

Yolen, Jane. *Welcome to the Green House.* Illus. by Laura Regan. New York: G. P. Putnam's, 1993.
Describes the tropical rainforest and the life found there.

Examples: ". . . a lunge of waking lizards, a plunge of silver fish; a flash of blue humming bird, a splash of golden toad; a slide of coral snake, a glide of butterflies; from the water's edge, from the rocky ledge; everywhere color threads through, spreads through the hot green house."

Other Devices: Analogy. Atmosphere. Imagery. Onomatopoeia. Pun.

Art Style: Realism/Expressionism.

Curriculum Tie-In: Science (Rainforest; Ecology).

IRONY

Contrast between expected outcomes or what appears to be and the actual way things turn out; a device useful to humorously comment upon the unpredictable nature of life. There are three main literary forms of irony:

Verbal.   Saying one thing and meaning its opposite.

As you come in from a raging blizzard you say, "Nice day, huh?"

Situation. Events turn out opposite to what is expected to happen or what seems appropriate under the circumstances.

A man believes he is the only human left on Earth; in despair he swallows sleeping tablets; just as he slips into unconsciousness, the telephone rings.

Dramatic. The reader perceives something that the characters in the story don't see or know. In picture books this may often be shown through illustrations.

SOURCES

Ada, Alma Flor. *The Golden Coin.* Illus. by Neil Waldman. Trans. from Spanish by Bernice Randall. New York: Atheneum, 1991.

Determined to steal an old woman's gold, a young thief follows her around the countryside and finds himself inadvertently helping others and being transformed in the process.

Examples: While the thief believes he is working hard to get to the woman's gold, he digs potatoes and tastes a home-cooked meal that makes him remember long ago. He picks corn and notices the beauty of a sunrise as he shakes hands and is warmed by the human touch. He gathers squash and beans and smiles to see a family of rabbits. He helps with a coffee harvest and enjoys the peaceful calm of the hillsides. When the gold finally comes into his hand, he quickly passes it on to someone else who "will need it more than I."

Other Devices: Ambiguity.

Art Style: Latin American Folk.

Curriculum Tie-In: Social Science (Ethics).

*Alexander, Lloyd. *The Fortune-Tellers*. Illus. by Trina Schart Hyman. New York: Dutton Children's Books, 1992.

A carpenter goes to a fortune-teller and finds the predictions about his future come true in an unusual way.

Examples: The mundane, one-fits-all fortune that he's given is actually self-fulfilling. When the fortune-teller turns up missing, the carpenter finds fame and fortune by accidentally stepping into his role. The good life comes to him because of mistaken identity and a belief that his fortune will come true.

Other Devices: Satire.

Art Style: Realism/Expressionism.

Alexander, Martha. *Nobody Asked Me if I Wanted a Baby Sister*. New York: Dial, 1971.

Oliver wants to give away his sister until, during a crying fit one day, she shows a clear preference for him. Suddenly, he finds her "a lot smarter than I thought."

Examples: Oliver is convinced his sister is a complete liability. But when the little girl will accept no comfort from anyone except him, he decides perhaps she does have some good qualities after all. All it took was her showing a need for him.

Art Style: Cartoon.

Curriculum Tie-In: Social Science (Jealousy; Siblings).

Allard, Harry. *It's So Nice to Have a Wolf Around the House*. Illus. by James Marshall. Garden City, NY: Doubleday, 1977.

A wolf answers an ad to be companion to an old man and his older pets. The companion does a wonderful job until he falls ill and must, himself, be nursed. Everyone benefits from the new arrangement.

Examples: The poor decrepit householder and his ancient pets, who can barely move around, suddenly become enlivened when they must nurse someone who is worse off than they.

Other Devices: Satire. Stereotype.

Art Style: Cartoon.

Curriculum Tie-In: Social Science (Prejudice; Forgiveness).

Allen, Judy. *Tiger*. Illus. by Tudor Humphries. Cambridge, MA: Candlewick Press, 1992.

When a rumor starts that there is a tiger in the woods, the villagers plan to kill it for the strength that will come to them from eating tiger meat and the riches they will earn from selling its hide.

Examples: Why not let the professional hunter do their work for them? They believe they see "a gun in his pack with a telephoto lens, so he doesn't have to get too close." But the person the villagers have put their faith in so they won't have to face the danger returns with photos, not a dead tiger.

Other Devices: Inference. Satire. Stereotype.

Art Style: Realism.

Curriculum Tie-In: Science (Endangered Species).

Asch, Frank. *Moon Bear*. New York: Charles Scribner's, 1978.
A bear who falls in love with the moon worries when it diminishes.

Examples: The bear believes he's helping the moon get fat by feeding it honey. When he finds out differently, he feels sad that he can't do anything for the moon, but the little birds, who are benefiting from the honey, tell the bear, "We still need you."

Other Devices: Ambiguity.

Art Style: Naive/Cartoon colored pen and ink.

Ball, Duncan. *Jeremy's Tail*. Illus. by Donna Rawlins. New York: Ashton Scholastic, 1990.
Jeremy is determined to pin the tail on the donkey at the birthday party. He is blindfolded and doesn't want any help.

Examples: After going through astonishing adventures determined to pin the tail on the donkey without cheating, he ends up placing the tail nearly perfectly. It is assumed he must have peeked. So, in spite of his effort, he is asked to try again and must begin the process all over.

Other Devices: Ambiguity. Inference.

Art Style: Folk.

*Carlstrom, Nancy White. *Fish and Flamingo*. Illus. by Lisa Desimini. Boston: Little, Brown & Co., 1993.
Two unlikely friends spend time together, help each other out, and tell stories about their lives.

Examples: When the friends must part, each wants to give the other a special gift that seems impossible. Flamingo wants Fish to witness the pink of a sunrise. Fish wants Flamingo to experience the silvery light of a night star shining on the edge of a wave. In the morning, when Fish and his friends gather at the water's surface to wave good-bye to Flamingo, they see only a mass of pink flying overhead as the flamingos migrate. Together they produce the effect of a pink sunrise, the gift Flamingo wanted Fish to have. Looking down to wave at his friend Fish, Flamingo sees only a churning mass of silver and recognizes that Fish has produced on the water's surface the effect of starlight. Neither friend knows he has given the special gift to the other.

Other Devices: Paradox.

Art Style: Expressionism paint.

Curriculum Tie-In: Social Science (Friendship).
Literature (Plot Balance).

Duvoisin, Roger. *Petunia.* New York: Knopf, 1950.
A silly goose carries around a book thinking that it will make her look smart.

> **Examples:** The more Petunia relies on the book, which she can not read, as her symbol for wisdom, the less she is successful helping her friends. Only when she decides to set aside the book and rely on her good common sense is she truly wise and helpful. A book that is unread does no good.
>
> **Other Devices:** Aphorism. Symbol.
>
> **Art Style:** Colored Cartoon
>
> **Curriculum Tie-In:** Social Science (Self-Discovery/Esteem; Values).

Edwards, Hazel. *Snail Mail.* Illus. by Rod Clement. Australia: Collins, 1986.
A mail-eating snail describes his life with "them" and his culinary interests.

> **Examples:** The snail who nibbles paper also chews on the lady's food magazine. It features escargot recipes she will never see.
>
> **Other Devices:** Alliteration. Inference. Poetic Justice. Pun.
>
> **Art Style:** Realism.

Ets, Marie Hall. *Play with Me.* New York: Viking, 1955.
A little girl tries to play with animals she finds in the meadow, but when she reaches, grabs, or runs toward them, they run away.

> **Examples:** Only when she gives up trying to make them play with her and sits silently on a rock by the pond, do the animals return. ". . . I didn't move and I didn't speak. . . . All of them—all of them, were playing with me."
>
> **Other Devices:** Imagery. Inference.
>
> **Art Style:** Naive/Cartoon pencil and charcoal drawings.
>
> **Curriculum Tie-In:** Science (Ecology).

Flack, Marjorie. *Angus and the Cat.* New York: Doubleday, 1931.
Angus the Scottie dog spends three days chasing the new cat that has come to live at this house. When the cat disappears, Angus misses his new friend.

> **Examples:** The cat troubles his life, but without her, life is boring and lonely. Actually, he needs to have her around.
>
> **Other Devices:** Inference. Paradox.
>
> **Art Style:** Expressionism colored line drawings
>
> **Curriculum Tie-In:** Social Science (Friendship; Acceptance and Respect).

Greenfield, Eloise. *First Pink Light.* Illus. by Jan Spivey Gilchrist. New York: Black Butterfly Children's Books, 1976, 1991.
Tyree wants to wait up to hear his father come home early in the morning. He and his mother work out a compromise so that he doesn't have to go to bed.

> **Examples:** When his mother suggests he "put on pajamas and sit in the big chair," he thinks he has won the test of wills. But the pillow and blanket felt "pretty good." Then the "pillow got softer and the blanket got warmer, and just before he felt his eyes close, he knew his mother had won. But he was too sleepy to care."
>
> **Art Style:** Expressionism gouache and pastels.
>
> **Curriculum Tie-In:** Social Science (Parent and Child).

Henkes, Kevin. *Chrysanthemum.* New York: Greenwillow, 1991.
Chrysanthemum loves her name, until she starts going to school, and the other children make fun of it.

> **Examples:** The name being ridiculed suddenly sounds beautiful to the children when they learn their "indescribable . . . something out of a dream" music teacher not only also has a flower's name, but loves the name "Chrysanthemum" and is going to name her own baby the same if it's a girl. Now the children adore flower names. "Call me Marigold." "I'm Carnation." "My name is Lily of the Valley." Etc.
>
> **Other Devices:** Poetic Justice.
>
> **Art Style:** Colored Cartoon.
>
> **Curriculum Tie-In:** Social Science (Self-Discovery/Esteem; Values).

Henkes, Kevin. *Julius the Baby of the World.* New York: Greenwillow, 1990.
Lilly is convinced that the arrival of her new baby brother is the worst thing that has happened in their house, until Cousin Garland comes to visit.

> **Examples:** Not until Garland damns Julius's pink nose, black eyes, and white fur with the same epithets she, herself, has used against the baby, does Lilly suddenly become defensive and protective of her brother. Things she formerly made fun of now get her proud support.
>
> **Art Style:** Cartoon.
>
> **Curriculum Tie-In:** Social Science (Siblings; Jealousy).

Hilton, Nette. *Dirty Dave.* Illus. by Roland Harvey. New York: Orchard Books, 1990.
Members of an outlaw family gain acceptance from the public because of the fine clothes their father makes for them.

> **Examples:** Respect isn't the result of the efforts of the fierce outlaw members of the family who bring riches and fame to the household. It's the quiet, excellent skills of father, who sews. Customers flock to make purchases. No more need to be bandits. Father makes them rich.

Other Devices: Stereotype (Reverse). Understatement.

Art Style: Cartoon.

Curriculum Tie-In: Social Science (Sexism).

Hutchins, Pat. *Rosie's Walk.* New York: Macmillan, 1968.
Rosie the hen strolls through the barnyard oblivious to the fox who follows her in spite of a series of mishaps.

> **Examples:** Time and again Rosie has close calls. But instead of gaining an easy chicken dinner, the determined fox misses his aim. The unaware chicken escapes without realizing there was ever any danger threatening her.
>
> **Other Devices:** Foreshadowing. Poetic Justice. Satire. Stereotype.
>
> **Art Style:** Expressionism.
>
> **Curriculum Tie-In:** Health and Safety (Accident Prevention).

Hutchins, Pat. *What Game Shall We Play?* New York: Greenwillow, 1990.
The animals ask each other what game they should play, but only Owl has an answer.

> **Examples:** While busily searching for one another to ask what game they should play, the animals are actually informally playing the very game that owl later suggests they play: hide and seek.
>
> **Other Devices:** Paradox.
>
> **Art Style:** Cartoon/Folk.

Johnston, Tony. *Goblin Walk.* Illus. by Bruce Degen. New York: G. P. Putnam's, 1991.
A little goblin has a series of frightening experiences while walking through the woods to his grandmother's house.

> **Examples:** Goblins are supposed to do the scaring, not the other way around. This one meets common creatures such as butterflies and bunnies and is terrorized by them. His grandma must walk him back home so these "bad" things don't scare him.
>
> **Other Devices:** Paradox. Point-Of-View.
>
> **Art Style:** Colored Cartoon.
>
> **Curriculum Tie-In:** Social Science (Fear).

Kahl, Virginia. *How Do You Hide a Monster?* New York: Charles Scribner's, 1971.
Townspeople join forces to lead astray a group of men sent to investigate a monster in their lake.

> **Examples:** Instead of cooperating to get rid of it, the people conspire to protect their monster. "We never need to worry when Phinney's about. He's the rare kind of friend we can't do without."
>
> **Other Devices:** Alliteration. Ambiguity.

Art Style: Colored Cartoon.

Curriculum Tie-In: Social Science (Cooperation).

Kahl. Virginia. *Plum Pudding for Christmas.* New York: Charles Scribner's, 1956.
After inviting the king to be their Christmas guest, the duchess and her daughters are unable to serve the promised plum pudding.

Examples: The duke feels morose at coming home without the promised gold or silk he has intended. But his family is far more pleased with what he does bring—the plums they need for their guest's pudding. He saves the day, not to mention his family's heads.

Other Devices: Alliteration. Foreshadowing. Internal Rhyme. Understatement.

Art Style: Colored Cartoon.

Curriculum Tie-In: History (Medieval Times).

Kasza, Keiko. *The Rat and the Tiger.* New York: G. P. Putnam's 1993.
In his friendship with Rat, Tiger takes advantage and bullies Rat because of his greater size. But, one day Rat stands up for his rights.

Examples: After Tiger destroys Rat's castle in a karate style kick, Rat refuses to be Tiger's friend. Only then does Tiger become a good fair-playing friend, making amends for his past injustices.

Other Devices: Foreshadowing.

Art Style: Colored Cartoon.

Curriculum Tie-In: Social Science (Friendship; Bullies).

Keller, Holly. *Henry's Happy Birthday.* New York: Greenwillow, 1990.
Relates the disappointments and eventual joy of Henry's birthday party.

Examples: The cake isn't chocolate like it's supposed to be; he must give up his silver-colored candy basket for cousin Gertie; he has to wear party clothes instead of his favorite play things; he is sure his gifts won't be what he wants; he is shoved out of the game, musical chairs. But the pink and white cake tastes good. The gifts are surprisingly good. It turns out to be a nice party after all.

Art Style: Cartoon.

Curriculum Tie-In: Social Science (Family Life).

Kellogg, Steven. *Pinkerton, Behave!* New York: Dial, 1977.
Pinkerton fails to learn behavior, but when he comes face to face with a burglar his bad habits become useful.

Examples: Normal commands won't work with Pinkerton. But, by reversing the commands, he responds and saves the day.

Other Devices: Ambiguity.

Art Style: Cartoon.

Kimmel, Eric. *Four Dollars and Fifty Cents.* Illus. by Glen Rounds. New York: Holiday House, 1989.

To avoid paying the Widow Macrae the four dollars and fifty cents he owes her, deadbeat cowboy Shorty Long plays dead and almost gets buried alive.

Examples: Even after Shorty Long gets a share of five hundred dollars in reward for recovering stolen money in a train robbery, he never settles up his four dollars and fifty cents debt at the Silver Dollar Cafe.

Other Devices: Allusion. Pun. Simile.

Art Style: Impressionism.

Curriculum Tie-In: Social Science (Foolish Behavior).

Kraus, Robert. *Milton the Early Riser.* Illus. by Jose Aruego and Ariane Aruego. New York: Windmill Books (E. P. Dutton), 1972.

Milton copes with his early morning loneliness in a manner that exhausts him by the time everyone else awakes.

Examples: A whirlwind had messed everything up while the animals slept. Because Milton is awake, he puts things to right before the others awake. But, when his mother says, "Wake up sleepy-head, . . Milton the early riser didn't hear a word." His family doesn't know he is worn out from all he'd already done that day.

Other Devices: Hyperbole. Pun.

Art Style: Colored Cartoon.

Leaf, Munro. *The Story of Ferdinand.* Illus. by Robert Lawson. New York: Viking, 1936.

Ferdinand is a bull who would rather sit and smell the flowers than fight.

Examples: The bull least likely to make a fighter is erroneously selected and labeled "Ferdinand the Fierce" because of his reaction to a bee sting that made him appear to be what he was not.

Other Devices: Foreshadowing. Satire.

Art Style: Expressionism/Cartoon.

Curriculum Tie-In: Social Science (Acceptance and Respect).

Lionni, Leo. *Frederick.* New York: Pantheon, 1967.

During fall food gathering, his friends don't feel Frederick is doing his share of the work. However, when the food later runs out and tempers fray in the dreary winter, it is Frederick's contributions that prove most welcome.

Examples: What makes the harsh winter season ultimately endurable is not the practical, dedicated gathering of food supplies, but rather the less valued gifts that Frederick brings. He offers "sun rays for cold dark winter days," because "winter is gray." He brings words for when "we'll run out of things to say." Being a dreamer has its useful side when times are tough.

Other Devices: Theme.

Art Style: Collage.

Curriculum Tie-In: Social Science (Values; Cooperation).

McNaughton, Colin. *Guess Who's Just Moved in Next Door?* New York: Random House, 1991.

A tour through a very peculiar neighborhood where an assortment of wacky neighbors from Superman to a ship of pirates reacts to the arrival of new neighbors.

Examples: The weird "regulars" worry that the new neighbors, who happen to be a normal human family, will lower property values, might be scary, could be ugly or crooks, etc. These very traits are the ones that the neighborhood folk have.

Other Devices: Allusion. Caricature. Parallel Story. Pun. Satire.

Art Style: Cartoon.

Novak, Matt. *Elmer Blunt's Open House.* New York: Orchard Books, 1992.

Several animals and a robber explore Elmer Blunt's home one day after he forgot to close the door on his way to work.

Examples: Though his home had been ransacked while he was gone, Elmer Blunt innocently cleans it all up, assuming that in his morning haste after oversleeping, he had left it untidy. He then goes to sleep "in his safe, quiet home," as the animals hiding under his bed creep away. He is unaware of any visitors.

Other Devices: Ambiguity. Pun. Understatement.

Art Style: Colored Cartoon.

***Parnall, Peter.** *The Mountain.* Garden City, NY: Doubleday, 1971.

The mountain, flowers, and moles should be kept just the way they are. To accomplish this, Congress passes a law making the mountain a national park. And, then a road is built. And, then the people come.

Examples: In an attempt to preserve nature, the decision to create a park out of the mountain actually results in its destruction. So many people come, and so many adjustments for them are necessary that the mountain loses its pristine natural character.

Other Devices: Satire. Theme.

Art Style: Expressionism/Cartoon line drawing.

Curriculum Tie-In: Science (Ecology).

Pinkwater, Daniel. *Doodle Flute.* New York: Macmillan, 1991.

Kevin Spoon acquires a doodle flute and makes a friend.

Examples: Kevin has everything a kid could want that money can buy. The only thing Mason has is a doodle flute. Kevin wants it but can't trade for or

buy it. Mason gives it to him. But, he can't play it. He begs Mason to teach
him how to play it. When they become co-owners of the instrument, they
also become buddies and Kevin is also happy.

Other Devices: Satire. Tone.

Art Style: Cartoon.

Curriculum Tie-In: Social Science (Values; Friendship).

Potter, Beatrix. *The Tale of Peter Rabbit.* New York: Frederick Warne & Co., 1902.
Disobedient Peter suffers consequences in Mr. McGregor's garden.

> **Examples:** Peter goes into the garden to be the hero his father failed to be.
> He barely returns home, frightened and chased away, "so tired that he flopped
> down upon the nice soft sand on the floor of the rabbit-hole and shut his
> eyes."
>
> **Other Devices:** Foreshadowing. Imagery. Metaphor. Onomatopoeia. Poetic
> Justice. Understatement.
>
> **Art Style:** Cartoon/Realism water color.
>
> **Curriculum Tie-In:** Social Science (Consequences; Parent and Child).

* **Rylant, Cynthia.** *An Angel for Solomon Singer.* Illus. by Peter Catalanotto. New
York: Orchard Books, 1992.
A lonely New York City resident finds companionship and good cheer at the
Westway Cafe where dreams come true.

> **Examples:** Circumstances hadn't changed, but each night that Solomon
> Singer went to the Westway Cafe, his sense of home became closer. "The
> streets began to move before him like fields of wheat." The building lights
> seemed to "twinkle and shine like stars." The voices of all who passed "sounded
> like the conversations of friendly crickets."
>
> **Other Devices:** Flash-Forward. Symbol.
>
> **Art Style:** Impressionism water color.
>
> **Curriculum Tie-In:** Social Science (Loneliness).

* **Say, Allen.** *Grandfather's Journey.* Boston: Houghton Mifflin, 1993. [Caldecott
Award]
A Japanese American man recounts his grandfather's journey to America, his
eventual longing to return to his homeland, and his restlessness when he does.
The man, too, learns how it feels to be torn by love for two different countries
and can empathize with his grandfather.

> **Examples:** Grandfather's love for two countries prevents him from feeling
> content in either land. When he is in one he longs for the other. In California
> he misses "the mountains and rivers of my childhood." But, back in Japan he
> can not forget the "mountains and rivers of California."

Other Devices: Aphorism. Atmosphere. Foreshadowing. Paradox. Parallel
Story. Symbol.

Art Style: Impressionism/Expressionism/Folk water color.

Curriculum Tie-In: Social Science (Cross-Cultures; Continuity of Life).

*Scieszka, Jon. *The Frog Prince Continued.* Illus. by Steve Johnson. New York: Viking, 1991.

After the frog turns into a prince, he and the princess do not live happily ever
after, so the prince decides to look for a witch to help him remedy the situation.

Examples: This human prince now longs for the happy life of a frog. But,
when he sets out to find a witch to turn him back into a frog, he decides to be
satisfied with what he has and is. Then he kisses his princess and "they both
turned into frogs. They hopped off happily ever after."

Other Devices: Allusion.

Art Style: Expressionism.

Slobodkina, Esphyr. *Caps for Sale.* New York: William Scott Inc., 1949.

A peddler takes a nap and awakes to find his merchandise has been stolen by
monkeys.

Examples: These copycat monkeys have frustrated every attempt of the peddler to retrieve his merchandise. Finally, in a gesture of disgust, he takes off
his own cap and flings it down. The monkeys, sitting high in the tree, faithfully follow his every action. By giving up on getting them back, the caps are
quite literally returned to him.

Other Devices: Paradox.

Art Style: Cartoon.

Spinelli, Eileen. *Somebody Loves You, Mr. Hatch.* Illus. by Paul Yalowitz. New
York: Bradbury, 1991.

An anonymous valentine changes the life of the unsociable Mr. Hatch, turning
him into a laughing friend who helps and appreciates all his neighbors.

Examples: Though the valentine came by mistake and was not really meant
for him, when Mr. Hatch believes that he's received a gift from a secret admirer, he becomes outgoing and friendly and soon makes many friendships he
did not have before the valentine came.

Other Devices: Inference.

Art Style: Naive/Cartoon.

Curriculum Tie-In: Social Science (Self-Discovery/Esteem; Loneliness).

Steig, William. *The Amazing Bone.* New York: Farrar Straus Giroux, 1976.

A talking bone saves a charming piglet from being food for a fox.

Examples: Pearl is amazed that a bone can talk. But the bone is merely flippant when she asks it how such a thing could happen. "I don't know,... I didn't make the world." Very soon the situation is regrettably turned on the bone, who charges the fox with no sense of shame. The fox says to him, "Why should I be ashamed? I can't help being the way I am. I didn't make the world."

Other Devices: Atmosphere. Caricature. Foreshadowing. Inference.

Art Style: Cartoon water color.

Steptoe, John. *Stevie.* New York: Harper & Row, 1969.
His mother takes a child-sitting job, but Robert is jealous and considers the child a useless nuisance.

Examples: Stevie interferes with his friendships, messes with his toys, makes his bed dirty, and gets him in trouble with his dad. But when Stevie is gone, instead of feeling relief, he can remember only the good things about having him around and truly misses him.

Other Devices: Inference. Paradox.

Art Style: Expressionism heavy black outlines suggestive of stained glass.

Curriculum Tie-In: Social Science (Self-Discovery/Esteem; Jealousy).

Thurber, James. *Many Moons.* Illus. by Louis Slobodkin. New York: Harcourt Brace & Co., 1943. [Caldecott Award]
The little Princess Lenore wants the moon. The Court Jester is the only one wise enough to get it for her after the Lord High Chancellor, the Royal Wizard, and Royal Mathematician fail.

Examples: The wise men of the palace can't satisfy the princess. But the Court Jester is wise enough to seek answers from Princess Lenore, herself, as he coaxes her to talk about the moon.

Other Devices: Paradox.

Art Style: Cartoon/Naive line drawing.

Titus, Eve. *Anatole.* Illus. by Paul Galdone. New York: McGraw-Hill, 1956.
A French mouse finds he can make a real contribution of thanks by assisting the cheese factory to improve its product.

Examples: People feel mice are "terrible," and a "disgrace." But Anatole proves this condemnation wrong. By tasting cheeses and anonymously applying quality labels on them, he can help the factory improve its product.

Art Style: Cartoon.

Curriculum Tie-In: Social Science (Self-Discovery/Esteem).

Tobias, Tobi. *Pot Luck.* Illus. by Nola Langner Malone. New York: Lothrop, Lee & Shepard, 1993.
Rachel learns her grandmother's definition of "pot luck" when she helps Gram prepare dinner for an old friend.

Examples: Though she has knocked herself out buying the best foods, cleaning the house, and cooking dinner, when her granddaughter wants to put a bow on the cat, Gram remarks, "Now we don't want to go making things so special."

Other Devices: Inference.

Art Style: Colored Cartoon pencil.

Curriculum Tie-In: Social Science (Friendship).

Zimelman, Nathan. *Treed by a Pride of Irate Lions.* Illus. by Toni Goffe. Boston: Little, Brown & Co., 1990.

Animals like Mother but not Father. Perhaps tame animals are too refined and Father must go among wild animals in Africa to find one that will love him.

Examples: Father comes to realize that it doesn't matter if animals don't like him. "It is enough that I am loved by my family." Then when father bends to kiss his youngest, Baby bites him.

Other Devices: Hyperbole. Understatement.

Art Style: Cartoon.

Zion, Gene. *Harry the Dirty Dog.* Illus. by Margaret Bloy Graham. New York: Harper & Row, 1956.

A white dog with black spots takes a tour of his town and gets so dirty he becomes unrecognizable as a black dog with white spots.

Examples: The threat of a bath causes Harry to bury the dreaded scrub brush. Only finding it again enables him to return to his beloved home. His people don't recognize him dirty. He must bathe so they will know him.

Other Devices: Inference.

Art Style: Naive/Cartoon.

METAPHOR

A suggested comparison between two unlike things for the purpose of pointing out an implied similarity of some sort between them; a device that suggests that the thing is this other thing.

Example: Tumbleweeds are the lost children of the desert.

SOURCES

Carlstrom, Nancy White. *Goodbye Geese.* Illus. by Ed Young. New York: Philomel, 1991.

As a child asks questions, his father explains what the coming of winter is like.

Examples: Like a human being, winter has an "icy stare" that freezes the rivers and ponds. Winter has feet that "walk through cracks" and "dance on the top of the roof." Winter's fingers have a "frosty grip that will tire the flowers" and put a "blanket of snow over the garden." Winter "wraps us in white." Winter's arms are as "strong as the wind's spirit" and as quiet as the "moon holding its breath." Winter's ears hear the geese spread their wings and fly south and hear "the beat of our hearts." Winter's voice is "as clean as new snow."

Art Style: Expressionism.

Curriculum Tie-In: Science (Seasons—Winter).

Chall, Marsha Wilson. *Up North at the Cabin.* Illus. by Steve Johnson. New York: Lothrop, Lee & Shepard, 1992.

Summer vacation up north at the cabin provides memorable experiences on the water, with the animals, and through the other faces of nature.

Examples: "I am a great gray dolphin. The lake is my ocean . . . rising in a sea of air-bubble balloons, I float on a carpet of waves . . . river spills over rocks and whispers to me . . . sling the canoe over our heads, its backbone to the sky, we trudge along, an armored beetle homeward bound."

Other Devices: Imagery. Simile.

Art Style: Impressionism paint.

Curriculum Tie-In: Science (Ecology).

*__**Gregory, Valiska.**__ *Through the Mickle Woods.* Illus. by Barry Moser. Boston: Little, Brown and Co., 1992.

After his wife's death, a grieving king journeys to an old bear's cave in the Mickle Woods, where he hears three stories that help him go on living.

Examples: "Winter drummed its fingers on the windows . . . my breath makes words in the air . . . flapping his arms like a bird the boy's shadow flies . . . moon peaked through the black fingers of the trees . . . orange sun deftly escapes the tangled web of branches."

Other Devices: Aphorism. Atmosphere. Inference. Pun. Simile. Symbol. Theme.

Art Style: Expressionism/Realism.

Curriculum Tie-In: Social Science (Death; Grief).

*__**Grifalconi, Ann.**__ *Kinda Blue.* Boston: Little, Brown and Co., 1993.

Sissy feels lonely until her Uncle Dan cheers her up by explaining that everything, even corn, needs special attention every now and then.

Examples: The corn plants: "corn children fling they leafy arms . . . wavin' hello . . . rows of dancers, silky white heads tossin' in the sunlight." Uncle says they "talks to me" though Sissy scoffs that they're only "rustlin' in the breeze."

The two walk "between gangly cornstalks, their leafy arms patting us friendly, like, as if to say hello."

Other Devices: Symbol. Tone.

Art Style: Impressionism water color, pastel, and colored pencil.

Curriculum Tie-In: Social Science (Acceptance and Respect; Loneliness).

MacDonald, Golden. *Little Island.* Illus. by Leonard Weisgard. Garden City, NY: Doubleday, 1946. [Caldecott Award]

Description of an island in foggy weather.

Examples: "Spiders sailing their webs against a gentle wind . . . violets with golden eyes . . . a little fur island in the air . . . howling, moaning, whistling wind."

Other Devices: Imagery. Paradox. Simile.

Art Style: Impressionism.

Curriculum Tie-In: Science (Geology).

Major, Beverly. *Over Back.* Illus. by Thomas B. Allen. New York: HarperCollins, 1993.

A young girl's favorite spot is over back, a place of pools and trees across the fields back behind the barn where the wonders of nature wait to be discovered each day.

Examples: "If you're not careful, the stones in the wall will growl at you . . . pine trees whispering over a carpet of soft brown needles."

Other Devices: Simile.

Art Style: Impressionism.

Curriculum Tie-In: Science (Ecology; Environment).

Parnall, Peter. *Alfalfa Hill.* Garden City, NY: Doubleday, 1975.

Winter comes in a whisper. The snow, hour after hour it fell, transforming a fall landscape into new arrangements.

Examples: "Caves of viny honeysuckle clumps . . . giant white mushrooms— ghosts, and marshmallows . . . green spruces reaching for the sky . . . hedgerows wandering through the woods."

Other Devices: Imagery. Simile.

Art Style: Expressionism pen and ink line drawing.

Curriculum Tie-In: Science (Seasons—Winter; Environment).

*Paterson, Katherine. *The Tale of the Mandarin Ducks.* Illus. by Leo Dillon and Diane Dillon. New York: Lodestar Books (Dutton), 1990.

A pair of mandarin ducks, separated by a cruel lord who wishes to possess the drake for his colorful beauty, rewards a compassionate couple who risk their lives to reunite the ducks.

Examples: Before the servants can be executed, "messengers" arrive. "It was obvious from their rich dress that the messengers were persons of great importance." They tell a tale that results in the release of the condemned. But when the released servants later try to thank them for their kindness, they see only "a pair of mandarin ducks" who "turned and seemed to bow," before flying off.

Other Devices: Theme.

Art Style: Folk (Japanese water color and pastel paintings similar to eighteenth-century woodcuts).

Potter, Beatrix. *The Tale of Peter Rabbit.* New York: Frederick Warne & Co., 1902.
Disobedient Peter suffers consequences in Mr. McGregor's garden.

Examples: Peter takes his medicine, literally and figuratively. He must have camomile tea because he has caught cold hiding in a watering can. And he must go to bed, missing the bread and milk and blackberries his good little siblings get as their just desserts.

Other Devices: Foreshadowing. Imagery. Irony. Onomatopoeia. Poetic Justice. Understatement.

Art Style: Cartoon/Realism water color.

Curriculum Tie-In: Social Science (Consequences; Parent and Child).

Radin, Ruth Yaffe. *High in the Mountains.* Illus. by Ed Young. New York: Macmillan, 1989.
Description of a day spent near Grandpa's house in the mountains.

Examples: The "mostly mist at the start of the day" in the high mountains is "really the spirits, old folks say, of those who lived there long ago . . . water from the melting snow polishes rocks and sings a song."

Other Devices: Imagery. Simile.

Art Style: Impressionism paint.

Curriculum Tie-In: Science (Ecology).

Ringgold Faith. *Tar Beach.* New York: Crown, 1991.
A young girl dreams of flying above her Harlem home, claiming all she sees for herself and her family.

Examples: Her "flying" enables her to escape the narrow confines of her cityscape. By releasing her imagination she can be "rich, like I owned all that I could see." Even the George Washington Bridge can be hers. Flying serves as the means to privileges that aren't possible through any other means.

Other Devices: Allusion. Symbol.

Art Style: Naive paint.

Curriculum Tie-In: Social Science (Discrimination; Race Relations).

Tresselt, Alvin. *Hide and Seek Fog.* Illus. by Roger Duvoisin. New York: Lothrop, Lee & Shepard, 1965.

The worst fog in 20 years temporarily disheartens grownups, but the children take it in stride.

Examples: Sailboats had to "creep home . . . afternoon sun turned to a pale daytime moon . . . mournful lost voices of the foghorns . . . damp cotton-wool thinned out . . . the islands changed to gold."

Other Devices: Imagery. Simile.

Art Style: Impressionism/Naive.

Tresselt, Alvin. *White Snow Bright Snow.* Illus. by Roger Duvoisin. New York: Lothrop, Lee & Shepard, 1947. [Caldecott Award]

A spring snow storm is described with lively text.

Examples: "Houses crouched together, their windows peeking out from under great white eyebrows . . . church steeple wore a pointed cap on its top."

Other Devices: Imagery. Simile.

Art Style: Naive.

Curriculum Tie-In: Science (Seasons—Winter; Environment).

*****Yolen, Jane.** *Encounter.* Illus. by David Shannon. New York: Harcourt Brace Jovanovich, 1992.

A Taino Indian boy on the island of San Salvador recounts the landing of Columbus and his men in 1492.

Examples: In the boy's dream he sees "three great-winged birds with voices like thunder." They "rode wild waves in our bay." The next day his dream apparently becomes reality when he sees "three great-sailed canoes floating in the bay." He watches as each "great canoe gave birth to many little ones that swam awkwardly to our shore." Later, he examines things the strangers have brought: a "sharp silver stick" that "bit my palm so hard the blood cried out," and "round pools to hold in the hand that gave a man back his face."

Other Devices: Atmosphere. Flash-Forward. Foreshadowing. Point-Of-View. Stereotype. Theme.

Art Style: Realism/Expressionism acrylic.

Curriculum Tie-In: History (Columbus-Discovery of America).

Yolen, Jane. *Greyling.* Illus. by David Ray. New York: Philomel, 1991.

A selchie, a seal transformed into a human form, lives on land with a lonely fisherman and his wife, until the day a great storm threatens the fisherman's life.

Examples: The moon touched down behind the water, "when the beach was a tan thread spun between the sea and plain; fear riding in her heart; waters gobbled up the little hut on the beach; roiling, boiling sea; little fingers of foam tore at his clothes."

Art Style: Expressionism.

ONOMATOPOEIA

Words that either imitate or suggest the meaning of the sounds they represent. "Slurp" sounds like and suggests the meaning associated with ingesting soup.

Example: E. B. White describes Wilbur the pig in *Charlotte's Web* as eating in the manner of "swishing" and "swooshing" his "slops."

SOURCES

Cole, Sheila. *When the Rain Stops.* Illus. by Henri Sorensen. New York: Lothrop, Lee & Shepard, 1991.
Setting off to pick blackberries, a child and her father encounter animals before a rain and afterward.

Examples: A blackbird goes "que-ee, que-ee." Rain goes "plippety-plippety, rat-a-tat-tat-tat" on windows. Cars "swish-swished" and water "dripped plip, plip, pling-pling." Water "gurgled and chortled." They walk through meadow grass "squish-squash." Birds "chirped and twittered."

Other Devices: Foreshadowing.

Art Style: Impressionism.

Curriculum Tie-In: Science (Rain).

Flack, Marjorie. *Angus and the Ducks.* New York: Doubleday, 1930.
A curious Scottish terrier wants to find out what made the noise coming from the other side of the hedge.

Examples: Angus feels in command when his "woo-oo-oof!!!" can send the ducks "all of a flutter." But, their "Hiss-s-s-s-s!" soon restores a small dog's proper place in the world's scheme.

Other Devices: Foreshadowing. Poetic Justice.

Art Style: Expressionism colored line drawings.

Curriculum Tie-In: Social Sciences (Consequences).

Flack, Marjorie. *Angus Lost.* New York: Doubleday, 1932.
A little Scottish terrier is bored with the same things at home and is curious to see what the outside world has to find.

Examples: The milk man's "rattle-rattle-clink-clink"; Angus's "patter-patter" following the milk man; owl's "Whoo-Whooo"; other dog's "Grrrruf"; goat's "Baa-aaaaa."

Other Devices: Foreshadowing. Point-Of-View.

Art Style: Expressionism colored line drawings.

Piper, Watty. *The Little Engine That Could.* Illus. by George Hauman and Doris Hauman. New York: Platt & Monk, 1954.

When the little red engine breaks down, it needs help to get its cargo for boys and girls over the mountain. Only the little blue engine offers its service. Doubtful at first but finally with determined confident effort, it pulls the cargo over the mountain.

> **Examples:** The sound of an engine puffing in labor seems to repeat the words: "I think I can."
>
> **Other Devices:** Stereotype. Theme.
>
> **Art Style:** Colored Cartoon.
>
> **Curriculum Tie-In:** Social Science (Values).

Potter, Beatrix. *The Tale of Peter Rabbit.* New York: Frederick Warne & Co., 1902.

Disobedient Peter suffers consequences in Mr. McGregor's garden.

> **Examples:** Mr. McGregor's hoe goes "scritch." Peter goes "lippity-lippity not very fast." Peter sneezes "kertyschoo." Mr. McGregor fetches a sieve "to pop upon the top of Peter."
>
> **Other Devices:** Foreshadowing. Imagery. Irony. Metaphor. Poetic Justice. Understatement.
>
> **Art Style:** Cartoon/Realism water color.
>
> **Curriculum Tie-In:** Social Science (Consequences; Parent and Child).

Seuss, Dr. *How the Grinch Stole Christmas.* New York: Random, 1957.

The Grinch thought stealing the trappings of Christmas would stop Christmas.

> **Examples:** "Grinch" is the nasty-sounding, heartless, fun-stealing creature who hates Christmas.
>
> **Other Devices:** Alliteration. Theme.
>
> **Art Style:** Cartoon.
>
> **Curriculum Tie-In:** Social Science (Values).

Yashima, Taro. *Umbrella.* New York: Viking, 1958.

Momo is three when she receives red rubber boots and an umbrella for her birthday. She eagerly looks forward to a chance to use them.

> **Examples:** When Momo hears and experiences for the first time what rain sounds like on her new umbrella, it is described: "Bon polo, pon polo pon polo, boto boto pon polo."
>
> **Other Devices:** Flash-Forward. Simile. Tone.
>
> **Art Style:** Impressionism paint.
>
> **Curriculum Tie-In:** Social Science (Self-Discovery/Esteem).

*Yolen, Jane. *Sky Dogs*. Illus. by Barry Moser. New York: Harcourt Brace Jovanovich, 1990.

A young motherless boy in a tribe of Blackfeet Indians is present when his people see horses for the first time.

Examples: "Grass beneath our feet sang swee-swash, swee-swash." The grass crunched with "sounds as loud as a careless man walking: snick-snack, snick-snack."

Other Devices: Point-Of-View.

Art Style: Realism/Expressionism.

Curriculum Tie-In: History (Native Americans—Blackfeet).

Yolen, Jane. *Welcome to the Green House*. Illus. by Laura Regan. New York: G. P. Putnam's, 1993.

Describes the tropical rainforest and the life found there.

Examples: "A-hoo, a-hoo, a-hoo" of the howler troop; "crinch-crunch" of long-horned beetles; "citter-chitter-rrrr" of golden lion tamarin.

Other Devices: Analogy. Atmosphere. Imagery. Internal Rhyme. Pun.

Art Style: Realism/Expressionism.

Curriculum Tie-In: Science (Rainforest; Ecology).

PARADOX

A statement that reveals a kind of unlikely truth although it seems at first to be self-contradictory and untrue.

Example: Good fences make good neighbors. (Fences do separate people, but since they define limits of people's property, fences prevent conflicts.)

SOURCES

*Baylor, Byrd. *Hawk, I'm Your Brother*. Illus. by Peter Parnall. New York: Charles Scribner's, 1976.

An Indian boy, whose great desire is to fly, feels he almost does so when he frees his pet hawk and watches him soar.

Examples: "It seemed to him he'd fly—if a hawk became his brother." Though he captured the bird for the magic and brotherhood, only by freeing it can he emphathize with the hawk's cry "to his brothers." Soon "brother to brother they call." The boy lifts his arms; his hair blows in the wind "and in his mind he's flying, too." Soon people notice "his eyes flash like a young hawk's eyes and there is sky reflected in those eyes." A sense of flying is achieved by freeing the captured hawk.

Art Style: Expressionism pen and ink line drawings.

Curriculum Tie-In: Social Science (Self-Discovery/Esteem).

Bemelmans, Ludwig. *Madeline.* New York: Viking, 1939.

Twelve little girls, and one of them brave and roguish, living together in a Paris house.

Examples: Having one's appendix out is not usually a fun event. Yet the little girls want to emulate Madeline and have the same operation she had. This is because when they visit her they find her surrounded with toys and candy and a scar to show off.

Art Style: Naive/Cartoon.

Curriculum Tie-In: Social Science (Self-Discovery/Esteem).

Carlstrom, Nancy White. *Fish and Flamingo.* Illus. by Lisa Desimini. Boston: Little, Brown & Co., 1993.

Two unlikely friends spend time together, help each other out, and tell stories about their lives.

Examples: Fish wishes to "cause a star to shine in the day for my friend to see." Flamingo wishes to "cause the sun to rise over my friend's head for him to see." Neither believes his parting gift is possible. Yet, when Flamingo and his migrating friends fly over Fish and his silvery friends at the ocean surface, there is the illusion of a pink dawn above and the illusion of a star on the waves below.

Other Devices: Irony.

Art Style: Expressionism paint.

Curriculum Tie-In: Social Science (Friendship).
Literature (Plot Balance).

Charlip, Remy, and Burton Supree. *Harlequin and the Gift of Many Colors.* Illus. by Remy Charlip. New York: Parents' Magazine Press, 1973.

On Carnival night everyone enjoys favorite things so that afterward they won't mind so much going without them for Lent, the time of giving up what is liked best.

Examples: By giving up some cloth from their own costumes, a little of what is dear to them, Harlequin's friends enable him to join in the festivities with a costume of his own. Everyone's fun is enhanced because "to think of having a good time without Harlequin seemed impossible." He is "clothed in the love of his friends."

Art Style: Renaissance Folk.

Curriculum Tie-In: History (The Jolly Trickster Harlequin of the diamond patch costume originated about 400 years ago when Carnival and Lent were important yearly events in Europe.).

Croll, Carolyn. *The Three Brothers.* A German folktale adapted and illus. by Carolyn Croll. New York: A Whitebird Book (G. P. Putnam's), 1991.
Unable to decide which of three sons will inherit the farm, a farmer father sets up a contest. Whoever can fill the barn before the day is done will be his heir.

> **Examples:** When the youngest son wins the contest, all sons win. Amos, the youngest, doesn't wish to live alone on the farm. He wants to share with his brothers. They all live happily together.
>
> **Other Devices:** Theme.
>
> **Art Style:** Pennsylvania Dutch Folk Motif.
>
> **Curriculum Tie-In:** Geography (Pennsylvania Dutch Culture).

Cutting, Michael. *The Little Crooked Christmas Tree.* Illus. by Ron Broda. New York: Scholastic, 1990.
A little tree sacrifices itself to a dove and her family. It loses a chance to be a Christmas tree and learns the true meaning of Christmas.

> **Examples:** By protecting the dove, the tree grows crooked and is rejected as a Christmas tree that would have been cut down and decorated briefly but then "thrown out, alone in the snow." By saving the bird, the tree is saved, too.
>
> **Other Devices:** Poetic Justice.
>
> **Art Style:** Collage paper and water color.

Edwards, Michelle. *A Baker's Portrait.* New York: Lothrop, Lee & Shepard, 1991.
Michelin paints portraits that do not flatter her sitters, but she learns an enduring lesson when she must paint her kindly aunt and uncle.

> **Examples:** When she paints portraits accurately she fails miserably. When she paints falling snow to represent her grandma she is successful. When she paints a chocolate cake and a challah as her uncle and aunt, the bakers, she has caught their essence most pleasingly without offending them by painting them truthfully.
>
> **Other Devices:** Symbol.
>
> **Art Style:** Expressionism.
>
> **Curriculum Tie-In:** Social Science (Acceptance and Respect; Family Life; Values).

Flack, Marjorie. *Angus and the Cat.* New York: Doubleday, 1931.
Angus the Scottie dog spends three days chasing the new cat that has come to live at this house, but when the cat disappears, Angus misses his new friend.

> **Examples:** The cat boxes his ears, takes his food, and sits in his sunshine. The cat is a nuisance. But, when it is gone, Angus finds he has nothing to do and needs the cat.
>
> **Other Devices:** Inference. Irony.

Art Style: Expressionism colored line drawings.

Curriculum Tie-In: Social Science (Friendship; Acceptance and Respect).

Gag, Wanda. *Millions of Cats.* New York: Coward-McCann, 1928.
The old man seeks a kitten for his wife and finds hundreds of cats, thousands of cats, millions and billions and trillions of cats.

> **Examples:** There is ample opportunity to secure a superior cat, but the "thin and scraggly" kitten from among all the beautiful ones is "the most beautiful cat in the whole world."
>
> **Other Devices:** Hyperbole. Theme.
>
> **Art Style:** Folk/Cartoon.

Goode, Diane. *Where's Our Mama?* New York: Dutton Children's Books, 1991.
A kindly gendarme conducts two children around Paris in search of their lost mother.

> **Examples:** When he asks what their mother looks like, he takes them at their word. She is "the most beautiful woman in the world; very strong; reads millions of books; famous for her voice; very slim; cooks the best food in the world; wears pretty hats; very smart." But the society lady, the librarian, the cook, the milliner, the teacher, the lion tamer are not Mama. She is all these things, but just Mama, too.
>
> **Art Style:** Expressionism.
>
> **Curriculum Tie-In:** Social Science (Parent and Child; Acceptance and Respect).

Graham, Margaret Bloy. *Be Nice to Spiders.* Eau Claire, WI: E. M. Hale, 1967.
A spider left at the gates of a zoo to be taken care of ends up taking care of the zoo animals.

> **Examples:** "Those webs make the place look a mess." So the zoo personnel believe they're cleaning up the zoo by removing all the spider webs in the cages. Soon the animals begin to "look miserable." It seems that without spiders, biting flies become a problem. The webs are welcomed back.
>
> **Art Style:** Cartoon.
>
> **Curriculum Tie-In:** Science (Spiders).

Helldorfer, M. C. *Cabbage Rose.* Illus. by Julie Downing. New York: Bradbury Press, 1993.
While painting pictures for the royal family, plain Cabbage falls in love with the prince and decides to use her magic brush to increase her own chances with him.

> **Examples:** Cabbage, in disguise as a beautiful lady, tells the prince she will paint him fine jewels that glitter like stars. He is strangely unimpressed. He misses plain Cabbage Rose and says the whole world is plain without her.

Cabbage breaks her magic brush and is herself again. "Some kind of magic ended then, but the people say another kind began."

Art Style: Realism water color.

Curriculum Tie-In: Social Science (Self-Discovery/Esteem).

Hutchins, Pat. *What Game Shall We Play?* New York: Greenwillow, 1990.
The animals ask each other what game they should play, but only Owl has an answer.

Examples: Though they don't realize it, the animals are playing hide and seek with each other all the while they pursue one another to ask what game they should play.

Other Devices: Irony.

Art Style: Cartoon/Folk.

Johnston, Tony. *Goblin Walk.* Illus. by Bruce Degen. New York: G. P. Putnam's, 1991.
A little goblin has a series of frightening experiences while walking through the woods to his grandmother's house.

Examples: All the things that should have made him repulsive: gnashing his teeth, growling out loud, snarling for joy, sticking out his tongue, making faces, and taking a basket of rocks, bugs, weeds, and thorns to his grandmother, only endear him to the reader because he is so very vulnerable on his walk. He comes upon a series of "bad" experiences. He sees a mouse, a squirrel, a bird, and other "frightening" creatures.

Other Devices: Irony. Point-Of-View.

Art Style: Colored Cartoon.

Curriculum Tie-In: Social Science (Fear).

Kroll, Virginia. *Masai and I.* Illus. by Nancy Carpenter. New York: Four Winds Press, 1992.
Linda, a little girl who lives in the city, learns in school about East Africa and the Masai. She imagines what her life might be like if she were Masai.

Examples: Wouldn't the differences be very great? Her brother goes to the faucet to fill a water pitcher. If he were Masai, he'd go to the water hole and bring back water in large gourds. She goes to the corner deli for sweets. The Masai go for honey at the bee tree. Her pet is a hamster. All the cows of the Masai herd would be as familiar as the hamster. She loves and respects her grandmother "just as I would if I were Masai." Her "smooth brown skin over high cheekbones and black eyes that slant up a little . . . would look just like this if I were Masai." The feeling of kinship is closer than it would seem because, really, all the important things are in common.

Other Devices: Inference.

Art Style: Expressionism/Realism.

Curriculum Tie-In: Geography (East African Culture).

Luttrell, Ida. *Three Good Blankets.* Illus. by Michael McDermott. New York: Atheneum, 1990.

To her grown children's dismay, an old woman shares her new blankets with her donkey, goat, and dog.

> **Examples:** Though she kept for herself only the ragged gray blanket, she is warmed because the goat gives twice as much milk, the donkey that is rested carries double the wood load, and the loyal dog keeping watch becomes the warmest cover of all.
>
> **Art Style:** Expressionism.
>
> **Curriculum Tie-In:** Social Science (Generosity).

MacDonald, Golden. *Little Island.* Illus. by Leonard Weisgard. Garden City, NY: Doubleday, 1946. [Caldecott Award]

Narration about an island in foggy weather.

> **Examples:** "It was good to be a Little Island. A part of the world and a world of its own all surrounded by the bright blue sea." Though the island in the ocean "was all surrounded by water, . . . all land is one land under the sea."
>
> **Other Devices:** Imagery. Metaphor. Simile.
>
> **Art Style:** Impressionism.
>
> **Curriculum Tie-In:** Science (Geology).

Ross, Christine. *Lily and the Present.* Boston: Houghton Mifflin, 1992.

Lily searches the store for a perfect big bright and beautiful present for her new baby brother.

> **Examples:** She finds a big crocodile that "once lurked in the murky Mississippi." She finds a bright chandelier with 149 light bulbs. She even finds a beautiful wedding cake. But these particular big, bright, and beautiful presents aren't quite suitable. She despairs of finding just the right big, bright, and beautiful gift. But, she does, and it only costs 25 cents—a big, bright, beautiful, red balloon!
>
> **Art Style:** Colored Cartoon.
>
> **Curriculum Tie-In:** Social Science (Siblings).

*Say, Allen. *Grandfather's Journey.* Boston: Houghton Mifflin, 1993. [Caldecott Award]

A Japanese American man recounts his grandfather's journey to America, his eventual longing to return to his homeland, and his restlessness when he does. The man, too, learns how it feels to be torn by love for two different countries and can empathize with his grandfather.

Examples: It is possible to love two lands equally, to be living in one and at the same time, longing to go "home" to the other. Grandfather, while in California, remembers "the mountains and rivers" of Japan. In Japan he remembers "the mountains and rivers of California." Neither land is quite home, yet the man is "homesick" for each.

Other Devices: Aphorism. Atmosphere. Foreshadowing. Irony. Parallel Story. Symbol.

Art Style: Impressionism/Expressionism/Folk water color.

Curriculum Tie-In: Social Science (Cross-Cultures; Continuity of Life).

Slobodkina, Esphyr. *Caps for Sale.* New York: William Scott, Inc., 1949.
A peddler takes a nap and awakes to find his merchandise has been stolen by monkeys.

Examples: Having run out of ideas for getting back his merchandise from the playful monkeys who have the caps on their own heads, the peddler pulls off his cap and flings it to the ground in anger. Then he walks away. The monkeys copy his action, throwing down their caps and walking away. By giving up, he is able to retrieve all his caps.

Other Devices: Irony.

Art Style: Cartoon.

Steptoe, John. *Stevie.* New York: Harper & Row, 1969.
When his mother takes on a baby-sitting job, and Robert learns Stevie will be staying at the house, he is first jealous of him and then sorry to have him gone.

Examples: Robert complains about Stevie not leaving his stuff alone, leaving dirty footprints all over his bed, making his friends chide him for baby-sitting and getting in the way, and being loud and causing his father to scold. In spite of all this aggravation, after Steven leaves, Robert can only remember how "he was a nice little guy . . . kinda like a little brother."

Other Devices: Inference. Irony.

Art Style: Expressionism heavy black outlines suggestive of stained glass.

Curriculum Tie-In: Social Science (Self-Discovery/Esteem; Jealousy).

Thurber, James. *Many Moons.* Illus. by Louis Slobodkin. New York: Harcourt Brace & Co., 1943. [Caldecott Award]
The little Princess Lenore wants the moon, and the Court Jester is the only one wise enough to get it for her after the Lord High Chancellor, the Royal Wizard, and Royal Mathematician fail.

Examples: The Princess, herself, is the only one who provides the advice on how it is possible to "get" the moon for her. And, she's the only one who can explain why it's possible to "have" the moon and still see the moon outside her window up in the sky. The Court Jester is just wise enough to listen to her talk, while the others rush out to put into practice their own knowledge.

Other Devices: Irony.

Art Style: Cartoon/Naive line drawing.

Yee, Paul. *Sing on New Snow, a Delicious Tale.* Illus. by Harvey Chan. New York: Macmillan, 1991.

Though she works seven days a week cooking in her father's restaurant, Maylin gets no credit for her fine cooking until the governor asks for re-creation of a dish in front of him.

> **Examples:** Side by side, the governor and Maylin fix the same dish. But they taste different. "What is your secret?" he demands. She explains that if both were to paint with paper and brush, their pictures would not be identical. "You cannot take this dish to China! . . . This is a dish of the New World . . . You cannot re-create it in the Old."
>
> **Art Style:** Impressionism/Expressionism water color.
>
> **Curriculum Tie-In:** History (American Chinatown Culture around 1900).

PARALLEL STORY

A narrative or picture story enclosed within another story upon which equal or even primary interest is centered.

SOURCES

Burningham, John. *Time to Get Out of the Bath, Shirley.* New York: Thomas Crowell, 1978.

During her bath, Shirley is off on a series of imaginative adventures, about which, her mother, tidying up the bathroom, has no idea.

> **Examples:** Shirley's mother nags with dull humdrum patter about leaving the soap in the bottom of the tub and which towel she's using and how messy she leaves her clothes around the floor, and how so much water gets splashed out. Meanwhile, in her imagination, Shirley has leaped astride her rubber duck and gone out the drain through the sewer line to a land of knighthood where she rides steeds and jousts successfully with the king and queen on inflated rubber ducks on a pond.
>
> **Art Style:** Cartoon/Impressionism.

Houghton, Eric. *Walter's Magic Wand.* Illus. by Denise Teasdale. New York: Orchard Books, 1989.

Feeling restless at the library, Walter combines his imagination with his magic wand to bring several exotic books to life and complicate the librarian's tidy existence.

Examples: Walter pokes and meddles with things on the librarian's desk and builds a castle with dictionaries. His mother keeps telling him to find a book and stop daydreaming. Meanwhile, he uses his imagination and magic wand. He brings to life a jungle with tigers, a desert island, and pirates in an ocean. The librarian is unphased; maybe his magic didn't really work. But when it's time to leave, his mother is pleased that he has found three books, and the librarian says his magic wand is too good to throw away. He notices a bit of seaweed poking from her collar and a palm leaf in her hair.

Art Style: Colored Cartoon.

Macauley, David. *Black and White.* Boston: Houghton Mifflin, 1990. [Caldecott Award]

Four brief stories about parents, trains, and cows intertwine but read separately also.

Examples: Elements in these special effect stories pass between each other. The Holstein cows serve as a shield to hide an escaping masked thief who turns up on the train. The cows on the track block the train's passage. The parents leave in the morning to catch the train to work. They carry newspapers which later become useful to relieve boredom for people waiting on the platform for the delayed train ride home.

Art Style: Cartoon/Impressionism.

McCloskey, Robert. *Blueberries for Sal.* New York: Viking, 1948.

Mother and Little Sal and Mother Bear and Little Bear on opposite sides of Blueberry Mountain go to pick blueberries and get all mixed up.

Examples: Each child follows its mother but gets tired, sits in "a large clump of bushes and eats berries." Each follows behind the other's mother. Each surprises the other's mother. And, each surprised mother "is old enough to be shy of . . ." Soon, each mother recognizes her youngster's sounds and they quickly reunite. Eventually, each family goes home down the opposite side of the mountain.

Art Style: Cartoon pen and ink.

Curriculum Tie-In: Social Science (Parent and Child).

McLeod, Emile. *The Bear's Bicycle.* Illus. by David McPhail. Boston: Little, Brown & Co., 1975.

A boy and his bear each ride bicycles in their own way.

Examples: The correct riding rules are demonstrated by the boy, but in parallel sequence the stuffed bear shows the wrong way to ride and the horrors of careless bicycle operation.

Art Style: Colored Cartoon ink drawings.

Curriculum Tie-In: Health and Safety (Accident Prevention).

McNaughton, Colin. *Guess Who's Just Moved in Next Door?* New York: Random House, 1991.

A tour through a very peculiar neighborhood where an assortment of wacky neighbors from Superman to a ship of pirates reacts to the arrival of new neighbors.

Examples: While the narration occurs, a pass-the-message secret moves through the pages getting more illogical until it ends up as it was originally started. Each window into each house displays an environment of outlandish residents doing their thing in a counterpoint to the narration.

Other Devices: Allusion. Caricature. Irony. Pun. Satire.

Art Style: Colored Cartoon.

Miles, Miska. *Hoagie's Rifle-Gun.* Illus. by John Schoenherr. Boston: Little, Brown & Co., 1970.

Hoagie never misses. But on the day another hunter has better success, he is jealous and angry and aims at Old Bob the bobcat. Something, fortunately, causes him to waste a bullet.

Examples: While the boys hunt with their rifle, Old Bob leaves the deserted shack and begins his own hunt. The boys miss an opportunity to get a rabbit that Old Bob gets. The boys resent his success. Finally, the boys go home, empty handed, electing not to investigate the deserted shack which they've looked into many times before and know to be empty. Old Bob continues his hunting and returns to the shack where he's taken up residence.

Other Devices: Theme.

Art Style: Impressionism/Realism pen and ink drawings.

Curriculum Tie-In: Social Sciences (Values; Ethics).

Raskin, Ellen. *Nothing Ever Happens on My Block.* New York: Atheneum, 1966.

Chester Filbert, a most unobservant child, complains that he will have to move away to find anything interesting happening.

Examples: As he sits on the sidewalk curb, he does not see all the things going on behind him on his block. A robber is caught, a fire is put out, a cat has kittens, a lady punishes practical jokers, a man builds a roof and sees it destroyed by lightning, and a house is infiltrated with witches, etc.

Art Style: Cartoon line drawing.

***Say, Allen.** *Grandfather's Journey.* Boston: Houghton Mifflin, 1993. [Caldecott Award]

A Japanese American man recounts his grandfather's journey to America, his eventual longing to return to his homeland, and his restlessness when he does. The man, too, learns how it feels to be torn by love for two different countries and can empathize with his grandfather.

Examples: The grandfather grows up in Japan and migrates to America. He brings to California a bride from his home village. He raises a daughter, and returns to Japan when she is nearly grown. The grandfather wishes to see California one last time but does not. The grandson is born in Japan and migrates to California when he is nearly grown. He marries and has a daughter. He, too, gets restless and must return to his homeland from time to time. He says, "I think I know my grandfather now."

Other Devices: Aphorism. Atmosphere. Foreshadowing. Irony. Paradox. Symbol.

Art Style: Impressionism/Expressionism/Folk water color.

Curriculum Tie-In: Social Science (Cross-Cultures; Continuity of Life).

PARODY

A humorous but recognizable imitation of another literary work for the sake of amusement or ridicule, sometimes gentle, sometimes not; the copied work's language, style, characters, plot, or theme may be mimicked.

Example: This humorous imitation of the plot in Edgar Allan Poe's gothic
story "The Fall of the House of Usher" is a poem by Reed Wittemore:
"It was big boxy wreck of a house
Owned by a classmate of mine named Rod Usher,
Who lived in the thing with his twin sister.
He was a louse and she was a souse."

SOURCES

Briggs, Raymond. *Jim and the Beanstalk*. New York: Coward-McCann, 1970.
It is years later and another curious climber finds the giant now beset with the inadequacies of old age and endeavors to fill his needs.

Examples: Though the giant would dearly love to eat the boy, he has no teeth. His hair is also gone, and his eyesight has failed. The other boy stole his golden harp and hen and "I've never really been happy since." The new boy gets him a wig, some glasses, and dentures. Only for a moment does the giant think back fondly on his former habits. But, under the circumstances, that would be unkind.

Other Devices: Ambiguity. Pun. Tone.

Art Style: Colored Cartoon.

Curriculum Tie-In: Social Science (Friendship).

Gerstein, Mordicai. *Anytime Mapleson and the Hungry Bears.* Illus. by Susan Yard Harris. New York: Harper & Row, 1990.

When he meets a family of hungry bears in the woods at the peak of maple sugaring time, Anytime Mapleson, who likes pancakes anytime, invites them home for some pancakes and maple syrup.

Examples: The bears in the forest seem to be ready to eat Anytime until he gives away all his clothes to them. They say, "I bet we're the best looking bears in the woods." When Anytime brings them home for pancakes they pass for his friend Harvey and Harvey's parents. They all eat lots of pancakes, but Anytime eats the most. The bears ate 1,000 pancakes "and were so stuffed they went back to the woods and slept for another month." Anytime ate 1,297 pancakes. Then he "drank a glass of milk and ate 537 more."

Art Style: Cartoon.

Johnston, Tony. *The Cowboy and the Black-Eyed Pea.* Illus. by Warren Ludwig. New York: G. P. Putnam's, 1992.

The wealthy daughter of a Texas rancher devises a plan to find a real cowboy among her many suitors.

Examples: In this western version of "The Princess and the Pea," it is the men being tested for their real cowboy-ness. A real cowboy, of course, is known for his sensitivity. At the least touch "he'll bruise like the petals of a desert rose." Each potential spouse gets an "itty-bitty black-eyed pea" beneath the saddle blanket on his horse. The one who keeps needing heaped up saddle blankets—50 of them—is, naturally, the "real" cowboy, whom she marries and lets run the spread.

Other Devices: Atmosphere. Caricature. Inference. Simile.

Art Style: Colored Cartoon.

***Scieszka, Jon.** *The True Story of the Three Little Pigs by A. Wolf.* Illus. by Lane Smith. New York: Viking Kestrel (Viking Penguin), 1989.

The wolf gives his own outlandish version of what really happened when he tangled with the three little pigs.

Examples: He didn't huff and puff; he sneezed because of a bad cold. And all he wanted was a cup of sugar to bake his granny a cake. But when the flimsy houses fell down on the pigs, he couldn't let good pork go to waste. And, he couldn't let the third pig insult his grandmother: "Your old granny can sit on a pin!" So when the cops drove up, of course he was trying to break down the pig's door. The rest is history, but "jazzed up."

Other Devices: Point-Of-View. Pun. Tone.

Art Style: Colored Cartoon/Collage.

Stern, Robert. *The House That Bob Built.* Illus. by Andrew Zega. New York: Rizzoli, 1991.

This is a retelling of the cumulative Mother Goose rhyme that describes a pleasant and comfortable house with an ocean view by an internationally recognized architect.

Examples: This story is not a hilarious take-off but a wonderful journey of discovery of meticulously detailed and furnished rooms.

Art Style: Impressionism.

Curriculum Tie-In: Science (Architectural Design).

* **Tolhurst, Marilyn.** *Somebody and the Three Blairs.* Illus. by Simone Abel. New York: Orchard Books, 1991.

In a reversal of the Goldilocks story, a bear explores the home of the Blair family while they are out.

Examples: "Somebody" finds the people breakfast food "too dry," "too noisy," and when the honey is found, "just right." The seats are "too hard," "too wobbly," and "just right." And, so it goes. Who could have created such havoc in the house? A burglar? A monster? No, "Issa big teddy bear," says baby Blair. Call the police, the fire department! Too late, "Somebody gone home . . . downa drain pipe."

Other Devices: Pun. Understatement.

Art Style: Colored Cartoon.

* **Wilsdorf, Anne.** *Princess.* New York: Greenwillow, 1993.

A girl proves that she is a real princess in an unusual way.

Examples: She must prove to be "genuine." The pea goes under the pile of mattresses. If she's not bruised in the morning, "that will be the end of her." But, of course, after falling out of bed and landing on the family pet, she does have the prerequisite bruises. The wedding is arranged at once and the shepherd girl, named "Princess" by her father, and Prince Leopold, a nice boy, but not very knowledgeable about sheep, her family thinks, live happily ever after.

Other Devices: Ambiguity. Foreshadowing. Pun. Satire.

Art Style: Cartoon water color.

* **Zemach, Harve.** *Duffy and the Devil.* Illus. by Margot Zemach. New York: Farrar Straus Giroux, 1973. [Caldecott Award]

A resourceful servant girl uses her wits to avoid admitting she can't spin and knit even when the game is up.

Examples: This version of Rumpelstiltskin has a robust Cornish flavor. Duffy can't spin or knit so a "squinney-eyed creature with a long tail" assures her he can handle "those little whilly-gogs and shizamagees." When it comes time to guess his name, the housekeeper plies him with beer. The name is revealed and Duffy is saved. But all the clothes he has knitted "turned to ashes." Duffy is not to be outdone; she loudly proclaims, "All my work! Gone up in smoke! I swear I'll never knit another thing ever again!" And she never does.

Other Devices: Poetic Justice. Tone.

Art Style: Folk/Cartoon water color.

Curriculum Tie-In: Social Science (Coping).

PERSONIFICATION

A figure of speech that assigns human qualities, actions, characteristics, or personality to an animal, an object, a natural force, or an idea.

Example: The two stores held a tête-à-tête across Main Street.

SOURCES

Burton, Virginia Lee. *The Little House.* Boston: Houghton Mifflin, 1942. [Caldecott Award]

A small house sitting on a hill is happy but wonders what life in the city is all about.

Examples: The little house watches the sun rise in the morning and she watches it set in the evening. She thinks about the city and wishes to see it. When the city surrounds her, she does not like it. She feels abandoned and sad when no one lives in the house. She is glad when it is fixed up again.

Other Devices: Analogy. Foreshadowing.

Art Style: Naive.

Curriculum Tie-In: Social Science (Values).

Ets, Marie Hall. *Gilberto and the Wind.* New York: Viking, 1963.

A child describes his experiences with the wind.

Examples: The wind whispers, grabs, plays with the wash, pulls out clothespins, breaks an umbrella, bangs a gate open and shut, races and runs over the top of the grass, helps fly kites, carries bubbles up in the air, sweeps without a broom, and gets tired out.

Art Style: Cartoon.

Curriculum Tie-In: Science (Meteorology; Wind).

Ichikawa, Satomi. *Nora's Duck.* New York: Philomel, 1991.

Nora finds a duckling in the woods and takes it to Doctor John, who provides love and care for many wild and domestic animals who have come to grief.

Examples: Though the story is reality oriented, Nora's companions, her doll, her teddy bear, and her dog speak to her.

Art Style: Colored Cartoon.

Curriculum Tie-In: Science (Animal Health).

Kitchen, Bert. *Tenrec's Twigs.* New York: Philomel, 1989.

Seized with doubts about the value of the small building he constructs out of twigs, Tenrec goes from one jungle animal to the next asking for opinions.

Examples: Each animal goes about its natural lifestyle but answers as though thinking like a human. The parrot squawks, "Useless! A waste of time," as it repeats what the grumpy warthog pronounced.

Art Style: Realism.

Mark, Jan. *Silly Tails.* Illus. by Tony Ross. New York: Atheneum, 1993.

Vegetables do not talk today thanks to vain and rude carrots who once hurled insults over the hedge separating their garden from formerly peaceable rabbits.

Examples: ". . . carrots never said anything important; the lettuces who were fat and vulgar; the cabbages who had big hearts but no brains; the turnips who were dull and earthy; and the radishes who were insignificant."

Other Devices: Foreshadowing.

Art Style: Colored Cartoon.

Steig, William. *Sylvester and the Magic Pebble.* New York: Windmill Books (Simon & Schuster), 1969. [Caldecott Award]

A magic pebble, a fierce lion, and a wish made in panic lead to separation from loved ones.

Examples: Sylvester Duncan, the donkey, collects pebbles as a hobby. His parents wear clothes, inquire of their animal neighbors when he is missing, and show human emotions when their son disappears. They knit, read, eat a picnic of alfalfa sandwiches, pickled oats, and timothy compote.

Other Devices: Foreshadowing. Imagery. Pun. Stereotype. Symbol. Theme.

Art Style: Cartoon water color.

Curriculum Tie-In: Social Science (Parent and Child).

POETIC JUSTICE

An outcome to a situation in which vice is punished and virtue is rewarded, usually in a manner appropriate to the situation.

Example: A bunch of hungry animals, each bent upon eating the one beneath him in strength and size, are all frightened away from their purpose by an army of tiny red ants whom everyone has ignored until these ants spoil their opportunity for a snack.

SOURCES

Aardema, Verna. *Why Mosquitoes Buzz in People's Ears.* Illus. by Leo Dillon and Diane Dillon. New York: Dial, 1975. [Caldecott Award]
Mosquito tells Iguana a nonsense tale that annoys Iguana and sets off a chain reaction that causes a jungle tragedy. Although all is eventually resolved, mosquito's guilty conscience causes it to adopt a worse habit.

Examples: The mosquito asks, "whining in people's ears," if the animals still blame her for the accidental death of the owl's baby. She gets an honest answer. She gets swatted in return.

Other Devices: Inference.

Art Style: Expressionism/African Folk.

Curriculum Tie-In: Social Science (Foolish Behavior).

Abolafia, Yossi. *Fox Tale.* New York: Greenwillow, 1991.
Donkey, Crow, and Rabbit join forces to prevent Fox from swindling Bear out of his jar of honey.

Examples: Fox tricks the animals out of cheese, sweet grapes, and chestnuts. When the table is turned, he must relinquish these things in order to retain his tail.

Other Devices: Allusion. Pun.

Art Style: Colored Cartoon.

Curriculum Tie-In: Social Science (Consequences; Cooperation).

Alexander, Martha. *Blackboard Bear.* New York: Dial, 1969.
Frustrated at not being allowed to play with the big kids, a small boy enters a satisfying fantasy that turns the tables on the elitist gang.

Examples: After being told he is too little and to go play with his teddy bear, the little boy tosses his stuffed toy out the window and draws an impressive, adult bear on the chalkboard. It joins him in play. Now the big kids want to hold his leash, pat him, or ride him. "Of course not," he tells them. And when he "feeds" the bear, it licks up chalk drawings of the older boys.

Art Style: Cartoon.

Curriculum Tie-In: Social Science (Anger; Self-Discovery/Esteem).

Armstrong, Jennifer. *Hugh Can Do.* Illus. by Kimberly Root. New York: Crown, 1992.
Hugh wants to seek his fortune in the city, but first he must find a way to pay the toll-taker at the bridge.

Examples: After much exertion to acquire a loaf of bread to pay the toll-taker, it seems, after all, that this payment will not suffice with the new toll-keeper. Still, all is not over. Hugh's past fair business dealings will stand him in good stead. His acquaintances invite him to climb aboard their wagon as they cross the bridge with one toll. ". . . Hugh knew, for certain, his fortune was made."

Other Devices: Atmosphere. Foreshadowing. Pun. Simile.

Art Style: Cartoon water color.

*Babbitt, Natalie. *Phoebe's Revolt.* New York: Farrar Straus and Giroux, 1968.
Stubborn Phoebe detests her dresses "of fluff and lace . . . and everything to do with girls." But when her father permits her to wear his clothes, they don't quite suit either.

Examples: After Phoebe's father lets her wear his plain clothes, she acknowledges they somehow "didn't seem so lovely now." But she is stuck with them for seven days according to his offer. "He had so nicely said she could, she knew she must, she felt she should. She couldn't spurn that hat and shirt." But this is not just a lesson to keep a girl in her place. Father gently provides the means to remind Mother about how she herself felt wearing restrictive girl things as a child. Soon mother and daughter both have practical play clothes.

Other Devices: Foreshadowing. Satire. Stereotype.

Art Style: Cartoon line drawing.

Curriculum Tie-In: Social Science (Acceptance and Respect; Anger; Self-Discovery/Esteem; Sexism).

Bottner, Barbara. *Bootsie Barker Bites.* Illus. by Peggy Rathmann. New York: G. P. Putnam's, 1992.
Bootsie Barker likes to play only intimidating games in which she can bite, until one day her friend comes up with a better game.

Examples: Bootsie brags she is a dinosaur. Her friend counters that she is a paleontologist who hunts dinosaur bones. Some special lighting effects convince the bully to run away.

Other Devices: Foreshadowing. Inference. Understatement.

Art Style: Colored Cartoon.

Curriculum Tie-In: Social Science (Bullies; Friendship).

Burton, Virginia Lee. *Mike Mulligan and His Steam Shovel.* Boston: Houghton Mifflin, 1939.
Mike Mulligan and his steam shovel Mary Anne make canals for boats, flat ground for trains, and airplane landing fields, but when gasoline, diesel, and electric shovels came along, the steam shovel becomes obsolete. There is only one last job left for Mike and Mary Anne.

Examples: Since the well-cared-for Mary Anne is obsolete, it is only fitting that after her last digging job she be refitted for a new role more suitable to the times. She stays in the basement she's dug and serves as the new building's furnace.

Other Devices: Foreshadowing.

Art Style: Cartoon/Naive.

Curriculum Tie-In: Science (Machine Technology).
Social Science (Values).

Corbalis, Judy. *The Cuckoo Bird.* Illus. by David Armitage. New York: HarperCollins, 1988.
A little girl and her grandmother try to outwit a shape-changing, greedy cuckoo bird who has tricked his way into their house.

Examples: The greedy cuckoo has eaten everything in the house. But the child outwits him by luring him out of the house taunting him with an apple. She throws the apple. He chases after it hollering, "Everything's for me." While he is out, the rightful owners reclaim their home and lock the door.

Other Devices: Inference. Theme.

Art Style: Expressionism.

Curriculum Tie-In: Health and Safety (Stranger Danger).

Cutting, Michael. *The Little Crooked Christmas Tree.* Illus. by Ron Broda. New York: Scholastic, 1990.
A little tree sacrifices itself to a dove and her family. It loses a chance to be a Christmas tree and learns the true meaning of Christmas.

Examples: Even though his crookedness prevents him from being taken as an indoor tree, the spruce is taken for planting in a yard. It receives decoration and is greatly admired. The dove returns on Christmas Eve and perches on the top.

Other Devices: Paradox.

Art Style: Collage paper and water color.

DePaola, Tomie. *The Quicksand Book.* New York: Holiday House, 1977.
A self-important young man insists on discussing the properties of quicksand and proper rescue efforts while his friend is struggling in it.

Examples: While jungle girl is sinking in quicksand and before he deigns to rescue her, jungle boy delivers a laborious lecture on the nature of quicksand and how to survive in it. When jungle boy accidentally falls into it himself, she coolly responds, "Now, now. Remember what you told me! Just keep calm, lie on your back, and float. I'll pull you out when I finish my tea."

Other Devices: Satire.

Art Style: Colored Cartoon.

Curriculum Tie-In: Science (Quicksand; Ecology; Environment).

DePaola, Tomie. *Strega Nona.* Englewood Cliffs: Prentice-Hall, 1975.
When Strega Nona leaves him alone with her magic pasta pot, her bumbling
apprentice Big Anthony is determined to show the townspeople how it works.

> **Examples:** Pasta is everywhere. Since the lad disobeys a directive never to
> touch the pasta pot, Strega Nona administers suitable punishment. ". . . you
> wanted pasta from my magic pasta pot, . . . and I want to sleep in my little bed
> tonight. So start eating." When the pasta is cleared out of her house, Big
> Anthony, with distended belly, is thoroughly sorry for ever touching the for-
> bidden pot.
>
> **Other Devices:** Foreshadowing. Tone.
>
> **Art Style:** Cartoon/European Middle Ages Folk.
>
> **Curriculum Tie-In:** Social Science (Consequences; Ethics).

De Regniers, Beatrice Schenk. *May I Bring a Friend?* Illus. by Beni Montresor.
New York: Atheneum, 1964. [Caldecott Award]
No matter whom the young friend brings to tea with him, the king and queen
welcome them.

> **Examples:** For their generous offers and kind welcome to tea and lunch and
> such, a return invitation comes to the king and queen to dine with everyone
> at the zoo.
>
> **Other Devices:** Hyperbole.
>
> **Art Style:** Impressionism.
>
> **Curriculum Tie-In:** Social Science (Acceptance and Respect).

Edwards, Hazel. *Snail Mail.* Illus. by Rod Clement. Australia: Collins, 1986.
A mail-eating snail describes his life with "them" and his culinary interests.

> **Examples:** Snail nibbles mail and accidentally eats a sample of Froth-A-Lot
> shampoo. Just a small payback for the damage he causes.
>
> **Other Devices:** Alliteration. Inference. Irony. Pun.
>
> **Art Style:** Realism.

Flack, Marjorie. *Angus and the Ducks.* New York: Doubleday, 1930.
A curious Scottish terrier wants to find out what made the noise coming from
the other side of the hedge.

> **Examples:** Angus's loud "Woo-oo-oof!!!" frightens the ducks and gains him
> a feeling of power. Their retaliatory "Hiss-s-s-s" reverses the situation, put-
> ting him back in his place.
>
> **Other Devices:** Foreshadowing. Onomatopoeia.
>
> **Art Style:** Expressionism colored line drawings.
>
> **Curriculum Tie-In:** Social Sciences (Consequences).

Hawkes, Kevin. *Then the Troll Heard the Squeak.* New York: Lothrop, Lee & Shepard, 1991.

Little Miss Terry wreaks havoc by jumping on the bedsprings at night, until a troll appears to set things right.

> **Examples:** Oblivious of the inconvenience her selfish pleasure causes, Terry's amusement is cut short when a troll living in the house devours her bed, effectively ending her ability to shake the house.
>
> **Art Style:** Expressionism.

Henkes, Kevin. *Chrysanthemum.* New York: Greenwillow, 1991.

Chrysanthemum loves her name, until she starts going to school and the other children make fun of it.

> **Examples:** Her opinion of her name is shaken by the children's cruelty, but when they all learn that their adored music teacher also has a long name that "scarcely fits on her name tag," and that she is named after a flower, too, the ridicule turns to envy.
>
> **Other Devices:** Irony.
>
> **Art Style:** Colored Cartoon.
>
> **Curriculum Tie-In:** Social Science (Self-Discovery/Esteem; Values).

Hutchins, Pat. *Rosie's Walk.* New York: Macmillan, 1968.

Rosie the hen strolls through the barnyard oblivious to the fox who follows her in spite of a series of mishaps.

> **Examples:** For trying to eat an innocent chicken, a fox endures getting hit with a rake, a fall into a pond and a haystack, a thump from a flour sack, and a mad ride on a cart into a bee hive. And, he doesn't get his prey.
>
> **Other Devices:** Foreshadowing. Irony. Satire. Stereotype.
>
> **Art Style:** Expressionism.
>
> **Curriculum Tie-In:** Health and Safety (Accident Prevention).

Johnston, Tony. *The Soup Bone.* Illus. by Margot Tomes. New York: Harcourt Brace Jovanovich, 1990.

Looking for a soup bone on Halloween, a little old lady finds a hungry skeleton instead.

> **Examples:** A skeleton scares an old lady and chases her because "of all things in the world, she was most afraid of skeletons." In her turn, she puts on her Halloween dog costume and frightens the skeleton because "of all things in the world, it was most afraid of dogs." When the two agree to stop scaring each other, they are glad for the company and "tired of talking to myself." Two lonely souls feel lucky.
>
> **Art Style:** Cartoon.
>
> **Curriculum Tie-In:** Social Science (Friendship; Fears).

Keats, Ezra Jack. *Goggles.* New York: Macmillan, 1969.
Peter found a pair of lensless motorcycle goggles, but he and his friend Archie must use their wits to keep them away from some bullies.

> **Examples:** The big boys come closer to the hideout. Soon Peter and Archie will be found. Peter tries a diversion. He yells to "Head for the parking lot!" The big boys are fooled. While they follow the false clue, Peter and Archie slip away with their treasure safe and sound.
>
> **Art Style:** Impressionism/Expressionism.
>
> **Curriculum Tie-In:** Social Science (Bullies).

Lamorisse, Albert. *The Red Balloon.* Garden City, NY: Doubleday, 1956.
A lonely boy and a red balloon become companions.

> **Examples:** When backed into a final corner by bullies, his loyalty to the beleaguered balloon brings him a delightful surprise. The balloon bursts, but a "revolt of all captive balloons" brings them rushing to him. They lift him away from his miserable life on "a wonderful trip all around the world." The bullies left behind have nothing.
>
> **Other Devices:** Atmosphere. Symbol.
>
> **Art Style:** Photography.
>
> **Curriculum Tie-In:** Social Science (Loneliness).

Lionni, Leo. *Inch by Inch.* New York: Obelensky Astor-Honor, 1960.
A clever inch worm uses his talent for measuring things to escape being eaten.

> **Examples:** The nightingale is so taken with her own song that she deservedly loses her chance to eat a juicy worm when she asks the inch worm to measure her song. He keeps her singing as he inches along out of her way to safety.
>
> **Other Devices:** Inference. Pun.
>
> **Art Style:** Collage.
>
> **Curriculum Tie-In:** Science (Measurement).

Olson, Arielle North. *Noah's Cats and the Devil's Fire.* Illus. by Barry Moser. New York: Orchard Books, 1992.
A rebuffed devil returns to Noah's ark in disguise ready to be the most troublesome passenger aboard.

> **Examples:** The devil disguises itself as a mouse in order to gain admittance aboard Noah's ark. It is only fitting that one of the cats pounces on it and eats it up.
>
> **Other Devices:** Pun. Satire. Tone.
>
> **Art Style:** Expressionism water color.
>
> **Curriculum Tie-In:** Literature (Pourquoi story).

Potter, Beatrix. *The Tale of Peter Rabbit.* New York: Frederick Warne & Co., 1902. Disobedient Peter suffers consequences in Mr. McGregor's garden.

> **Examples:** Peter stuffs himself on forbidden food, though there is no shortage at home. He gets sick and then can't enjoy the legitimate bread his mother buys or the berries his siblings bring home. He's in bed, having been dosed with medicine while the others eat the goodies.
>
> **Other Devices:** Foreshadowing. Imagery. Irony. Metaphor. Onomatopoeia. Understatement.
>
> **Art Style:** Cartoon/Realism water color.
>
> **Curriculum Tie-In:** Social Science (Consequences; Parent and Child).

Reiser, Lynn. *Dog and Cat.* New York: Greenwillow, 1991.
A dog learns never to chase cats.

> **Examples:** The conclusion of the confrontation is satisfying. The dog who once dreamed of chasing cats is thoroughly disabused of this notion by the remarkable talents of his small but mighty neighbor. The cat turns into a "scary thing" that puffs its tail, arches its back, glares at the dog, and leaps on the dog's neck. The dog can't shake off this horror. He finally figures out what it is when it jumps off, and he sees the cat's tail disappearing under the hedge.
>
> **Other Devices:** Foreshadowing.
>
> **Art Style:** Cartoon.
>
> **Curriculum Tie-In:** Social Science (Consequences).

*__Zemach, Harve.__ *Duffy and the Devil.* Illus. by Margot Zemach. New York: Farrar Straus Giroux, 1973. [Caldecott Award]
A resourceful servant girl uses her wits to avoid admitting she can't spin and knit even when the game is up.

> **Examples:** When the devil is thwarted and can't claim Duffy, he takes final revenge by turning to ashes all the knitting he's done over the past three years. But, clever Duffy turns the situation to her advantage and doesn't admit defeat. "All my work! Gone up in smoke! I swear I'll never knit another thing ever again!" And, she never does.
>
> **Other Devices:** Parody. Tone.
>
> **Art Style:** Folk/Cartoon water color.
>
> **Curriculum Tie-In:** Social Science (Coping).

Zemach, Harve. *The Judge.* Illus. by Margot Zemach. New York: Farrar Straus Giroux, 1969.
A judge's mistrust of people leads to a disastrous confrontation with a monster.

> **Examples:** Allegations against the hapless defendants are made by the judge, who stubbornly refuses to believe a monster is coming. He accuses everyone of being a scoundrel, a nincompoop, a dimwit, a dunce. He locks them all up,

and there is no one to defend him against the monster that gets him. The prisoners walk away.

Other Devices: Caricature. Foreshadowing. Hyperbole. Satire. Theme.

Art Style: Expressionism.

Curriculum Tie-In: Social Science (Consequences; Foolish Behavior).

POINT-OF-VIEW

The perspective from which the story is seen and told; three principal vantage points are most commonly employed.

Omniscient. This is the ability to see into minds and record thoughts of characters and make comments about either one or several of them so that the reader may come to know more of their situation than does any single character in it.

> George, anxiously hoping that no one was watching him, placed a carefully wrapped package on an empty park bench. But Molly, who was walking home, saw him and couldn't help thinking that he was acting strangely.

Third Person (Limited Omniscient). Here, the central observer of the story limits interpretation to what is seen or heard without additional comment about the character motive or thoughts; this thus limits the knowledge available to the reader.

> As George placed the carefully wrapped package on the park bench, he looked up and saw Molly walking across the street.

First Person. The view and thoughts are solely through one character telling the story, (I); this view can only reveal what the character sees and is told by others.

> As I placed the carefully wrapped package on the park bench, I looked up and saw Molly waling across the street. I hoped that she hadn't seen me.

SOURCES

Baylor, Byrd. *Everybody Needs a Rock.* Illus. by Peter Parnall. New York: Charles Scribner's, 1974.

A child explains 10 rules for selecting your own personal rock.

> **Examples:** She says she feels "sorry for kids who don't have a rock for a friend" and that's why "I'm giving them my own ten rules for finding a rock" that can be kept "as long as you can, maybe forever." She advises anyplace will do for finding a rock "even an alley, even a sandy road." While you're hunting for one don't worry about barking dogs or buzzing bees because "the worst thing

you can do is go rock hunting when you are worried." You have to get down close to the rock so you "look a rock right in the eye. Otherwise don't blame me if you can't find a good one." If the rock is too small, "It will only be easy to lose or a mouse might eat it, thinking that it is a seed." You need to sniff a rock to tell whether it came from middle of earth or ocean or mountain top. "You'll find grown-ups can't tell these things. Too bad for them. They just can't smell as well as kids can."

Art Style: Expressionism/Surrealism pen and ink line drawings.

*Bedard, Michael. *Emily.* Illus. by Barbara Cooney. New York: Doubleday Book for Young Readers, 1992.

When a mother and child pay a visit to their reclusive neighbor Emily, who stays in her house writing poems, there is an exchange of special gifts.

Examples: With the arrival of the mysterious letter from the recluse across the street, the child-narrator remarks on many of life's mysteries: the dull, dead-looking lily bulbs that have "a hidden life," mysterious adults like children who hide themselves because maybe they're afraid, the yellow house that "slipped down behind the hedge as we came near," and the "little bit of sherry left in the glass was the color of Emily's eyes."

Other Devices: Imagery.

Art Style: Naive.

Curriculum Tie-In: Literature (Emily Dickinson).

Booth, Barbara D. *Mandy.* Illus. by Jim Lamarche. New York: Lothrop, Lee & Shepard, 1991.

Hearing-impaired Mandy risks going out into the scary night during an impending storm to look for her beloved grandmother's lost pin.

Examples: Mandy's unique perception of the world lends a special perspective to things the hearing take for granted. To test what her mother's "sweet and soft" voice must be like she puts a marshmallow to her ear. How silly to stop dancing when music stops in the radio box if you still feel like dancing. If leaves make small noises like Grandma says, then tree branches must make really loud noises. Maybe the reason people didn't come much to the woods is because the woods are full of noise and hurt peoples' ears. Night is lonely because she can't sign or see anyone's lips.

Other Devices: Atmosphere.

Art Style: Impressionism

Curriculum Tie-In: Health and Safety (Hearing Impaired).

*Briggs, Raymond. *Father Christmas.* New York: Coward, 1973.

The evening shows a rather disgruntled Santa on his annual rounds.

Examples: "I hate winter; Blooming snow; Blooming cold; Roll on summer; Keep still you silly deers; Blooming soot; Blooming chimneys; Getting a blooming cold; Awful tie—horrible socks." After finishing his rounds, he returns gratefully home, turns on radio music, has a hot bath, and "lovely" food and drink. His mood is much improved.

Other Devices: Allusion.

Art Style: Colored Cartoon.

Brown, Ruth. *The Picnic.* New York: Dutton Children's Books, 1992.

Rabbit is first to sense danger. Everyone scrambles into Rabbit's hole when unwelcome visitors and their pesky dog unleash some frightening surprises.

> **Examples:** Underground, the animals huddle close together "as footsteps echoed louder above them." Suddenly, everything goes black "when a cookie and picnic cloth block the rabbit hole opening. The huge face of a baby tells Mole "who was used to finding her way in the dark" that "danger was very near." Then comes a nose and pink tongue and some sharp teeth and a pair of scrabbling claws "that sent dirt and mud flying everywhere." Only when "water gushed into the hole," does the foreign danger end. Rain is "driving away the dog and his people." The art shows events from the perspective of the animals in the hole.
>
> **Art Style:** Impressionism/Expressionism/Realism paint.

Browne, Anthony. *Changes.* New York: Knopf, 1990.

As he waits at home for his parents to return, a young boy ponders his father's remark, "Things are going to change around here," and begins to imagine all kinds of changes in the world around him.

> **Examples:** The changes he imagines reflect his confusion and curiosity. Maybe the tea kettle will sprout cat ears in its handle or the bed slippers will grow crow wings or beaks. Could the bathroom sink have a human face rather than its normal appointments? The couch might become an alligator, the chair a gorilla. Maybe the soccer ball he kicks is actually an enormous egg. The boy sees a very unpredictable world. But not once does he imagine what the real change will be. In comes Mom with a baby. "Hello love. . . . This is your sister."
>
> **Art Style:** Realism/Surrealism.

Bunting, Eve. *The Wall.* Illus. by Ronald Himler. New York: Clarion (Houghton Mifflin), 1990.

A boy and his father visit the Vietnam Veterans Memorial to find the name of the boy's dead grandfather.

> **Examples:** The boy sees reflections of trees and clouds in the shiny black wall. He sees a wheelchair veteran wearing a "soldier's shirt," an old couple crying and comforting each other, "flowers old as my grandma," and other things "laid against the wall." He finds his grandpa's name. The printing is better than he could do and the wall is warm. He hears a grandfather tell a little boy to "button your jacket. It's cold." And, he wishes his own grandfather was there to talk to.

Other Devices: Atmosphere.

Art Style: Realism.

Curriculum Tie-In: History (Vietnam Memorial).

Social Science (War).

Fatio, Louise. *The Happy Lion.* Illus. by Roger Duvoisin. New York: McGraw-Hill, 1954.

The French townspeople, friendly when the Happy Lion is in his cage, run in fear of him when he leaves it to visit his town friends.

Examples: When the door of his home is accidentally left open, the lion says, "I don't like that. Anyone may walk in." On the city streets he is puzzled by the reactions he encounters. "What a silly way to say bonjour," he thinks when his friend Monsieur Dupont says "Hooooohh" and faints onto the sidewalk. How impolite the ladies are to run away, "as if an ogre were after them." He begins to assume, "This must be the way people behave when they are not at the zoo."

Art Style: Cartoon.

Flack, Marjorie. *Angus Lost.* New York: Doubleday, 1932.

A little Scottish terrier is bored with the same things at home and is curious to see what the outside world has to find.

Examples: Angus wonders "what kind of animals cars are." The car comes at Angus and he woofs. The car honks back, but then it "ran away." He sees two eyes up in a tree. The owl's "Whoo-Whoo" frightens him.

Other Devices: Foreshadowing. Onomatopoeia.

Art Style: Expressionism colored line drawings.

Freeman, Don. *Corduroy.* Viking, 1968.

A toy teddy bear finds a home with Lisa.

Examples: The toy steps on an escalator and wonders, "Could this be a mountain?" The furniture floor seems to him a palace. The missing button on his overall strap appears to be stuck to a mattress, "tied down tight."

Art Style: Colored Cartoon.

Curriculum Tie-In: Social Science (Friendship; Loneliness).

Johnston, Tony. *Goblin Walk.* Illus. by Bruce Degen. New York: G. P. Putnam's, 1991.

A little goblin has a series of frightening experiences while walking through the woods to his grandmother's house.

Examples: To a goblin, a mouse or squirrel can be awful. He "snarls" for joy, "gnashes" his teeth, and does other repulsive acts, but is scared of a fluttering butterfly.

Other Devices: Irony. Paradox.

Art Style: Cartoon.

Curriculum Tie-In: Social Science (Fear).

Kitamura, Satoshi. *UFO Diary.* New York: Farrar Straus Giroux, 1989.

A UFO is lost in space, until it spots a strange blue planet. Zooming in for a closer look, the UFO discovers a curious creature watching it. The two become friends and explore together.

Examples: The strange looking "creature" shows the traveler "his relations": squirrels, lizards, birds, rabbits, etc. He "dropped him home"—on top of the roof of a highrise apartment. He receives a "present" from the creature. It is yellow and grew in the field where they met—a dandelion.

Art Style: Cartoon.

Konigsburg, E. L. *Samuel Todd's Book of Great Inventions.* New York: Atheneum, 1991.

Samuel Todd shows some inventions that make his day easier and better, including velcro, a thermos bottle, training wheels, backpacks, and mittens.

Examples: Samuel Todd observes the world from a fresh, thought-provoking perspective. The great inventions are not the telephone and TV, because they just "come with the house." He is impressed with things like mirrors so you can "make sure I am still Samuel Todd," or belt loops to keep up pants, "but two would have been enough."

Art Style: Expressionism/Impressionism paint.

Lyon, George Ella. *Cecil's Story.* Illus. by Peter Catalanotto. New York: Orchard Books, 1991.

A boy thinks about the possible scenarios that exist for him at home if he father goes off to fight in the Civil War.

Examples: He might have to stay with neighbors; he'd cry only at night, wiping his face on his shirt tail; he'd have to take care of Mama and do the farm work; the plow might be troublesome, the high handles. Etc.

Other Devices: Flash-Forward.

Art Style: Expressionism.

McCloskey, Robert. *Make Way for Ducklings.* New York: Viking, 1941. [Caldecott Award]

The mallard family causes consternation when it takes up residence in the city.

Examples: The mallards see a pleasure boat with a swan ornament which hid the boat's motor. They interpret this unfamiliar spectacle as "a strange enormous bird . . . pushing a boat full of people." The bird seems "too proud to answer" their polite greeting. There are "horrid things" (children on bicycles) "rushing about," making the park "no place for babies."

Other Devices: Caricature. Foreshadowing.

Art Style: Cartoon.

Curriculum Tie-In: Literature (Pacing of Story).

*Melmed, Laura Krauss. *The First Song Ever Sung*. Illus. by Ed Young. New York: Lothrop, Lee & Shepard, 1993.

Animal and human friends provide lyrical answers to a young boy's musical query.

Examples: Each time a child asks what was the first song ever sung, the answer reflects the spirit of the speaker. From his father he hears that the first song was strong, a warrior's song, a friend's song. From his sister's view, the first song was a swinging, jumping, twirling rope song. The minnows tell him the first song was a ripple, splash, pebble song. Etc.

Art Style: Impressionism.

Ryder, Joanne. *Winter Whale*. Illus. by Michael Rothman. New York: Morrow Junior Books (Just-For-A-Day Series), 1991.

A child transforms into the animal for a day and discovers what life is like as a whale; also bear and goose. Others in the series: *Lizard in the Sun*, 1990; *White Bear, Ice Bear*, 1989; *Catching the Wind*, 1989.

Examples: The child experiences in first-person point of view what it feels like to be the various animals who can soar, live in shaggy fur, feel the hot sun on dry leathery skin, and splash heavily in an ocean.

Other Devices: Imagery.

Art Style: Expressionism.

Curriculum Tie-In: Science (Ecology).

*Say, Allen. *Tree of Cranes*. Boston: Houghton Mifflin, 1991.

A Japanese boy learns of Christmas when his mother decorates a pine tree with paper cranes.

Examples: The child is puzzled and concerned because his mother is preoccupied with the paper crane tree decorations. What does it mean? She must still be angry with him because he disobeyed and went to the neighbor's pond. Now he cannot understand why she is digging a hole in the garden. He is uninformed about Christmas trees and customs.

Other Devices: Atmosphere. Flash-Forward. Inference.

Art Style: Oriental Folk/Realism.

Curriculum Tie-In: Social Science (Cross-Cultures).

*Scieszka, Jon. *The True Story of the 3 Little Pigs by A. Wolf*. Illus. by Lane Smith. New York: Viking Kestrel (Viking Penguin), 1989.

The wolf gives his own outlandish version of what really happened when he tangled with the three little pigs.

Examples: It all started with "a sneeze and a cup of sugar." He needed the sugar to make a cake for "dear old granny." He went to borrow from his pig neighbor, whose straw house fell down killing the occupant after he sneezed. And, it was "a shame to leave a perfectly good ham dinner lying there in the straw." And so it happened at each house. The reporters were responsible for the way they "jazzed up the story." He was really "framed."

Other Devices: Parody. Pun. Tone.

Art Style: Colored Cartoon/Collage.

Sendak, Maurice. *Where the Wild Things Are.* New York: Harper & Row, 1963. [Caldecott Award]

Max is a little boy dressed in a wolf suit sent to his room for behaving ferociously. Suddenly, the walls disappear, and he finds himself in a magic forest of wild creatures.

Examples: With power and control at his command, it is Max's turn to be fiercest of the wild things and to order them to bed without their supper as had happened to him. Nothing they say will persuade him to stay with them when he has decided to leave them.

Other Devices: Hyperbole. Inference. Theme.

Art Style: Expressionism pen and ink colored drawings.

Curriculum Tie-In: Social Sciences (Anger; Consequences; Forgiveness; Parent and Child; Self-Discovery/Esteem).

Stanley, Diane. *Siegfried.* Illus. by John Sanford. New York: Little Rooster (Bantam), 1991.

When a cuckoo clock invades Siegfried's peace and calls him names, the cat wages war against it.

Examples: The "cuckoo" sound seems like an insult to Siegfried. He dares the bird to come out and watches for it, pacing and "thinking dark thoughts." When he finally snatches the bird, the clock box comes crashing down on him. His family feels sorry the accident happened. They fix the clock but the bird no longer calls "cuckoo." It whirrs, and the clock doesn't bong; it clicks. Siegfried considers those sounds acceptable. "It doesn't purr very well. . . . But, after all, it's only a bird." He decides to "let it stay, now that it had learned how to behave."

Art Style: Expressionism.

Woolf, Virginia. *Nurse Lugton's Curtain.* Illus. by Julie Vivas. New York: Gulliver Books (Harcourt Brace Jovanovich), text: 1982, illus.: 1991.

As Nurse Lugton dozes, the animals on the patterned curtain she is sewing come alive.

Examples: In the point of view of the "blue stuff" animals and people, "they could see her, from their windows, towering over them. She had a face like the side of a mountain with great precipices and avalanches, and chasms for her eyes and hair and nose and teeth."

Other Devices: Simile.

Art Style: Expressionism.

* **Yolen, Jane.** *Encounter.* Illus. by David Shannon. New York: Harcourt Brace Jovanovich, 1992.

A Taino Indian boy on the island of San Salvador recounts the landing of Columbus and his men in 1492.

Examples: The boy describes the invasion of Columbus. Three great-sailed canoes "gave birth to many little ones that swam awkwardly to our shore. The baby canoes spat out many strange creatures, men but not men." They had "hair growing like bushes on their chins." They "hid their bodies in colors like parrots." The bells they brought were "hollow shells with tongues that sang chinga-chunga." Mirrors were "round pools to hold in the hand that gave a man back his face." They carried "sticks that sound like thunder and could kill a parrot many paces away."

Other Devices: Atmosphere. Flash-Forward. Foreshadowing. Metaphor. Stereotype. Theme.

Art Style: Realism/Expressionism acrylic.

Curriculum Tie-In: History (Columbus-Discovery of America).

* **Yolen, Jane.** *Sky Dogs.* Illus. by Barry Moser. New York: Harcourt Brace Jovanovich, 1990.

A young motherless boy in a tribe of Blackfeet Indians is present when his people see horses for the first time.

Examples: The strange beings came near and the narrator was frozen in fear. "I was glad when the newest baby cried . . . I was glad when his mother sang softly to him, for then I could listen to the words of his cradleboard song, and they comforted me." Thinking the creatures were large dogs, the people "rubbed their noses with good backfat, which made them sneeze." Throwing sticks for them to chase startled them. Finally, the animals "put their faces into the prairie grass, eating loudly so we would know how to feed them."

Other Devices: Onomatopoeia.

Art Style: Realism/Expressionism.

Curriculum Tie-In: History (Native Americans—Blackfeet).

PUN

A humorous use of a word or phrase to suggest two or more meanings at the same time; puns can involve three kinds of word play.

1. Words spelled or pronounced the same but with different meanings.

Example: "Now we must all *hang* together or we will surely *hang* separately."—Ben Franklin (If the revolutionaries did not remain united, their individual lives would be in danger.)

2. Words based on homonyms.

Example: lone/loan

3. Words based on close similarities in sound or meaning.

Example: Teacher to Child: You're a disturbing element today, Mike.
Child to Mother: She called me a scurvy elephant today!

SOURCES

Abolafia, Yossi. *Fox Tale.* New York: Greenwillow, 1991.
Donkey, Crow, and Rabbit join forces to prevent Fox from swindling Bear out of his jar of honey.

Examples: In this fox "tale," fox must give up the things he's cheated from his friends in order to retain his "tail."

Other Devices: Allusion. Poetic Justice.

Art Style: Colored Cartoon.

Curriculum Tie-In: Social Science (Consequences; Cooperation).

Armstrong, Jennifer. *Hugh Can Do.* Illus. by Kimberly Bulcken Root. New York: Crown, 1992.
Hugh wants to seek his fortune in the city, but first he must find a way to pay the toll-taker at the bridge.

Examples: Though the effect is something more than double meaning, the words connect with the occupation of each laborer who talks to Hugh. For example, the baker calls young Hugh a "Muffinhead." He smiles "with a dusty sneeze." The miller "grits" his teeth on a piece of rock candy and smiles "with a grating laugh." The tailor calls him "Ripsnorter" and smiles with a "needly grin."

Other Devices: Atmosphere. Foreshadowing. Poetic Justice. Simile.

Art Style: Cartoon water color.

Curriculum Tie-In: Social Science (Coping).

Briggs, Raymond. *Jim and the Beanstalk.* New York: Coward-McCann, 1970.
Later in the life of the giant, another curious climber finds the giant now beset with the inadequacies of old age and endeavors to fill his needs.

Examples: "Don't you have any glasses?" asked Jim.
"Only beer glasses," said the Giant.
"I mean reading glasses," said Jim.

Other Devices: Ambiguity. Parody. Tone.

Art Style: Colored Cartoon.

Curriculum Tie-In: Social Science (Friendship).

Cameron, Polly. *I Can't Said the Ant.* New York: Coward-McCann, 1961.
An ant, encouraged by a kitchen battalion of 89 objects, comes to the rescue of a fallen teapot.

> **Examples:** When the teapot exclaims at the end of her harrowing experience, "Polly put the kettle on," the reader notes both the reference to the author's name and the famous nursery rhyme.
>
> **Other Devices:** Allusion. Internal Rhyme. Theme.
>
> **Art Style:** Cartoon.
>
> **Curriculum Tie-In:** Science (Lever and Pulley).

Daly, Niki. *Mama, Papa, and Baby Joe.* New York: Viking Penguin, 1991.
A family goes on an adventure shopping trip described in action-packed pictures full of unlikely hilarious detail.

> **Examples:** The "Retail Store" sells? Tails! Of course.
>
> **Other Devices:** Alliteration. Allusion. Tone.
>
> **Art Style:** Cartoon.

DePaola, Tomie. *Nanna Upstairs and Nanna Downstairs.* New York: G. P. Putnam's, 1973.
Tommy loved weekly visits to his grandmother downstairs and his great-grandmother upstairs. When Nanna upstairs dies, it is the closeness of his loving family that comforts him and helps him accept her death.

> **Examples:** After his great grandmother dies, Tommy sees a shooting star, and his mother suggests it might be a "kiss from Nanna Upstairs." Later when he is grown up and his grandmother has also died, he sees another shooting star and thinks, "Now you are both Nanna Upstairs." The reference is to the upstairs of their home on Earth and the "upstairs" of a heavenly home.
>
> **Other Devices:** Atmosphere. Flash-Forward.
>
> **Art Style:** Cartoon.
>
> **Curriculum Tie-In:** Social Science (Death; Aging; Grandparents).

Edwards, Hazel. *Snail Mail.* Illus. by Rod Clement. Australia: Collins, 1986.
A mail-eating snail describes his life with "them" and his culinary interests.

> **Examples:** Snail watches the postman with a bag of mail, bicycling up the hill with his "meals on wheels." He accidentally eats a sample of Froth-A-Lot shampoo, and now he froths a lot.
>
> **Other Devices:** Alliteration. Inference. Irony. Poetic Justice.
>
> **Art Style:** Realism.

Freeman, Don. *Dandelion*. New York: Viking, 1964.
Jennifer Giraffe sends out party invitations that read, "Come as you are," but that doesn't stop Dandelion from indulging in a make-over.

> **Examples:** After learning his lesson he promises, "never again to turn myself into a stylish dandy." Dandelion brings dandelions to his hostess.
> **Other Devices:** Foreshadowing. Theme.
> **Art Style:** Cartoon.
> **Curriculum Tie-In:** Social Science (Self-Discovery/Esteem).

***Gregory, Valiska.** *Through the Mickle Woods*. Illus. by Barry Moser. Boston: Little, Brown and Company, 1992.
After his wife's death, a grieving king journeys to an old bear's cave in the Mickle Woods, where he hears three stories that help him go on living.

> **Examples:** When his jester tries to lighten the king's mood by making bird shadows with his arms in the winter sun, the king somberly says, "I have had enough of shadows," referring to the recent death of his wife. Says the king when painful memories begin to awaken in him, "I do not think I can bear to remember all of it." The bear rounds on him, "Can you bear to remember less?" For the sake of his life he must face all the memories.
> **Other Devices:** Aphorism. Atmosphere. Inference. Metaphor. Simile. Symbol. Theme.
> **Art Style:** Expressionism/Realism.
> **Curriculum Tie-In:** Social Science (Death; Grief).

Johnson, Crockett. *Harold and the Purple Crayon*. New York: Harper & Row, 1955.
Harold draws his way into magical adventures.

> **Examples:** The crayon dropped on the floor and Harold dropped off to sleep. Harold made his bed and "drew" up the covers. Harold "made land" without much trouble.
> **Art Style:** Cartoon.

Kimmel, Eric. *Four Dollars and Fifty Cents*. Illus. by Glen Rounds. New York: Holiday House, 1989.
To avoid paying the Widow Macrae the four dollars and fifty cents he owes her, deadbeat cowboy Shorty Long plays dead and almost gets buried alive.

> **Examples:** "Shorty saw stars, but not the ones in the sky." His "stars" result from his injuries. He's been a "dead"beat for years, but he finds himself close to the real thing (dead) when he crawls into a coffin to hide from his creditors.
> **Other Devices:** Allusion. Irony. Simile.
> **Art Style:** Impressionism.
> **Curriculum Tie-In:** Social Science (Foolish Behavior).

Koller, Jackie French. *Mole and Shrew Step Out.* Illus. by Stella Ormai. New York: Atheneum, 1992.

Mole commits a comic blunder regarding a fancy ball, but his good friend Shrew sticks by him.

> **Examples:** Mole seeks to outfit himself in "tie and tails." He asks silk worm "a great spinner of tales" to provide one for him.
>
> **Other Devices:** Ambiguity.
>
> **Art Style:** Cartoon water color.
>
> **Curriculum Tie-In:** Social Science (Friendship).

Kraus, Robert. *Milton the Early Riser.* Illus. by Jose Areugo and Ariane Areugo. New York: Windmill Books (E. P. Dutton), 1972.

Milton copes with his early morning loneliness in a manner that exhausts him before everyone else awakes.

> **Examples:** Milton's jumping and tricks didn't awaken anyone, but when he "sang up a storm" one came and "the mountains shook, the trees trembled."
>
> **Other Devices:** Hyperbole. Irony.
>
> **Art Style:** Colored Cartoon.

Lionni, Leo. *Inch by Inch.* New York: Obelensky Astor-Honor, 1960.

A clever inch worm uses his talent for measuring things to escape being eaten.

> **Examples:** Inch by inch, he inches out of sight. He measures himself safely out of the songbird's reach.
>
> **Other Devices:** Inference. Poetic Justice.
>
> **Art Style:** Collage.
>
> **Curriculum Tie-In:** Science (Measurment).

Lionni, Leo. *Matthew's Dream.* New York: Knopf, 1991.

A visit to an art museum inspires a young mouse to become a painter.

> **Examples:** Matthew chooses to name his greatest work of art "My Dream." It is a representation of the dream he had after visiting the art museum years ago. That dream set him on to his life's career. He realizes his dream come true in the culmination of his best work.
>
> **Other Devices:** Analogy.
>
> **Art Style:** Collage.

McNaughton, Colin. *Guess Who's Just Moved in Next Door?* New York: Random House, 1991.

A tour through a very peculiar neighborhood where an assortment of wacky neighbors from Superman to a ship of pirates reacts to the arrival of new neighbors.

> **Examples:** Many peculiar lines such as the following: —I only stole a calender; I got twelve months. —Mabel is sweeping. Would you like a hand,

Mabel? A hand is hung up in the mad scientist's room. —A hump-backed man keeps the belfry tidy; I've a "hunch" I know him well.

Other Devices: Allusion. Caricature. Irony. Parallel Story. Satire.

Art Style: Colored Cartoon.

Nicholson, William. *Clever Bill.* New York: Farrar, 1977.
A little girl's toy soldier refuses to be left behind when the girl goes to visit her aunt.

Examples: A toy soldier named Clever Bill Davis can play cymbals but has other talents as well. Though he is left behind, he manages to run cross country to meet the girl's train at its arrival, proving just how "clever" he really is.

Art Style: Impressionism woodcut and paint.

Novak, Matt. *Elmer Blunt's Open House.* New York: Orchard Books, 1992.
Several animals and a robber explore Elmer Blunt's home when he forgets to close the door on his way to work.

Examples: Indeed, "guests" do arrive at Elmer Blunt's "Open House." But he did not invite them, did not know they came, and did not know he left his door open by mistake.

Other Devices: Ambiguity. Irony. Understatement.

Art Style: Colored Cartoon.

Olson, Arielle North. *Noah's Cats and the Devil's Fire.* Illus. by Barry Moser. New York: Orchard Books, 1992.
A rebuffed devil returns to Noah's ark in disguise ready to be the most troublesome passenger aboard.

Examples: The cats on board heard the devil-mouse cackle and they "pussy-footed" toward a pile of hay to seek the creature.

Other Devices: Poetic Justice. Satire. Tone.

Art Style: Expressionism water color.

Curriculum Tie-In: Literature (Pourquoi Story).

Peet, Bill. *The Spooky Tail of Prewitt Peacock.* Boston: Houghton Mifflin, 1972.
Prewitt's scraggly tail feathers are no source of pride, and then they grow into a ridiculous frightening fan. The other peacocks chase him off until he saves the day when they encounter old Travis the Tiger.

Examples: Because the tail's fierceness frightens the tiger away, the other peacocks ask Prewitt to be their new leader. They are "behind" him 100 percent. And Prewitt knows why, "but just the same he couldn't help being proud."

Art Style: Colored Cartoon.

Curriculum Tie-In: Social Science (Discrimination; Acceptance and Respect; Values).

Polacco, Patricia. *Just Plain Fancy.* New York: Little Rooster (Bantam), 1990.
Naomi, an Amish girl whose elders have impressed upon her the importance of adhering to the simple ways of her people, is horrified when one of her hen eggs hatches into an extremely fancy bird.

> **Examples:** Although no one quite knew how Fancy came to be hatched by Henny, "Plainly, it was a miracle . . . and sometimes miracles are just Plain Fancy!"
>
> **Other Devices:** Foreshadowing.
>
> **Art Style:** Expressionism.
>
> **Curriculum Tie-In:** Geography (Amish Culture).

*Scieszka, Jon. *The True Story of the 3 Little Pigs by A. Wolf.* Illus. by Lane Smith. New York: Viking Kestrel (Viking Penguin), 1989.
The wolf gives his own outlandish version of what really happened when he tangled with the three little pigs.

> **Examples:** The maligned, witty, and mostly innocent wolf only wanted to borrow a cup of sugar from his neighbors. "He wouldn't give me even one little cup for my dear sweet old granny's birthday cake. What a pig!" At the story's conclusion, the hapless wolf is still begging for a loan of a cup of sugar. He is doing this behind bars in the "Pig Penn."
>
> **Other Devices:** Parody. Point-Of-View. Tone.
>
> **Art Style:** Colored Cartoon/Collage.

Steig, William. *Sylvester and the Magic Pebble.* New York: Windmill Books (Simon & Schuster), 1969. [Caldecott Award]
A magic pebble, a fierce lion, and a wish made in panic lead to separation from loved ones.

> **Examples:** Through an unfortunate wish, Sylvester turns into a stone. He then tries to talk but has no voice. "He was stone-dumb."
>
> **Other Devices:** Foreshadowing. Imagery. Personification. Stereotype. Symbol. Theme.
>
> **Art Style:** Cartoon water color.
>
> **Curriculum Tie-In:** Social Science (Parent and Child).

*Tolhurst, Marilyn. *Somebody and the Three Blairs.* Illus. by Simone Abel. New York: Orchard Books, 1991.
In a reversal of the Goldilocks story, a bear explores the home of the human three Blairs while they are out.

> **Examples:** The play on "Somebody" refers on occasion to the bear's name, to an unknown intruder, and to the need for a clearheaded rational person to do sensible action. "Somebody came to the door." "Somebody's been eating my Crispies." "Somebody phone the police." An inquisitive bear visits the

human "Three Blairs"—Mama, Papa, and Baby. (Not to be confused with the Three Bears of the familiar version.)

Other Devices: Parody. Understatement.

Art Style: Colored Cartoon.

Ward, Lynd. *The Biggest Bear.* Boston: Houghton Mifflin Co., 1952. [Caldecott Award]

Johnny Orchard goes out to acquire a bearskin, comes home with a cute little cub instead, and has to contend with its growing appetite.

Examples: In reference to the family name: "Better a bear in the orchard than an Orchard in the bear." The only apple trees in the valley "were known as Orchard's orchard."

Other Devices: Foreshadowing. Stereotype. Understatement.

Art Style: Realism/Impressionism.

Curriculum Tie-In: History (Nineteenth-Century America Frontier Life).

***Wilsdorf, Anne.** *Princess.* New York: Greenwillow, 1993.

A girl proves that she is a real princess in an unusual way.

Examples: The prince has a difficult time finding the right princess, a "certified genuine" princess until he discovers "Princess," a stranger who says that's what her father calls her. She turns out to be "exactly the one I have been looking for."

Other Devices: Ambiguity. Foreshadowing. Parody. Satire.

Art Style: Cartoon water color.

Yolen, Jane. *Welcome to the Green House.* Illus. by Laura Regan. New York: G. P. Putnam's, 1993.

Describes the tropical rainforest and the life found there.

Examples: "Welcome to the green house. Welcome to the hot house." Like the glass-enclosed artificial world, the tropical rainforest is home to a myriad of species all bunched together in one steamy, lively environment.

Other Devices: Analogy. Atmosphere. Imagery. Internal Rhyme. Onomatopoeia.

Art Style: Realism/Expressionism.

Curriculum Tie-In: Science (Ecology; Rainforest).

SATIRE

The act of criticizing or ridiculing weaknesses, characteristics, and wrongdoings of humans (clothing, fads, political problems, etc.), groups, and institutions; a device for exaggerating faults for the purpose of showing how absurd they are. Satire can be in a tone of scorn, amusement, or contempt to get across the point.

SOURCES

*Alexander, Lloyd. *The Fortune-Tellers*. Illus. by Trina Schart Hyman. New York: Dutton Children's Books, 1992.

A carpenter goes to a fortune-teller and finds the predictions about his future come true in an unusual way.

Examples: Dissatisfied in his trade, a young carpenter puts his faith in a fortune-teller who spouts the predictable fortune with some useless caveats: he will be rich, if he earns large sums of money; he will marry, if she agrees; he will be happy, if he can avoid being miserable. It sounds easy. And, it is. There seems nothing more sure of success than becoming the fortune-teller, his conduit to the good life.

Other Devices: Irony.

Art Style: Realism/Expressionism.

Allard, Harry. *It's So Nice to Have a Wolf Around the House*. Illus. by James Marshall. Garden City, NY: Doubleday, 1977.

A wolf answers an ad to be companion to an old man and his older pets. The companion does a wonderful job until he falls ill and must, in turn, be nursed. Everyone benefits from the new arrangement.

Examples: This gentle spoof on the nature and reputation of the wolf shows that being considered bad and being good are mostly in the eye of the one labeling. "I always wanted to be good, but everyone expected me to be bad because I'm a wolf." So he has to rob banks. When he collapses from "frayed nerves," the doctor tells the man and his pets that "you've got a very sick wolf on your hands." Everyone pitches in, and everyone becomes healthy together.

Other Devices: Irony. Stereotype.

Art Style: Cartoon.

Curriculum Tie-In: Social Science (Prejudice; Forgiveness).

Allen, Judy. *Tiger*. Illus. by Tudor Humphries. Cambridge, MA: Candlewick Press, 1992.

When a rumor starts that there is a tiger in the woods, the villagers plan to kill it. Eating the meat, they believe, will make them brave, and selling its skin will make them rich. So, when another rumor begins that a famous hunter is coming to town, the villagers decide to ask him to hunt the tiger for them.

Examples: The men of the village desire benefits from the tiger but decide to avoid the danger that goes along with a tiger hunt. They relinquish control to the famous "hunter" and put their faith in the stranger. The tiger is found and "shot" but is not brought back to the village because the hunter has his own agenda. He is a photographer. The old ways of destructive greed, especially without effort, are no match against modern environmental values.

Other Devices: Inference. Irony. Stereotype.

Art Style: Realism.

Curriculum Tie-In: Science (Endangered Species).

*Babbitt, Natalie. Phoebe's Revolt. *New York: Farrar Straus Giroux, 1968.*
Stubborn Phoebe detests her dresses "of fluff and lace . . . and everything to do with girls." But when her father permits her to wear his clothes they don't quite suit either.

Examples: Each generation finds its clothes restrictive. What Phoebe wants is not to literally wear her father's clothes. She wants the freedom of move- ment that she thinks they represented. She is "prone to having notions of her own." The female adults around her are baffled by her attitude until her own mother is gently reminded how, as a child, she had not liked the things she was expected to wear. With this realization, she and Phoebe are outfitted with "girl" clothes that allow room for play.

Other Devices: Foreshadowing. Poetic Justice. Stereotype.

Art Style: Cartoon.

Curriculum Tie-In: Social Science (Acceptance and Respect; Anger; Self-Discovery/Esteem; Sexism).

Bright, Robert. *Georgie. Garden City, NY: Doubleday, 1944.*
A personable little ghost is unhappy until reunited with the home that needs him to haunt it.

Examples: This story illustrates the opposite of the usual concept of the rela- tionship between ghosts and the houses they haunt. The house can't function without Georgie "keeping everything as it should be." The people and cat depend on Georgie to make the appropriate creaks and squeaks so they know when it's bedtime, when it's time for the cat to prowl, when it's time for the owl to wake up. Too bad the householders decide to do some home mainte- nance. Now, Georgie can't do his job and must find another house to haunt. Life isn't "much fun." Happiness is restored when their mutual relationship is restored.

Other Devices: Stereotype (Reverse).

Art Style: Cartoon.

DePaola, Tomie. *The Quicksand Book. New York: Holiday House, 1977.*
Discusses the composition of quicksand and rescue procedures.

Examples: A self-important young man refuses to rescue a girl who has fallen into quicksand until he subjects her to a long lecture on the property of quick- sand and how to survive a fall into it. When he, in turn, tumbles into it, he can only remember to holler "Help, help."

Other Devices: Poetic Justice.

Art Style: Colored Cartoon.

Curriculum Tie-In: Science (Quicksand; Ecology; Environment).

Hilton, Nette. *A Proper Little Lady.* Illus. by Cathy Wilcox. New York: Orchard Books, 1989.

Annabella feels like a proper little lady in her fancy clothes but finds them a bit inconvenient when she goes out and gets embroiled in messy fun.

Examples: Clothes don't make the person. Annabella can wear play things—jeans, shirt, and sneakers—and still be a "proper little lady."

Art Style: Cartoon.

Curriculum Tie-In: Social Science (Sexism).

Hutchins, Pat. *Rosie's Walk.* New York: Macmillan, 1968.

Rosie the hen strolls through the barnyard oblivious to the fox who follows her in spite of a series of mishaps.

Examples: The famed cunning and clever maneuvering of the fox is debunked as a clumsy bushy tail is foiled again and again in his many tries to nab a hen for his dinner. On the other hand, the equally famed bumbling, inept chicken who uses no skills and artifice leads a charmed existence and escapes being snatched. So much for alert skill vs. foggy carelessness.

Other Devices: Foreshadowing. Irony. Poetic Justice. Stereotype.

Art Style: Expressionism.

Curriculum Tie-In: Health and Safety (Accident Prevention).

Leaf, Munro. *The Story of Ferdinand.* Illus. by Robert Lawson. New York: Viking, 1936.

Ferdinand is a bull who would rather sit and smell the flowers than fight.

Examples: While Ferdinand grows sleek and plump, his fellow bulls become scarred and anxious from sparring so much. The bullfight is a gala affair with much pomp and showing off besides fierce fighting. Ferdinand is chosen because he looks like a prize fighter. Unfortunately, there is much ado over nothing, because he refuses to fight. Everyone is mad, except Ferdinand who goes home to live doing what he likes best.

Other Devices: Foreshadowing. Irony.

Art Style: Expressionism/Cartoon.

Curriculum Tie-In: Social Science (Acceptance and Respect).

McNaughton, Colin. *Guess Who's Just Moved in Next Door?* New York: Random House, 1991.

A tour through a very peculiar neighborhood where an assortment of wacky neighbors from Superman to a ship of pirates reacts to the arrival of new neighbors.

Examples: Society is being chastized for worrying about who and what will ruin a neighborhood. Bigotry and false stereotypes are held up for ridicule. It's the crook who accuses the new neighbors of being crooks. The Hell's Angel believes property values will go down. The Frankenstein monster calls them "unnatural." Ghosts call them scary.

Other Devices: Allusion. Caricature. Irony. Parallel Story. Pun.

Art Style: Colored Cartoon.

Olson, Arielle North. *Noah's Cats and the Devil's Fire.* Illus. by Barry Moser. New York: Orchard Books, 1992.

A rebuffed devil returns to Noah's ark in disguise ready to be the most troublesome passenger aboard.

Examples: The story pokes fun at the underlying seriousness of one tiny mouse that could have posed a deadly threat to all of creation. The devil mouse intends to gnaw a hole in the bottom of the ship so the animals would drown. It makes the mistake of eliciting help from the two real mice on board. "Noah might not have noticed the beginning of a mouse hole. He might not have seen bits of wood on the floor. But Noah did notice three mice." One of the cats catches and eats it, but quickly spits it out into the sea. (It is hot!) The cat, to this day, has some devil fire inside it. Its eyes glow in the dark and its fur makes sparks when stroked.

Other Devices: Poetic Justice. Pun. Tone.

Art Style: Expressionism water color.

Curriculum Tie-In: Literature (Pourquoi Story).

*Parnall, Peter. *The Mountain.* Garden City, NY: Doubleday, 1971.

The mountain, flowers, and moles should be kept just the way they are. To accomplish that, Congress passed a law making the mountain a national park. And, then a road was built. And, then people came.

Examples: A few people at first, a few toilets, water fountains, picnic tables, parking lots, food stands, litter and clutter, and eventual destruction of the area where "this is a flower trying to grow on the mountain that stood in the West." Preservation measures meant its downfall.

Other Devices: Irony. Theme.

Art Style: Expressionism/Cartoon line drawing.

Curriculum Tie-In: Science (Ecology).

Pinkwater, Daniel. *Doodle Flute.* New York: Macmillan, 1991.

Kevin Spoon acquires a doodle flute and makes a friend.

Examples: Those who "have it all" aren't to be envied. They are never satisfied, because there is always something that they still desire. And, if that something can't be purchased, it's bound to be the thing desired most. Having it all is never enough until the human element is included. Kevin finally gets it all when he and Mason become friends.

Other Devices: Irony. Tone.

Art Style: Cartoon.

Curriculum Tie-In: Social Science (Values; Friendship).

Pomerantz, Charlotte. *The Piggy in the Puddle.* Illus. by James Marshall. New York: Macmillan, 1974.

A piggy refuses to get out of a mud puddle. Her family tries unsuccessfully to get her to come out and finally join her in the puddle.

Examples: Pleasure in this case is the opposite of soap and cleanliness. This is what fuddy-duddy Daddy and fiddle-faddle Mommy and silly-billy brother learn.

Art Style: Cartoon.

Curriculum Tie-In: Social Science (Family Life).

Williams, Jay. *Everyone Knows What a Dragon Looks Like.* Illus. by Mercer Mayer. New York: Four Winds, 1976.

Because of the road sweeper's belief in him, a dragon saves the city of Wu from the Wild Horsemen invaders.

Examples: This cautionary tale is an indictment against hidebound society. It is unwise to overlook unexpected sources for help. A government full of authority can be all puffery and no substance. Accept wisdom from grass roots and don't assume only those in power have all the answers. In this case, each councilor is sure a dragon must look like himself, and each is foolishly mistaken.

Other Devices: Simile.

Art Style: Expressionism/Folk.

Curriculum Tie-In: Social Science (Foolish Behavior).

*****Wilsdorf, Anne.** *Princess.* New York: Greenwillow, 1993.

A girl proves that she is a real princess in an unusual way.

Examples: Prince Leopold must vanquish all the evil monsters who guard the "certified, genuine" princesses. Having done so, he finds none of them worth fighting for. And, in the end, he selects a bride with whom he "has a lot in common," even if she isn't genuine.

Other Devices: Ambiguity. Foreshadowing. Parody. Pun.

Art Style: Cartoon water color.

Zemach, Harve. *The Judge.* Illus. by Margot Zemach. New York: Farrar Straus Giroux, 1969.

A judge's mistrust of people leads to a disastrous confrontation with a monster.

Examples: The fair, righteous Court Justice takes testimony and refuses to acknowledge its truth. Innocent citizens are punished for doing their civic duty. The arrogant judge presumes guilt without justifiable cause and lives (briefly) to regret his injustice.

Other Devices: Caricature. Foreshadowing. Hyperbole. Poetic Justice. Theme.

Art Style: Expressionism.

Curriculum Tie-In: Social Science (Consequences; Foolish Behavior).

SIMILE

Explicit comparison from one unlike thing to another that shares some common recognizable similarity; this device uses "like," "as," "such as," and "than" to set them off.

Example: Mad as a hornet; laughed like a hyena; lower than a snake's belly in a wagon rut.

SOURCES

Ackerman, Karen. *The Banshee.* Illus. by David Ray. New York: Philomel, 1990. One night the Banshee comes to the village in search of a lonely soul to keep her company.

Examples: "Night settles like dust across a mantelpiece. The main road is washed in a silvery moonlight. Sounds are as even and peaceful as bedtime prayers."

Other Devices: Tone:

Art Style: Expressionism.

Armstrong, Jennifer. *Hugh Can Do.* Illus. by Kimberly Bulcken Root. New York: Crown, 1992. Hugh wants to seek his fortune in the city, but first he must find a way to pay the toll-taker at the bridge.

Examples: "Hugh was poor as a rabbit but quick as a fox; rips sewn up nice as a hanky; needle this apron as fast as a hummingbird; ground as fine as diamond dust; baked as hot as a coal; empty pickets as bare as a bone; bounding like a hare."

Other Devices: Atmosphere. Foreshadowing. Poetic Justice. Pun.

Art Style: Cartoon water color.

Curriculum Tie-In: Social Science (Coping).

Chall, Marsha Wilson. *Up North at the Cabin.* Illus. by Steve Johnson. New York: Lothrop, Lee, & Shepard, 1992.

Summer vacation up north at the cabin provides memorable experiences on the water, with the animals, and through the other faces of nature.

> **Examples:** "Houses of logs that look like shiny pretzels; bull moose like a house on stilts . . . mighty as a diesel engine; smack the water like an angry northern pike; blood thumps through my head like old Ojibway drums."
>
> **Other Devices:** Imagery. Metaphor.
>
> **Art Style:** Impressionism paint.
>
> **Curriculum Tie-In:** Science (Ecology).

Chaucer, Geoffrey. *Chanticleer and the Fox.* Adapted and illus. by Barbara Cooney. New York: Crowell, 1958. [Caldecott Award]

A moral tale about a rooster who listened to flattery.

> **Examples:** "The rooster's comb was turreted like a castle wall; his bill was black and shone like jet; his legs and toes were like azure; his nails whiter than a lily; his feathers like burnished gold; his voice merrier than the merry organ that plays in church; his crowing more trustworthy than a clock."
>
> **Other Devices:** Aphorism. Foreshadowing. Understatement.
>
> **Art Style:** Cartoon scratchboard with color overlay.
>
> **Curriculum Tie-In:** Social Science (Values; Consequences).

Doherty, Berlie. *Snowy.* Illus. by Keith Bowen. New York: Dial Books for Young Readers, 1992.

When the other children bring their pets to school, Rachel feels left out because she can't bring in the horse that pulls the barge on which she lives.

> **Examples:** "Snowy the horse has long hair like feathers around his hooves; he's big as a mountain; he smells like a haystack; the barge glides along the canal just like a painted swan."
>
> **Art Style:** Impressionism pastels.

Freschet, Berniece. *The Web in the Grass.* Illus. by Roger Duvoisin. New York: Charles Scribner's, 1972.

A fragile and friendless little spider lives out her life in a strangely silent and busy beauty.

> **Examples:** "Water droplets sparkling like bright jewels caught in a fairy net; sun shone on the silken threads billowing bright as new-washed silver; like wisps of smoke."
>
> **Other Devices:** Imagery.
>
> **Art Style:** Collage.
>
> **Curriculum Tie-In:** Science (Spiders).

Goble, Paul. *The Girl Who Loved Wild Horses*. Scarsdale: Bradbury, 1978. [Caldecott Award]

A romantic tale of a Native American girl who ran free with wild horses on the plains.

Examples: "Horses swept like a brown flood across hills and through valleys; eyes shone like cold stars; hooves struck as fast as lightning; mane and tail floating like wispy clouds about her."

Other Devices: Imagery. Symbol.

Art Style: Native American Folk Motif.

Curriculum Tie-In: History (Native Americans).

Goudey, Alice E. *The Day We Saw the Sun Come Up*. Illus. by Adrienne Adams. New York: Charles Scribner's, 1961.

Two children get up early to witness the sun through a day's cycle.

Examples: "The sun caused the eastern sky to be streaked with pearly-pink just like the inside of a scallop shell; the sun hung like a great ball made of fire; shadows like small dark pools."

Art Style: Impressionism/Colored Cartoon.

Curriculum Tie-In: Science (Sun).

*****Gregory, Valiska.** *Through the Mickle Woods*. Illus. by Barry Moser. Boston: Little, Brown & Co., 1992.

After his wife's death, a grieving king journeys to an old bear's cave in the Mickle Woods, where he hears three stories that help him go on living.

Examples: "Cloak around him like a crow folding black wings; icicles hung like daggers from the roof; opal ring flecked blue as the boy's eyes; words written plain as footsteps in the snow; breathed out like a dragon; snow looks like sugar in the moonlight; yellow cinders danced like summer bees; bear large and golden as a haystack."

Other Devices: Aphorism. Atmosphere. Inference. Metaphor. Pun. Symbol. Theme.

Art Style: Expressionism/Realism.

Curriculum Tie-In: Social Science (Death; Grief).

Johnston, Tony. *The Cowboy and the Black-Eyed Pea*. Illus. by Warren Ludwig. New York: G. P. Putnam's Sons, 1992.

The wealthy daughter of a Texas rancher devises a plan to find a real cowboy among her many suitors.

Examples: "Flock like flies to pralines; bruise like the petals of a desert rose; fresh as a Texas morning; tall as a mountain; mustache as big as tarnation; spurs the size of tambourines; prideful as a rooster; hissed mean as a snake; swelled with swagger like a horned toad; as hard as petrified grits."

Other Devices: Atmosphere. Caricature. Inference. Parody.

Art Style: Colored Cartoon.

Kimmel, Eric. *Four Dollars and Fifty Cents.* Illus. by Glen Rounds. New York: Holiday House, 1989.

To avoid paying the Widow Macrae the four dollars and fifty cents he owes her, deadbeat cowboy Shorty Long plays dead and almost gets buried alive.

> **Examples:** ". . . lay him out flatter 'n the bottom of a skillet; broker 'n a mess of eggs; deader 'n a Christmas tree in August; shot out of that graveyard faster than fireworks."
>
> **Other Devices:** Allusion. Irony. Pun.
>
> **Art Style:** Impressionism.
>
> **Curriculum Tie-In:** Social Science (Foolish Behavior).

MacDonald, Golden. *Little Island.* Illus. by Leonard Weisgard. Garden City, NY: Doubleday, 1946. [Caldecott Award]

Narration about an island in foggy weather.

> **Examples:** "Waves as big as glassy mountains; snow fell like a quiet secret in the night cold and still."
>
> **Other Devices:** Imagery. Metaphor. Paradox.
>
> **Art Style:** Impressionism.
>
> **Curriculum Tie-In:** Science (Geology).

Mahy, Margaret. *Keeping House.* Illus. by Wendy Smith. New York: Margaret K. McElderry Books (Macmillan), 1991.

Lizzie Firkin has no time to keep house because she works at night at a famous club singing and tap dancing and playing trombone. So she is too tired to sweep the floor or clean cupboards.

> **Examples:** "Unsuccessful songs lay scattered like autumn leaves over the floor; vacuum cleaner sulked under the stairs like a dog that has given up hope of ever being taken for a walk; bottles of hair dye like soldiers."
>
> **Other Devices:** Atmosphere. Hyperbole. Inference. Stereotype.
>
> **Art Style:** Impressionism.

Major, Beverly. *Over Back.* Illus. by Thomas B. Allen. New York: HarperCollins, 1993.

A young girl's favorite spot is over back, a place of pools and trees across the fields back behind the barn, where the wonders of nature wait to be discovered each day.

> **Examples:** "Rocks scattered as if a giant had thrown a handful of pebbles; pale-pink flowers like little new stars that have been wakened from a nap; smell the flowers the way you keep looking at a rainbow until it's gone; frog

eggs feel like Jell-O; soft brown pine needles like a blanket covering their toes; wait coiled and ready as a grasshopper."

Other Devices: Metaphor.

Art Style: Impressionism.

Curriculum Tie-In: Science (Ecology; Environment).

Parnall, Peter. *Alfalfa Hill.* Garden City, NY: Doubleday, 1975.
Winter comes in a whisper. The snow, hour after hour, falls, transforming an autumn landscape into new arrangements.

Examples: "Like a world full of cotton the snow muffled all sound."

Other Devices: Imagery. Metaphor.

Art Style: Expressionism pen and ink line drawing.

Curriculum Tie-In: Science (Seasons—Winter; Environment).

Radin, Ruth Yaffe. *High in the Mountains.* Illus. by Ed Young. New York: Macmillan, 1989.
Description of a day spent near Grandpa's house in the mountains.

Examples: "My shadow very long, just like a giant lying down; road wraps like elastic around each slope."

Other Devices: Imagery. Metaphor.

Art Style: Impressionism paint.

Curriculum Tie-In: Science (Ecology).

Rosenberg, Liz. *Monster Mama.* Illus. by Stephen Gammell. New York: Philomel (Putnam & Grosset), 1993.
Patrick Edward's fierce mother helps him deal with some obnoxious bullies.

Examples: "Broke the baseball bat like a loaf of stale bread; zoomed out of her cave like a fast-moving freight train."

Other Devices: Ambiguity. Aphorism. Hyperbole. Inference.

Art Style: Expressionism.

Curriculum Tie-In: Social Science (Parent and Child).

Tresselt, Alvin. *Hide and Seek Fog.* Illus. by Roger Duvoisin. New York: Lothrop, Lee & Shepard, 1965. [Caldecott Award]
The worst fog in 20 years temporarily disheartens grownups, but the children take it in stride.

Examples: "The fog twisted about the cottages like slow-motion smoke; sailboats bobbled like corks."

Other Devices: Imagery. Metaphor.

Art Style: Impressionism/Naive.

Tresselt, Alvin. *White Snow Bright Snow.* Illus. by Roger Duvoisin. New York: Lothrop, Lee & Shepard, 1947. [Caldecott Award]

A spring snow storm is described with lively text.

Examples: "Automobiles like fat raisins buried in snowdrifts."

Other Devices: Imagery. Metaphor.

Art Style: Naive.

Curriculum Tie-In: Science (Seasons—Winter; Environment).

Turnbull, Ann. *The Tapestry Cats.* Illus. by Carol Morley. Boston: Little, Brown & Co., 1992.

Subdued by her mother, who always knows what is best for her, a princess dreams of having pet cats.

Examples: "Silver the tapestry cat was as secret as moonlight and as quick as thought. Gold was the tapestry cat as warm as honey and as heavy as sleep."

Other Devices: Ambiguity. Inference.

Art Style: Naive.

Turner, Ann. *Rainflowers.* Illus. by Robert J. Blake. New York: A Charlotte Zolotow Book (HarperCollins), 1992.

Animals, trees, flowers—all react to a thunderstorm and its aftermath.

Examples: "Queen Anne's Lace flew out like wash in a tearing wind; horses danced like foals; robins bloomed like flowers in the wet, black trees."

Other Devices: Imagery.

Art Style: Impressionism.

Curriculum Tie-In: Science (Rain).

Warnock, Natalie Kinsey. *When Spring Comes.* Illus. by Stacey Schuett. New York: Dutton Children's Books, 1993.

A child living on a farm in the early 1900s describes some of the activities that mark the approach of spring.

Examples: ". . . earth dark and moist as chocolate; strawberries that glisten like rubies; sparks, like stars, stream from the runners."

Other Devices: Imagery.

Art Style: Expressionism acrylic and pastel.

Curriculum Tie-In: Science (Seasons—Spring; Ecology).

Williams, Jay. *Everyone Knows What a Dragon Looks Like.* Illus. by Mercer Mayer. New York: Four Winds, 1976.

Because of the road sweeper's belief in him, a dragon saves the city of Wu from the Wild Horsemen invaders.

Examples: "The dragon was taller than the tallest tree or tallest tower; color of sunset shining through the rain; claws and teeth glittered like diamonds; eyes noble like those of a proud horse."

Other Devices: Satire.

Art Style: Expressionism/Folk.

Curriculum Tie-In: Social Science (Foolish Behavior).

Woolf, Virginia. *Nurse Lugton's Curtain.* Illus. by Julie Vivas. New York: Gulliver Books (Harcourt Brace Jovanovich), text: 1982, illus.: 1991.

As Nurse Lugton dozes, the animals on the patterned curtain she is sewing come alive.

Examples: "She had a face like the side of a mountain with great precipices and avalanches, and chasms for her eyes and hair and nose and teeth."

Other Devices: Point-Of-View.

Art Style: Expressionism.

Wright, Betty Ren. *The Cat Next Door.* Illus. by Gail Owens. New York: Holiday House, 1991.

After Grandma dies, the annual visit to her summer cabin is not the same. But, the cat next door remembers how things used to be and cheers a grieving grandchild.

Examples: "Flowers that curved like a waterfall over the path; gulls rode waves bobbing like my bathtub toys."

Other Devices: Imagery. Symbol.

Art Style: Realism/Expressionism.

Curriculum Tie-In: Social Science (Grief; Grandparents; Death).

Yashima, Taro. *Umbrella.* New York: Viking, 1958.

Momo is three when she receives red rubber boots and an umbrella for her birthday. She eagerly looks forward to a chance to use them.

Examples: "Raindrops were jumping all over like the tiny people dancing."

Other Devices: Flash-Forward. Onomatopoeia. Tone.

Art Style: Impressionism painting.

Curriculum Tie-In: Social Science (Self-Discovery/Esteem).

STEREOTYPE/REVERSE STEREOTYPE

Fixed generalized ideas about characters and situations such as plots of predictable formula or recognizable pattern; stereotype is also used when persons are typed rather than presented as unique and are denied full range of qualities and characteristics.

Reverse stereotype is the opposite of the expected.

Example: Instead of a lady's group creating a winning quilt at the fair, a man's group takes honors for winning the quilt.

SOURCES

Allard, Harry. *It's So Nice to Have a Wolf Around the House.* Illus. by James Marshall. Garden City, NY: Doubleday, 1977.

A wolf answers an ad to be companion to an old man and his older pets. The companion does a wonderful job until he falls ill and must be nursed in turn. Everyone benefits from the arrangement.

> **Examples:** The wolf has gotten a bad rap in literature and in nature. Not all wolves want to be bad. This one wants nothing more than to be a house servant.
>
> **Other Devices:** Irony. Satire.
>
> **Art Style:** Cartoon.
>
> **Curriculum Tie-In:** Social Science (Prejudice; Forgiveness).

Allen, Judy. *Tiger.* Illus. by Tudor Humphries. Cambridge, MA: Candlewick Press, 1992.

When a rumor starts that there is a tiger in the woods, the villagers plan to kill it. Eating the meat, they believe, will make them brave, and selling its skin will make them rich. So when another rumor begins that a famous hunter is coming to town, the villagers decide to ask him to hunt the tiger for them.

> **Examples:** This is one famous "hunter" who stalks prey not with a powerful weapon, but with a camera. Instead of destroying a creature for meat that produces momentary strength or a hide that creates temporary wealth, the new approach is to enjoy nature through a photo that can be appreciated forever while the natural world stays intact.
>
> **Other Devices:** Inference. Irony. Satire.
>
> **Art Style:** Realism.
>
> **Curriculum Tie-In:** Science (Endangered Species).

*Babbitt, Natalie. *Phoebe's Revolt.* New York: Farrar Straus Giroux, 1968.

Stubborn Phoebe detests her dresses "of fluff and lace . . . and everything to do with girls." But when her father permits her to wear his clothes they don't quite suit either.

> **Examples:** Phoebe objected to girl clothes but found boy clothes "didn't seem so lovely now . . . the lure was gone." Must her choice be either clothes too restrictive or clothes oversized? Fortunately, Phoebe's mother remembers being unhappy with the clothes she had to wear as a little girl. A seamstress fixes up both mother and daughter with feminine clothing that allows physical activity.

Other Devices: Foreshadowing. Poetic Justice. Satire.

Art Style: Cartoon.

Curriculum Tie-In: Social Science (Acceptance and Respect; Anger; Self-Discovery/Esteem; Sexism).

Backovsky, Jan. *Trouble in Paradise.* New York: Tambourine Books, 1992.
When the world famous big game hunter sets forth on his most challenging expedition yet—a trip to unexplored Paradise Island—he discovers the wily animals have no plans to visit a zoo any time soon.

    Examples: Rather than the game hunter capturing the animals, the animals "spent their time thinking of ways to welcome him." In the end, the game hunter is very happy to leave and the animals are happy to see him go.

    Art Style: Colored Cartoon.

Bright, Robert. *Georgie.* Garden City, NY: Doubleday, 1944.
A personable little ghost is unhappy until reunited with the home that needs him to haunt it.

    Examples: When Georgie loses his job, he goes next door to haunt. But he is frightened because at this place it is "so awfully gloomy." The big door groans, and the big stairway moans, and the resident is "crotchety." Georgie is happy to return to his own house and get things back to normal.

    Other Devices: Satire.

    Art Style: Cartoon.

DePaola, Tomie. *Oliver Button Is a Sissy.* New York: Harcourt Brace Jovanovich, 1979.
His classmates' taunts don't stop Oliver Button from doing what he likes best.

    Examples: His father tells Oliver, who likes to sing, dance, and put on costumes, to "go out and play baseball or football or basketball. Any kind of ball." When Oliver joins dance class, his father justifies it as "exercise." The boys at school tease him because the girls scold them for messing with his tap shoes. They taunt that he's "gotta have help from girls." Only when he performs in a talent show is his individuality affirmed.

    Art Style: Cartoon.

    Curriculum Tie-In: Social Science (Acceptance and Respect; Self-Discovery/Esteem; Sexism).

Handforth, Thomas. *Mei Li.* Garden City, NY: Doubleday, 1938. [Caldecott Award]
A resourceful young girl wheedles and buys her way along on a New Year's fair trip to the city and concludes the best part of the trip is getting home.

    Examples: Girls aren't allowed to leave home. But after bribing her brother, she goes to the city. She wants a firecracker but lets her sneering brother shoot it off because she's afraid to do it. She lets him throw her lucky penny at the priest's little bell because "I'm sure I could never hit it." She crawls inside a goose basket to protect her brother's thrush when she is frightened by a hawk-shaped kite, something she has never seen before. Her uncle gives her grudging praise for bravely protecting the bird but chides her fear of the "hawk." At home she is happy with her fate—her kingdom will be her own house and everyone inside are her "loyal, loving subjects."

Other Devices: Ambiguity.

Art Style: Impressionism/Chinese Folk.

Curriculum Tie-In: Social Science (Sexism).

Hilton, Nette. *Dirty Dave.* Illus. by Roland Harvey. New York: Orchard Books, 1990.

In this reverse stereotype, members of an outlaw family gain acceptance from the public because of the fine clothes their father makes for the public.

Examples: Mother, sister, and brother are tough, fierce, and rough. But, father doesn't go on stick ups. He stays home and sews.

Other Devices: Irony. Understatement.

Art Style: Cartoon.

Curriculum Tie-In: Social Science (Sexism).

Hutchins, Pat. *Rosie's Walk.* New York: Macmillan, 1968.

Rosie the hen strolls through the barnyard oblivious to the fox who follows her in spite of a series of mishaps.

Examples: In this reversal of expectations, the smart capable fox becomes inept, careless, and frustrated. The foolish, unaware chicken escapes capture.

Other Devices: Foreshadowing. Irony. Poetic Justice. Satire.

Art Style: Expressionism.

Curriculum Tie-In: Health and Safety (Accident Prevention).

Isadora, Rachel. *Max.* New York: Macmillan, 1976.

Max finds a new way to warm up for his Saturday baseball game—his sister's dancing class.

Examples: In spite of himself, Max is intrigued by the dance movements. He begins to imitate them and is soon invited to join the class, stretching, leaping, and having fun. The author justifies dance as a "warm-up" for the Saturday baseball games.

Art Style: Cartoon.

Curriculum Tie-In: Social Science (Sexism).

Johnston, Tony. *The Promise.* Illus. by Pamela Keaveney. New York: A Charlotte Zolotow Book (HarperCollins), 1992.

When Mr. Gates was a boy, a rancher gave him a calf as reward for being helpful with cattle care and for obviously loving them. That boy grew up to buy and raise cattle for a living. Many years later when it is his turn to return the favor, it is a girl who gets a chance to become a cattle rancher.

Other Devices: Flashback. Foreshadowing. Inference.

Art Style: Impressionism.

Mahy, Margaret. *Keeping House.* Illus. by Wendy Smith. New York: Margaret K. McElderry Books (Macmillan), 1991.

Lizzie Firkin has no time to keep house because she works at night at a famous club singing and tap dancing and playing trombone. So she is too tired to sweep the floor or clean cupboards.

Examples: This career girl calls in a housekeeper—a male.

Other Devices: Atmosphere. Hyperbole. Inference. Simile.

Art Style: Impressionism.

Paxton, Tom. *Engelbert the Elephant.* Illus. by Steven Kellogg. New York: Morrow Junior Books, 1990.

An elephant's dancing skills and good manners surprise everyone at the royal ball, including the queen.

Examples: People panic at the thought of an elephant at the ball. They expect to be trampled. But the mannerly eating and gentlemanly bow and graceful dancing "in the very nicest way" overcome prejudice. A good time is had by all. Even the other jungle animals participate after the ball, "and the frolicking that followed is still talked about today."

Art Style: Cartoon.

Curriculum Tie-In: Social Science (Prejudice).

Piper, Watty. *The Little Engine That Could.* Illus. by George Hauman and Doris Hauman. New York: Platt & Monk, 1954.

When the little red engine breaks down, it needs help to get its cargo for boys and girls over the mountain. Only the little blue engine offers its service.

Examples: The proud, capable train, which seems most promising, proves, nevertheless, a disappointment. The weak, unlikely train rises to the task and succeeds against all odds.

Other Devices: Onomatopoeia. Theme.

Art Style: Colored Cartoon.

Curriculum Tie-In: Social Science (Values).

Steig, William. *Sylvester and the Magic Pebble.* New York: Windmill Books (Simon & Schuster), 1969. [Caldecott Award]

A magic pebble, a fierce lion, and a wish made in panic lead to separation from loved ones.

Examples: Sexism is apparent when household scenes show mother wearing an apron and sweeping and knitting while father is reading a newspaper and books. Mother "set out the picnic food on the rock" while father "walked aimlessly about." Mrs. Duncan "cried a lot" and Mr. Duncan did his best "to soothe her."

Other Devices: Foreshadowing. Imagery. Personification. Pun. Symbol. Theme.

Art Style: Cartoon water color.

Curriculum Tie-In: Social Science (Parent and Child).

Van Allsburg, Chris. *The Widow's Broom.* New York: Houghton Mifflin, 1992.
A witch's worn-out broom serves a widow well, until her neighbors decide it's wicked and must be destroyed.

Examples: "The men who saw it seemed to agree, it probably was a wicked thing. But their wives pointed out that it was a great help to the widow." Because the men had no history with household drudgery, they could not perceive the broom's value. The women had no such problem seeing its worth. To them "evil" does not characterize a description of its activities.

Other Devices: Allusion. Inference.

Art Style: Impressionism.

Ward, Lynd. *The Biggest Bear.* Boston: Houghton Mifflin, 1952. [Caldecott Award]
Johnny Orchard goes out to acquire a bearskin, comes home with a cute little cub instead, and has to contend with its growing appetite.

Examples: Mountain men shoot bears with pride and tack their trophy skin to the outside wall of their barns. The boy is expected to do the correct thing about the bear problem he has brought home. He must shoot it, of course.

Other Devices: Foreshadowing. Pun. Understatement.

Art Style: Realism/Impressionism.

Curriculum Tie-In: History (Nineteenth-Century America Frontier Life).

***Yashima, Taro.** *Crow Boy.* New York: Viking, 1955.
A misunderstood, shy student earns the respect of his fellow classmates after being ignored for years. A new teacher shows them the boy has much to offer.

Examples: Schools tend to teach to the "standard" average person who fits into the system. "Different" individuals are quickly branded, as Chibi is, "slow-poke" or "stupid." What he knows and the skills he has are not the kind that can be measured in school. Even though he relates very well to his world, he is not honored for these things until a sensitive teacher helps students be aware of other kinds of knowledge.

Other Devices: Theme. Tone. Understatement.

Art Style: Impressionism pastel pencil.

Curriculum Tie-In: Social Science (Acceptance and Respect).

*Yolen, Jane. *Encounter*. Illus. by David Shannon. New York: Harcourt Brace Jovanovich, 1992.

A Taino Indian boy on the island of San Salvador recounts the landing of Columbus and his men in 1492.

Examples: The strange chief's eyes are "blue and gray like the shifting sea." Even those men with "dark human eyes looked away, like dogs before they are driven from the fire." Their ships are described as "great-winged birds with voices like thunder."

Other Devices: Atmosphere. Flash-Forward. Foreshadowing. Metaphor. Point-Of-View. Theme.

Art Style: Realism/Expressionism acrylic

Curriculum Tie-In: History (Discovery of America-Columbus).

Zolotow, Charlotte. *A Father Like That.* Illus. by Ben Shecter. New York: Harper, 1971.

A boy describes his ideal father.

Examples: There is an element of sexism in the child's concept of both his mother, who is present in his world, and his father, who is not. His father would call him "Old Man." Mother would stay at home waving to her two men who walk off together each morning on important business. Father carries a briefcase and together "we made another day, the two of us." Father would make a drink for him and mother and he'd "make her" sit down with him before dinner. When they would do dishes together, father has to clown around with dish balancing tricks to make the task more tolerable to the male psyche. Mother shows impassive horror at their sport. When the boy and father play checkers before bedtime, father would overrule mother's concern with "oh, just one more."

Art Style: Cartoon.

Curriculum Tie-In: Social Science (Sexism; Parent and Child).

Zolotow, Charlotte. *William's Doll.* Illus. by William Pene Du Bois. New York: Harper & Row, 1972.

William is not a sissy. He just wants a doll so he can practice being like his father.

Examples: William wants to relate to a doll "just as though he were its father and it were his child." His brother calls him creepy. The boy next door accuses him of being a sissy. His father gets him a basketball and electric train and remarks, "Why does he need a doll?" Only his grandmother understands that William needs one "so he can practice being a father." Playing into the natural order, the author shows that typically males don't or won't understand this. Typically grandmothers are endued with the necessary heightened senses and must go against odds to get the message across.

Art Style: Cartoon/Impressionism.

Curriculum Tie-In: Social Science (Self-Discovery/Esteem; Acceptance and Respect; Sexism).

SYMBOL

Any person, object, or action that has additional meaning beyond itself to represent or stand for a more abstract emotion or idea.

Example: Great Conestogas, white against the sky:
Listen to the rumble as the East goes by
—Jessamyn West "Conestoga Wagons."

SOURCES

Duvoisin, Roger. *Petunia.* New York: Knopf, 1950.
A silly goose carries around a book thinking that it will make her look smart.

Examples: For Petunia the book stands for wisdom and respect, which she desires. She expects to be wise because she recalls hearing, "He who owns Books and loves them is wise."

Other Devices: Aphorism. Irony.

Art Style: Cartoon.

Curriculum Tie-In: Social Science (Values; Self-Discovery/Esteem).

Edwards, Michelle. *A Baker's Portrait.* New York: Lothrop, Lee & Shepard, 1991.
Michelin paints portraits that do not flatter her sitters, but she learns an enduring lesson when she must paint her kindly aunt and uncle.

Examples: It won't do to paint the real thing. All she can see is aunt's missing teeth and uncle's big belly. Then uncle shares with her how his wife is like a piece of chocolate cake, sweet on the outside and rich on the inside. He says he is her challah, a little crusty on the outside but soft inside and always tasting as good as the day it's baked. Now she knows what to paint. The lovely cake and bread are big hits. And, she is pronounced ready to paint her grandmother, a woman of pale blue beady eyes, cold wrinkled hands, windy voice, and white soft hair. Perhaps a portrait showing the first snow of winter would capture her perfectly.

Other Devices: Paradox.

Art Style: Expressionism.

Curriculum Tie-In: Social Science (Acceptance and Respect; Family Life; Values).

Glass, Andrew. *Charles T. McBiddle.* New York: Doubleday Books for Young Readers (Delacorte), 1993.

Charles T. McBiddle persists in trying to learn to ride his bike, despite a nasty little creature's attempt to undermine his confidence.

Examples: Charles imagines how full of pride his parents and brother will be when he can ride his bike without the training wheels. But he falls off because "nothing is holding this stupid bike up." That's when he encounters "a tiny creature who looked like a very ugly chipmunk." This monster symbolizes his fear and doubts about his ability to succeed. It suggests he should give up. Maybe his mother thinks he's "still too little." His dad doesn't think he's "quite ready yet." With each new doubt, the creature grows bigger and looms more frightening. It sneers that he's wasting his time, he might fall, his mom wishes he'd give up. But Charles gets back on the bike, and "the monster shriveled a little." And keeps shriveling when he keeps trying to ride. In spite of continued harassment Charles keeps going until he is strong and confident and makes "the victory cry of the great ape."

Art Style: Expressionism.

Curriculum Tie-In: Social Science (Self-Discovery/Esteem).

Goble, Paul. *The Girl Who Loved Wild Horses.* Scarsdale: Bradbury, 1978. [Caldecott Award]

A romantic tale of a Native American girl who ran free with the wild horses on the plains.

Examples: "People noticed that she understood horses in a special way." They represent freedom and happiness to her. She so closely identifies with them that eventually she assimilates fully with them. The horses become her relatives, and she goes to live among them.

Other Devices: Imagery. Simile.

Art Style: Native American Folk Motif.

Curriculum Tie-In: History (Native Americans).

*Gregory, Valiska. *Through the Mickle Woods.* Illus. by Barry Moser. Boston: Little, Brown & Co., 1992.

After his wife's death, a grieving king journeys to an old bear's cave in the Mickle Woods, where he hears three stories that help him go on living.

Examples: When the story begins, the "moon can only peak" through the clutches of "the black fingers of the trees." At the end, when the king's spirit awakens, "the orange sun deftly escapes the tangled web of branches." From the tentative moon to bright sun, the king has emerged from deep gloom to lively interest in the world about him. Life has triumphed over death.

Other Devices: Aphorism. Atmosphere. Inference. Metaphor. Pun. Simile. Theme.

Art Style: Expressionism/Realism.

Curriculum Tie-In: Social Science (Death; Grief).

*Grifalconi, Ann. *Kinda Blue.* Boston: Little, Brown & Co., 1993.
Sissy feels lonely until her Uncle Dan cheers her up by explaining that everything, even corn, needs special attention now and then.

> **Examples:** Uncle Dan shows Sissy how people and corn plants are similar. They're individuals. "See now? Every one's different. . . . Just the way we be." And they can feel "kinda blue," too. "See? This one be drooping. . . . Sometimes we needs somebody to pay 'tention to us—water us when we be sad!"
>
> **Other Devices:** Metaphor. Tone.
>
> **Art Style:** Impressionism water color, pastel, and colored pencil.
>
> **Curriculum Tie-In:** Social Science (Acceptance and Respect; Loneliness).

Ikeda, Daisaku. *The Cherry Tree.* Illus. by Brian Wildsmith. English version by Geraldine McCaughrean. New York: Knopf, 1992.
After a war destroys their Japanese village and kills their father, Taichi and Yumiko find hope by nursing a cherry tree through a harsh winter and seeing it blossom into new life.

> **Examples:** The tree brings the villagers together in a spirit of new hope. When the cherry tree came back to life, so did the village. The "bombs had shattered their world into a thousand pieces." Now, "life was everything they had dared to hope for."
>
> **Other Devices:** Aphorism.
>
> **Art Style:** Impressionism line drawings.
>
> **Curriculum Tie-In:** Social Science (Coping; War).

Lamorisse, Albert. *The Red Balloon.* Garden City, NY: Doubleday, 1956.
A lonely boy and a red balloon become companions.

> **Examples:** Denied the usual pets, Pascal, with no brothers or sisters, finds and keeps a red balloon, which serves in place of friend or pet. Even when his mother tries to throw it away, the faithful balloon doesn't fly away because "friends will do all kinds of things for you." The balloon even sacrifices itself when a gang of boys attacked Pascal.
>
> **Other Devices:** Atmosphere. Poetic Justice.
>
> **Art Style:** Photography.
>
> **Curriculum Tie-In:** Social Science (Loneliness).

Lionni, Leo. *Little Blue and Little Yellow.* New York: Ivan Obolensky, 1959.
Splashes of color and abstract forms tell the story of Little Blue and his friend Little Yellow, whose hug turns them green.

> **Examples:** Separate minds (the blue and yellow splotches) can have a good life, but by joining forces they can create something better or more interesting. The way new ideas form is by sharing and combining.

Art Style: Expressionism.

Curriculum Tie-In: Social Science (Cooperation).

Oppenheim, Shulamith Levy. *The Lily Cupboard.* Illus. by Ronald Himler. New York: A Charlotte Zolotow Book (HarperCollins), 1992.

Miriam, a young Jewish girl, is forced to leave her parents and hide with strangers in the country during the German occupation of Holland.

> **Examples:** When Miriam learns she must leave her parents, her "heart feels like the little stone lantern in our garden, heavy, without a candle." She realizes her "heart doesn't have a candle in it either." The rabbit that she keeps in the country comes to stand for her chances to return home. Like her parents who have gone to great lengths to protect her life, Miriam transfers this devotion to the rabbit. She believes she must keep the creature protected and even risks her own life taking him into the safety cupboard with her. "I have to keep him with me. Mama and Papa wouldn't go without him."
>
> **Other Devices:** Inference.
>
> **Art Style:** Impressionism water color gouache.
>
> **Curriculum Tie-In:** History (German Occupation—Netherlands). Social Science (War).

Ringgold, Faith. *Tar Beach.* New York: Crown, 1991.

A young girl dreams of flying above her Harlem home, claiming all she sees for herself and her family.

> **Examples:** Tar Beach, the rooftop where her family and friends have evening picnics, represents city recreational alternatives to real moonlight beaches.
>
> **Other Devices:** Allusion. Metaphor.
>
> **Art Style:** Naive.
>
> **Curriculum Tie-In:** Social Science (Race Relations; Discrimination).

Rosen, Michael J. *Elijah's Angel.* A Story for Hanukkah and Christmas. Illus. by Aminah Robinson. New York: Harcourt Brace Jovanovich, 1992.

At Christmas-Hanukkah time, a Christian woodcarver gives a carved angel to a young Jewish friend, who struggles with accepting the Christmas gift until he realizes that friendship means the same in any religion.

> **Examples:** The angel given by Elijah and the Menorah given in return represent the friendship between unlikely people, a black Christian and a white Jew. The footprints that "connected our house and his barbershop in a perfect dotted line" were also a connection of oneness.
>
> **Art Style:** Expressionism.
>
> **Curriculum Tie-In:** Social Science (Race Relations; Cross-Cultures).

*Rylant, Cynthia. *An Angel for Solomon Singer.* Illus. by Peter Catalanotto. New York: Orchard Books, 1992.

A lonely New York City resident finds companionship and good cheer at the Westway Cafe, where dreams come true.

Examples: Solomon Singer was drawn to the Westway Cafe because "he was from the Midwest and liked to imagine he was, each day, making his way west." Inside the menu, it read, ". . . where all your dreams come true." The friendly waiter, Angel, slowly transformed Solomon into a happier person who was eventually able to see in the New York City streets something of the moving fields of wheat and night stars and friendly cricket sounds of Indiana.

Other Devices: Flash-Forward. Irony.

Art Style: Impressionism water color.

Curriculum Tie-In: Social Science (Loneliness).

Sanders, Scott Russell. *Warm as Wool.* Illus. by Helen Cogancherry. New York: Bradbury Press, 1992.

When Betsy Ward's family moves to Ohio from Connecticut in 1803, she brings along a sockful of coins to buy sheep so that she can gather wool, spin cloth, and make clothes to keep her children warm.

Examples: ". . . when a herd of sheep drifted by the cabin one day in spring, Betsy Ward imagined each animal a walking blanket." The sheep represent warmth in this harsh, cold land. Her family can "be dressed from head to toe in wool."

Art Style: Realism.

Curriculum Tie-In: History (Nineteenth-Century America—Frontier Life).

*Say, Allen. *Grandfather's Journey.* Boston: Houghton Mifflin, 1993. [Caldecott Award]

A Japanese American man recounts his grandfather's journey to America, his eventual longing to return to his homeland, and his restlessness when he does. The man, too, learns how it feels to be torn by love for two different countries and can empathize with his grandfather.

Examples: In each home grandfather keeps caged birds, which serve as a link to the best memories of the other home. In California, he "surrounded himself with songbirds, but he could not forget." In Japan "he raised warblers and silvereyes, but he could not forget." The birds are always a little bit of home, until the war ravages his Japanese city, forcing him to return to the village of his childhood. But he "never kept another songbird," and died before he could "see California one more time."

Other Devices: Aphorism. Atmosphere. Foreshadowing. Irony. Paradox. Parallel Story.

Art Style: Impressionism/Expressionism/Folk water color.

Curriculum Tie-In: Social Science (Cross-Cultures; Continuity of Life).

Scheller, Melanie. *My Grandfather's Hat.* Illus. by Keiko Narahashi. New York: Margaret K. McElderry Books (Macmillan), 1992.

A boy's relationship with his grandfather is remembered through vignettes with a 17-year-old hat.

> **Examples:** The hat clearly represents the love, mutual respect, tolerance, and sharing that the boy and old man have in common. Even when the grandfather forgets and leaves his hat on the sofa and the boy forgets and squashes it flat, the incident affords them an opportunity for bonding. Though "its too big for me now, someday, when I grow up, I will wear my grandfather's hat." Here is affirmation that this person is someone worth emulating.
>
> **Other Devices:** Flash-Forward.
>
> **Art Style:** Impressionism.
>
> **Curriculum Tie-In:** Social Science (Acceptance and Respect; Aging; Grandparents).

Steig, William. *Sylvester and the Magic Pebble.* New York: Windmill Books (Simon & Schuster), 1969. [Caldecott Award].

A magic pebble, a fierce lion, and a wish made in panic lead to separation from loved ones.

> **Examples:** The "flaming, red, shiny and perfectly round pebble" that Sylvester finds proves magic. But the wishes it can grant pale beside the reality of family and loved ones. When their unity is restored, "no magic is now needed" that this family does not already have.
>
> **Other Devices:** Foreshadowing. Imagery. Personification. Pun. Stereotype. Theme.
>
> **Art Style:** Cartoon water color.
>
> **Curriculum Tie-In:** Social Science (Parent and Child).

Wright, Betty Ren. *The Cat Next Door.* Illus. by Gail Owens. New York: Holiday House, 1991.

After grandma dies, the annual visit to her summer cabin is not the same. But the cat next door remembers how things used to be and cheers a grieving grandchild.

> **Examples:** The cat serves as a stable link to bridge the time before grandma died and the present time. The cat demonstrates with her new kittens that life continues even after sad changes. Some happy things remain the same— the orange flowers, shining silver lake, cat whiskers tickling your chin, gulls riding the waves. These are things that all make "splendiferous" days.
>
> **Other Devices:** Imagery. Simile.
>
> **Art Style:** Realism/Expressionism.
>
> **Curriculum Tie-In:** Social Science (Grief; Grandparents; Death).

THEME

The underlying meaning of a literary work, a particular truth about life or humanity, which the author is trying to make the reader see. Plot is a pattern of events—what happens—but theme is the meaning—what it's about.

   Example: Plot—young soldier during his first battle. Theme—war is futile; fighting solves nothing.

SOURCES

*Baylor, Byrd. *Your Own Best Secret Place*. Illus. by Peter Parnall. New York: Charles Scribner's, 1979.
   A girl discovers that the hollow at the foot of a cottonwood tree was first someone else's secret place before it was hers. She begins to understand how William Cottonwood felt there.

   Examples: The author's sensitive writing suggests that everyone shares a connectedness. First, William Cottonwood uses a hollow tree as a special place. The girl who comes upon it later feels spiritual kinship with him. Others offer a sense of their own special place with her in widely different locales—a hay bale stack in Montana, a white, open sand dune in Yuma, Arizona. The feelings of being part of someone else's world are similar and universal.

   Other Devices: Imagery. Tone.

   Art Style: Expressionism pen and ink line drawings.

   Curriculum Tie-In: Social Science (Acceptance and Respect; Continuity of Life; Self-Discovery/Esteem).
   Geography (American Southwest).

Benson, Patrick. *Little Penguin*. New York: Philomel, 1990.
   Comparing herself to the larger Emperor penguins, Pip the Adelie penguin feels unhappy with her size until an encounter with a huge sperm whale puts things in perspective for her.

   Examples: Playful and mischievous, Pip notices the Emperor penguins her age are "much bigger than Pip." But so is the huge sperm whale. They play together. Next time she walks past the Emperors, she has come to terms with her size. "They're big, but not so big." Friendship is what matters, and that goes beyond appearances.

   Art Style: Expressionism pen and ink water color drawings.

   Curriculum Tie-In: Social Science (Friendship; Self-Discovery/Esteem; Acceptance and Respect).

Brown, Margaret Wise. *The Runaway Bunny.* Illus. by Clement Hurd. New York: Harper & Row, 1942.

Once there was a little bunny who wanted to run away. His mother says, "I will run after you. For you are my little bunny." Though he thinks of all kinds of things to become to escape his mother, he finally concludes, "I might just as well stay where I am and be your little bunny."

Examples: The little bunny demonstrates both a need for independence and close loving ties. This is the way with all children.

Art Style: Impressionism/Cartoon.

Curriculum Tie-In: Social Science (Acceptance and Respect; Self-Discovery/Esteem; Parent and Child).

Cameron, Polly. *I Can't Said the Ant.* New York: Coward-McCann, 1961.

An ant, encouraged by a kitchen battalion of 89 objects, comes to the rescue of a fallen teapot.

Examples: By persistence and combined efforts, "we quickly made plans on just what to do." Because, "to figure that out we all had to think." When one can't accomplish something alone, it's time to gather friends together.

Other Devices: Allusion. Internal Rhyme. Pun.

Art Style: Colored Cartoon.

Curriculum Tie-In: Science (Lever and Pulley).

Corbalis, Judy. *The Cuckoo Bird.* Illus. by David Armitage. New York: HarperCollins, 1988.

A little girl and her grandmother try to outwit a shape-changing, greedy cuckoo bird who has tricked his way into their house.

Examples: This cautionary tale warns that danger can be disguised in innocent-appearing form. "Many an older and wiser person than you has been tricked by the Cuckoo Bird," says the comforting grandmother.

Other Devices: Inference. Poetic Justice.

Art Style: Expressionism.

Curriculum Tie-In: Health and Safety (Stranger Danger).

Croll, Carolyn. *The Three Brothers.* A German folktale adapted and illus. by Carolyn Croll. New York: A Whitebird Book (G. P. Putnam's), 1991.

Unable to decide which of three sons will inherit the farm, a farmer sets up a contest. Whoever can fill the barn before the day is done will be his heir.

Examples: Happiness cannot be achieved in isolation. Sharing one another's life and understanding each other's work is the route to personal satisfaction. When the younger son wins the contest, he invites the other brothers to share the farm with him.

Other Devices: Paradox.

Art Style: Pennsylvania Dutch Folk Motif.

Curriculum Tie-In: Geography (Pennsylvania Dutch Culture).

Fife, Dale H. *The Empty Lot.* Illus. by Jim Arnosky. San Francisco: Sierra Club Books (Little, Brown & Co.), 1991.

Inspecting an empty, partially wooded lot before selling it, Harry finds it occupied by many live creatures.

Examples: Natural undeveloped spaces have value that are important over and above financial considerations.

Art Style: Cartoon.

Curriculum Tie-In: Science (Ecology).

Flack, Marjorie, and Kurt Weise. *The Story about Ping.* New York: Viking, 1933.

Ping enjoys life on the boat with his relatives except for the Spank that hits the last duck to go aboard at night after a day of foraging.

Examples: Sometimes it's better to bravely accept unavoidable and unpleasant situations rather than avoid them and risk something even worse.

Art Style: Colored Cartoon.

Curriculum Tie-In: Social Science (Self-Discovery/Esteem; Consequences; Ethics).

Fowler, Susi Gregg. *Fog.* Illus. by Jim Fowler. New York: Greenwillow Books (William Morrow), 1992.

A visitation by deep fog traps a family in their house and causes them to rediscover their love of making music.

Examples: "Well, being quiet is sure showing us what a lot of work there is to do," Mama says. There are dripping faucets, mice to catch, rooms to clean up, a dog to bathe. But on a gloomy fog-bound day grandma knows that it's more important to do something fun. Soon everyone is brightening the day making music. Sometimes it's necessary to remind ourselves that pleasure belongs in life.

Other Devices: Atmosphere.

Art Style: Expressionism.

Curriculum Tie-In: Social Science (Family Life; Values).

Freeman, Don. *Dandelion.* New York: Viking, 1964.

Jennifer Giraffe sends out party invitations that read, "Come as you are." But that doesn't stop Dandelion from indulging in a make-over.

Examples: It never works out well to try to be something you're not. In this case, Dandelion's friends don't recognize him and reject him at the party.

Other Devices: Foreshadowing. Pun.

Art Style: Cartoon.

Curriculum Tie-In: Social Science (Self-Discovery/Esteem).

Gag, Wanda. *Millions of Cats.* New York: Coward-McCann, 1928.

The old man seeks a kitten for his wife and finds hundreds of cats, thousands of cats, millions and billions and trillions of cats.

Examples: In all the world, the one that belongs to you is by far the best of all.

Other Devices: Hyperbole. Paradox.

Art Style: Cartoon/Folk.

*****Gregory, Valiska.** *Through the Mickle Woods.* Illus. by Barry Moser. Boston: Little, Brown & Co., 1992.

After his wife's death, a grieving king journeys to an old bear's cave in the Mickle Woods, where he hears three stories that help him go on living.

Examples: After reflecting, the king chooses life over death. This tale celebrates the resilient capacity of the human spirit to choose love and life over dark rejection and spiritual despair. Life, after all, is "threads of sunlight fine as silk and cobwebs gray as skulls." Life is both "full of woe and gladness."

Other Devices: Aphorism. Atmosphere. Inference. Metaphor. Pun. Simile. Symbol.

Art Style: Expressionism/Realism.

Curriculum Tie-In: Social Science (Death; Grief).

Haseley, Dennis. *Ghost Catcher.* Illus. by Lloyd Bloom. New York: Laura Geringer Book (HarperCollins), 1991.

An allegory of emotional growth and human kinship in which Ghost Catcher solves people's problems and they in turn help him.

Examples: Human beings need each other to keep lives and spirits whole. Pride of superiority and reliance on unique self-sufficiency can bring disaster. Ghost Catcher thinks because he has no shadow, he is impervious to the shadow world. He rejects villagers' help. But he finds himself alone in a place that causes him fear, anger, and sadness. His friends restore him to reality. The next time anyone needs help he does not go by himself, "You and I, we better go get her," he says.

Art Style: Expressionism/African Folk.

Curriculum Tie-In: Social Science (Values; Self-Discovery/Esteem).

Hill, Elizabeth Starr. *Evan's Corner.* Illus. by Nancy Grossman. New York: Holt, Rinehart and Winston, 1967.

Evan wants a place of his own to be lonely, waste time, and have peace and quiet. But when he gets his own corner fixed up, he's not totally happy with it.

Examples: Evan learns that to be content with himself, it is not enough to fix up his own corner. He needs, also, to "step out now, and help somebody else." After he helps his little brother to fix up a corner just right for him, he experiences fulfillment.

Art Style: Impressionism.

Curriculum Tie-In: Social Science (Generosity; Siblings).

Karl, Jean. *The Search for the Ten-Winged Dragon.* Illus. by Steve Cieslawski. New York: Doubleday, 1990.

A young apprentice toy maker's search for a fantastical creature leads him on an unusual journey of adventure and self-discovery.

> Examples: To release his powers of creative imagination in the toy-making business, a boy is advised to find a ten-winged dragon. After failing to find one in the dimension of reality, he finally discovers that by relaxing and forgetting about his task, his own internal powers of memory and imagination combine to produce, in the clouds above his head, the very dragon he is searching for. Once released, his imagination picks out dragons in stream water ripples, patterns of leaves, and wayside stones. A "big bubble of dragons filled him from head to toe." Some things cannot be forced through empirical evidence.

> Art Style: Expressionism/Realism.

> Curriculum Tie-In: Social Science (Self-Discovery/Esteem).

Lionni, Leo. *Alexander and the Wind-Up Mouse.* New York: Pantheon, 1969.

Alexander thinks it would be more pleasant to be an appreciated wind-up toy than a hated real mouse until he sees what fate the toy faces when new toys arrive.

> Examples: Freedom, even with danger, is preferable to momentary popularity which is dependent on whim. Accept one's self with the good and bad rather than wish to live someone's else's life and risk facing an equal, if not worse, fate.

> Other Devices: Foreshadowing.

> Art Style: Collage.

> Curriculum Tie-In: Social Science (Self-Discovery/Esteem).

Lionni, Leo. *Frederick.* New York: Pantheon, 1967.

During the mouse fall food gathering, his friends don't feel Frederick is doing his share of the work, but when the food runs out and tempers fray during the dreary winter, it is Frederick's contributions that prove most welcome.

> Examples: Life that centers on only practical needs is not enough for a complete life. Beauty, poetry, and imagination are equally necessary. Frederick "spoke of the sun," and they "began to feel warmer." They "saw colors as clearly as if they had been painted in their minds" when he described blue periwinkles, red poppies in yellow wheat, and green leaves of the berry bush.

> Other Devices: Irony.

> Art Style: Collage.

> Curriculum Tie-In: Social Science (Values; Cooperation).

Marshall, James. *George and Martha.* Boston: Houghton Mifflin, 1972.

Friendship is a delicate thing, even when it exists between two not so delicate hippos. They delight in having someone who will tell you the truth and go to great lengths to spare your feelings.

Examples: It was hard for George to tell Martha he hated split pea soup, but Martha says, "Friends should always tell each other the truth." So they share chocolate chip cookies, instead. George is forced to get out of the air balloon basket so it will fly when Martha suggests that perhaps "the basket is too heavy." These two support each other in loving gentleness.

Art Style: Cartoon.

Curriculum Tie-In: Social Science (Friendship; Acceptance and Respect).

*Miles, Miska. *Annie and the Old One.* Illus. by Peter Parnall. Boston: Little, Brown & Co., 1971.

A Navajo girl tries to stop the passage of time when her grandmother announces that after "the new rug is taken from the loom, I will go to Mother Earth."

Examples: Despite her efforts to prevent the finishing of the new rug, Annie's grandmother tells her, "You have tried to hold back time. This cannot be done. . . . Earth, from which good things come for the living creatures on it. Earth, to which all creatures finally go." Annie begins to understand that "she was part of the earth and the things on it. She would always be a part of earth, just as her grandmother has always been, . . . always be, always and forever."

Other Devices: Inference.

Art Style: Expressionism.

Curriculum Tie-In: Social Science (Death; Aging; Grandparents).
Geography (Native American Navajo Culture).

Miles, Miska. *Hoagie's Rifle-Gun.* Illus. by John Schoenherr. Boston: Little, Brown, 1970.

Hoagie never misses. But on the day another hunter has better success, he is jealous and angry and aims at something off-limits, Old Bob the bobcat. Something causes him to waste a bullet.

Example:
"You can't shoot a thing when you know it by name!" So, no matter how hungry the boys, they are grateful the bullet missed. They think boiled potatoes are just fine. They like boiled potatoes. Doing the right thing cures their hunger.

Other Devices: Parallel Story.

Art Style: Impressionism/Realism pen and ink drawings.

Curriculum Tie-In: Social Science (Values; Ethics).

*Parnall, Peter. *The Mountain*. Garden City, NY: Doubleday, 1971.

The mountain, flowers, and moles should be kept just the way they are. To accomplish that, Congress passes a law making the mountain a national park. And, then a road is built. And, then people come.

> **Examples:** Too much "love" is destroying natural wilderness. Limits on use and access are necessary to preserve what is left.
>
> **Other Devices:** Irony. Satire.
>
> **Art Style:** Expressionism/Cartoon line drawing.
>
> **Curriculum Tie-In:** Science (Ecology).

*Paterson, Katherine. *The Tale of the Mandarin Ducks*. Illus. by Leo Dillon and Diane Dillon. New York: Lodestar Books (Dutton), 1990.

A pair of Mandarin ducks, separated by a cruel lord who wishes to possess the drake for his colorful beauty, rewards a compassionate couple who risk their lives to reunite the ducks.

> **Examples:** Compassion for other living creatures and commitment through sharing life's hurdles are expressed through the ducks and the kitchen maid. When the drake "began to droop, the kitchen maid noted, 'He is grieving for his mate,' . . . for she was wise in the customs of wild creatures." For releasing the duck, the maid is punished severely. In turn, the reunited ducks help her. Mutual help is part of healthy living.
>
> **Other Devices:** Metaphor.
>
> **Art Style:** Folk (Japanese water color and pastel paintings similar to eighteenth-century woodcuts).

Petersham, Maud, and Miska Petersham. *The Circus Baby*. New York: Macmillan, 1950.

A mother elephant tries to teach her baby to eat like a human being. The results are disastrous.

> **Examples:** Living naturally is better than trying to copy the ways of others. "My child, you do not have to learn to eat as the circus people do because, after all, you are an elephant."
>
> **Art Style:** Cartoon.
>
> **Curriculum Tie-In:** Social Science (Self-Discovery/Esteem; Acceptance and Respect; Parent and Child; Values).

Piper, Watty. *The Little Engine That Could*. Illus. by George Hauman and Doris Hauman. New York: Platt & Monk, 1954.

When the little red engine breaks down, it needs help to get its cargo for boys and girls over the mountain. Only the little blue engine offers its service.

> **Examples:** Being courageous enough to try and determined enough to stick with a difficult task are the ways toward satisfaction and success. The less promising ones among us deserve a chance and often succeed where those more likely to succeed fail.

Other Devices: Onomatopoeia. Stereotype.

Art Style: Colored Cartoon.

Curriculum Tie-In: Social Science (Values).

Rathmann, Peggy. *Ruby the Copycat.* New York: Scholastic, 1991.
Ruby insists on copying Angela, until her teacher helps her discover her own creative resources.

> **Examples:** Ruby learns that her own unique talents offer her more satisfaction than trying to copy the activities and appearance of others. Ruby can hop better than just about anyone.
>
> **Other Devices:** Foreshadowing.
>
> **Art Style:** Cartoon.
>
> **Curriculum Tie-In:** Social Science (Self-Discovery/Esteem; Acceptance and Respect).

Rosenberg, Liz. *The Scrap Doll.* Illus. by Robin Ballard. New York: A Charlotte Zolotow Book (HarperCollins), 1991.
A little girl fixes up her mother's old scrap doll and learns that one made at home with love can be much better than the most beautiful store-bought doll.

> **Examples:** The doll was Ugly Old Thing until fixed up. Now it seemed to belong on her bed better than on the dresser or in the closed shoe box where she once wanted to hide it. Meaning adds value to an object.
>
> **Other Devices:** Inference.
>
> **Art Style:** Cartoon.
>
> **Curriculum Tie-In:** Social Science (Values).

Sendak, Maurice. *Where the Wild Things Are.* New York: Harper & Row, 1963. [Caldecott Award]
Max is a little boy dressed in a wolf suit sent to his room for behaving ferociously. Suddenly the walls disappear and he finds himself in a magic forest of wild creatures.

> **Examples:** Feeling fierce in his wolf suit, Max defies his mother. Her chastisement results in punishment that causes Max to lash out in anger. But, when his anger is spent, he wants "to be where someone loved him best of all." An expression of anger does not bring an end to love.
>
> **Other Devices:** Hyperbole. Inference. Point-Of-View.
>
> **Art Style:** Expressionism pen and ink colored drawings.
>
> **Curriculum Tie-In:** Social Science (Self-Discovery/Esteem; Anger; Consequences; Forgiveness; Parent and Child).

Seuss, Dr. *How the Grinch Stole Christmas.* New York: Random, 1957.
Grinch thought stealing the trappings of Christmas would stop Christmas.

Examples: Christmas is not dependent upon stores and money. "Maybe Christmas perhaps means a little bit more."

Other Devices: Alliteration. Onomatopoeia.

Art Style: Cartoon.

Curriculum Tie-In: Social Science (Values).

Steig, William. *Sylvester and the Magic Pebble.* New York: Windmill Books (Simon & Schuster), 1969. [Caldecott Award]
A magic pebble, a fierce lion, and a wish made in panic lead to separation from loved ones.

Examples: The best wish of all must inevitably be companionship with loved ones. The possibility of wonderful wishes for "anything I want" means nothing without the love of family first.

Other Devices: Foreshadowing. Imagery. Personification. Pun. Stereotype. Symbol.

Art Style: Cartoon water color.

Curriculum Tie-In: Social Science (Parent and Child).

Velthuijs, Max. *Elephant and Crocodile.* Trans. by Anthea Bell. New York: Farrar Straus Giroux, 1990.
A wall separates two musical artists who can not abide one another's noise until the wall comes down and they cooperate. Their consequent duets make them world famous. More can be accomplished together than separately.

Art Style: Cartoon.

Curriculum Tie-In: Social Science (Cooperation; Anger).

Viorst, Judith. *Alexander and the Terrible, Horrible, No Good, Very Bad Day.* Illus. by Ray Cruz. New York: Atheneum, 1976.
When nothing goes right for Alexander, he dreams of leaving it all behind and going to Australia where it's bound to be better.

Examples: Mom doesn't give too much credence to a day of tough luck. One can't run away from the bad things in life. They're common to everyone anywhere—"even in Australia."

Art Style: Colored Cartoon.

Curriculum Tie-In: Social Science (Self-Discovery/Esteem; Anger; Family Life).

Williams, Garth. *The Chicken Book.* New York: Delacorte, 1946, 1970.
Some baby chicks express wishes for food and grit.

Examples: To get anything in life, effort must be expended to achieve it. Wishing is not enough. Success is more likely to those who "scratch" for their needs.

Other Devices: Analogy. Foreshadowing.

Art Style: Expressionism/Cartoon.

*Yashima, Taro. *Crow Boy*. New York: Viking, 1955.
A misunderstood, shy student earns the respect of his fellow classmates after being ignored for years. A new teacher shows them the boy has much to offer.

Examples: People need to be valued for themselves. No one can judge another's worth without understanding that person's life. No one understands the nature of his environment better than the "Crow Boy" who can imitate the bird and discuss accurately its life.

Other Devices: Stereotype. Tone. Understatement.

Art Style: Impressionism pastel pencil.

Curriculum Tie-In: Social Science (Acceptance and Respect).

Yolen, Jane. *The Emperor and the Kite*. Illus. by Ed Young. Cleveland: World, 1967.
Because she is tiny, the emperor's youngest daughter is dismissed as insignificant. When disaster strikes, she alone proves her loyalty and service.

Examples: Don't underestimate unlikely individuals. Given opportunity, they demonstrate abilities usually attributed to more likely persons.

Art Style: Expressionism/Chinese Folk Motif.

Curriculum Tie-In: Social Science (Prejudice; Discrimination; Sexism).

*Yolen, Jane. *Encounter*. Illus. by David Shannon. New York: Harcourt Brace Jovanovich, 1992.
A Taino Indian boy on the island of San Salvador recounts the landing of Columbus and his men in 1492.

Examples: In the boy's dream, the "great-winged birds" with "sharp white teeth" in their mouths and "voices like thunder" portend the arrival of strangers "from the sky" who sail in on great canoes and show the "serpent's smile—no lips and all teeth." These strangers "touched our golden nose rings and our golden armbands but not the flesh of our faces or arms." They came with no respect for the people but barely concealed greed for their possessions. The strangers gave trivial gifts of "singing shells and tiny balls on strings." Noticeably, the "sharp stick that made his blood cry out" and the "darts that sprang from sticks with a sound like thunder that could kill a parrot many paces away" were not given as gifts. The strangers were politely laughed at behind their backs for their odd clothing, but the final cruel joke was the strangers': capture and destruction of the island people.

Other Devices: Atmosphere. Flash-Forward. Foreshadowing. Metaphor. Point-Of-View. Stereotype.

Art Style: Realism/Expressionism acrylic.

Curriculum Tie-In: History (Discovery of America—Columbus).

Zemach, Harve. *The Judge.* Illus. by Margot Zemach. New York: Farrar Straus Giroux, 1967.

A judge's mistrust of people leads to a disastrous confrontation with a monster.

Examples: Arrogance can be one's undoing. Don't presume superior knowledge and then dismiss evidence to the contrary. There is something of the pride-goeth-before-a-fall truism in this tale of a public official who refuses to listen and pays the price.

Other Devices: Caricature. Foreshadowing. Hyperbole. Poetic Justice. Satire.

Art Style: Expressionism.

Curriculum Tie-In: Social Science (Consequences; Foolish Behavior).

TONE

Author's attitude toward his or her subject and audience revealed by choice of words and details.

> **Example:** "Afoot and light-hearted I take to the open road, healthy, free, the world before me."   —Walt Whitman, "Song of the Open Road."
> (Tone is positive about life and upbeat.)

SOURCES

Ackerman, Karen. *The Banshee.* Illus. by David Ray. New York: Philomel, 1990.

At night the Banshee comes to a village in search of a lonely soul to keep her company.

Examples: There is a juxtaposition of tenderness and loving spirit among the village folk that is far more powerful than the compelling touch of the mysterious Banshee. When her sad song slips across a window ledge, a mother lifts her baby from its crib and holds him close to her. The Banshee turns away.

Other Devices: Simile.

Art Style: Expressionism.

*Baylor, Byrd. *Your Own Best Secret Place.* Illus. by Peter Parnall. New York: Charles Scribner's, 1979.

A girl discovers that the hollow at the foot of a cottonwood tree was first someone else's secret place before it was hers. She begins to understand how William Cottonwood felt there.

Examples: Maybe he left those things behind because "I think that leaving things you like means you'll be back." The girl respects his privacy and "never looked in the can again." She adds her contribution to the special place without infringing on the former tenant. She lists all the birds and animals she sees "from where I sit inside his tree looking out." The list is there "for him to read when he comes home." The author demonstrates respect and appreciation for life and those who impact on nature.

Other Devices: Imagery. Theme.

Art Style: Expressionism pen and ink line drawings.

Curriculum Tie-In: Social Science (Self-Discovery/Esteem; Acceptance and Respect; Continuity of Life).
Geography (American Southwest).

Briggs, Raymond. *Jim and the Beanstalk.* New York: Coward-McCann, 1970.
As a sequel to Jack, another curious climber finds the giant now beset with the inadequacies of old age and endeavors to fill his needs.

Examples: A bit of black humor comes through this "reformed" giant. He used to enjoy eating "a nice juicy boy" but hasn't any teeth now. When he gets fixed up, he feels his old stirrings return. "You better go now before I feel like fried boy again." The boy, too, isn't a helpless lad unaware of reality. He hopes he could get breakfast at the "top of the plant." He hopes the giant has cornflakes.

Other Devices: Ambiguity. Parody. Pun.

Art Style: Colored Cartoon.

Curriculum Tie-In: Social Science (Friendship).

Daly, Niki. *Mama, Papa, and Baby Joe.* New York: Viking Penguin, 1991.
A family's adventure on a shopping trip is described in action-packed pictures full of unlikely hilarious detail.

Examples: The author makes ordinary shopping seem a funny, goofy, nonsensical, light-hearted experience. ". . . oozy-poosy tube of toothpaste; Chicken Licken and Pudding Pack; sticky icky licking baby; in fatty Boom Boom's Take Away; Quickero Backero tiddly-pom."

Other Devices: Alliteration. Allusion. Pun.

Art Style: Cartoon.

DePaola, Tomie. *Strega Nona.* Englewood Cliffs: Prentice-Hall, 1975.
When Strega Nona leaves him alone with her magic pasta pot, her bumbling apprentice Big Anthony is determined to show the townspeople how it works.

Examples: She's got her uses even though folks "talked about her in whispers." She is good with "headaches, and husbands and warts." But when Big Anthony wants respect from the community, he is spurned. "Big Anthony was angry and that wasn't a very good thing to be." There is folksy, gently sardonic humor in this tale of justice dispensed.

Other Devices: Foreshadowing. Poetic Justice.

Art Style: Cartoon/European Middle Ages Folk.

Curriculum Tie-In: Social Science (Consequences; Ethics).

Francoise. *Jeanne-Marie Counts Her Sheep.* New York: Charles Scribner's, 1951.
Jeanne-Marie may buy a bright red hat with a blue feather. She may take a ride
on the Merry-Go-Round. She may even get a little house! Such wonderful things
may be bought if Patapon, her sheep, has a lamb or two or three—or more.

> **Examples:** The author, in language expressing warm, gentle, mutual devo-
> tion, shows what would make an appealing wish list and provides an accom-
> modating sheep. Though disappointed that Patapon gives birth to only one
> lamb, the girl won't show she's unhappy because the sheep is obviously so
> pleased with her little lamb.

Art Style: Naive.

Curriculum Tie-In: Social Science (Acceptance and Respect).

*Grifalconi, Ann. *Kinda Blue.* Boston: Little, Brown & Co., 1993.
Sissy feels lonely until her Uncle Dan cheers her up by explaining that everything, even corn, needs special attention every now and then.

> **Examples:** Without becoming maudlin, the author's language shows that her
> uncle knows why she's "kinda blue." "What you doin' over there, Sissy Honey? . . .
> Scratchin in the ground like ol' wet hen?" He compares the care of corn to
> people. "So, even when you thinks nobody cares, even when you wishes you
> had your own papa to watch over you and take care of you . . . never you mind!
> We be there, takin' care!"

Other Devices: Metaphor. Symbol.

Art Style: Impressionism water color, pastel, and colored pencil.

Curriculum Tie-In: Social Science (Acceptance and Respect; Loneliness).

*Jordon, Mary Kate. *Losing Uncle Tim.* Illus. by Judith Friedman. Niles, IL: Albert
Whitman, 1989.
Daniel struggles to accept beloved Uncle Tim's impending death from AIDS,
and finds his favorite grownup has left him a legacy of joy and courage.

> **Examples:** No nonsense and directly gentle is the approach to this frighten-
> ing subject. Their relationship has been loving. "I was good at stretching my
> legs to go faster, and Uncle Tim was good at stepping small to go slower."
> When his uncle sells a favorite toy at the antique store, Daniel is sad. Uncle
> Tim asks Daniel what other toys he especially cares about. Daniel tells him
> and he says, "I'll remember." Those items are later bequeathed to Daniel after
> Tim's death. And Uncle Tim won't let Daniel "throw" the checkers game.
> Daniel knows the end is near when Uncle Tim gives him the checkers set to
> take home. "You can teach somebody else how to play."

Art Style: Realism.

Curriculum Tie-In: Health and Safety (AIDS).
Social Science (Death; Grief).

Jukes, Mavis. *I'll See You in My Dreams.* Illus. by Stacey Schuett. Knopf, 1993.
A girl preparing to visit her seriously ill uncle in the hospital imagines being a
skywriter and flying over his bed with a message of love.

Examples: At the time of day when the sky "is pink and blue, the colors of
dusk or dawn," the girl would carefully prepare for flight, as would her uncle,
and she'd write "Good-bye" in clouds. Later, across the moon she'd write "I
love you. . . . I'll see you in my dreams." But she isn't a skywriter. "She's a little
kid." So she will do what a little kid can do. She won't be afraid to go into the
hospital in spite of the two old men there who walk about looking up saying
"aaah!" And, she won't be afraid of the old woman who asks everyone where
she should sit. She might even tell her to sit on the bench with her Mom and
her. "He might not know that she was standing there. But she would know
that she was standing there." She would see her uncle one last time.

Art Style: Impressionism paint.

Curriculum Tie-In: Social Science (Death; Grief).

Kennedy, Richard. *The Porcelain Man.* Illus. by Marcia Sewall. Boston: Little,
Brown & Co., 1986.
Every time the poor girl mends the broken porcelain vase, it becomes something different, and personal, providing another means of escaping from her
dreary existence of mending junk.

Examples: The author's sardonic view of the girl's life is given spirited interest whenever the porcelain vase performs one of its mystical changes. The
father does his best to keep her chained to his service. "It's dog-eat-dog out
there. The world is full of bottle-snatchers, ragmongers, and ratrobbers. Believe you me!" The man is totally mercenary. When he learns the porcelain
man can speak and move, he remarks, "I'll make a cage for him and take him
to the county fair. I'll charge a dollar to see him." But the porcelain man has
other ideas. "Gracious," she says as he "encircled her in his arms and kissed
her." "Whoa!" bellows the father as he breaks a chair over the head of the
porcelain man. The battle for the girl is on. The father is no match for persistent love.

Other Devices: Inference. Understatement

Art Style: Colored Cartoon.

Mantinband, Gerda. *The Blabbermouths.* Illus. by Paul Borovsky. New York:
Greenwillow, 1992.
Although he swears not to reveal the source of his new-found wealth, a poor
farmer can't help telling his wife, and then a neighbor, and soon even the chief
magistrate finds out.

Examples: An innocent fool is saved from himself by his wife's shrewdness. The chest, "chock-full of gold pieces," shows the author's whimsical, droll attitude toward her subject. An old woman tells the farmer, "You can set me free and do yourself some good into the bargain." When the wife warns her husband "not to breathe a word of this to a living soul," he replies indignantly, "Do you think I am a blabbermouth?" Then he goes on to prove he is.

Other Devices: Foreshadowing.

Art Style: Naive

Curriculum Tie-In: Social Science (Foolish Behavior).

Martin, Jacqueline Briggs. *Good Times on Grandfather Mountain.* Illus. by Susan Gaber. New York: Orchard Books, 1992.

Mountain man Washburn insists on looking on the bright side of things, even as disaster after disaster befalls him.

Examples: The old man is apparently beloved by his neighbors. When there is nothing left to do but make music, he "fiddled old-time songs about losing and finding, quick little jigs about greedy grasshoppers and silly chickens, and slow songs about watchful stars." The neighbors bring hammers and tools as well as harmonicas and musical saws. They know how to accept disaster and have a good time and recover from hard times. Old Washburn can even "whittle a party out of a blown-down cabin." The spirit of upbeat determination comes through the lilting language.

Other Devices: Atmosphere.

Art Style: Expressionism.

Curriculum Tie-In: Social Science (Coping).

Mayer, Mercer. *There's a Nightmare in My Closet.* New York: Dial, 1968.

"One night I decided to get rid of my nightmare once and for all."

Examples: If you decide to get rid of a bothersome nightmare by shooting him, you have an unhappy, crying nightmare on your hands, so you have to tuck him in bed with you. And what if your closet hides yet another nightmare? The "bed's not big enough for three." This practical, matter-of-fact discussion demystifies the all-powerful, controlling fear of closet bogeymen and makes the topic humorous and manageable.

Art Style: Cartoon pen and ink.

Curriculum Tie-In: Social Science (Fear).

McLerran, Alice. *Roxaboxen.* Illus. by Barbara Cooney. New York: Lothrop, Lee & Shepard, 1991.

A hill covered with rocks and wooden boxes becomes an imaginary town for Marion, her sisters, and their friends.

Examples: The nostalgic pleasures of a favorite play site are depicted. This is a wonderful place created out of nothing. It becomes a vital place that lasts past childhood into fond memories. A tin box full of pebbles is buried trea-sure. "Old wooden boxes could be shelves or tables or anything you wanted." "For a car all you needed was something round for a steering wheel." A horse is a stick "you could gallop anywhere." "Not one of them ever forgot Roxaboxen."

Art Style: Naive.

Curriculum Tie-In: Social Science (Nostalgia).

Ness, Evaline. *Sam, Bangs, & Moonshine.* New York: Holt, Rinehart and Win-ston, 1966. [Caldecott Award]

Sam dreams rich and lovely dreams, but her father calls them moonshine. Tho-mas, a young friend, doesn't know about moonshine. He takes her words for truth, and then there is trouble.

Examples: Sam is a lonely child who deliberately remakes the world to suit her fantasies. "Sam said her mother was a mermaid, when everyone knew she was dead." She tells people she has a fierce lion and baby kangaroo, but her only pet is a cat "who could talk if and when he wanted to." Her father wants her to talk "real." He warns that "moonshine spells trouble." But later when trouble comes and Sam admits she fibbed, her father becomes thoughtful when she says, "I almost believed I did have a baby kangaroo." He acknowl-edges there "is good moonshine and bad moonshine" and brings her a gerbil that looks like a miniature kangaroo. Because of Sam, Thomas has lost his bicycle and is ill. She asks her Dad if he thinks she should give it to Thomas. The author has shown her change from self-centered concern to active car-ing for someone else.

Art Style: Expressionism prints.

Curriculum Tie-In: Social Science (Self-Discovery/Esteem; Consequences; Ethics; Loneliness).

Oakley, Graham. *The Church Cat Abroad.* New York: Atheneum, 1973.

For the sake of their friends two mice and a cat set out to become high paid actors so they will earn enough money to fix their leaking church vestry roof.

Examples: Much tongue-in-cheek language. For example: Sampson the church cat "didn't chase mice; some of his best friends were mice." "At the moment things were a bit slack for smirking cats and ballet-dancing mice." "Sampson did the Cheshire Cat's smile from Alice in Wonderland. He did it twice because it didn't last very long."

Other Devices: Allusion. Understatement.

Art Style: Colored Cartoon.

Olson, Arielle North. *Noah's Cats and the Devil's Fire.* Illus. by Barry Moser. New York: Orchard Books, 1992.

A rebuffed devil returns to Noah's ark in disguise, ready to be the most troublesome passenger aboard.

> **Examples:** The author shares confidentially with the reader that after Noah built the mighty ark, ". . . the minute he finished, guess what happened?" Potentially frightening subjects are discussed in an easy, jocular camaraderie in this Pourquoi story.
>
> **Other Devices:** Poetic Justice. Pun. Satire.
>
> **Art Style:** Expressionism water color.
>
> **Curriculum Tie-In:** Literature (Pourquoi Story).

Pinkwater, Daniel. *Doodle Flute.* New York: Macmillan, 1991.

Kevin Spoon acquires a doodle flute and makes a friend.

> **Examples:** The author has a sardonic attitude toward his characters. When Kevin says he wants the flute, Mason replies, "I know you do." But he doesn't give it to him in trade or purchase. He gives it because Kevin asks and "That's just the kind of guy I am." But, after it's gone he won't teach Kevin to play it because "I don't own one." "What's the point of being a doodle flute player if you haven't got a doodle flute?" The only way Kevin will learn to play is by sharing ownership with his new friend.
>
> **Other Devices:** Irony. Satire.
>
> **Art Style:** Cartoon.
>
> **Curriculum Tie-In:** Social Science (Values; Friendship).

Ratz de Tagyos, Paul. *A Coney Tale.* New York: Clarion Books (Houghton Mifflin), 1992.

The inhabitants of a rabbit village in seventeenth-century Flanders discover the biggest carrot in the world and work to dig it up.

> **Examples:** "Coneys love nothing better than feeding. Not much has changed about that for hundreds of years." There is jovial teasing about rabbit habits and characteristics. The town boasts a "pad repair shop" for "hopper" foot relief and an ear care center showing a poster demonstrating "ear floss" use. The problem of the huge carrot is hard to handle because "coneys are better at feeding than at thinking." When the carrot is finally pulled free it goes soaring to a field outside the village but "no coneys were hurt, as they are generally a rather bouncy group."
>
> **Other Devices:** Hyperbole.
>
> **Art Style:** Colored Cartoon.

Scieszka, Jon. The True Story of the Three Little Pigs by A. Wolf. *Illus. by Lane Smith. New York: Viking Kestrel, 1989.*

The wolf gives his own outlandish version of what really happened when he tangled with the three little pigs.

Examples: Irreverant, ghoulish narration. "It's not my fault wolves eat cute little animals like bunnies and sheep and pigs. . . . If cheeseburgers were cute, folks would probably think you were Big and Bad, too." The first little pig's house fell in on him and killed him "dead as a doornail," and it seemed "like a shame to leave a perfectly good ham dinner lying there in the straw. So I ate it up. Think of it as a big cheeseburger just lying there."

Other Devices: Parody. Point-Of-View. Pun.

Art Style: Colored Cartoon/Collage.

Smucker, Anna Egan. *No Star Nights.* Illus. by Steve Johnson. New York: Knopf, 1989.

A young girl growing up in a steel mill town in the 1950s describes her childhood and how it was affected by the local industry.

Examples: In this very harsh, dangerous, and unhealthy environment, children accepted the reality with feelings of nostalgia. We "couldn't see the stars in the nightime sky because the furnaces of the mill turned the darkness into a red glow." Regular life went on: ball games in Pittsburgh, 4th of July parades, as well as gritty graphite that could sting bare legs and get in eyes. There were days when smoke was "so thick you couldn't see anything clearly." The mountains they climbed were slag heaps.

Art Style: Impressionism.

Curriculum Tie-In: History (Steel Mills America).

Vozar, David. *Yo, Hungry Wolf! A Nursery Rap.* Illus. by Betsy Lewin. New York: Delacorte, 1993.

A retelling in rap verse of "The Three Little Pigs," "Little Red Riding Hood," and "The Boy Who Cried Wolf."

Examples: The vernacular rap style contains asides to the reader (or fellow wolves). "Wolves everywhere, you know me, the meanest wolf in history!" "Pardon me for interrupting this rhyme. But I've been off these pages, biding my time. Throughout this book I've had barely a meal, but this bakery story could be a good deal."

Other Devices: Internal Rhyme.

Art Style: Colored Cartoon.

Yashima, Taro. Crow Boy. *New York: Viking, 1955.*

A misunderstood, shy student earns the respect of his fellow classmates after being ignored for years. A new teacher shows them the boy has much to offer.

Examples: The boy's strange dedication to an education that largely bewilders him is eloquently shown. "Even when it rained or stormed, he still came trudging along, wrapped in a raincoat from dried zebra grass." Though "he was left alone in the study time" and "he was left alone in the play time," he persists. His only reaction to snubs is his ability to "make his eyes cross-eyed so that he was able not to see whatever he did not want to see." In quiet unemotional language, respect grows for this child who left his home for school at dawn and arrived home at sunset "every day for six long years."

Other Devices: Stereotype. Theme. Understatement.

Art Style: Impressionism paint.

Curriculum Tie-In: Social Science (Acceptance and Respect).

Yashima, Taro. *Umbrella.* New York: Viking, 1958.

Momo is three when she receives red rubber boots and an umbrella for her birthday. She eagerly looks forward to a chance to use them.

Examples: The importance to Momo of this grown-up gift is sensitively, and winsomely, portrayed. When the rain finally comes, she is so excited, she "pulled the boots onto her bare feet." The day is momentous because not only was she using the umbrella for the first time, she also "walked alone, without holding either her mother's or her father's hand." And, she "used to forget her mittens or her scarf so easily—but not her umbrella."

Other Devices: Flash-Forward. Onomatopoeia. Simile.

Art Style: Impressionism paint.

Curriculum Tie-In: Social Science (Self-Discovery/Esteem).

***Zemach, Harve.** *Duffy and the Devil.* Illus. by Margot Zemach. New York: Farrar Straus Giroux, 1973. [Caldecott Award]

A resourceful servant girl uses her wits to avoid admitting she can't spin and knit, even when the game is up.

Examples: Droll, hilarious folk style: "The door of the cottage flew open and out ran a blubbering, bawling girl chased by an old woman who was clouting her with a broom and shouting, 'You lazy bufflehead, you!'" "Squire Lovel could see that Duffy and the woman would be glad to get quit of one another." When Duffy proves unable to spin wool "an oogly little squinny-eyed creature with a long tail" appeared remarking "I'll do the spinning for you, and the knitting, too. How'd you like that?" Three years later it didn't seem like Duffy would be able to correctly guess his name. He "started jibing and jeering at her, grinning and winking and behaving all cock-a-hoop."

Other Devices: Parody. Poetic Justice.

Art Style: Folk/Cartoon water color.

Curriculum Tie-In: Social Science (Coping).

UNDERSTATEMENT

The act of presenting something as less significant than it really is.

Example: There seems to be a slight discrepancy in your bookkeeping statements.

SOURCES

Agee, Jon. *The Return of Freddy Le Grand.* New York: Farrar Straus Giroux, 1992.
Pilot Freddy's adventures come full circle when he is found and befriended by
the farm couple who rescued him the first time he crashed.

> **Examples:** The grateful Freddy wants to pay back Sophie and Albert for their
> kind hospitality by "helping" around the farm. But, the pig shed he built is
> unsuitable; his attempts to milk a cow don't work. He "could see that farm
> life was not for him. Sophie and Albert agreed."
>
> **Other Devices:** Foreshadowing.
>
> **Art Style:** Cartoon.

Bottner, Barbara. *Bootsie Barker Bites.* Illus. by Peggy Rathmann. New York: G. P.
Putnam's, 1992.
Bootsie Barker likes to play only intimidating games in which she can bite,
until one day her friend comes up with a better game.

> **Examples:** When she has torn the book about turtles to shreds, her friend
> remarks, "Bootsie hates turtles." Bootsie yells that they are playing nicely. "I
> can't yell anything"— because Bootsie's hand is clamped over her mouth.
> When Bootsie finally leaves for good, the girl doesn't have to wish her on a
> rocket trip to outer space, "Although if she does go, it's fine with me."
>
> **Other Devices:** Foreshadowing. Inference. Poetic Justice.
>
> **Art Style:** Colored Cartoon.
>
> **Curriculum Tie-In:** Social Science (Bullies; Friendship).

Brown, Ruth. *Our Puppy's Vacation.* New York: E. P. Dutton, 1987.
The quintessential Labrador puppy has a busy first day exploring the English
Cornwall countryside with her family.

> **Examples:** ". . . an old tree was a problem for her in more ways than one."
> She can't climb it with the kids and a swarm of bees flies out of a hold in it
> near her. "She makes friends—sometimes easily, sometimes not so easily." A
> cow licks her but a dirty-mouthed pig makes her stand off a bit.
>
> **Art Style:** Realism/Impressionism paint.

Chaucer, Geoffrey. *Chanticleer and the Fox.* Adapted and illus. by Barbara Cooney. New York: Thomas Crowell, 1958. [Caldecott Award]
A moral tale about a rooster who listened to flattery.

> **Examples:** Speaking of the rooster's parents, the fox remarked in a decep-
> tively friendly manner that they "did me the great honor of visiting my house."
> When Chanticleer laid eyes on the fox, he "had no desire to crow."
>
> **Other Devices:** Aphorism. Foreshadowing. Simile.
>
> **Art Style:** Cartoon scratchboard with color overlay.
>
> **Curriculum Tie-In:** Social Science (Values; Consequences).

Fleischman, Paul. *Time Train.* Illus. by Claire Ewart. New York: A Charlotte Zolotow Book (HarperCollins), 1991.
A class takes a field trip back through time to observe living dinosaurs in their natural habitat.

> **Examples:** "We knew we were in for an unusual trip," says the modern narra-
> tor as he views out the train window at a scene of early 1900s Philadelphia.
> Later, the "new passengers" at Pittsburgh are dressed in Civil War Union
> attire. Then the engineer is "busy" in the morning with buffalo on the track.
> They notice the "weather had changed" to deep snow. A mammoth is watch-
> ing the train pass. Later still, giant dragon flies indicate the "weather had
> warmed up quite a bit." And, so it goes backward in time until they frolic
> with dinosaurs, riding them, playing ball, etc. At trip's end, Dad asks if they
> had seen any dinosuars. "One or two," they reply.
>
> **Other Devices:** Foreshadowing.
>
> **Art Style:** Expressionism.
>
> **Curriculum Tie-In:** History (Pre-History).

Hilton, Nette. *Dirty Dave.* Illus. by Roland Harvey. New York: Orchard Books, 1990.
Members of an outlaw family gain acceptance from the public because of the fine clothes their father makes for the public.

> **Examples:** The family demand and shout and get what they want. They bel-
> low, roar, and holler. But father stays quietly home. The garments he makes
> impress travelers. When people ask about the tailor, the reply is simply, "Their
> Dad loves to sew."
>
> **Other Devices:** Irony. Stereotype (Reverse).
>
> **Art Style:** Cartoon.
>
> **Curriculum Tie-In:** Social Science (Sexism).

Hilton, Nette. *Prince Lachlan.* Illus. by Ann James. New York: Orchard Books, 1990.
Noisy Prince Lachlan saves the day when his antics frighten off the Great One, who wants to steal the king's throne.

Examples: When the noisy, somewhat destructive, bumbling prince crashes home, his queen mother says he's home. "I know," says the king. When the noisy prince booms, blasts, and strums his toys, the queen says, "Prince Lachlan loves music." "I know," sighs the king. When the prince's games "zing! and ouch!," the queen remarks that the prince loves games. "I know," says the king. When the Great One covets the king's throne, the king says, "I know." When the Great One flees from Prince Lachlan's calamitous behavior, the prince wonders why the Great One ran away. The queen says, "We'll never know." The king says, "I know."

Art Style: Cartoon.

Kahl, Virginia. *Plum Pudding for Christmas.* New York: Charles Scribner's, 1956.
After inviting the king to be their Christmas guest, the duchess and her daughters are unable to serve the promised plum pudding.

Examples: When the king says he'll cut off their heads if the pudding isn't right, the duchess remarks, ". . . though we don't often use 'em, it will come as a shock when the time comes to lose 'em.'" The duke returns to his family without the promised head of a foe and feels himself in disgrace. He says his adversary turned out to be "a person like me. If I cut off his head, it might ruin his figger . . . besides he was bigger."

Other Devices: Alliteration. Foreshadowing. Internal Rhyme. Irony.

Art Style: Colored Cartoon.

Curriculum Tie-In: History (Medieval Times).

Kennedy, Richard. *The Porcelain Man.* Illus. by Marcia Sewall. Boston: Little, Brown & Co., 1976.
Everytime the poor girl mends the broken porcelain vase, it becomes something different and useful to use as a means of escape from her dreary existence, mending junk her father drags home.

Examples: The jealous father smashes a chair "squarely on top of the head of the porcelain man with a blow that shattered him from head to toe." "Godamighty!" the father says. "I've fractured his skull."

Other Devices: Inference. Tone.

Art Style: Colored Cartoon.

Mahy, Margaret. *The Boy Who Was Followed Home.* Illus. by Steven Kellogg. New York: Franklin Watts, Inc., 1975.
A witch's pill is supposed to cure Robert of the hippopotamuses who daily follow him home from school. But there is one disadvantage to the treatment.

Examples: All the way home a hippo follows Robert. At the doorstep, Robert "thought his mother would not like this," so "he shooed it away." His disgruntled father remarks, "People should keep their hippos chained up and not allow them to go climbing into other people's goldfish pools. . . . It was

quite a big pool, but with four hippos in it, it seemed quite small." Looking at
the situation, Robert's mother thinks, "That seems quite a few." The witch
who helps clear up the problem "was not very respectable-looking," but, these
are desparate times. Robert is rather sorry to lose the hippos but "very pleased"
with their replacements—giraffes.

Other Devices: Foreshadowing.

Art Style: Cartoon pen and ink.

Novak, Matt. *Elmer Blunt's Open House.* New York: Orchard Books, 1992.
Several animals and a robber explore Elmer Blunt's home when he forgets to
close the door on his way to work.

Examples: "The thief explored Elmer Blunt's house." He actually helped himself to its contents.

Other Devices: Ambiguity. Irony. Pun.

Art Style: Colored Cartoon.

Oakley, Graham. *The Church Cat Abroad.* New York: Atheneum, 1973.
For the sake of their friends, two mice and a cat set out to become high paid
actors so they will earn enough money to fix their leaking church vestry roof.

Examples: The people of the church didn't seem to care about their vestry
roof. The church mice, on the other hand, "who lived in the vestry, cared
about it a great deal." After figuring out how long (200 years, 6 months, 3
weeks, and 4 days) it would take to earn enough money to repair the roof,
they thought, "This seemed a depressing prospect." As they set off on their
journey, they asked their friends "not to keep tea waiting" for them because
their destination was the South Sea Islands, and they "might get held up in
the rush hour traffic."

Other Devices: Allusion. Tone.

Art Style: Colored Cartoon.

Parnall, Peter. *The Great Fish.* Garden City, NY: Doubleday, 1973.
A beloved grandfather's poetic explanation for the cause of spawning salmon
that saved the Indians from starvation is a poignant reminder of a heritage lost.

Examples: The grandfather has explained why the salmon came upstream to
be captured by the starving Indians, but in explanation for why they stopped
coming, he simply says, "A mother's tears are not enough." The illustrations
show a stream polluted by various toxic substances.

Other Devices: Imagery. Inference.

Art Style: Expressionism pen and ink line drawing.

Curriculum Tie-In: Science (Environment; Ecology).

Potter, Beatrix. *The Tale of Peter Rabbit.* New York: Frederick Warne & Co., 1902.
Disobedient Peter suffers consequences in Mr. McGregor's garden.

Examples: Mother Rabbit tells Peter not to go into Mr. McGregor's garden. She hints why not: "Your father had an accident there." She then becomes direct: "He was put in a pie by Mrs. McGregor." But, Peter does go into the garden, and when he sees the white cat he "thought it best to go away without speaking to her." The watering can becomes a hiding place for Peter. But, it is not ideal. "It would have been a beautiful thing to hide in, if it had not had so much water in it." For a time, Peter gorges on garden vegetables. Then, "feeling rather sick, he went to look for some parsley."

Other Devices: Foreshadowing. Imagery. Irony. Metaphor. Onomatopoeia. Poetic Justice.

Art Style: Cartoon/Realism water color.

Curriculum Tie-In: Social Science (Consequences; Parent and Child).

***Tolhurst, Marilyn.** *Somebody and the Three Blairs.* Illus. by Simone Abel. New York: Orchard Books, 1991.

In a reversal of the Goldilocks story, a bear explores the home of the three Blairs while they are out.

Examples: Baby Blair's comments lend stolid reality to his parents' growing hysteria as they follow a trail of destruction in their ransacked home. He says in matter-of-fact ways, "All gone!" when he lifts the honey jar. "Busted," when he observes his high chair. "Naughty," when he sees the food spilled. "Lotta water," when he observes the bathroom flood. "Issa big teddy bear," when he sees Somebody in his bed. His parents shriek that the bear has escaped from the zoo, "escaped from the circus!" Baby observes, "Iss escaped downa drainpipe." When his parents shout for somebody to "phone the police!" for somebody to "call the fire department!" Baby announces, "Somebody gone home."

Other Devices: Parody. Pun.

Art Style: Colored Cartoon.

Ward, Lynd. *The Biggest Bear.* Boston: Houghton Mifflin, 1952. [Caldecott Award] Johnny Orchard goes out to acquire a bearskin, comes home with a cute little cub instead, and has to contend with its growing appetite.

Examples: In typical northeastern stoicism and unemotional speech, the bear's destructive eating habits are described as "the bear liked the milk that was meant for the calves." "Mother got pretty upset when he started looking for things on the kitchen shelves." Then "Mr. Carroll got pretty upset when the bear spent the night in his cornfield." He "had a wonderful time with the bacons and hams in the Pennells' smokehouse."

Other Devices: Foreshadowing. Pun. Stereotype.

Art Style: Realism/Impressionism.

Curriculum Tie-In: History (Nineteenth-Century America—Frontier Life).

Wells, Rosemary. *Benjamin and Tulip.* New York: Dial, 1973.
Benjamin is bullied by Tulip until he has nothing to lose and earns her respect
by fighting back.

Examples: Benjamin comes into the store all muddy because of an earlier
confrontation with Tulip. After taking his order, the storekeeper remarks,
"How about some soap?" Tulip smashes the watermelon he was bringing home.
When Benjamin's Aunt Fern later asks where it is, he says, "Back a ways." On
his second trip to bring home watermelon, he zips up a tree to avoid Tulip,
who threatens him. He replies, "I've got all night, . . . I won't get dinner now
anyway."

Other Devices: Inference.

Art Style: Cartoon pen and ink.

Curriculum Tie-In: Social Science (Bullies; Friendship; Anger; Self-Discov-
ery/Esteem).

***Yashima, Taro.** *Crow Boy.* New York: Viking, 1955.
A misunderstood, shy student earns the respect of his fellow classmates after
being ignored for years. A new teacher shows them the boy has much to offer.

Examples: The days are fruitless. He "found many ways, one after another,
to kill time and amuse himself." Every day his lunch is the same, "a rice ball
wrapped in a radish leaf." But in the end, "He was the only one in our class
honored for perfect attendance through all six years." With the least to gain
from his schooling, he has been the most dedicated.

Other Devices: Stereotype. Theme. Tone.

Art Style: Impressionism pastel pencil.

Curriculum Tie-In: Social Science (Acceptance and Respect).

Zimelman, Nathan. *Treed by a Pride of Irate Lions.* Illus. by Toni Goffe. Boston:
Little, Brown & Co., 1990.
Animals like Mother, but not Father. Perhaps tame animals are too refined, and
Father must go among wild animals in Africa to find one that will love him.

Examples: "Animals did not like Father." Dogs and cats bite. Horses kick.
Every single animal, wild or tame, abuses Father. He doesn't seem to have
rapport with animals.

Other Devices: Hyperbole. Irony.

Art Style: Cartoon.

RESOURCE TITLES AND LITERARY DEVICES

❋ ❋ ❋ ❋ ❋ ❋ ❋ ❋ ❋ ❋

Albert's Toothache, E. P. Dutton, 1974.
Williams, Barbara
Ambiguity

Alexander and the Terrible, Horrible, No Good, Very Bad Day, Atheneum, 1976.
Viorst, Judith
Theme

Alexander and the Wind-Up Mouse, Pantheon, 1969.
Lionni, Leo
Foreshadowing. Theme

Alfalfa Hill, Doubleday, 1975.
Parnall, Peter
Imagery. Metaphor. Simile

Alison's Zinnia, Greenwillow, 1990.
Lobel, Anita
Alliteration

All the Lights in the Night, Tambourine Books, 1992.
Levine, Arthur A.
Ambiguity

... Along Came Eric, Lothrop, Lee & Shepard, 1991.
Clarke, Gus
Foreshadowing. Inference

Amazing Bone (The), Farrar Straus Giroux, 1976.
Steig, William
Atmosphere. Caricature. Foreshadowing. Inference. Irony

Anatole, McGraw-Hill, 1956.
Titus, Eve
Irony

Andy and the Lion, Viking, 1938.
Daugherty, James
Foreshadowing

*Angel for Solomon Singer (An), Orchard Books, 1992.
Rylant, Cynthia
Flash-Forward. Irony. Symbol

Angus and the Cat, Doubleday, 1931.
Flack, Marjorie
Inference. Irony. Paradox

Angus and the Ducks, Doubleday, 1930.
Flack, Marjorie
Foreshadowing. Onomatopoeia. Poetic Justice

Angus Lost, Doubleday, 1932.
Flack, Marjorie
Foreshadowing. Onomatopoeia. Point-Of-View

193

Annie and the Old One, Little, Brown,
1971.
Miles, Miska
Inference. Theme

Anytime Mapleson and the Hungry Bears,
Harper & Row, 1990.
Gerstein, Mordicai
Parody

Baker's Portrait (A), Lothrop, Lee &
Shepard, 1991.
Edwards, Michelle
Paradox. Symbol

Banshee (The), Philomel, 1990.
Ackerman, Karen
Simile. Tone

Be Nice to Spiders, E. M. Hale, 1967.
Graham, Margaret Bloy
Paradox

Bear's Bicycle (The), Little, Brown, 1975.
McLeod, Emile W.
Parallel Story

Bedtime for Frances, Harper & Row, 1960.
Hoban, Russell
Inference

Benjamin and Tulip, Dial, 1973.
Wells, Rosemary
Inference. Understatement

Ben's Trumpet, Greenwillow, 1979.
Isadora, Rachel
Inference

Biggest Bear (The), Houghton Mifflin,
1952. [Caldecott Award]
Ward, Lynd
**Foreshadowing. Pun. Stereotype.
Understatement**

Bike Trip, HarperCollins, 1992.
Maestro, Betsy
Imagery

Blabbermouths (The), Greenwillow, 1992.
Mantinband, Gerda
Foreshadowing. Tone

Black and White, Houghton Mifflin, 1990.
[Caldecott Award]
Macauley, David
Parallel Story

Blackboard Bear, Dial, 1969.
Alexander, Martha
Poetic Justice

Blueberries for Sal, Viking, 1948.
McCloskey, Robert
Parallel Story

*Blumpoe the Grumpoe Meets Arnold the
Cat*, Little, Brown, 1990.
Okimoto, Jean Davies
Allusion. Inference

Bootsie Barker Bites, G. P. Putnam's, 1992.
Bottner, Barbara
**Foreshadowing. Inference. Poetic
Justice. Understatement**

Boy Who Was Followed Home (The),
Franklin Watts, 1975.
Mahy, Margaret
Foreshadowing. Understatement

Cabbage Rose, Bradbury, 1993.
Helldorfer, M. C.
Paradox

Caps for Sale, William Scott, 1949.
Slobodkina, Esphyr
Irony. Paradox

Careful with That Ball, Eugene! Orchard
Books, 1991.
Riddle, Tohby
Flash-Forward. Hyperbole

Cat in the Hat (The), Random, 1957.
Seuss, Dr.
Foreshadowing. Hyperbole. Imagery

Cat Next Door (The), Holiday House,
1991.
Wright, Betty Ren
Imagery. Simile. Symbol

Cataract of Lodore (The), Henry Holt,
1992.
Southey, Robert
Internal Rhyme

Cecil's Story, Orchard Books, 1991.
Lyon, George Ella
Flash-Forward. Point-Of-View

Changes, Knopf, 1990.
Browne, Anthony
Point-Of-View

Chanticleer and the Fox, Crowell, 1958.
[Caldecott Award]
Chaucer, Geoffrey, adapted by Barbara Cooney
Aphorism. Foreshadowing. Simile. Understatement

Charles T. McBiddle, Doubleday, 1993.
Glass, Andrew
Symbol

Charlie's House, Viking Penguin, 1989.
Schermbrucker, Reviva
Flashback. Inference

Cherry Tree (The), Knopf, 1992.
Ikeda, Daisaku
Aphorism. Symbol

Chicken Book (The), Delacorte, 1970.
Williams, Garth
Analogy. Foreshadowing. Theme

Chrysanthemum, Greenwillow, 1991.
Henkes, Kevin
Irony. Poetic Justice

Church Cat Abroad (The), Atheneum, 1973.
Oakley, Graham
Allusion. Tone. Understatement

Circus Baby (The), Macmillan, 1950.
Petersham, Maud, and Miska Petersham
Theme

Clever Bill, Farrar, 1977.
Nicholson, William
Pun

Coney Tale (A), Houghton Mifflin, 1992.
Ratz de Tagyos, Paul
Hyperbole. Tone

Corduroy, Viking, 1968.
Freeman, Don
Point-Of-View

Country Crossing, Atheneum, 1991.
Aylesworth, Jim
Imagery

Cowboy and the Black-Eyed Pea (The),
G. P. Putnam's, 1992.
Johnston, Tony
Atmosphere. Caricature. Inference. Parody. Simile

*Crow Boy, Viking, 1955.
Yashima, Taro
Stereotype. Theme. Tone. Understatement

Cuckoo Bird (The), HarperCollins, 1988.
Corbalis, Judy
Inference. Poetic Justice. Theme

Dandelion, Viking, 1964.
Freeman, Don
Foreshadowing. Pun. Theme

Dawn, Farrar Straus Giroux, 1974.
Shulevitz, Uri
Atmosphere. Imagery

Day We Saw the Sun Come Up (The),
Charles Scribner's, 1961.
Goudey, Alice E.
Simile

Dirty Dave, Orchard Books, 1990.
Hilton, Nette
Irony. Stereotype-Reverse. Understatement

Dog and Cat, Greenwillow, 1991.
Reiser, Lynn
Foreshadowing. Poetic Justice

Doodle Flute, Macmillan, 1991.
Pinkwater, Daniel
Irony. Satire. Tone

*Duffy and the Devil, Farrar Straus Giroux, 1973. [Caldecott Award]
Zemach, Harve
Parody. Poetic Justice. Tone

Each Peach Pear Plum, Viking Kestrel, 1978.
Ahlberg, Janet, and Allan Ahlberg
Allusion

Elephant and Crocodile, Farrar Straus Giroux, 1990.
Velthuijs, Max
Theme

Elijah's Angel, Harcourt Brace Jovanovich, 1992.
Rosen, Michael J.
Symbol

Elmer Blunt's Open House, Orchard
  Books, 1992.
  Novak, Matt
  Ambiguity. Irony. Pun. Understatement

*Emily, Doubleday, 1992.
  Bedard, Michael
  Imagery. Point-Of-View

Emperor and the Kite (The), World, 1967.
  Yolen, Jane
  Theme

Empty Lot (The), Little, Brown, 1991.
  Fife, Dale
  Theme

*Encounter, Harcourt Brace Jovanovich,
  1992.
  Yolen, Jane
  **Atmosphere. Flash-Forward.
  Foreshadowing. Metaphor. Point-Of-
  View. Stereotype. Theme.**

Engelbert the Elephant, Morrow, 1990.
  Paxton, Tom
  Stereotype

Eppie M. Says ... , Macmillan, 1990.
  Dunrea, Olivier
  Atmosphere

Evan's Corner, Holt Rinehart and
  Winston, 1967.
  Hill, Elizabeth Starr
  Theme

Everybody Needs a Rock, Charles
  Scribner's, 1974.
  Baylor, Byrd
  Point-Of-View

Everyone Asked about You, Philomel,
  1990.
  Gross, Theodore Faro
  Hyperbole. Internal Rhyme

*Everyone Knows What a Dragon Looks
  Like*, Four Winds, 1976.
  Williams, Jay
  Satire. Simile

*Father Christmas, Coward, 1973.
  Briggs, Raymond
  Allusion. Point-Of-View

Father Like That (A), Harper, 1971.
  Zolotow, Charlotte
  Stereotype

Feathers for Lunch, Harcourt Brace
  Jovanovich, 1990.
  Ehlert, Lois
  Inference

First Pink Light, Black Butterfly Children's
  Books, 1991.
  Greenfield, Eloise
  Irony

**First Song Ever Sung (The)*, Lothrop,
  Lee, & Shepard, 1993.
  Melmed, Laura Krauss
  Point-Of-View

**Fish and Flamingo*, Little, Brown, 1993.
  Carlstrom, Nancy White
  Irony. Paradox

Fishing at Long Pond, Greenwillow, 1991.
  George, William T.
  Imagery

Fog, Greenwillow, 1992.
  Fowler, Susi Gregg
  Atmosphere. Theme

Fortunately, Four Winds, 1964.
  Charlip, Remy
  Hyperbole

**Fortune-Tellers (The)*, Dutton, 1992.
  Alexander, Lloyd
  Irony. Satire

Four Dollars and Fifty Cents, Holiday
  House, 1989.
  Kimmel, Eric A.
  Allusion. Irony. Pun. Simile

Fox Tale, Greenwillow, 1991.
  Abolafia, Yossi
  Allusion. Poetic Justice. Pun

Frederick, Pantheon, 1967.
  Lionni, Leo
  Irony. Theme

**Frog Prince Continued (The)*, Viking,
  1991.
  Scieszka, Jon
  Allusion. Irony

Garden of Abdul Gasazi (The), Houghton
   Mifflin, 1979.
   Van Allsburg, Chris
   Inference

George and Martha, Houghton Mifflin,
   1972.
   Marshall, James
   Theme

Georgie, Doubleday, 1944.
   Bright, Robert
   Satire. Stereotype-Reverse

Ghost Catcher, HarperCollins, 1991.
   Haseley, Dennis
   Theme

Gilberto and the Wind, Viking, 1963.
   Ets, Marie Hall
   Personification

Girl Who Loved Wild Horses (The),
   Bradbury, 1978. [Caldecott Award]
   Goble, Paul
   Imagery. Simile. Symbol

Go Fish, Viking Penguin, 1991.
   Dickens, Lucy
   Inference

Goblin Walk, G. P. Putnam's, 1991.
   Johnston, Tony
   Irony. Paradox. Point-Of-View

Goggles, Macmillan, 1969.
   Keats, Ezra Jack
   Poetic Justice

Golden Coin (The), Atheneum, 1991.
   Ada, Alma Flor
   Ambiguity. Irony

Good Times on Grandfather Mountain,
   Orchard Books, 1992.
   Martin, Jacqueline Briggs
   Atmosphere. Tone

Goodbye Geese, Philomel, 1991.
   Carlstrom, Nancy White
   Metaphor

Gracie, Greenwillow, 1993.
   Ballard, Robin
   Flashback

*Grandfather's Journey, Houghton Mifflin,
   1993. [Caldecott Award]
   Say, Allen
   **Aphorism. Atmosphere. Foreshadow-
   ing. Irony. Paradox. Parallel Story.
   Symbol**

Grandpa's Town, Kane/Miller, 1991.
   Nomura, Tukaaki
   Inference

Great Fish (The), Doubleday, 1973.
   Parnall, Peter
   Imagery. Inference. Understatement

Greyling, Philomel, 1991.
   Yolen, Jane
   Metaphor

Guess Who's Just Moved in Next Door?
   Random House, 1991.
   McNaughton, Colin
   **Allusion. Caricature. Irony. Parallel
   Story. Pun. Satire**

Happy Lion (The), McGraw-Hill, 1954.
   Fatio, Louise
   Point-Of-View

Harlequin and the Gift of Many Colors,
   Parents' Magazine Press, 1973.
   Charlip, Remy, and Burton Supree
   Paradox

Harold and the Purple Crayon, Harper &
   Row, 1955.
   Johnson, Crockett
   Pun

Harry the Dirty Dog, Harper & Row, 1956.
   Zion, Gene
   Inference. Irony

*Hawk, I'm Your Brother, Charles
   Scribner's, 1976.
   Baylor, Byrd
   Paradox

Henry's Happy Birthday, Greenwillow,
   1990.
   Keller, Holly
   Irony

Hide and Seek Fog, Lothrop, Lee, &
   Shepard, 1965.
   Tresselt, Alvin
   Imagery. Metaphor. Simile

High in the Mountains, Macmillan, 1989.
Radin, Ruth Yaffe
Imagery. Metaphor. Simile

Hoagie's Rifle-Gun, Little, Brown, 1970.
Miles, Miska
Parallel Story. Theme

Home Place, Macmillan, 1990.
Dragonwagon, Crescent
Flashback. Imagery

House That Bob Built (The), Rizzoli, 1991.
Stern, Robert
Parody

How Do You Hide a Monster? Charles Scribner's, 1971.
Kahl, Virginia
Alliteration. Ambiguity. Irony

How the Grinch Stole Christmas, Random, 1957.
Seuss, Dr.
Alliteration. Onomatopoeia. Theme

Hugh Can Do, Crown, 1992.
Armstrong, Jennifer
Atmosphere. Foreshadowing. Poetic Justice. Pun. Simile

I Can't Said the Ant, Coward-McCann, 1961.
Cameron, Polly
Allusion. Internal Rhyme. Pun. Theme

Iktomi and the Berries, a Plains Indian Story, Orchard Books, 1989.
Goble, Paul
Caricature

I'll See You in My Dreams, Knopf, 1993.
Jukes, Mavis
Tone

Inch by Inch, Obelensky Astor-Honor, 1960.
Lionni, Leo
Inference. Poetic Justice. Pun

It's So Nice to Have a Wolf Around the House, Doubleday, 1977.
Allard, Harry
Irony. Satire. Stereotype

Jeanne-Marie Counts Her Sheep, Charles Scribner's, 1951.
Francoise (Seignobosc, Francoise)
Tone

Jeremy's Tail, Ashton Scholastic, 1990.
Ball, Duncan
Ambiguity. Inference. Irony

Jim and the Beanstalk, Coward-McCann, 1970.
Briggs, Raymond
Ambiguity. Parody. Pun. Tone

Judge (The), Farrar Straus Giroux, 1969.
Zemach, Harve
Caricature. Foreshadowing. Hyperbole. Poetic Justice. Satire. Theme

Julius the Baby of the World, Greenwillow, 1990.
Henkes, Kevin
Irony

Just Like Max, Knopf, 1990.
Ackerman, Karen
Flash-Forward

Just Plain Fancy, Bantam, 1990.
Polacco, Patricia
Foreshadowing. Pun

Keeping House, Macmillan, 1991.
Mahy, Margaret
Atmosphere. Hyperbole. Inference. Simile. Stereotype

*Kinda Blue, Little, Brown, 1993.
Grifalconi, Ann
Metaphor. Symbol. Tone

Lentil, Viking, 1940.
McCloskey, Robert
Foreshadowing

Lily and the Present, Houghton Mifflin, 1992.
Ross, Christine
Paradox

Lily Cupboard (The), HarperCollins, 1992.
Oppenheim, Shulamith Levy
Inference. Symbol

Little Blue and Little Yellow, Ivan
Obolensky, 1959.
Lionni, Leo
Symbol

Little Crooked Christmas Tree (The),
Scholastic, 1990.
Cutting, Michael
Paradox. Poetic Justice

Little Engine That Could (The), Platt &
Monk, 1954.
Piper, Watty
Onomatopoeia. Stereotype. Theme

Little House (The), Houghton Mifflin,
1942. [Caldecott Award]
Burton, Virginia Lee
Analogy. Foreshadowing. Personification

Little Island, Doubleday, 1946. [Caldecott
Award]
MacDonald, Golden
Imagery. Metaphor. Paradox. Simile

Little Penguin, Philomel, 1990.
Benson, Patrick
Theme

*Losing Uncle Tim, Albert Whitman,
1989.
Jordon, Mary Kate
Tone

Lunch, Henry Holt, 1992.
Fleming, Denise
Inference

Madeline, Viking, 1939.
Bemelmans, Ludwig
Paradox

Make Way for Ducklings, Viking, 1941.
[Caldecott Award]
McCloskey, Robert
**Caricature. Foreshadowing. Point-Of-
View**

Mama, Papa, and Baby Joe, Viking
Penguin, 1991.
Daly, Niki
Alliteration. Allusion. Pun. Tone

Mandy, Lothrop, Lee, & Shepard, 1991.
Booth, Barbara D.
Atmosphere. Point-Of-View

Many Moons, Harcourt Brace, 1943.
[Caldecott Award]
Thurber, James
Irony. Paradox

Masai and I, Four Winds Press, 1992.
Kroll, Virginia
Inference. Paradox

Matthew's Dream, Knopf, 1991.
Lionni, Leo
Analogy. Pun

Max, Macmillan, 1976.
Isadora, Rachel
Stereotype

May I Bring a Friend? Atheneum, 1964.
[Caldecott Award]
De Regniers, Beatrice Schenk
Hyperbole. Poetic Justice

Mei Li, Doubleday, 1938. [Caldecott
Award]
Handforth, Thomas
Ambiguity. Stereotype

Mike Mulligan and His Steam Shovel,
Houghton Mifflin, 1939.
Burton, Virginia Lee
Foreshadowing. Poetic Justice

Million Fish ... More or Less (A), Knopf,
1992.
McKissack, Patricia
Caricature. Foreshadowing. Hyperbole. Inference

Millions of Cats, Coward-McCann, 1928.
Gag, Wanda
Hyperbole. Paradox. Theme

Milton the Early Riser, E. P. Dutton, 1972.
Kraus, Robert
Hyperbole. Irony. Pun

Mirette on the High Wire, G. P. Putnam's,
1992. [Caldecott Award]
McCully, Emily Arnold
Atmosphere. Inference

Mole and Shrew Step Out, Atheneum,
1992.
Koller, Jackie French
Ambiguity. Pun

Monster Mama, Philomel, 1993.
  Rosenberg, Liz
  Ambiguity. Aphorism. Hyperbole. Inference. Simile
Moon Bear, Charles Scribner's, 1978.
  Asch, Frank
  Ambiguity. Irony
Moon Glows, Little, Brown, 1990.
  ver Dorn, Berthea
  Atmosphere
*Moon Was the Best (The), Greenwillow, 1993.
  Zolotow, Charlotte
  Atmosphere. Imagery
*Mountain (The), Doubleday, 1971.
  Parnall, Peter
  Irony. Satire. Theme
Mr. & Mrs. Pig's Evening Out, Atheneum, 1976.
  Rayner, Mary
  Inference
My Brown Bear Barney in Trouble, Greenwillow, 1993.
  Butler, Dorothy
  Inference
My Grandfather's Hat, Macmillan, 1992.
  Scheller, Melanie
  Flash-Forward. Symbol
My Noah's Ark, Harper & Row, 1978.
  Goffstein, M. B.
  Allusion. Atmosphere
Mystery of the Missing Red Mitten (The), Dial, 1974.
  Kellogg, Steven
  Flashback
Nanna Upstairs and Nanna Downstairs, G. P. Putnam's, 1973.
  DePaola, Tomie
  Atmosphere. Flash-Forward. Pun
Night Tree, Harcourt Brace Jovanovich, 1991.
  Bunting, Eve
  Foreshadowing
Nine Days to Christmas, Viking, 1959.
  [Caldecott Award]
  Ets, Marie Hall, and Aurora Labastida
  Atmosphere

No Star Nights, Knopf, 1989.
  Smucker, Anna Egan
  Tone
Noah's Cats and the Devil's Fire, Orchard Books, 1992.
  Olson, Arielle North
  Poetic Justice. Pun. Satire. Tone
Nobody Asked Me if I Wanted a Baby Sister, Dial, 1971.
  Alexander, Martha
  Irony
Nora's Duck, Philomel, 1991.
  Ichikawa, Satomi
  Personification
Nothing Ever Happens on My Block, Atheneum, 1966.
  Raskin, Ellen
  Parallel Story
Nurse Lugton's Curtain, Harcourt Brace Jovanovich, 1991.
  Woolf, Virginia
  Point-Of-View. Simile
Obadiah the Bold, Viking, 1965.
  Turkle, Brinton
  Inference
Old Hannibal and the Hurricane, Hyperion, 1991.
  Amoss, Berthe
  Alliteration. Hyperbole. Internal Rhyme
Oliver Button Is a Sissy, Harcourt Brace Jovanovich, 1979.
  DePaola, Tomie
  Stereotype
One Monday Morning, Charles Scribner's, 1967.
  Shulevitz, Uri
  Inference
One Morning in Maine, Viking, 1952.
  McCloskey, Robert
  Atmosphere. Inference
One of Three, Orchard Books, 1991.
  Johnson, Angela
  Atmosphere

One Small Blue Bead, Charles Scribner's, 1992.
Baylor, Byrd
Flashback. Flash-Forward

Our Puppy's Vacation, E. P. Dutton, 1987.
Brown, Ruth
Understatement

Over Back, HarperCollins, 1993.
Major, Beverly
Metaphor. Simile

Ox-Cart Man, Viking, 1979. [Caldecott Award]
Hall, Donald
Atmosphere

Petunia, Knopf, 1950.
Duvoisin, Roger
Aphorism. Irony. Symbol

*Phoebe's Revolt, Farrar Straus Giroux, 1968.
Babbitt, Natalie
Foreshadowing. Poetic Justice. Satire. Stereotype

Picnic (The), Dutton, 1992.
Brown, Ruth
Point-Of-View

Piggy in the Puddle (The), Macmillan, 1974.
Pomerantz, Charlotte
Satire

Pinkerton, Behave! Dial, 1979.
Kellogg, Steven
Ambiguity. Irony

Play with Me, Viking, 1955.
Ets, Marie Hall
Imagery. Inference. Irony

Plum Pudding for Christmas, Charles Scribner's, 1956.
Kahl, Virginia
Alliteration. Foreshadowing. Internal Rhyme. Irony. Understatement

Pocketful of Cricket (A), Holt Rinehart Winston, 1964.
Caudill, Rebecca
Atmosphere. Imagery

Porcelain Man (The), Little, Brown, 1976.
Kennedy, Richard
Inference. Tone. Understatement

Pot Luck, Lothrop, Lee, & Shepard, 1993.
Tobias, Tobi
Inference. Irony

·Prince Lachlan, Orchard Books, 1990.
Hilton, Nette
Understatement

*Princess, Greenwillow, 1993.
Wilsdorf, Anne
Ambiguity. Foreshadowing. Parody. Pun. Satire

Promise (The), HarperCollins, 1992.
Johnston, Tony
Flashback. Foreshadowing. Inference. Stereotype-Reverse

Proper Little Lady (A), Orchard Books, 1989.
Hilton, Nette
Satire

Quicksand Book (The), Holiday House, 1979.
DePaola, Tomie
Poetic Justice. Satire

Rain Drop Splash, Lothrop, Lee, & Shepard, 1946.
Tresselt, Alvin
Imagery

Rain Puddle (The), Lothrop, Lee, & Shepard, 1965.
Holl, Adelaide
Inference

Rainflowers, HarperCollins, 1992.
Turner, Ann
Imagery. Simile

Rat and the Tiger (The), G. P. Putnam's, 1993.
Kasza, Keiko
Foreshadowing. Irony

Return of Freddy Le Grand (The), Farrar Straus Giroux, 1992.
Agee, Jon
Foreshadowing. Understatement

Red Balloon (The), Doubleday, 1956.
Lamorisse, Albert
Atmosphere. Poetic Justice. Symbol

Rosie and the Rustlers, Farrar Straus
Giroux, 1989.
Gerrard, Roy
Internal Rhyme

Rosie's Walk, Macmillan, 1968.
Hutchins, Pat
**Foreshadowing. Irony. Poetic Justice.
Satire. Stereotype**

Roxaboxen, Lothrop, Lee, & Shepard,
1991.
McLerran, Alice
Tone

Ruby the Copycat, Scholastic, 1991.
Rathmann, Peggy
Foreshadowing. Theme

Runaway Bunny (The), Harper & Row,
1942.
Brown, Margaret Wise
Theme

Sachiko Means Happiness, Children's Book
Press, 1990.
Sakai, Kimiko
Foreshadowing. Inference

Sam, Bangs, and Moonshine, Holt,
Rinehart and Winston, 1966.
[Caldecott Award]
Ness, Evaline
Tone

Samuel Todd's Book of Great Inventions,
Atheneum, 1991.
Konigsburg, E. L.
Point-Of-View

Scrap Doll (The), HarperCollins, 1991.
Rosenberg, Liz
Inference. Theme

Search for the Ten-Winged Dragon (The),
Doubleday, 1990.
Karl, Jean
Theme

*She Come Bringing Me That Little Baby
Girl*, Lippincott, 1974.
Greenfield, Eloise
Inference

Sheep in a Shop, Houghton Mifflin, 1991.
Shaw, Nancy
Alliteration. Allusion

Shortcut, Greenwillow, 1992.
Crews, Donald
**Atmosphere. Foreshadowing.
Inference**

Shrek, Farrar Straus Giroux, 1990.
Steig, William
**Alliteration. Hyperbole. Internal
Rhyme**

Siegfried, Bantam, 1991.
Stanley, Diane
Point-Of-View

Sign Painter's Dream (The), Crown, 1993.
Roth, Roger
Allusion

Silly Tails, Atheneum, 1993.
Mark, Jan
Foreshadowing. Personification

Sing on New Snow, A Delicious Tale,
Macmillan, 1991.
Yee, Paul
Paradox

*Sky Dogs, Harcourt Brace Jovanovich,
1990.
Yolen, Jane
Onomatopoeia. Point-Of-View

Snail Mail, Collins, 1986.
Edwards, Hazel
**Alliteration. Inference. Irony. Poetic
Justice. Pun**

Snowy, Dial, 1992.
Doherty, Berlie
Simile

Snowy Day (The), Viking, 1962.
[Caldecott Award]
Keats, Ezra Jack
Atmosphere. Imagery

Solomon's Secret, Dial, 1989.
Pirotta, Saviour
Flashback

*Somebody and the Three Blairs, Orchard
Books, 1991.
Tolhurst, Marilyn
Parody. Pun. Understatement

Somebody Loves You, Mr. Hatch, Bradbury,
1991.
Spinelli, Eileen
Inference. Irony

Someday a Tree, Houghton Mifflin, 1993.
Bunting, Eve
Foreshadowing. Inference

Song of the Boat, Thomas Crowell, 1975.
Graham, Lorenz
Atmosphere

Soup Bone (The), Harcourt Brace
Jovanovich, 1990.
Johnston, Tony
Poetic Justice

Spooky Tail of Prewitt Peacock (The),
Houghton Mifflin, 1972.
Peet, Bill
Pun

Stevie, Harper & Row, 1969.
Steptoe, John
Inference. Irony. Paradox

Stone Men, Greenwillow, 1993.
Weiss, Nicki
Flashback

Story about Ping (The), Viking, 1933.
Flack, Marjorie, and Kurt Weise
Theme

Story of Ferdinand (The), Viking, 1936.
Leaf, Munro
Foreshadowing. Irony. Satire

Strega Nona, Prentice-Hall, 1975.
DePaola, Tomie
Foreshadowing. Poetic Justice. Tone

Sun's Day (The), Harper & Row, 1989.
Gerstein, Mordicai
Alliteration

Swimmy, Pantheon, 1963.
Lionni, Leo
Analogy

Sylvester and the Magic Pebble, Simon &
Shuster, 1969. [Caldecott Award]
Steig, William
**Foreshadowing. Imagery. Personification. Pun. Stereotype. Symbol.
Theme**

Tale of Peter Rabbit (The), Frederick
Warne, 1902.
Potter, Beatrix
**Foreshadowing. Imagery. Irony.
Metaphor. Onomatopoeia. Poetic
Justice. Understatement**

*Tale of the Mandarin Ducks (The),
Dutton, 1990.
Paterson, Katherine
Metaphor. Theme

Tapestry Cats (The), Little, Brown, 1992.
Turnbull, Ann
Ambiguity. Inference. Simile

Tar Beach, Crown, 1991.
Ringgold, Faith
Allusion. Metaphor. Symbol

Tenrec's Twigs, Philomel, 1989.
Kitchen, Bert
Personification

Then the Troll Heard the Squeak, Lothrop,
Lee, & Shepard, 1991.
Hawkes, Kevin
Poetic Justice

There's a Nightmare in My Closet, Dial,
1968.
Mayer, Mercer
Tone

Three Brothers (The), G. P. Putnam's,
1991.
Croll, Carolyn
Paradox. Theme

Three Good Blankets, Atheneum, 1990.
Luttrell, Ida
Paradox

*Through the Mickle Woods, Little, Brown,
1992.
Gregory, Valiska
**Aphorism. Atmosphere. Inference.
Metaphor. Pun. Simile. Symbol.
Theme**

Tidy Lady, Harcourt Brace Jovanovich,
1989.
Lindbergh, Anne
Hyperbole

Tidy Titch, Greenwillow, 1991.
Hutchins, Pat
Foreshadowing

Tiger, Candlewick Press, 1992.
Allen, Judy
Inference. Irony. Satire. Stereotype

Widow's Broom (The), Houghton Mifflin, 1992.
Van Allsburg, Chris
Allusion. Inference. Stereotype

William's Doll, Harper & Row, 1972.
Zolotow, Charlotte
Stereotype

Wing Shop (The), Holiday House, 1991.
Woodruff, Elvira
Foreshadowing

Winter Whale, Morrow, 1991.
Ryder, Joanne
Imagery. Point-Of-View

World That Jack Built (The), Dutton, 1991.
Brown, Ruth
Atmosphere

Yo, Hungry Wolf! A Nursery Rap, Doubleday, 1993.
Vozar, David
Internal Rhyme. Tone

**Your Own Best Secret Place*, Charles Scribner's, 1979.
Baylor, Byrd
Imagery. Theme. Tone

ALL-AGES RESOURCES

* * * * * * * * * *

... *Along Came Eric*, 1991
    Clarke, Gus
Angel for Solomon Singer (An), 1992
    Rylant, Cynthia
Annie and the Old One, 1971
    Miles, Miska
Crow Boy, 1955
    Yashima, Taro
Duffy and the Devil, 1973 [Caldecott
    Award]
    Zemach, Harve
Emily, 1992
    Bedard, Michael
Encounter, 1992
    Yolen, Jane
Father Christmas, 1973
    Briggs, Raymond
First Song Ever Sung (The), 1993
    Melmed, Laura Krauss
Fish and Flamingo, 1993
    Carlstrom, Nancy White
Fortune-Tellers (The), 1992
    Alexander, Lloyd
Frog Prince Continued (The), 1991
    Scieszka, Jon
Grandfather's Journey, 1993 [Caldecott
    Award]
    Say, Allen

Hawk, I'm Your Brother, 1976
    Baylor, Byrd
Kinda Blue, 1993
    Grifalconi, Ann
Losing Uncle Tim, 1989
    Jordon, Mary Kate
Moon Was the Best (The), 1993
    Zolotow, Charlotte
Mountain (The), 1971
    Parnall, Peter
Phoebe's Revolt, 1968
    Babbitt, Natalie
Princess, 1993
    Wilsdorf, Anne
Sky Dogs, 1990
    Yolen, Jane
Somebody and the Three Blairs, 1991
    Tolhurst, Marilyn
Tale of the Mandarin Ducks (The), 1990
    Paterson, Katherine
Through the Mickle Woods, 1992
    Gregory, Valiska
Tree of Cranes, 1991
    Say, Allen
True Story of the Three Little Pigs (The),
    1989
    Scieszka, Jon
Your Own Best Secret Place, 1979
    Baylor, Byrd

ARTISTIC STYLES
AND TECHNIQUES
USED IN
RESOURCES

❋ ❋ ❋ ❋ ❋ ❋ ❋ ❋ ❋ ❋

CARTOON

*Alexander and the Terrible, Horrible, No
Good, Very Bad Day*
Viorst, Judith

*... Along Came Eric
Clarke, Gus

Amazing Bone (The)
Steig, William

Anatole
Titus, Eve

Andy and the Lion
Daugherty, James

Anytime Mapleson and the Hungry Bears
Gerstein, Mordicai

Be Nice to Spiders
Graham, Margaret Bloy

Bear's Bicycle (The)
McLeod, Emile W.

Bedtime for Frances
Hoban, Russell

Benjamin and Tulip
Wells, Rosemary

Bike Trip
Maestro, Betsy

Black and White
Macauley, David
(and Impressionism)

Blackboard Bear
Alexander, Martha

Blueberries for Sal
McCloskey, Robert

*Blumpoe the Grumpoe Meets Arnold the
Cat*
Okimoto, Jean Davies

Bootsie Barker Bites
Bottner, Barbara

Boy Who Was Followed Home (The)
Mahy, Margaret

Caps for Sale
Slobodkina, Esphyr

Careful with That Ball, Eugene!
Riddle, Tohby

Cat in the Hat (The)
Seuss, Dr.

Cataract of Lodore (The)
Southey, Robert

Chanticleer and the Fox
Chaucer, Geoffrey, as adapted by
Barbara Cooney

Chicken Book (The)
Williams, Garth
(and Expressionism)

Chrysanthemum
  Henkes, Kevin
Church Cat Abroad (The)
  Oakley, Graham
Circus Baby (The)
  Petersham, Maud, and Miska
  Petersham
Coney Tale (A)
  Ratz de Tagyos, Paul
Corduroy
  Freeman, Don
Cowboy and the Black-Eyed Pea (The)
  Johnston, Tony
Dandelion
  Freeman, Don
Day We Saw the Sun Come Up (The)
  Goudey, Alice E.
  (and Impressionism)
Dirty Dave
  Hilton, Nette
Dog and Cat
  Reiser, Lynn
Doodle Flute
  Pinkwater, Daniel
Duffy and the Devil
  Zemach, Harve
  (and Folk)
Each Peach Pear Plum
  Ahlberg, Janet, and Allan Ahlberg
Elephant and Crocodile
  Velthuijs, Max
Elmer Blunt's Open House
  Novak, Matt
Empty Lot (The)
  Fife, Dale H.
Engelbert the Elephant
  Paxton, Tom
Eppie M. Says ...
  Dunrea, Olivier
  (and Surrealism)
*Father Christmas
  Briggs, Raymond
Father Like That (A)
  Zolotow, Charlotte

Fox Tale
  Abolafia, Yossi
George and Martha
  Marshall, James
Georgie
  Bright, Robert
Gilberto and the Wind
  Ets, Marie Hall
Go Fish
  Dickens, Lucy
Goblin Walk
  Johnston, Tony
Guess Who's Just Moved in Next Door?
  McNaughton, Colin
Happy Lion (The)
  Fatio, Louise
Harold and the Purple Crayon
  Johnson, Crockett
Harry the Dirty Dog
  Zion, Gene
  (and Naive)
Henry's Happy Birthday
  Keller, Holly
How Do You Hide a Monster?
  Kahl, Virginia
How the Grinch Stole Christmas
  Seuss, Dr.
Hugh Can Do
  Armstrong, Jennifer
I Can't Said the Ant
  Cameron, Polly
It's So Nice to Have a Wolf Around the House
  Allard, Harry
Jim and the Beanstalk
  Briggs, Raymond
Julius the Baby of the World
  Henkes, Kevin
Lentil
  McCloskey, Robert
  (and Impressionism)
Lily and the Present
  Ross, Christine
Little Engine That Could (The)
  Piper, Watty

Madeline
  Bemelmans, Ludwig
  (and Naive)
Make Way for Ducklings
  McCloskey, Robert
Mama, Papa, and Baby Joe
  Daly, Niki
Many Moons
  Thurber, James
  (and Naive)
Max
  Isadora, Rachel
Mike Mulligan and His Steam Shovel
  Burton, Virginia Lee
  (and Naive)
Millions of Cats
  Gag, Wanda
  (and Folk)
Milton the Early Riser
  Kraus, Robert
Mole and Shrew Step Out
  Koller, Jackie French
Moon Bear
  Asch, Frank
  (and Naive)
*Mountain (The)
  Parnall, Peter
  (and Expressionism)
Mr. & Mrs. Pig's Evening Out
  Rayner, Mary
My Brown Bear Barney in Trouble
  Butler, Dorothy
My Noah's Ark
  Goffstein, M. B.
  (and Naive)
Mystery of the Missing Red Mitten (The)
  Kellogg, Steven
Nanna Upstairs and Nanna Downstairs
  De Paola, Tomie
Nobody Asked Me if I Wanted a Baby Sister
  Alexander, Martha
Nora's Duck
  Ichikawa, Satomi
Nothing Ever Happens on My Block
  Raskin, Ellen

Old Hannibal and the Hurricane
  Amoss, Berthe
Oliver Button Is a Sissy
  De Paola, Tomie
One Monday Morning
  Shulevitz, Uri
  (and Impressionism)
One Morning in Maine
  McCloskey, Robert
  (and Impressionism)
Petunia
  Duvoisin, Roger
*Phoebe's Revolt
  Babbitt, Natalie
Piggy in the Puddle (The)
  Pomerantz, Charlotte
Pinkerton, Behave!
  Kellogg, Steven
Play with Me
  Ets, Marie Hall
  (and Naive)
Plum Pudding for Christmas
  Kahl, Virginia
Porcelain Man (The)
  Kennedy, Richard
Pot Luck
  Tobias, Tobi
Prince Lachlan
  Hilton, Nette
*Princess
  Wilsdorf, Anne
Proper Little Lady (A)
  Hilton, Nette
Quicksand Book (The)
  De Paola, Tomie
Rain Drop Splash
  Tresselt, Alvin
  (and Naive)
Rat and the Tiger (The)
  Kasza, Keiko
Return of Freddy Le Grand (The)
  Agee, Jon
Ruby the Copycat
  Rathmann, Peggy

Runaway Bunny (The)
  Brown, Margaret Wise
  (and Impressionism)
Scrap Doll (The)
  Rosenberg, Liz
Sheep in a Shop
  Shaw, Nancy
Shrek
  Steig, William
Silly Tails
  Mark, Jan
*Somebody and the Three Blairs
  Tolhurst, Marilyn
Somebody Loves You, Mr. Hatch
  Spinelli, Eileen
  (and Naive)
Soup Bone (The)
  Johnston, Tony
Spooky Tail of Prewitt Peacock (The)
  Peet, Bill
Stone Men
  Weiss, Nicki
  (and Naive)
Story about Ping (The)
  Flack, Marjorie, and Kurt Weise
Story of Ferdinand (The)
  Leaf, Munro
  (and Expressionism)
Strega Nona
  De Paola, Tomie
  (and Folk)
Sun's Day (The)
  Gerstein, Mordicai

Sylvester and the Magic Pebble
  Steig, William
Tale of Peter Rabbit (The)
  Potter, Beatrix
  (and Realism)
There's a Nightmare in My Closet
  Mayer, Mercer
Tidy Titch
  Hutchins, Pat
Time to Get Out of the Bath, Shirley
  Burningham, John
  (and Impressionism)
Treed by a Pride of Irate Lions
  Zimelman, Nathan
Trouble in Paradise
  Backovsky, Jan
*True Story of the Three Little Pigs (The)
  Scieszka, Jon
  (and Collage)
UFO Diary
  Kitamura, Satoshi
Walter's Magic Wand
  Houghton, Eric
What Game Shall We Play?
  Hutchins, Pat
  (and Folk)
William's Doll
  Zolotow, Charlotte
  (and Impressionism)
Yo, Hungry Wolf! A Nursery Rap
  Vozar, David

COLLAGE

Alexander and the Wind-Up Mouse
  Lionni, Leo
Frederick
  Lionni, Leo
Inch by Inch
  Lionni, Leo
Little Crooked Christmas Tree (The)
  Cutting, Michael
Matthew's Dream
  Lionni, Leo

Snowy Day (The)
  Keats, Ezra Jack
Swimmy
  Lionni, Leo
*True Story of the Three Little Pigs (The)
  Scieszka, Jon
  (and Cartoon)
Web in the Grass (The)
  Freschet, Berniece

EXPRESSIONISM

Alfalfa Hill
  Parnall, Peter

Alison's Zinnia
  Lobel, Anita

Angus and the Cat
  Flack, Marjorie

Angus and the Ducks
  Flack, Marjorie

Angus Lost
  Flack, Marjorie

Annie and the Old One
  Miles, Miska

Baker's Portrait (A)
  Edwards, Michelle

Banshee (The)
  Ackerman, Karen

Ben's Trumpet
  Isadora, Rachel
  (and Impressionism and Realism)

Cat Next Door (The)
  Wright, Betty Ren
  (and Realism)

Cecil's Story
  Lyon, George Ella

Charles T. McBiddle
  Glass, Andrew

Charlie's House
  Schermbrucker, Reviva

Chicken Book (The)
  Williams, Garth
  (and Cartoon)

Country Crossing
  Aylesworth, Jim

Cuckoo Bird (The)
  Corbalis, Judy

Elijah's Angel
  Rosen, Michael J.

Emperor and the Kite (The)
  Yolen, Jane
  (and Folk)

Encounter
  Yolen, Jane
  (and Realism)

Everybody Needs a Rock
  Baylor, Byrd
  (and Surrealism)

Everyone Knows What a Dragon Looks Like
  Williams, Jay
  (and Folk)

First Pink Light
  Greenfield, Eloise

Fish and Flamingo
  Carlstrom, Nancy White

Fog
  Fowler, Susi Gregg

Fortune-Tellers (The)
  Alexander, Lloyd
  (and Realism)

Frog Prince Continued (The)
  Scieszka, Jon

Ghost Catcher
  Haseley, Dennis
  (and Folk)

Goggles
  Keats, Ezra Jack
  (and Impressionism)

Good Times on Grandfather Mountain
  Martin, Jacqueline Briggs

Goodbye Geese
  Carlstrom, Nancy White

Grandfather's Journey
  Say, Allen
  (and Folk and Impressionism)

Grandpa's Town
  Nomura, Tukaaki
  (and Folk)

Great Fish (The)
  Parnall, Peter

Greyling
  Yolen, Jane

Hawk, I'm Your Brother
  Baylor, Byrd

Judge (The)
  Zemach, Harve

Just Plain Fancy
  Polacco, Patricia

Little Blue and Little Yellow
  Lionni, Leo
Little Penguin
  Benson, Patrick
Lunch
  Fleming, Denise
Masai and I
  Kroll, Virginia
  (and Realism)
Million Fish ... More or Less (A)
  McKissack, Patricia
  (and Impressionism)
Monster Mama
  Rosenberg, Liz
*Mountain (The)
  Parnall, Peter
  (and Cartoon)
Noah's Cats and the Devil's Fire
  Olson, Arielle North
Nurse Lugton's Curtain
  Woolf, Virginia
Picnic (The)
  Brown, Ruth
  (and Impressionism and Realism)
Pocketful of Cricket (A)
  Caudill, Rebecca
Rosie and the Rustlers
  Gerrard, Roy
Rosie's Walk
  Hutchins, Pat
Sam, Bangs, & Moonshine
  Ness, Evaline
Samuel Todd's Book of Great Inventions
  Konigsburg, E. L.
  (and Impressionism)
Search for the Ten-Winged Dragon (The)
  Karl, Jean
  (and Realism)
She Come Bringing Me That Little Baby Girl
  Greenfield, Eloise
Siegfried
  Stanley, Diane
Sign Painter's Dream (The)
  Roth, Roger

Sing on New Snow, a Delicious Tale
  Yee, Paul
  (and Impressionism)
*Sky Dogs
  Yolen, Jane
  (and Realism)
Solomon's Secret
  Pirotta, Saviour
Stevie
  Steptoe, John
Story of Ferdinand (The)
  Leaf, Munro
  (and Cartoon)
Then the Troll Heard the Squeak
  Hawkes, Kevin
Three Good Blankets
  Luttrell, Ida
*Through the Mickle Woods
  Gregory, Valiska
  (and Realism)
Tidy Lady
  Lindbergh, Anne
Time Train
  Fleischman, Paul
Welcome to the Green House
  Yolen, Jane
  (and Realism)
When Spring Comes
  Warnock, Natalie Kinsey
Where the Wild Things Are
  Sendak, Maurice
Where's Our Mama?
  Goode, Diane
Who Is the Beast?
  Baker, Keith
Why Mosquitoes Buzz in People's Ears
  Aardema, Verna
  (and Folk)
Winter Whale
  Ryder, Joanne
*Your Own Best Secret Place
  Baylor, Byrd

FOLK

*Duffy and the Devil
  Zemach, Harve
  (and Cartoon)

Emperor and the Kite (The)
  Yolen, Jane
  (and Expressionism)

Everyone Asked about You
  Gross, Theodore Faro

Everyone Knows What a Dragon Looks Like
  Williams, Jay
  (and Expressionism)

Feathers for Lunch
  Ehlert, Lois

Ghost Catcher
  Haseley, Dennis
  (and Expressionism)

Girl Who Loved Wild Horses (The)
  Goble, Paul

Golden Coin (The)
  Ada, Alma Flor

*Grandfather's Journey
  Say, Allen
  (and Expressionism and Impressionism)

Grandpa's Town
  Nomura, Tukaaki
  (and Expressionism)

Harlequin and the Gift of Many Colors
  Charlip, Remy, and Burton Supree

Iktomi and the Berries, a Plains Indian Story
  Goble, Paul

Jeremy's Tail
  Ball, Duncan

Mei Li
  Handforth, Thomas
  (and Impressionism)

Millions of Cats
  Gag, Wanda
  (and Cartoon)

Nine Days to Christmas
  Ets, Marie Hall

Roxaboxen
  McLerran, Alice

Song of the Boat
  Graham, Lorenz

Strega Nona
  De Paola, Tomie
  (and Cartoon)

*Tale of the Mandarin Ducks (The)
  Paterson, Katherine

Three Brothers (The)
  Croll, Carolyn

*Tree of Cranes
  Say, Allen
  (and Realism)

What Game Shall We Play?
  Hutchins, Pat
  (and Cartoon)

Why Mosquitoes Buzz in People's Ears
  Aardema, Verna
  (and Expressionism)

IMPRESSIONISM

Albert's Toothache
  Williams, Barbara

All the Lights in the Night
  Levine, Arthur A.

*Angel for Solomon Singer (An)
  Rylant, Cynthia

Ben's Trumpet
  Isadora, Rachel
  (and Expressionism and Realism)

Biggest Bear (The)
  Ward, Lynd
  (and Realism)

Black and White
  Macauley, David
  (and Cartoon)

Cherry Tree (The)
  Ikeda, Daisaku

Clever Bill
  Nicholson, William
*Crow Boy
  Yashima, Taro
Dawn
  Shulevitz, Uri
Day We Saw the Sun Come Up (The)
  Goudey, Alice E.
  (and Cartoon)
Evan's Corner
  Hill, Elizabeth Starr
*First Song Ever Sung (The)
  Melmed, Laura Krauss
Four Dollars and Fifty Cents
  Kimmel, Eric A.
Garden of Abdul Gasazi (The)
  Van Allsburg, Chris
Goggles
  Keats, Ezra Jack
  (and Expressionism)
*Grandfather's Journey
  Say, Allen
  (and Folk and Expressionism)
Hide and Seek Fog
  Tresselt, Alvin
  (and Naive)
High in the Mountains
  Radin, Ruth Yaffe
Hoagie's Rifle-Gun
  Miles, Miska
  (and Realism)
Home Place
  Dragonwagon, Crescent
House That Bob Built (The)
  Stern, Robert A. M.
I'll See You in My Dreams
  Jukes, Mavis
Just Like Max
  Ackerman, Karen
  (and Realism)
Keeping House
  Mahy, Margaret
*Kinda Blue
  Grifalconi, Ann

Lentil
  McCloskey, Robert
  (and Cartoon)
Lily Cupboard (The)
  Oppenheim, Shulamith Levy
Little Island
  MacDonald, Golden
Mandy
  Booth, Barbara D.
May I Bring a Friend?
  De Regniers, Beatrice Schenk
Mei Li
  Handforth, Thomas
  (and Folk)
Million Fish ... More or Less (A)
  McKissack, Patricia
  (and Expressionism)
Mirette on the High Wire
  McCully, Emily
Moon Glows
  ver Dorn, Berthea
My Grandfather's Hat
  Scheller, Melanie
No Star Nights
  Smucker, Anna Egan
Obadiah the Bold
  Turkle, Brinton
One Monday Morning
  Shulevitz, Uri
  (and Cartoon)
One Morning in Maine
  McCloskey, Robert
  (and Cartoon)
One Small Blue Bead
  Baylor, Byrd
  (and Realism)
Our Puppy's Vacation
  Brown, Ruth
  (and Realism)
Over Back
  Major, Beverly
Picnic (The)
  Brown, Ruth
  (and Expressionism and Realism)

Promise (The)
Johnston, Tony
Rainflowers
Turner, Ann
Runaway Bunny (The)
Brown, Margaret Wise
(and Cartoon)
Sachiko Means Happiness
Sakai, Kimiko
(and Realism)
Samuel Todd's Book of Great Inventions
Konigsburg, E. L.
(and Expressionism)
Shortcut
Crews, Donald
Sing on New Snow, a Delicious Tale
Yee, Paul
(and Expressionism)
Snowy
Doherty, Berlie
Someday a Tree
Bunting, Eve

Time of Wonder
McCloskey, Robert
Time to Get Out of the Bath, Shirley
Burningham, John
(and Cartoon)
Umbrella
Yashima, Taro
Up North at the Cabin
Chall, Marsha Wilson
When the Rain Stops
Cole, Sheila
White Wave, A Chinese Tale
Wolkstein, Diane
Widow's Broom (The)
Van Allsburg, Chris
William's Doll
Zolotow, Charlotte
(and Cartoon)
Wing Shop (The)
Woodruff, Elvira
World That Jack Built (The)
Brown, Ruth

NAIVE

Blabbermouths (The)
Mantinband, Gerda
Emily
Bedard, Michael
Fortunately
Charlip, Remy
Gracie
Ballard, Robin
Harry the Dirty Dog
Zion, Gene
(and Cartoon)
Hide and Seek Fog
Tresselt, Alvin
(and Impressionism)
Jeanne-Marie Counts Her Sheep
Francoise
Little House (The)
Burton, Virginia Lee

Madeline
Bemelmans, Ludwig
(and Cartoon)
Many Moons
Thurber, James
(and Cartoon)
Mike Mulligan and His Steam Shovel
Burton, Virginia Lee
(and Cartoon)
Moon Bear
Asch, Frank
(and Cartoon)
My Noah's Ark
Goffstein, M. B.
(and Cartoon)
Ox-Cart Man
Hall, Donald
Play with Me
Ets, Marie Hall
(and Cartoon)

Rain Drop Splash
  Tresselt, Alvin
  (and Cartoon)
Rain Puddle (The)
  Holl, Adelaide
Roxaboxen
  McLarren, Alice
Somebody Loves You, Mr. Hatch
  Spinelli, Eileen
  (and Cartoon)

Stone Men
  Weiss, Nicki
  (and Cartoon)
Tapestry Cats (The)
  Turnbull, Ann
Tar Beach
  Ringgold, Faith
White Snow Bright Snow
  Tresselt, Alvin

PHOTOGRAPHY

Red Balloon (The)
  Lamorisse, Albert

Moon was the Best (The)
  Zolotow, Charlotte

REALISM

Ben's Trumpet
  Isadora, Rachel
  (and Expressionism and Impressionism)
Biggest Bear (The)
  Ward, Lynd
  (and Impressionism)
Cabbage Rose
  Helldorfer, M. C.
Cat Next Door (The)
  Wright, Betty Ren
  (and Expressionism)
Changes
  Browne, Anthony
  (and Surrealism)
Encounter
  Yolen, Jane
  (and Expressionism)
Fishing at Long Pond
  George, William T.
Fortune-Tellers (The)
  Alexander, Lloyd
  (and Expressionism)
Hoagie's Rifle-Gun
  Miles, Miska
  (and Impressionism)

Just Like Max
  Ackerman, Karen
  (and Impressionism)
Losing Uncle Tim
  Jordon, Mary Kate
Masai and I
  Kroll, Virginia
  (and Expressionism)
Night Tree
  Bunting, Eve
One of Three
  Johnson, Angela
One Small Blue Bead
  Baylor, Byrd
  (and Impressionism)
Our Puppy's Vacation
  Brown, Ruth
  (and Impressionism)
Picnic (The)
  Brown, Ruth
  (and Expressionism and Impressionism)
Sachiko Means Happiness
  Sakai, Kimiko
  (and Impressionism)

Search for the Ten-Winged Dragon (The)
   Karl, Jean
   (and Expressionism)
Sky Dogs
   Yolen, Jane
   (and Expressionism)
Snail Mail
   Edwards, Hazel
Tale of Peter Rabbit (The)
   Potter, Beatrix
   (and Cartoon)
Tenrec's Twigs
   Kitchen, Bert
Through the Mickle Woods
   Gregory, Valiska
   (and Expressionism)

Tiger
   Allen, Judy
Tree of Cranes
   Say, Allen
   (and Folk)
Wall (The)
   Bunting, Eve
Warm as Wool
   Sanders, Scott Russell
Welcome to the Green House
   Yolen, Jane
   (and Expressionism)

SURREALISM

Changes
   Browne, Anthony
   (and Realism)
Eppie M. Says ...
   Dunrea, Olivier
   (and Cartoon)

Everybody Needs a Rock
   Baylor, Byrd
   (and Expressionism)

CURRICULUM TIE-INS FOR RESOURCES

❖ ❖ ❖ ❖ ❖ ❖ ❖ ❖ ❖

GEOGRAPHY

American Southwest
Your Own Best Secret Place, Baylor, Byrd

Amish Culture
Just Plain Fancy, Polacco, Patricia

East African Culture
Masai and I, Kroll, Virginia

Japanese Culture
Grandpa's Town, Nomura, Tukaaki

Maine
One Morning in Maine, McCloskey, Robert

Mexican Culture
Nine Days to Christmas, Ets, Marie Hall [Caldecott Award]

Native American Navajo Culture
Annie and the Old One, Miles, Miska

Paris, France
The Moon Was the Best, Zolotow, Charlotte

Pennsylvania Dutch Culture
The Three Brothers, Croll, Carolyn

West African Culture
Song of the Boat, Graham, Lorenz

HEALTH AND SAFETY

Accident Prevention
The Bear's Bicycle, McLeod, Emile W.
Bike Trip, Maestro, Betsy
Rosie's Walk, Hutchins, Pat

AIDS
Losing Uncle Tim, Jordon, Mary Kate

Alzheimer's Disease
Sachiko Means Happiness, Sakai, Kimiko

Hearing Impaired
Mandy, Booth, Barbara D.

Maturation
One Morning in Maine, McCloskey,
  Robert

Stranger Danger
The Cuckoo Bird, Corbalis, Judy
Mr. & Mrs. Pig's Evening Out, Rayner,
  Mary

HISTORY

American Chinatown Culture-1900s
Sing on New Snow, A Delicious Tale, Yee,
  Paul

Columbus-Discovery of America
Encounter, Yolen, Jane

German Occupation-Netherlands
The Lily Cupboard, Oppenheim,
  Shulamith Levy

Harlequin-Clown
Harlequin and the Gift of Many Colors,
  Charlip, Remy

Jewish Emigration from Russia, 1914
All the Lights in the Night, Levine, Arthur
A.

Medieval Times
Plum Pudding for Christmas, Kahl, Virginia

Native Americans
The Girl Who Loved Wild Horses, Goble,
  Paul [Caldecott Award]

*Iktomi and the Berries, a Plains Indian
  Story*, Goble, Paul
Sky Dogs, Yolen, Jane

**Nineteenth-Century America—
Frontier Life**
The Biggest Bear, Ward, Lynd [Caldecott
  Award]
Ox-Cart Man, Hall, Donald
Warm as Wool, Sanders, Scott Russell

**Nineteenth-Century New England—
Quaker Life**
Obadiah the Bold, Turkle, Brinton

Pre-History
One Small Blue Bead, Baylor, Byrd
Time Train, Fleischman, Paul

Steel Mills-America
No Star Nights, Smucker, Anna Egan

Vietnam Memorial
The Wall, Bunting, Eve

LITERATURE

Emily Dickinson
Emily, Bedard, Michael

Pacing of Story
Make Way for Ducklings, McCloskey,
  Robert [Caldecott Award]

Plot Balance
Fish and Flamingo, Carlstrom, Nancy
White

Pourquoi Story
Noah's Cats and the Devil Fire, Olson,
  Arielle North

MUSIC

Jazz
Ben's Trumpet, Isadora, Rachel

SCIENCE

Animal Health
Nora's Duck, Ichikawa, Satomi

Architectural Design
The House That Bob Built, Stern, Robert

Bird and Plant Identification
Feathers for Lunch, Ehlert, Lois

Ecology
The Empty Lot, Fife, Dale H.
Fishing at Long Pond, George, William T.
The Great Fish, Parnall, Peter
High in the Mountains, Radin, Ruth Yaffe
The Mountain, Parnall, Peter
Over Back, Major, Beverly
Play with Me, Ets, Marie Hall
A Pocketful of Cricket, Caudill, Rebecca
The Quicksand Book, DePaola, Tomie
Someday a Tree, Bunting, Eve
Time of Wonder, McCloskey, Robert
   [Caldecott Award]
Up North at the Cabin, Chall, Marsha
   Wilson
Welcome to the Green House, Yolen, Jane
When Spring Comes, Warnock, Natalie
   Kinsey
Winter Whale, Ryder, Joanne
The World That Jack Built, Brown, Ruth

Endangered Species
Tiger, Allen, Judy

Environment
Alfalfa Hill, Parnall, Peter
Dawn, Shulevitz, Uri
The Great Fish, Parnall, Peter
Over Back, Major, Beverly
The Quicksand Book, DePaola, Tomie

Rain Drop Splash, Tresselt, Alvin
White Snow Bright Snow, Tresselt, Alvin
   [Caldecott Award]
The World That Jack Built, Brown, Ruth

Geology
The Cataract of Lodore, Southey, Robert
Little Island, MacDonald, Golden
   [Caldecott Award]
Rain Drop Splash, Tresselt, Alvin

Lever and Pulley
I Can't Said the Ant, Cameron, Polly

Machine Technology
Mike Mulligan and His Steam Shovel,
   Burton, Virginia Lee

Measurement
Inch by Inch, Lionni, Leo

Meteorology
Dawn, Shulevitz, Uri
Gilberto and the Wind, Ets, Marie Hall
Rain Drop Splash, Tresselt, Alvin

Quicksand
The Quicksand Book, DePaola, Tomie

Rain
Rain Drop Splash, Tresselt, Alvin
Rainflowers, Turner, Ann
When the Rain Stops, Cole, Sheila

Rainforest
Welcome to the Green House, Yolen, Jane

Seasons-Spring
When Spring Comes, Warnock, Natalie Kinsey

Seasons-Winter
Alfalfa Hill, Parnall, Peter
Goodbye Geese, Carlstrom, Nancy White
The Snowy Day, Keats, Ezra Jack
White Snow Bright Snow, Tresselt, Alvin [Caldecott Award]

Spiders
Be Nice to Spiders, Graham, Margaret Bloy

The Web in the Grass, Freschet, Berniece

Sun
Dawn, Shulevitz, Uri
The Day We Saw the Sun Come Up, Goudey, Alice E.
The Sun's Day, Gerstein, Mordicai

Trees
Someday a Tree, Bunting, Eve

Wind
Gilberto and the Wind, Ets, Marie Hall

SOCIAL SCIENCE

Acceptance and Respect
Albert's Toothache, Williams, Barbara
Angus and the Cat, Flack, Marjorie
A Baker's Portrait, Edwards, Michelle
The Circus Baby, Petersham, Maud and Miska Petersham
*Crow Boy, Yashima, Taro
George and Martha, Marshall, James
Jeanne-Marie Counts Her Sheep, Francoise
*Kinda Blue, Grifalconi, Ann
Little Penguin, Benson, Patrick
May I Bring a Friend? DeRegniers, Beatrice Schenk [Caldecott Award]
My Grandfather's Hat, Scheller, Melanie
Oliver Button Is a Sissy, DePaola, Tomie
One of Three, Johnson, Angela
*Phoebe's Revolt, Babbitt, Natalie
Ruby the Copycat, Rathmann, Peggy
The Runaway Bunny, Brown, Margaret Wise
Shrek, Steig, William
The Spooky Tail of Prewitt Peacock, Peet, Bill
The Story of Ferdinand, Leaf, Munro
Where's Our Mama? Goode, Diane
William's Doll, Zolotow, Charlotte
*Your Own Best Secret Place, Baylor, Byrd

Aging
*Annie and the Old One, Miles, Miska

My Grandfather's Hat, Scheller, Melanie
My Noah's Ark, Goffstein, M. B.
Nanna Upstairs and Nanna Downstairs, DePaola, Tomie

Anger
Alexander and the Terrible, Horrible, No Good, Very Bad Day, Viorst, Judith
Benjamin and Tulip, Wells, Rosemary
Blackboard Bear, Alexander, Martha
Elephant and Crocodile, Velthuijs, Max
*Phoebe's Revolt, Babbitt, Natalie
Where the Wild Things Are, Sendak, Maurice [Caldecott Award]

Bullies
Benjamin and Tulip, Wells, Rosemary
Bootsie Barker Bites, Bottner, Barbara
Goggles, Keats, Ezra Jack
The Rat and the Tiger, Kasza, Keiko

Consequences
Angus and the Ducks, Flack, Marjorie
Chanticleer and the Fox, Chaucer, Geoffrey (Barbara Cooney) [Caldecott Award]
Dog and Cat, Reiser, Lynn
Fox Tale, Abolafia, Yossi
The Judge, Zemach, Harve

Sam, Bangs, & Moonshine, Ness, Evaline
  [Caldecott Award]
The Story about Ping, Flack, Marjorie, and
  Kurt Weise
Strega Nona, DePaola, Tomie
The Tale of Peter Rabbit, Potter, Beatrix
Where the Wild Things Are, Sendak,
  Maurice [Caldecott Award]

Continuity of Life
*Grandfather's Journey, Say, Allen
  [Caldecott Award]
Home Place, Dragonwagon, Crescent
Just Like Max, Ackerman, Karen
Your Own Best Secret Place, Baylor, Byrd

Cooperation
Elephant and Crocodile, Velthuijs, Max
Fox Tale, Abolafia, Yossi
Frederick, Lionni, Leo
How Do You Hide a Monster? Kahl,
  Virginia
Little Blue and Little Yellow, Lionni, Leo
Swimmy, Lionni, Leo

Coping
The Cherry Tree, Ikeda, Daisaku
*Duffy and the Devil, Zemach, Harve
Good Times on Grandfather Mountain,
  Martin, Jacqueline Briggs
Hugh Can Do, Armstrong, Jennifer

Courage
Mirette on the High Wire, McCully, Emily
  Arnold [Caldecott Award]

Cross-Cultures
Elijah's Angel, Rosen, Michael J.
*Grandfather's Journey, Say, Allen
  [Caldecott Award]
Tree of Cranes, Say, Allen

Death
*Annie and the Old One, Miles, Miska
The Cat Next Door, Wright, Betty Ren
I'll See You in My Dreams, Jukes, Mavis
*Losing Uncle Tim, Jordon, Mary Kate

Nanna Upstairs and Nanna Downstairs,
  DePaola, Tomie
*Through the Mickle Woods, Gregory,
  Valiska

Discrimination
The Emperor and the Kite, Yolen, Jane
The Spooky Tail of Prewitt Peacock, Peet,
  Bill
Tar Beach, Ringgold, Faith
Who Is the Beast? Baker, Keith

Divorce
Gracie, Ballard, Robin

Ethics
The Cat in the Hat, Seuss, Dr.
The Golden Coin, Ada, Alma Flor
Hoagie's Rifle-Gun, Miles, Miska
Sam, Bangs, & Moonshine, Ness, Evaline
  [Caldecott Award]
The Story about Ping, Flack, Marjorie, and
  Kurt Weise
Strega Nona, DePaola, Tomie

Family Life
Albert's Toothache, Williams, Barbara
*Alexander and the Terrible, Horrible, No
  Good, Very Bad Day*, Viorst, Judith
A Baker's Portrait, Edwards, Michelle
Fog, Fowler, Susi Gregg
Gracie, Ballard, Robin
Henry's Happy Birthday, Keller, Holly
Just Like Max, Ackerman, Karen
*Kinda Blue, Grifalconi, Ann
*Phoebe's Revolt, Babbitt, Natalie
The Piggy in the Puddle, Pomerantz,
  Charlotte

Fear
Goblin Walk, Johnston, Tony
Shortcut, Crews, Donald
The Soup Bone, Johnston, Tony
There's a Nightmare in My Closet, Mayer,
  Mercer

Foolish Behavior

The Blabbermouths, Mantinband, Gerda
Everyone Knows What a Dragon Looks Like, Williams, Jay
Four Dollars and Fifty Cents, Kimmel, Eric A.
Iktomi and the Berries, A Plains Indian Story, Goble, Paul
The Judge, Zemach, Harve
Why Mosquitoes Buzz in People's Ears, Aardema, Verna

Forgiveness

It's So Nice to Have a Wolf Around The House, Allard, Harry
Where the Wild Things Are, Sendak, Maurice [Caldecott Award]

Friendship

Angus and the Cat, Flack, Marjorie
Benjamin and Tulip, Wells, Rosemary
Bootsie Barker Bites, Bottner, Barbara
Corduroy, Freeman, Don
Doodle Flute, Pinkwater, Daniel
Fish and Flamingo, Carlstrom, Nancy White
George and Martha, Marshall, James
Jim and the Beanstalk, Briggs, Raymond
Little Penguin, Benson, Patrick
Mole and Shrew Step Out, Koller, Jackie French
Pot Luck, Tobias, Tobi
The Rat and the Tiger, Kasza, Keiko
The Soup Bone, Johnston, Tony

Generosity

Evan's Corner, Hill, Elizabeth Starr
Three Good Blankets, Luttrell, Ida

Grandparents

*Annie and the Old One, Miles, Miska
The Cat Next Door, Wright, Betty Ren
Grandpa's Town, Nomura, Tukaaki
My Grandfather's Hat, Scheller, Melanie
Nanna Upstairs and Nanna Downstairs, DePaola, Tomie

Grief

The Cat Next Door, Wright, Betty Ren
I'll See You in My Dreams, Jukes, Mavis
*Losing Uncle Tim, Jordon, Mary Kate
*Through the Mickle Woods, Gregory, Valiska

Jealousy

*... Along Came Eric, Clarke, Gus
Julius the Baby of the World, Henkes, Kevin
Nobody Asked Me if I Wanted a Baby Sister, Alexander, Martha
One of Three, Johnson, Angela
She Come Bringing Me That Little Baby Girl, Greenfield, Eloise
Stevie, Steptoe, John

Loneliness

*An Angel for Solomon Singer, Rylant, Cynthia
Blumpoe the Grumpoe Meets Arnold the Cat, Okimoto, Jean Davies
Corduroy, Freeman, Don
*Kinda Blue, Grifalconi, Ann
One Monday Morning, Shulevitz, Uri
The Red Balloon, Lamorisse, Albert
Sam, Bangs, & Moonshine, Ness, Evaline [Caldecott Award]
Somebody Loves You, Mr. Hatch, Spinelli, Eileen

Nostalgia

Country Crossing, Aylesworth, Jim
Roxaboxen, McLerran, Alice

Parent and Child

Bedtime for Frances, Hoban, Russell
Blueberries for Sal, McCloskey, Robert
The Circus Baby, Petersham, Maud and Miska Petersham
A Father Like That, Zolotow, Charlotte
First Pink Light, Greenfield, Eloise
Monster Mama, Rosenberg, Liz
One of Three, Johnson, Angela
The Runaway Bunny, Brown, Margaret Wise

Sylvester & The Magic Pebble, Steig, William [Caldecott Award]
The Tale of Peter Rabbit, Potter, Beatrix
Where the Wild Things Are, Sendak, Maurice [Caldecott Award]
Where's Our Mama? Goode, Diane

Prejudice
The Emperor and the Kite, Yolen, Jane
Engelbert the Elephant, Paxton, Tom
It's So Nice to Have a Wolf Around The House, Allard, Harry

Race Relations
Elijah's Angel, Rosen, Michael J.
Tar Beach, Ringgold, Faith

Self-Discovery/Esteem
Alexander and the Terrible, Horrible, No Good, Very Bad Day, Viorst, Judith
Alexander and the Wind-Up Mouse, Lionni, Leo
Anatole, Titus, Eve
Bedtime for Frances, Hoban, Russell
Benjamin and Tulip, Wells, Rosemary
Blackboard Bear, Alexander, Martha
Cabbage Rose, Helldorfer, M. C.
Charles T. McBiddle, Glass, Andrew
Chrysanthemum, Henkes, Kevin
The Circus Baby, Petersham, Maud and Miska Petersham
Dandelion, Freeman, Don
Ghost Catcher, Haseley, Dennis
Hawk, I'm Your Brother, Baylor, Byrd
Little Penguin, Benson, Patrick
Madeline, Bemelmans, Ludwig
A Million Fish ... More or Less, McKissack, Patricia
Oliver Button Is a Sissy, DePaola, Tomie
One of Three, Johnson, Angela
Petunia, Duvoisin, Roger
Phoebe's Revolt, Babbitt, Natalie
Ruby the Copycat, Rathmann, Peggy
The Runaway Bunny, Brown, Margaret Wise
Sam, Bangs, & Moonshine, Ness, Evaline [Caldecott Award]

The Search for the Ten-Winged Dragon, Karl, Jean
Somebody Loves You, Mr. Hatch, Spinelli, Eileen
Stevie, Steptoe, John
The Story about Ping, Flack, Marjorie, and Kurt Weise
Umbrella, Yashima, Taro
Where the Wild Things Are, Sendak, Maurice [Caldecott Award]
Who Is the Beast? Baker, Keith
William's Doll, Zolotow, Charlotte
Your Own Best Secret Place, Baylor, Byrd

Sexism
Dirty Dave, Hilton, Nette
The Emperor and the Kite, Yolen, Jane
A Father Like That, Zolotow, Charlotte
Max, Isadora, Rachel
Mei Li, Handforth, Thomas [Caldecott Award]
Oliver Button Is a Sissy, DePaola, Tomie
Phoebe's Revolt, Babbitt, Natalie
A Proper Little Lady, Hilton, Nette
William's Doll, Zolotow, Charlotte

Siblings
... Along Came Eric, Clarke, Gus
Evan's Corner, Hill, Elizabeth Starr
Julius the Baby of the World, Henkes, Kevin
Lily and the Present, Ross, Christine
Nobody Asked Me if I Wanted a Baby Sister, Alexander, Martha
One of Three, Johnson, Angela
She Come Bringing Me That Little Baby Girl, Greenfield, Eloise

Values
A Baker's Portrait, Edwards, Michelle
Chanticleer and the Fox, Chaucer, Geoffrey (Barbara Cooney) [Caldecott Award]
Chrysanthemum, Henkes, Kevin
The Circus Baby, Petersham, Maud, and Miska Petersham
Doodle Flute, Pinkwater, Daniel
Fog, Fowler, Susi Gregg
Frederick, Lionni, Leo

Ghost Catcher, Haseley, Dennis
Hoagie's Rifle-Gun, Miles, Miska
How the Grinch Stole Christmas, Seuss, Dr.
The Little Engine That Could, Piper, Watty
The Little House, Burton, Virginia Lee
  [Caldecott Award]
Mike Mulligan and His Steam Shovel,
  Burton Virginia Lee
My Noah's Ark, Goffstein, M. B.
Petunia, Duvoisin, Roger

The Scrap Doll, Rosenberg, Liz
The Spooky Tail of Prewitt Peacock, Peet,
  Bill

War

The Cherry Tree, Ikeda, Daisaku
The Lily Cupboard, Oppenheim,
  Shulamith Levy
The Wall, Bunting, Eve

INDEX

❋ ❋ ❋ ❋ ❋ ❋ ❋ ❋ ❋ ❋